WHAT <u>STUDENTS</u> ARE SAYING ABOUT *SPEAK UP!*

Easy to read, good fluidity, logical order, relatable examples and anecdotes.

—Sarah Le Clair, Student

I found it highly engaging. I wasn't bored or zoning out because the material kept my attention, unlike other textbooks I've used.

—Dana Schmitz, Student

The tone of the book is easygoing, so it helps me feel reassured about my anxiety that's naturally associated with taking Speech.

—Matthew Pactao, Student

When I learned something new, it captivated me.

—Jon Hongpananon, Student

The images really helped me understand what the text was saying—like a visual summary.

—Olivia Baney, Student

Speak Up

AN ILLUSTRATED GUIDE TO PUBLIC SPEAKING

Fourth Edition

Douglas M. Fraleigh
California State University–Fresno

Joseph S. Tuman
San Francisco State University

With Illustrations by
Peter Arkle

 bedford/st.martin's
Macmillan Learning
Boston | New York

For Bedford/St. Martin's

Vice President, Editorial, Macmillan Learning Humanities: Edwin Hill
Publisher for Communication: Erika Gutierrez
Development Manager: Susan McLaughlin
Senior Developmental Editor: Julia Bartz
Senior Production Editor: Peter Jacoby
Media Producer: Melissa Skepko-Masi
Senior Production Supervisor: Jennifer Wetzel
Marketing Manager: Kayti Corfield
Copy Editor: Rosemary Winfield
Indexer: Kirsten Kite
Permissions Editor: Linda Winters
Senior Art Director: Anna Palchik
Text Design: Jerilyn Bockorick
Cover Design: William Boardman
Cover Illustrations: Peter Arkle
Composition: Cenveo Publisher Services
Printing and Binding: LSC Communications

Manufactured in the United States of America.

1   0   9   8   7   6
f   e   d   c   b   a

For information, write: Bedford/St. Martin's, 75 Arlington Street,
Boston, MA 02116   (617-399-4000)

ISBN 978-1-319-03065-0

Joe

For my wife, Kirsten: With every new book, there are more reasons to appreciate your love and patience.

Doug

To my family, the source of inspiration for all of my writing.

BRIEF CONTENTS

ABOUT THE AUTHORS AND ILLUSTRATOR:

<u>DOUGLAS M. FRALEIGH</u> is a professor and chair of the Communication Department at California State University-Fresno, where he also teaches in the Smittcamp Family Honors College and serves as assessment coordinator for the College of Arts and Humanities. His teaching and research interests include freedom of speech, argumentation, and public discourse. He is coauthor of *Let's Communicate: An Illustrated Guide to Human Communication* and *Freedom of Expression in the Marketplace of Ideas.* Before becoming chair, he was active in speech and debate coaching at Fresno State, Cornell, UC Berkeley, and California State University-Sacramento. He holds a juris doctor from UC Berkeley and a BA from CSU Sacramento. When not busy teaching, writing, and administrating, he looks forward to running, reading, family time (especially plays and sporting events), and hanging out with his dogs.

<u>JOSEPH S. TUMAN</u> is a professor and former chair of the Department of Communication Studies at San Francisco State University, where he received the Jacobus tenBroek Society Award, a statewide award for Excellence in Teaching. He has also taught at the University of California at Berkeley, the New School, and the University of Paris II, and has published widely in the field of communication studies (including coauthoring *Let's Communicate: An Illustrated Guide to Human Communication*). Joseph has appeared regularly on local and national network television and radio as a political analyst since 1984. He has served on the boards of several nonprofits in Oakland, and in 2014 he was one of the leading candidates in the mayoral race. Currently, he serves as an advisor and expert analyst regarding terrorism and social media for the North Atlantic Treaty Organization. In his spare time, he is an avid triathlete and marathoner.

<u>PETER ARKLE</u> is a freelance illustrator who grew up in Scotland and received a BA in illustration from St. Martin's School of Art and an MA from the Royal College of Art (both in London). His clients include magazines (the *New Yorker, Canadian Business, Time,* and the *Harvard Business Review*), newspapers (the *New York Times* and the *Wall Street Journal*), sports brands (Nike and Brooks Running), scientists (the Howard Hughes Medical Institute), lawyers (Kennedys Law), whisky makers (anCnoc Highland Single Malt Scotch Whisky), hotels (Morgans Hotel Group), and other enterprises that keep his life interesting. He just published a book, *All Black Cats Are Not Alike,* with his wife, Amy Goldwasser. To see more of Peter's work, please visit peterarkle.com.

PREFACE

As longtime teachers of public speaking and former coaches of forensics, we have spent more than seventy combined years teaching students about the power of speech in their own lives and its value in shaping our society. In creating the first edition of *Speak Up*, we distilled our best practices while transmitting our passionate commitment to the craft of public speaking. Our goal was to create a product that would grab students' attention while meeting the teaching and learning needs of students, colleagues, and friends across the communication discipline.

We recognized that covering the vast field of public speaking—from classical rhetoric and contemporary theory to the specific steps of researching, preparing, and delivering a speech—can be a tremendous challenge given the time constraints of the course. Instructors need teaching materials that are comprehensive yet flexible enough to work with a variety of teaching styles. At the same time, students want a book that is engaging, fun, and affordable.

Keeping these challenges in mind, we came up with a three-part plan. First, we would make sure to include both traditional and compelling content. The organization would seamlessly integrate with instructors' syllabi, and the accessible language and current examples would engage students. Second, we would team up with the brilliant Peter Arkle to develop illustrations that would illuminate concepts much more efficiently than would photographs. Professors have since confirmed that these are smart, pedagogically effective learning tools, and students have told us that the fun images actually motivate them to read more of the text. Third, we would aim to be affordable for students, with a resulting cost at less than half the price of most traditional introductory speech texts.

We have continued to emphasize these goals in every revision. For our fourth edition, we also wanted to add resources that would help students understand the process of developing and presenting a successful speech. Each edition of *Speak Up* has emphasized the idea that effective speeches are the result of a series of good choices. To help bring this idea to life for students, we created a new feature—**Speech Choices**—which uses case studies to follow two students, Mia and Jacob, as they go through each stage of developing their speeches. As students consider each case study (in Chapters 1 to 3, 5 to 14, and 16 to 17), they are asked to analyze their own choices as they use the chapter content to develop their speeches. We also included the full-length videos of Mia's and Jacob's speeches (with assignable questions) so that students can see how their choices influenced the final product. Students can access these videos in *Speak Up*'s online course space, **LaunchPad**. Finally, we included more materials in LaunchPad—such as speech clips with assignable questions, class discussion questions, and suggested activities—so that instructors can further integrate this case study feature into their classrooms.

That's not all we updated. Because our students will be preparing and delivering speeches in a digital age, we have added and updated material on using online resources effectively to prepare a speech and deliver a mediated presentation. Our discussion of the strengths and weaknesses of digital research sources has been expanded. We've also increased examples and illustrations that depict mediated speech contexts. In Launch-Pad, instructors can access an expanded array of videos and activities. Our improved media program also has been revised and strengthened in terms of core functionality. We are excited about how the program has evolved.

In response to instructors who would like to empower their students to apply their public speaking skills in their communities, we have added material on civic engagement. This concept is introduced in Chapter 1, and examples and illustrations that show speakers using course concepts to participate in civic engagement are incorporated throughout the text.

We also received feedback from instructors that their students faced challenges using research and citing sources in their speech outlines. To address those challenges, we've inserted new material on the nature of academic research and the types of sources that college instructors tend to prefer. We also added text content and a full-page illustration to show students how to quote and paraphrase sources and how to distinguish appropriate paraphrasing from plagiarism.

NEW TO THIS EDITION

Speech Choices, a brand-new case study feature, guides students through the speech-making process. As they follow the case studies, students can see how Mia's and Jacob's choices affect their final speeches and are asked to think of what they would do in similar situations. The feature comes with two brand-new, professional full-length speech videos with assignable questions, further video clips with questions, in-class discussion questions, and activities that instructors can use in the classroom, which are all available in LaunchPad.

New and extensive coverage focuses on technology, civic engagement, and citing sources. Given the importance of these topics, we've included them in nearly every chapter. We've added and updated material on using online resources effectively to prepare speeches and deliver mediated presentations and have added technology-based examples throughout the text. In response to comments from instructors who would like to empower their students to apply their public speaking skills in their communities, we have added new content and many new examples on civic engagement. We've also inserted new material on the nature of academic research, the types of sources that college instructors tend to prefer, and ways to distinguish appropriate paraphrasing from plagiarism.

Updated text includes cutting-edge issues and freshened popular culture examples that will keep students engaged. New examples focus on technology (such as a TED talk on bionic limb technology to show the power of presentation aids) and on areas that engage students (such as students who present speeches on women in comedy).

Extensive updates have been made to the online course space, LaunchPad. LaunchPad has been updated to include video tools, two new full-length speech videos, new quizzing capabilities, and an improved LearningCurve interface.

- **Two new full-length videos for the Speech Choices case studies** look at how emigrants use smartphones to navigate their journeys and why student athletes should be paid. They include assignable questions and sixteen new clips from the two speeches that take a closer look at public speaking concepts. These videos are in addition to the hundreds of speech videos already in our library.

- **LearningCurve, our adaptive quizzing and personalized learning program, has gotten a facelift.** In every chapter, call-outs prompt students to tackle the game-like LearningCurve quizzes to test their knowledge and reinforce learning of the material. Based on research into how students learn, LearningCurve motivates students to engage with course materials and provides reporting tools that let you see what content students have mastered and adapt your teaching plan to their needs. LearningCurve's questions have been revised for this edition, and it now has a beautiful new interface, making it even more effective and enjoyable to use.

- **New quizzing capabilities** allow you to search and create quizzes by chapter, question type, level of difficulty, and Bloom's level. The Review & Modify tab is designed to make editing your quiz easier, and the order of the tabs is now even more intuitive.

- **Video tools** make it easy to create video assignments and evaluate videos using rubrics and time-based comments. Instructors and students can upload videos, embed clips from YouTube, and use publisher-supplied videos in your own assignments.

- The interactive **Personal Report of Communication Apprehension** and **Personal Report of Public Speaking Anxiety** allow students to measure their levels in these areas.

Curriculum solutions: customize for your needs. Get in touch to find your solutions. Go to **macmillanlearning.com/catalog/preview /curriculumsolutions** to learn more.

DIGITAL AND PRINT FORMATS

Whether it's a print, digital, or value option, choose the best format for you. For more information on these resources, please visit the online catalog at **macmillanlearning.com**.

LaunchPad for *Speak Up*. LaunchPad is a digital platform that dramatically enhances teaching and learning. LaunchPad combines the full e-book, videos, quizzes and self-assessments, instructor's resources, and LearningCurve adaptive quizzing. To get access to all multimedia resources, package LaunchPad with the print book, using ISBN 978-1-319-11539-5. To order LaunchPad on its own, use ISBN 978-1-319-06261-3.

***Speak Up* as a print text.** To get the most out of the book, package LaunchPad at a significant discount with the text.

***Speak Up* e-book option.** *Speak Up* is available in a range of new e-book formats for computers, tablets, and e-readers. For information, see **macmillanlearning.com**.

RESOURCES FOR STUDENTS AND INSTRUCTORS

Online Resources for Students

To find more information about these resources or to learn about package options, please visit the online catalog at **macmillanlearning.com**.

LaunchPad helps students learn, study, and apply public speaking concepts. Digital resources for *Speak Up* are available in LaunchPad, a dynamic digital platform that combines a collection of relevant video clips, self-assessments, e-book content, and LearningCurve adaptive quizzes in a simple design. LaunchPad has been updated to include video tools, two new full-length speech videos, new quizzing capabilities, and an improved LearningCurve interface. **LaunchPad can be packaged with the book, purchased separately, and integrated with course management systems. See more on the inside back cover of this book.**

Print Resources for Students
Outlining and Organizing Your Speech
Merry Buchanan, University of Central Oklahoma

This student workbook provides step-by-step guidance for preparing informative, persuasive, and professional presentations. It gives students many opportunities to practice the critical skills of conducting audience analysis, dealing with communication apprehension, selecting a speech topic and purpose, researching support materials, organizing and outlining, developing introductions and conclusions, enhancing language and delivery, and preparing and using presentation aids.

The Essential Guide Series

This series of brief booklets gives instructors flexibility and support in designing courses. Each booklet begins with a useful overview of an important speech topic and then addresses the essential concepts and skills that students need to master that topic. The Essential Guides can be packaged with *Speak Up*.

The Essential Guide to Presentation Software, **Second Edition,** by Allison Bailey, University of North Georgia, and Rob Patterson, University of Virginia

The Essential Guide to Rhetoric, by William M. Keith, University of Wisconsin–Milwaukee, and Christian O. Lundberg, University of North Carolina–Chapel Hill

The Essential Guide to Interpersonal Communication, by Dan O'Hair, University of Kentucky, and Mary O. Wiemann, Emeritus, Santa Barbara City College

The Essential Guide to Group Communication, **Second Edition,** by Dan O'Hair, University of Kentucky, and Mary O. Wiemann, Emeritus, Santa Barbara City College

The Essential Guide to Intercultural Communication, by Jennifer Willis-Rivera, University of Wisconsin–River Falls

Media Career Guide: Preparing for Jobs in the Twenty-first Century, **Tenth Edition, by Sherri Hope Culver, Temple University** Practical, student friendly, and revised to include the most recent statistics on the job market, this guide includes a comprehensive directory of media jobs, practical tips, and career guidance for students who are considering a major in the media industry.

Research and Documentation in the Electronic Age, Sixth Edition Diana Hacker, Prince George's Community College, and Barbara Fister, Gustavus Adolphus College

This handy booklet covers everything that students need for college research assignments at the library and on the Internet, including advice for finding and evaluating Internet sources.

Resources for Instructors

To find more information or to order or download the instructor resources, please visit the online catalog at **macmillanlearning.com**. The *Instructor's Manual*, *Electronic Test Bank*, and Lecture Slides are also available on LaunchPad at **macmillanhighered.com/speakup4e**.

Instructor's Manual

Nancy Fraleigh, Fresno City College

This comprehensive online *Instructor's Manual* includes teaching notes on managing, organizing, and integrating assessment in a public speaking course; sample syllabi; chapter outlines; discussion questions; more information and activities for the new Speech Choices case study feature; personal writing assignments; classroom activities; media resources; and ready-to-print activities.

Electronic Test Bank

Nancy Fraleigh, Fresno City College

   Speak Up offers a complete testing program that is available for Windows and Macintosh environments. Each chapter includes multiple-choice, true/false, short-answer, and essay questions. This easy-to-use *Electronic Test Bank* also identifies the level of difficulty for each question, includes the book page where the answer can be found, and connects every question to a learning objective.

Lecture Slides for *Speak Up*

These lecture slides can be used in class. They include the chapters' main ideas, many illustration examples, and explanations from the text.

Curriculum Solutions

You can customize course solutions for your students' needs at Curriculum Solutions. Learn more at **macmillanlearning.com/catalog/preview /curriculumsolutions**.

The Communication COMMunity

Created by instructors for instructors, the Communication COMMunity is an ideal online forum for interacting with fellow educators—including Macmillan authors—in your discipline. Join ongoing conversations about course preparation, presentations, assignments, assessments, teaching with media, and keeping pace with and influencing new directions in your field. The Communication COMMunity includes exclusive access to classroom resources, blogs, webinars, professional development opportunities, and more.

ESL Students in the Public Speaking Classroom: A Guide for Teachers, Second Edition

Robbin Crabtree, Loyola Marymount University, and David Allen Sapp, Fairfield University

   This guidebook provides support for new and experienced instructors of public speaking courses whose classrooms include students who are learning English as a second language and other linguistically diverse students. Based on landmark research and years of their own teaching experience, the authors provide insights about the variety of non-native English-speaking students (including speakers of global English varieties), practical techniques that can be used to help these students succeed in their assignments, and ideas for leveraging this cultural asset for the education of all students in the public speaking classroom.

ACKNOWLEDGMENTS

We would like to offer special thanks to Joan Feinberg, former co-president of Macmillan Learning, and Denise Wydra, former president of Bedford/St. Martin's, for convening the meeting that gave birth to this project, providing an exceptional team of editorial and developmental support, and seeing multiple editions of our book all the way through to completion. Publisher for Communication Erika Gutierrez has done a marvelous job working with us to brainstorm, select, and refine new ideas for developing and marketing each edition of the book. We would also like to thank Macmillan Higher Education's Vice President of Editorial Edwin Hill and Development Manager Susan McLaughlin. Shepherding any textbook from manuscript to production is a daunting task, even more so when working with an innovative idea that creates new challenges. We appreciate their enthusiasm and professionalism, which enabled us to complete the project on time.

It was also an absolute pleasure to continue our collaboration with professional artist Peter Arkle. Peter's ability to depict our ideas in pictures is simply amazing. His illustrations are a large part of what makes this text provocative, fun, and engaging.

For the fourth edition of *Speak Up*, we were very pleased to have Julia Bartz continue on the team as our Senior Editor. Julia devoted countless hours working with us on ideas for additions, updates, and revisions of the text and illustrations. She also contributed greatly to the addition of new online resources to accompany this edition. She kept everything well organized and on schedule as we worked together on two book projects simultaneously. She contributed many excellent ideas for updates and revisions, along with masterful work on line-by-line rewrites. Editorial Assistant Mary Jane Chen also deserves a huge round of thanks for her focus, enthusiasm, and attention to detail. We are very thankful to the incredible professionals who guided the production and design of *Speak Up*, including Senior Art Director Anna Palchik. Senior Production Editor Peter Jacoby expertly guided the process from manuscript through pages, delivering page proofs with great efficiency and helping us with the tricky business of making each page look its best. Picking up where Peter left off, Senior Production Supervisor Jennifer Wetzel put in the hard and careful work needed to turn hundreds of manuscript pages with more than five hundred illustrations into a finished product, as did Director of Rights and Permissions Hilary Newman, who lined up permissions for the book's sample speeches.

Beyond collaborating with the many people who helped to produce this book, we have been fortunate to work with a crackerjack marketing team. We love working with Marketing Manager Kayti Corfield, who helped develop our marketing and sales message.

We want to thank Nancy Fraleigh of Fresno City College for her expert work revising the *Instructor's Manual* and *Electronic Test Bank* for our fourth edition. She worked hard to revise content and test questions to reflect changes in our new edition. Her work has built on the strong foundation created by Steve Vrooman of Texas Lutheran University and Chrys Egan of Salisbury University, who authored the instructor materials for the first edition. Many thanks also to Bruce Sherwin and Linda DeMasi of Publishers Solutions for all their help with the ancillary program.

We are also grateful to the many reviewers and class testers who gave us feedback on *Speak Up* and helped us make it even better. The input of our colleagues in the public speaking profession played a central role in our decisions for revising the prior edition, and they offered both validation for what was working and constructive suggestions for improvement. For the fourth edition, we would like to thank Shawn Apostel, Bellarmine University; Joseph Bailey, Hardin-Simmons University; Lisa Coleman, Southwest Tennessee Community College; Erica Cooper, Roanoke College; Wade Cornelius, New Mexico State University; Paul Crowley, Spartanburg Community College; Carolyn Cunningham, Gonzaga University; Cheri Hampton-Farmer, Findlay University; Anne Helms, Alamance Community College; Seth Horning, DePaul University; Allison Horrell, Spartanburg Community College; Stan McKinney, Campbellsville University; Raymond Ozley, Montevallo University; Rasha Ramzy, Georgia State University; Ian Sheeler, Indiana University–Purdue University Indianapolis; Harvey Ussach, Bristol Community College; and Patti Vorndran, Delaware County Community College.

We would like to thank our own speech teachers and forensics coaches for their contributions to our development as public speakers and teachers. We thank our faculty colleagues for their support and understanding as we balance teaching, writing, and other academic responsibilities.

We are grateful for the many students and forensics team members who have worked with us to develop and present speeches over the past thirty-six years, and we hope that our book will help a new generation of students gain public speaking skills and confidence.

Our friendship began at the 1977 Governor's Cup Speech and Debate Tournament in Sacramento, California. This is our seventh major book project, and it continues to be both a privilege and a pleasure to write together. Our families have been exceptional at supporting our work and serving as sounding boards for ideas. Our kids—Douglas, Helen, Nate, and Whitney—have their own careers now, but we continue to value their strategic input (and input from their significant others) as we make revisions. For thirty-plus years our wives, Kirsten and Nancy, have encouraged and supported our writing and contributed valuable ideas to our projects. Needless to say, their love and patience have sustained us through all our collaborations. We appreciate the opportunity to continue to share ideas and write with each other—something we will do long after *Speak Up* is (hopefully) in its tenth edition.

CONTENTS

Veni vidi vici.

JULIUS CAESAR

2   DEVELOPING YOUR FIRST SPEECH   35

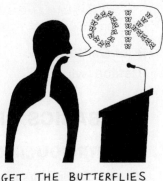

GET THE BUTTERFLIES FLYING IN FORMATION

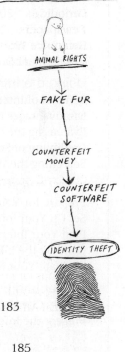

10 INTRODUCTIONS AND CONCLUSIONS   279

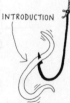

11 OUTLINING YOUR SPEECH 305

12 LANGUAGE AND STYLE 333

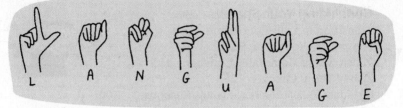

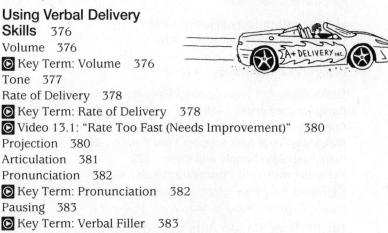

15 MEDIATED PUBLIC SPEAKING 435

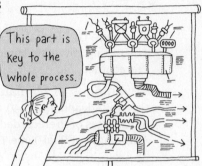

Speak Up

AN ILLUSTRATED GUIDE TO PUBLIC SPEAKING

INTRODUCING PUBLIC SPEAKING

"Public speaking is right for you."

In 2008, Malala Yousafzai was a ten-year-old student in the Swat Valley region of Pakistan. After the Taliban prohibited girls' education in the region in early 2009, Malala began to blog about the importance of education for girls. The British Broadcasting Company published her writings using the pseudonym Gul Makai ("corn flower") for ten months. A year later, Malala began to speak in public to advocate for girls' education—using her real name this time. She became well known around the world, especially after the *New York Times* featured her in a documentary[1] and South African archbishop Desmond Tutu nominated her for the 2011 International Children's Peace Prize.[2]

In October 2012, a Taliban shooter attempted to end Malala's life. Although suffering a gunshot to her head, Malala survived, and the violent attack did not deter her from continuing to speak out. Four months later, as she recovered in a British hospital, Malala delivered a message to the public: "I want every girl, every child, to be educated."[3] Since then, Ms. Yousafzai has been steadfast in her public advocacy for girls' rights and education, delivering one of her most noteworthy speeches when she shared the 2014 Nobel Peace Prize.[4]

Malala Yousafzai's story is a unique example of how public speaking can change the world. In more everyday situations, public speaking is still a vital skill for anyone looking to inform, influence, or persuade others—which is why it's often a required course in colleges and universities. Public speaking is also highly prized in most professions.

For example, as the supervisor of a team developing a new video game, you may have to deliver a presentation to a group of managers updating them on the team's progress. As a leader in a nonprofit environmental organization, you may need to give a talk during a major fund-raising dinner to influence potential donors to open their wallets. If you work as a director of social media for a company, you may need to explain the rollout of a new campaign to managers in several different regional offices, using videoconferencing technology to communicate with all managers simultaneously. Despite this, many college graduates enter the work world without any experience in public speaking. As Marilyn Mackes, executive director of the National Association of Colleges and Employers, noted, "For more than ten years, we've asked employers about key skills, and they have consistently named communication skills as critical, yet have also said that this is something many candidates lack."[5] A public speaking course helps you master skills that will enable you not only to advance in your career but also to excel in other courses (especially your major) *and* make valuable contributions in other areas of your life—such as taking an active role in the community.

Of course, you may find the thought of giving a speech terrifying. If so, you're not alone. A survey by Randolph H. Whitworth and Claudia Cochran[6] found that public speaking is Americans' number one fear, and another researcher noted that many people find it "even scarier than rattlesnakes."[7] But there's good news: you *can* learn to master public speaking—just as most people learn to read, ride a bicycle, or keep up with the latest technology. In our fifty-plus years of teaching public speaking, we've seen thousands of students gain confidence and lose their fear of public speaking as they acquire experience with it.

This book walks you through the steps you need to follow in order to create and deliver an effective speech—one that gets a favorable response from your listeners. In the chapters that follow, we explain each step in clear terms and show you how to make smart choices at each stage of the speech preparation process. We supplement these

explanations with illustrations that depict key points—which, besides being entertaining, are designed to help you grasp and remember the most important concepts in the book.

But before we jump into the process of preparing and delivering an effective speech, we will take a few moments to explore the field of public speaking itself. In this chapter, we take a closer look at the benefits of studying public speaking. We also survey its rich tradition and consider the highlights of contemporary trends in the study of public speaking.

WHAT IS PUBLIC SPEAKING?

What is public speaking, exactly? When done effectively, this activity has several characteristics that distinguish it from other types of communication.

Public Speaking Features Communication between a Speaker and an Audience. In public speaking, the speaker does most of the talking, while the audience primarily listens. However, that does not mean audience members don't respond to what they're hearing. Audience members may smile, frown, or look puzzled. Talented speakers recognize these signals and modify their message if needed—for example, clarifying a point when they notice confused expressions on their listeners' faces. Audience members might even respond with more than just silent facial expressions. For instance, they may applaud the speaker or shout out words of encouragement and appreciation if they're pleased with or excited by the speaker's message. Or they may boo or heckle the speaker if they disagree with the message. However, in public speaking, even the most energetic interjections are usually brief. For the majority of the speech, the speaker "has the floor."

Public Speaking Is Audience Centered. In public speaking, the presenter chooses his or her message with the audience's interests and needs in mind. Good speakers consider what topic would be appropriate for their audience on a particular occasion. They also develop their message in a way that their audience will find interesting and understandable.

For example, suppose you recently got a job as a product developer at a furniture company. You've asked to meet with members of your

YOU ARE A PUBLIC SPEAKER WHEN

company's management team to discuss a new line of dorm furniture that you'd like to launch. At the meeting, you want to persuade your listeners to approve funding for a proposed line. In preparing your speech, you think about what members of the management team care about most: the company's profitability—its ability to increase revenues while reducing costs. So you develop explanations for how the proposed campaign will enhance profitability ("This new line will increase sales by 10 percent over the next two quarters, cut our expenses by 5 percent, and lead to a 6 percent increase in profitability"). You make sure to avoid sales-style language (such as "This new design is bold and provocative") because you know that such language will hold little interest for your business-oriented listeners.

Public Speaking Emphasizes the Spoken Word. Any speaker can supplement her or his speech with pictures, charts, videos, handouts, objects, or even a live demonstration. However, public speakers devote most of their time to *speaking* to their audience. The spoken word plays the central role in their message, although speakers use gestures, posture, voice intonation, eye contact, other types of body language, and even presentation aids to heighten the effect of their words.

YOU ARE NOT A PUBLIC SPEAKER WHEN

Public Speaking Is Usually a Prepared Presentation. Few public speakers simply walk up to the lectern or podium and make up their talk as they go. The best speakers choose their topic in advance, carefully consider what they might say about that topic, and then select the best ideas for the audience they will be addressing. They organize those ideas, choose their words carefully, and practice delivering the speech before the big day. Even people who suspect that they may be called on to deliver an impromptu speech—for example, at a community-service awards dinner—know how to quickly piece together a few comments as they step to the front of the room.

WHY STUDY PUBLIC SPEAKING?

As you make your way through life—completing your degree, advancing in your career, establishing yourself in a neighborhood or community—you will sometimes find yourself in situations in which you need to express your ideas to others. By studying and practicing public speaking, you can learn to deliver effective presentations in each of these contexts. Public speaking skills give you the power to share your ideas and bring about needed change in the world around you.

Public speaking skills can also come in handy in everyday situations. As you become more comfortable with public speaking, you will find yourself more confident about asking a question at a meeting or speaking up when hanging out with new coworkers. You will also be equipped

PUBLIC SPEAKING SKILLS COME IN HANDY...

IN THE CLASSROOM

IN YOUR CAREER

to speak on the fly if you are asked to give a toast, accept an award, or make a presentation at the last minute.

Using Public Speaking as a Student

Of course, you'll need to start practicing your public speaking skills to get through this class. But the skills you acquire by working your way through this book will also help you as you complete your degree and participate in additional educational opportunities throughout your life. Those later opportunities may include adult-education workshops, higher-level degrees, or professional development courses. Instructors in all types of courses may ask students to stand up on the first day of class and introduce themselves as well as explain what they hope to get from the class.

Many instructors also require students to deliver oral presentations on research projects and other coursework. Students with strong public speaking skills can share their findings more effectively than those with a limited background in presenting speeches. Think about students who have given oral presentations in your classes. Most likely you've noticed that those who give thoughtfully crafted and skillfully delivered presentations make a better impression on the instructor *and* the rest of the class. Equally important, the information they offer is probably more useful to listeners than information delivered by less skilled speakers.

> ©️ To see an example of a speech in a course on Communication and Technology, try Video Activity 1.1, "Gender-Based Responses in Sports Chatrooms."

As you approach graduation, your college may require you to deliver an oral presentation to show what you have learned. For example,

IN THE COMMUNITY

WHEN YOU LEAST EXPECT IT

engineering majors may need to explain their senior project to a panel of local construction managers, or business majors might have to pitch an idea for a product to a faculty committee. Colleges are increasingly requiring seniors to submit a portfolio of their work in order to assess student learning,[8] often requiring a videotape of an oral presentation among other assignments.

Public speaking skills also enhance your ability to participate in campus activities. If you belong to an organization or a club, team, sorority, or fraternity, you may want to speak out at a group meeting or represent your group before the student senate or other campus organizations. When you present an effective speech to these audiences, you boost your chances of achieving your goal—whether it's persuading your sorority to take up a new social cause or convincing the student senate to fund a campus job fair related to your major.

Using Public Speaking in Your Career

A knack for public speaking is one of the most important assets you can possess in the workplace. According to the National Association of Col-

leges and Employers' 2015 Job Outlook survey, verbal communication skills and ability to work in a team are two of the qualities that employers are most likely to seek in potential job candidates.[9] Employees agree that communication skills are important. In the survey "Making the Grade? What American Workers Think Should Be Done to Improve Education," 87 percent of the 1,014 U.S. adult workers surveyed rated communication skills as very important for performing their jobs.[10]

The importance of public speaking is not limited to careers that might first come to mind, such as law or politics. In *Listen. Write. Present.*, a book on effective communication in scientific and technical fields, authors Stephanie Roberson Barnard and Deborah St. James emphasize that workers in these careers need to practice public speaking so that they will be comfortable when presenting, and able to tailor their presentations to audience needs.[11] No matter which career path you choose, you'll almost certainly need public speaking skills. Consider the following examples:

- A city engineer addresses an angry crowd of citizens at a city council meeting, following a news report that a heavily traveled local bridge has safety issues. The engineer calmly reassures the public that repairs will be made immediately, using lay terms to describe the repairs in a way that the audience can understand.

- An information technology professional creates a podcast for a company's sales force, explaining how to use a new software app to track prospective customers.

- An elementary school teacher encounters a roomful of parents who are skeptical about a new math curriculum, which differs markedly from how they learned math in "the good old days." The teacher clearly and energetically presents research results defending the curriculum, and the parents happily accept the new method.

Baseball Hall of Famer Lou Gehrig was planning to major in engineering at Columbia University before the Yankees came calling, and neither of those career paths made public speaking likely. Nevertheless, he delivered one of the most compelling presentations in American history. After being diagnosed with amyotrophic lateral sclerosis (ALS), he was honored in a ceremony at Yankee Stadium. His eloquent remarks, sometimes called the "Gettysburg Address of baseball,"[12] are perhaps even more memorable than his four Most Valuable Player awards. This video can be found on YouTube if you'd like to view it (search for "Gehrig's Farewell Address").

Using Public Speaking in Your Community

Beyond work or school, you may wear many different hats in your community. For example, you might be active in service organizations, athletic leagues, clubs, religious groups, or political committees. If you're a parent, you may find yourself taking on leadership roles in your children's schools, sports teams, clubs, or other activities. You may also decide to get involved in a social cause you feel passionate about. In each of these endeavors, public speaking skills can help you.

For example, Tammy Duckworth, a Black Hawk helicopter pilot, received a Purple Heart military medal for being wounded in action after her aircraft was hit by a grenade near Baghdad in 2004. When she returned to the United States, she decided to enter public service. While running for Congress in 2006, she delivered campaign speeches on health care, gas prices, and the economy. Although Duckworth lost the election, she made an impression. She was asked to speak at the 2008 Democratic National Convention and was appointed the Department of Veterans Affairs assistant secretary for public and intergovernmental affairs from 2009 to 2011, where she advocated for veterans' issues such as therapy for post-traumatic stress disorder. In 2012, Duckworth ran for Congress again and used public speaking skills to defend her perspectives on a diverse set of issues, including the economy, Medicare, and contraceptive policy. These skills paid off again. Duckworth was elected twice, and in a March 30, 2015, YouTube video, she announced her candidacy for the Senate in 2016.[13]

To play an active role in issues that concern you, you also will need to speak out. The health of a democratic, self-governing society depends on **civic engagement**, or active public participation in political affairs and social and community organizations. Public speaking skills facilitate civic engagement. College students who actively participate in public discussion or political activities are more likely to be confident in their ability to make a difference in their communities.[14]

Throughout life, you may also be asked to speak in less formal situations—for example, by offering a wedding toast or presenting an award to a friend or colleague who is retiring. In each of these cases, the skills you learn in a public speaking class will help ensure that others hear and respect your views.

PUBLIC SPEAKING: A GREAT TRADITION

For centuries, people around the world have studied the art and practice of public speaking and used public address to inform, influence, and persuade others. As far back as the fifth century BCE, all adult male

citizens in the Greek city-state of Athens had a right to speak out in the assembly and vote on proposals relating to civic matters. Sometimes as many as six thousand citizens attended these meetings.[15] Indeed, the ancient Greeks were the first people to think formally about rhetoric and to teach it as a subject. A century later, the Greek scholar Aristotle wrote *Rhetoric*, a systematic analysis of the art and practice of public speaking. Many of Aristotle's ideas influence the study of public speaking even today. Later, in first-century BCE Rome, senators vehemently debated the issues of the day. Cicero, a Roman politician, was a renowned orator and a prolific writer on rhetoric, the craft of public speaking. Another noteworthy Roman rhetorician, Quintilian, emphasized the ideal of an ethical orator—the good person speaking well.

The tradition of public speaking was not limited to Greece and Rome: it's been practiced in many regions throughout history. From the time

MEDIEVAL AFRICAN KINGDOM
(NEAR PRESENT-DAY MALI)

of Confucius in the fifth century BCE until the end of the third century BCE, China enjoyed an intellectual climate whose energy rivaled that of ancient Greece.[16] Scholars traveling throughout China passionately advocated a variety of systems of political and economic philosophy. In fifteenth-century western Africa, traveling storytellers recited parables and humorous stories, while in northeastern Africa, Islamic scholars embarked on lecture tours attended by large crowds.[17] On feast days in one African kingdom (near present-day Mali), it was traditional for a bard to dress in a bird's-head mask and deliver a speech encouraging the king to live up to his predecessors' high standards.[18] In seventeenth-century India, a speaker's words were valued over other means of communication, and inscribed versions of the messages were referred to as "treasure houses of the Goddess of Speech."[19] Native Americans prized oratory, too; indeed, many deemed oratorical ability a more important leadership quality than even bravery in battle.[20]

The United States also has a rich history of public speaking. During the Great Awakening of the 1730s and 1740s, preachers sought to revive waning religious zeal in the colonies, often preaching in fields to accommodate the many listeners. During the American Revolution in the second half of the eighteenth century, colonists took to the streets to passionately decry new taxes and also launched the Boston Tea Party, in which they dressed as Mohawk Indians, boarded three ships in Boston Harbor, and hurled the vessels' cargoes of tea overboard. In the 1770s and 1780s, political leaders in each of the states energetically debated the merits of ratifying the U.S. Constitution and the Bill of Rights.

In the nineteenth century, public speaking became a hallmark of American society, as people debated political issues, expanded their knowledge, and even entertained one another. Political debates drew particularly large and enthusiastic crowds, such as the debates between Abraham Lincoln and Stephen Douglas during the Illinois Senate election. More than fifteen thousand people gathered to hear the contenders in Freeport, Illinois—a town with just five thousand residents.[21]

The antislavery movement of this time also used public speaking to drive major social change. Frederick Douglass, a former slave who moved audiences with his depictions of life under slavery, counted among the most compelling antislavery speakers. Women also actively participated in the American Anti-Slavery Society, holding offices and delivering public lectures. Angelina Grimké was just one eloquent orator who won audience members' commitment to the antislavery cause with graphic descriptions of the slave abuse she had witnessed while growing up in South Carolina. Other women—such as Elizabeth Cady Stanton, Susan B. Anthony, and Lucy Stone—took leadership roles in the women's suffrage movement, which arose in the mid-1800s and continued into the early 1900s. These able orators used fiery speeches to convince Americans that women deserved the right to cast a ballot at the polls—a radical notion at the time.[22]

During the twentieth century, public address continued to play a key role in American and world affairs, especially from political leaders throughout both world wars and the Great Depression. In August 1963, 250,000 people gathered near the Lincoln Memorial in Washington, D.C., to hear Martin Luther King Jr. deliver his "I Have a Dream" speech,[23] an address that instantly excited the imaginations of people around the world. In June of that same year, President John F. Kennedy traveled to Berlin to speak to an audience of over 400,000, voicing his support for those blocked in by the Berlin Wall—built by East German leaders after World War II to prevent emigration to the West. Kennedy famously showed his solidarity with Berliners by declaring *"Ich bin ein Berliner"* ("I am a Berliner").

Twenty-four years later, President Ronald Reagan traveled to the Brandenburg Gate in Berlin and challenged Russian leader Mikhail Gorbachev with the iconic words, "Mr. Gorbachev, tear down this wall!" The wall was finally opened in 1989. In the 1990s, the Million Man and the Million Woman marches culminated in public speeches by activists on such issues as job creation, human rights, and respect for African Americans.[24] And within minutes of the June 26, 2015, ruling that the Constitution protected the right of same-sex couples to marry, a crowd gathered outside the U.S. Supreme Court building, where lead plaintiff Jim Obergefell addressed supporters and the Washington, D.C., Gay Men's Chorus sang the national anthem.

Today, new means of digital communication (such as social media, smartphones, and videoconferences) allow people to use technology to connect with distant audiences almost instantaneously. Nevertheless, from

presidential State of the Union addresses to Academy Awards acceptance speeches, public speaking before live audiences remains an important part of our social fabric.

PUBLIC SPEAKING: A DYNAMIC DISCIPLINE

Clearly, public speaking has a long history, and many of the principles taught by ancient scholars such as Aristotle are still relevant today. However, it's also a dynamic discipline that has evolved to reflect changes in society. In this section, we highlight several of these major changes—new ways of depicting the public speaking process, ever-expanding channels for communication, greater awareness of audiences' cultural diversity, new emphasis on the importance of critical thinking in preparing a speech, and increasing attention to ethics in public address.

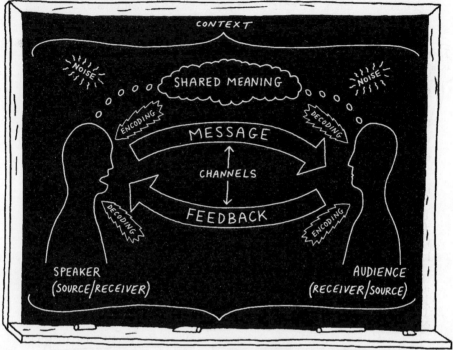

A MODEL OF COMMUNICATION

From Linear to Transactional: Evolving Views of the Public Speaking Process

At the dawn of the modern communication disciplines, scholars viewed all forms of communication—including public speaking—as a linear process. In their view, a speech was a one-way flow of ideas from speaker

WE ARE ALL CHANNELS

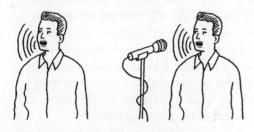

to audience. That is, the speaker "injected" listeners with his or her ideas, much as a doctor injects a patient with a vaccine.

A linear model includes several key elements. Specifically, a person with an idea to express is the **source**, and the ideas that he or she conveys to the audience constitute the **message**. The source must **encode** the message, meaning that he or she chooses **verbal** and **non-verbal symbols** to express the ideas. Verbal symbols are the words that the source uses. Nonverbal symbols are the means of making a point without the use of words, such as hand gestures, eye contact, and facial expressions.

The source communicates the encoded message through a **channel**, the medium of delivery. For example, to deliver their message, speakers can use their voices to address a small group, rely on a microphone or the broadcast airwaves to give a speech to a huge crowd, or even podcast a speech so that it can be heard at different times in different locations.

In the linear model, sources communicate their message to one or more **receivers**, who try to make sense of the message by decoding. To **decode**, receivers process the source's verbal and nonverbal symbols and form their own perception of the message's meaning.

Noise (also called **interference**) is a phenomenon that disrupts communication between source and receiver. Noise may be caused by external sources (for example, when a speech is drowned out by a fleet of jets roaring overhead). But noise also can originate internally—within the source or his or her listeners. For instance, a student giving an oral presentation in class might forget key elements in her speech if she is preoccupied with a recent argument with a coworker. Meanwhile, several members of her audience might have difficulty focusing on her message if they, too, are distracted by their own thoughts and concerns.

Today, scholars have modified this view to consider communication—including public speaking—to be transactional and not a one-way activity. Although many of the elements of the linear model remain in play, a **transaction** is a communicative exchange in which all participants continuously send *and* receive messages.[25] For example, suppose you're about to deliver a speech. As you organize your notes at the lectern, you notice a man yawning in the front row of your audience. In this case, the man is both a receiver of your message and a sender of his own message: "I hope you're not planning to talk for two hours."

Participants in a public speaking transaction can also send and receive messages by providing **feedback** in the form of verbal or nonverbal responses. An audience member who shouts "Right on!" in response to a compelling point in a speech is giving feedback. People listening to a speech can also provide nonverbal feedback. For example, an audience member can lean forward to express interest, nod vigorously to show agreement, fold her arms to signal disagreement, or adopt a puzzled look to convey confusion.

SHARED MEANING

In the transactional model of communication, the participants in a public speaking exchange seek to create **shared meaning**—a common understanding with little confusion and few misinterpretations.[26] Good public speakers don't merely try to get their point of view across to their audience. Instead, they strive to improve their own knowledge, seek understanding, and develop agreements when they communicate with others.[27]

For example, suppose an audience member nods when the speaker says, "We can easily put our privacy at risk on Facebook." The speaker must assume the role of *receiver* and decode the message behind that nod. The nod could mean either "I agree" or "Well, duh, we all know that. Move on!" To better decode the message, a speaker may look for additional cues, such as signs of understanding or boredom on the faces of other audience members. Imagine that the speaker determines that the nod conveys agreement that this potential loss of privacy is a serious problem. He or she might respond by saying, "Because we agree that using Facebook can put our privacy at risk, let's take a look at how we can protect ourselves." Audience members then smile and nod. Now, audience and speaker have created shared meaning.

New Technologies, New Channels

For thousands of years, public speaking was conducted exclusively face-to-face. Whether we consider our ancient ancestors planning a hunt around a campfire or Susan B. Anthony calling for equal rights for nineteenth-century women, speaker and audience were at the same location.

The rise of new communication technologies changed this, providing speakers with ever-expanding options for bringing their message to an audience. In 1923, Calvin Coolidge delivered the first presidential address broadcast on radio,[28] and just twenty-four years later, President Harry S. Truman delivered the first televised presidential address.[29] In the late twentieth century, the development of the Internet introduced even more channels for public speaking. Speakers now can present live speeches

to remote audiences using videoconferencing or VoIP (voice over Internet protocol) technologies such as Skype, Google Hangouts, or MegaChat. They also can create podcasts or make digital recordings of their speeches available on platforms such as YouTube. These options are growing so fast that by the time this book is published, there undoubtedly will be more possibilities. If you are enrolled in an online speech class, you probably will have the chance to use some of these digital technologies to present your speeches. In Chapter 15, we discuss how to do this effectively.

Although technological innovation presents many options for speakers to reach audiences, face-to-face public speaking is unlikely to go the way of the passenger pigeon or landline phone any time soon. The connection that is created when speaker and audience are physically present is very powerful. As former secretary of state Hillary Clinton explained, "Even though we live in the age of so-called virtual reality, where I could do a video-conference with anybody in the world in government, I could even be satellite-beamed into a personal appearance somewhere, . . . nothing substitutes for showing up."[30]

Awareness of Audiences' Cultural Diversity

Most effective and ethical public speakers today take into account the cultural backgrounds of their listeners. By **culture**, we mean the values, traditions, and rules for living that are passed from generation to generation.[31] Culture is learned, and it influences all aspects of a person's life, including religious practices, use of language, food choices, dress, and ways of communicating with others.

In the United States, public speakers have increasingly needed to consider the range of cultures represented by their audience members as American society has grown more culturally diverse. A 2012 Census Bureau Report concluded that forty million U.S. residents, or 13 percent, were born in another country—the highest percentage in over ninety years.[32] The number of minority and non-Hispanic white newborns is now about equal, and the Census Bureau estimates that by 2043, there will be no majority ethnic group in the United States.[33] These trends are exemplified by a recent *National Geographic* map displaying the most common last names in the United States. Jones, Smith, and Anderson are prominent, as are Garcia, Martinez, Nguyen, and Kim.[34]

This trend is not limited to "gateway" states such as California, New York, and Florida: Nguyen is also the fourth most frequent name among

Nebraska home buyers.[35] Communication scholars have recognized the importance of understanding and relating to persons from diverse cultures. Myron Lustig and Jolene Koester note that it is no longer likely that your clients, customers, coworkers, or neighbors have the same values, customs, or first language that you do. Your career success and personal satisfaction will depend increasingly on how well you can communicate with persons from other cultures.[36]

The most effective public speakers are sensitive to their audience members' cultural backgrounds. For example, they avoid biased language and ethnic jokes. They also adapt their delivery to acknowledge their awareness of different cultural norms regarding communication. For example, audience members from one particular culture might interpret extensive eye contact as rude or disrespectful, while individuals from another culture might welcome it. Savvy speakers take pains to identify the cultural norms of their audience and customize their presentation accordingly.

> ▶ **Try Video Activity 1.2, "Humanity 4 Haitian Development," to see an example of a speech targeted to a college audience.**

An audience member's culture not only influences how she or he perceives a speaker's behavior but also affects the person's **worldview**—the "lens" through which she or he sees and interprets reality. Worldview, in turn, influences how listeners respond to a speaker's message. For example, suppose your audience members' culture maintains a worldview that says, "It's not polite to challenge a speaker's claims." In this case, your listeners may decline to ask questions during or after your speech because (to their thinking) asking questions might appear to challenge you and therefore is disrespectful to you. But without questions, you don't have the feedback you need to assess whether your listeners have understood you. Listeners' worldviews also can affect how they respond to a speaker's ideas during a presentation.

For instance, the issue of whether childhood vaccinations should be mandatory has become increasingly controversial,[37] reflecting a difference in worldviews. Persons opposed to mandatory vaccinations are more likely to distrust the medical profession and believe, instead, that parents have a right to decide this question for their own children. There is a greater chance they will believe that vaccines have serious side effects and may not even work. They will tend to doubt that their own children are at risk of contracting the disease that the vaccine is

CONFLICTING WORLDVIEW PROBLEM

supposed to prevent.[38] People who support mandatory vaccinations will have a very different worldview. They are more likely to trust the medical profession and their own doctor's recommendation. They also tend to agree that vaccines are safe and effective. Some supporters remember their own early experiences when measles and other diseases were common and recall that the number of cases declined significantly after vaccines were introduced.[39]

Where do you stand on the vaccinations debate? It depends on your worldview. More important, where does your *audience* stand on the topic that you're discussing in your speech? By understanding your listeners' worldviews, you can more easily gauge their likely reaction to your speech—and craft an appropriate and effective message.

Emphasis on Critical Thinking

In addition to encouraging greater attention to cultural awareness, scholars of public speaking have begun emphasizing the importance of critical thinking skills for speakers who are preparing presentations. **Critical thinking** refers to the analysis and evaluation of ideas based on reliability, truth, and accuracy. When you are engaged in critical thinking, you

CRITICAL THINKING MEANS EVALUATING THE IDEAS OF OTHERS
AND YOUR OWN ASSUMPTIONS

carefully evaluate the evidence and reasoning presented in the message.[40] You also are open-minded about your own ideas and assumptions and subject them to the same analysis that you apply to others' viewpoints.[41]

Before you present ideas to an audience, you should feel confident that those ideas are reasonable. Rather than assuming that your beliefs are true, suspend judgment and consider other perspectives. For example, suppose you are interested in speaking about a law that requires companies to pay for new countermeasures to keep customers' personal data safe from hackers. You could research the perspectives of information technology professionals, businesses affected by the law, consumer protection organizations, legal scholars, and economists. Carefully consider the ideas of each group, and modify your opinions when new ideas make sense.

To use critical thinking, you also would evaluate the probable truth of the claims you plan to make. Anybody can make a claim, but not all claims are based on careful analysis. For example, if you are researching the ability of new technology to keep information safe from hackers, the views of a highly regarded cybersecurity consultant are more likely to be accurate than those of an angry customer who posted a rant on social media.

A Focus on Free and Ethical Communication

Public speaking also involves careful consideration of the rights and responsibilities that come into play when individuals are free to express their ideas in a public forum. **Freedom of expression**—the right to share one's ideas and opinions free from government censorship—is vital in a democratic society, where self-governance depends on both the free flow of information and open debate.

SPEECH CHOICES

TWO CASE STUDIES

What can you do to prepare and present an effective speech? What practices might hold you back? Throughout this book, we'll consider the examples of Mia and Jacob—two college students who are enrolled in two different public speaking classes. We'll follow these students as they move through every step in the speechmaking process, from picking a topic to working on their delivery. You can use their ideas and plan to avoid their pitfalls as you prepare your own speeches. At the end of the book, you can see Mia and Jacob's final outlines and speeches. On LaunchPad, you can watch full-length videos of them giving their speeches.

To introduce Mia and Jacob, let's take a look at the "introductory biographical" speech that they had to give on their second day of class. Based on these five-minute speeches, the students in their class learned the following about Mia and Jacob:

MIA
Introductory Speech

- Career interest: sports medicine
- Favorite sport: soccer
- Hobbies: researching family history, volunteering with an animal rescue organization
- Favorite app: Instagram, so she can keep up with her favorite female comedians
- Weekend activity: attending church, which has many parishioners from different parts of the world

JACOB
Introductory Speech

- Favorite college basketball team: Kentucky Wildcats
- Favorite professional basketball player: Anthony Davis, who played one year at Kentucky before leaving to play professional ball
- Sport played in high school: baseball
- Favorite Web site: The Onion

YOUR TURN:
What important parts of your life would you share in an introductory speech? How would you share these in a way that interests your classmates?

YOUR TURN:
How do you think Mia's and Jacob's interests might affect their choice of speech topics to present in class?

For more questions and activities for this case study, please go to LaunchPad at macmillanhighered.com/speakup4e.

Although you are guaranteed the right to express your ideas freely, as a public speaker you also have a responsibility to express your ideas ethically. **Ethics** refers to a group's shared beliefs about what behaviors are correct or incorrect. Protecting freedom of expression and encouraging the ethical use of that right are increasingly important concerns in the field of public discourse. The principles endorsed by the National Communication Association include the following:

- "We advocate truthfulness, accuracy, honesty, and reason as essential to the integrity of communication."
- "We endorse freedom of expression, diversity of perspective, and tolerance of dissent to achieve the informed and responsible decision making fundamental to a civil society."[42]

Concerns about free expression and ethics are not a new consideration in public speaking. In the first century CE, the Roman rhetorician Quintilian argued that parents and teachers should strive to produce "the good person speaking well." That is, communicators should be virtuous, moral, and focused on the public good, in addition to being effective orators.[43] Today, as unethical communication has increased in the United States, people have stepped up their demands for ethical public speaking. Americans are tired of politicians, lawyers, and multimillionaire chief executive officers who blatantly lie to the public. Recent polling indicates that a majority of Americans no longer have a high level of trust in a wide range of institutions—not only the usual suspects, such as corporations and government, but also schools and organized religion.[44] The online world also has led to new modes of unethical communication, such as trolling (posting incendiary comments to start arguments) and catfishing (misrepresenting one's identity to online contacts).

Consequently, ethics have begun playing an increasingly prominent role in the study of communication as well as other disciplines. As it turns out, there's far more to public speaking than just presenting your message in a way that induces your audience to agree with you and take the actions you have advocated. You must also treat your listeners ethically. That means telling the truth, helping your audience make a well-informed decision about your topic, avoiding manipulative reasoning, and incorporating research materials properly in your speech. We discuss ethical public speaking further in Chapter 3.

CHAPTER REVIEW

"Public speaking is right for you."

In this chapter, we introduced the field of public speaking. Key elements of public speaking are communication between speaker and audience, a focus on the audience by the speaker, an emphasis on the spoken word, and a prepared presentation. We also examined the benefits of mastering public speaking—in the classroom, on the job, in your community, and in everyday situations.

Next, we turned to the rich tradition of public speaking, citing examples from across time (including ancient Greece and Rome) and from around the world (such as China, Africa, India, and the United States).

We also examined the ways in which public speaking as a discipline has evolved to reflect changes in society. We provided examples of several contemporary developments in the field—new ways of viewing the public speaking process, the effects of changing technologies, an emphasis on understanding your audience's cultural background, the usefulness of critical thinking when you're planning your speech, and the importance of protecting freedom of expression and making ethical use of that freedom.

 LaunchPad
macmillan learning

LaunchPad for *Speak Up* offers videos and encourages self-assessment through adaptive quizzing. Go to **macmillanhighered.com/speakup4e** to get access to:

 LearningCurve Adaptive Quizzes

 Video clips that help you understand public speaking concepts

---

Key Terms

civic engagement *12*

source *19*

message *19*

encode *19*

verbal symbol *19*

nonverbal symbol *19*

channel *19*

receiver *19*

Review Questions

1. Describe the four basic characteristics that distinguish public speaking from other forms of communication.
2. Name and explain three ways in which becoming a competent public speaker can positively affect your life and career.
3. Define civic engagement, and explain how it is an important part of democratic self-government.
4. Describe the great tradition of public speaking. Offer some examples of rhetoric playing a role in world events.
5. What is the transactional model of communication? How does it differ from the linear model?
6. How is new technology changing the nature of public speaking?
7. Why is it important to consider culture when analyzing an audience?
8. In what ways can you employ critical thinking in a public speaking situation?
9. Why is it important for speakers to behave ethically?

Critical Thinking Questions

1. In what ways might becoming a more effective and confident speaker affect your life? How could it affect your performance in classes? Help you in your career? Enable you to make a difference in your community?
2. What kinds of public speaking situations are you exposed to on a daily basis? What kind of feedback do you provide to the speaker? How might this feedback affect the speaker's message?

3. Consider your public speaking class as an audience. In what ways are the people in the group alike? In what ways are they diverse?

4. Think of a time you believed that a speaker was being honest with the audience and another time when you thought the speaker was not being honest. What differences between the two speakers led you to these conclusions?

5. Name one person whom you believe to be an effective public speaker. What are the main characteristics that make him or her effective?

Activities

1. ▟ Review the illustration "A Model of Communication" on page 18. Then think of a speaker's message that could be misinterpreted. Answer the following questions: What was the speaker's message? How might an audience member decode a different message from the one that the speaker intended? What feedback might that audience member give to the speaker? Could the speaker clarify her or his idea to help create shared meaning?

2. In small groups, develop a list of situations in which you could suddenly be called on to give an unanticipated speech. The occasion might be a wedding toast, a tribute at the retirement party of a favorite teacher, a presentation of an award, or a plea to the city council about an issue that concerns you. Have each group member select one situation and prepare a brief (one-minute) speech to deliver to the group.

3. Consider a career of interest to you. Then identify a scenario for that career in which you may be called on to speak. Jot down two or three main ideas that you would express in that speech.

4. Search for and watch President George W. Bush's address to Congress after the attacks of September 11, 2001. What assumptions does he seem to be making about the worldview of his audience? How does he seek to establish shared meaning with audience members? Based on the audience's feedback, which parts of his speech are the most successful in creating shared meaning?

Study Plan

_____

_____

_____

_____

_____

_____

_____

_____

_____

_____

_____

_____

_____

_____

_____

_____

_____

_____

_____

_____

_____

_____

_____

DEVELOPING YOUR FIRST SPEECH

2

66Preparation and perseverance are the keys to a successful speech.**99**

On August 28, 1963, tens of thousands of Americans traveled huge distances to join the March on Washington for Jobs and Freedom. Gathering at the Lincoln Memorial, they sang protest songs and hymns and listened to speeches by civil rights leaders.[1] After nearly three hours, the final orator stood at the lectern, with the Lincoln Memorial in the background, and addressed an audience of about 250,000 people.[2]

The speaker, Martin Luther King Jr., told the audience, "I have a dream . . . a dream big enough to include all Americans."[3] The dream that King shared—one in which people would "not be judged by the color of their skin but by the content of their character"—had his listeners cheering and weeping as he concluded his address. Covered by major television networks and newspapers, the speech captured the imaginations of people around the world. In the aftermath of the March on Washington, Congress passed civil rights legislation that banned discrimination in public facilities, in laws or practices pertaining to voting rights, and by employers.

King's "I Have a Dream" speech has won renown among speech scholars as the greatest oral presentation of the twentieth century. A gifted public speaker, King won his first oratorical contest when he was just fifteen years old.[4] Yet he still diligently prepared for the March on Washington speech, putting more care into it than he'd put into any of his previous public addresses.[5] Indeed, he typically invested much time in speech preparation, writing multiple drafts of his Nobel Peace Prize acceptance speech and spending as many as fifteen hours preparing a typical Sunday sermon.[6]

The careful attention that King gave to preparing his addresses illustrates an important lesson that can benefit all public speakers, whether they have experience or are new to public speaking: *preparation and perseverance are the keys to a successful speech*. We have found that students who have a well-organized plan for speech preparation, and who devote enough time to following that plan, become more effective speakers than those who rely solely on natural talent and confidence.

In this chapter, we provide a preview of the speech preparation process. We begin by discussing the importance of preparation. Next, we cover five major considerations you should keep in mind while preparing a public address. We then lay out steps you can follow to deliver a successful speech early in the term. Finally, we offer tips for minimizing speech anxiety.

YOU ARE NOT PREPARED WHEN...

You waited until the last minute.

You focused on length, not quality.

WHY PREPARE?

For beginning speakers, preparation is crucial. The more rigorously you prepare your speech, the more likely you'll avoid three common problems that inexperienced public speakers typically encounter:

- *Leaving too little time for planning and practicing.* Students who wait until the last minute to develop their speeches usually deliver weaker addresses than their better-prepared classmates. Why? If you put off your assignment until just before the due date, you can't plan or practice your presentation. And without a plan or sufficient practice, you risk losing track of your thoughts while delivering your speech.

- *Focusing on length rather than quality.* Beginners sometimes focus more on meeting time requirements than on developing their ideas. They write down the first thoughts that come to mind or simply insert chunks of researched material. They don't consider what information might be most interesting, useful, or convincing to their listeners, nor do they try to organize their ideas in a way that their audience can easily follow. The result? A disjointed, lackluster presentation.

- *Failing to follow the assignment.* A speech may impress a classroom full of beginning speakers if it's delivered well and includes interesting details. Yet it will not succeed if it fails to meet your instructor's assignment regarding such matters as which topics are acceptable, how the speech should be organized, and how many sources are required. Make sure to clarify such expectations before preparing your speech.

Fortunately, you don't have to succumb to these challenges. This chapter introduces steps of the speechmaking process that will help you avoid these stumbling blocks and deliver a successful speech.

CAREFULLY "FILED"
ASSIGNMENT
DESCRIPTION

You did not follow the assignment.

THE CLASSICAL APPROACH TO SPEECH PREPARATION

The speech preparation process that we outline in this book is based on principles of rhetoric that have been taught and learned for over 2,400 years. As we noted in Chapter 1, Aristotle wrote a systematic analysis of rhetorical practices in the fourth century BCE. Cicero (106–43 BCE)—a Roman lawyer, a politician, and one of history's most famed orators—elaborated on these concepts. During this time, rhetoric was a highly prized skill that citizens used to present and defend their ideas in public forums.

In his treatise *De inventione*, Cicero maintained that effective speakers attend to five key matters while preparing a speech—*invention, arrangement, style, memory,* and *delivery.* Contemporary scholars refer to these five concepts as the **classical canons of rhetoric**. These five canons form the basis of speech preparation to this day. Here, we take a closer look at each one:

- **Invention** is the generation of ideas for use in a speech, including both the speaker's own thoughts on the topic and ideas from other sources. Speakers generate a large number of ideas for their speeches and then choose those that will best serve their purpose

CLASSICAL CANONS OF RHETORIC

ΕΫΡΕΣΙΣ   ΤΑΞΙΣ   ΛΕΞΙΣ   ΜΝΗΜΗ   ΫΠΟΚΡΙΣΙΣ
INVENTION   ARRANGEMENT   STYLE   MEMORY   DELIVERY

in an ethical manner. Talented speakers select the best ideas for a particular speech based on their analysis of their audience, their choice of topic and purpose, the research they conduct, and the evidence they gather.

- **Arrangement** refers to the structuring of ideas to convey them effectively to an audience; today, we refer to this as *organization*. Most speeches have three main parts—an introduction, a body, and a conclusion—with the body serving as the core of the speech and containing the main points. Effective speakers arrange the ideas in the body so that the message will be clear and memorable to the audience.

- **Style** is the choice of language that will best express a speaker's ideas to the audience. Through effective style, speakers state their ideas clearly, make their ideas memorable, and avoid bias.

- **Memory** (also known as *preparation*) is somewhat analogous to practice and refers to the work that speakers do to remain in command of their material when they present a speech.[7] This canon originally emphasized techniques for learning speeches by heart and creating mental stockpiles of words and phrases that speakers could inject into presentations where appropriate.[8] In contemporary settings, speakers seldom recite speeches from memory; instead, they rely on notes to remind themselves of key ideas that they can deliver conversationally.

- **Delivery** refers to the speaker's use of his or her voice and body during the actual presentation of a speech. A strong delivery—one in which the speaker's voice, hand gestures, eye contact, and movements are appropriate for the audience and setting—can make a powerful impression. Chapter 13 covers delivery skills in detail.

The five canons—invention, arrangement, style, memory, and delivery—inform the steps you will follow to prepare and deliver an effective speech. Next, we discuss how to use these principles to craft a speech. This material in Chapter 2 serves two purposes. First, it introduces you to the steps in the preparation process for any speech. Second, it covers information about each step that will help you prepare for an early-in-the-term speech that has been assigned before you have covered the later chapters in more detail.

PREPARING AND DELIVERING YOUR FIRST SPEECH

It's happened: you've just begun this course, and already your instructor has assigned your first speech. Often, this first assignment is designed to be an icebreaker—a speech introducing a classmate, for example, or a talk about yourself. Such assignments are usually focused on giving students an opportunity to speak in front of the class in a low-pressure situation as well as a chance to get to know one another better. Other instructors may begin with a more substantive assignment, such as a three- to five-minute speech describing a hero in your community or an artifact that is significant to your culture. In either case, because the speech comes early in the term, you will not be expected to be familiar with all of the concepts in this book. However, your professor will have covered some of these topics and will expect to see you apply them in your presentation.

COMMON FIRST SPEECH ASSIGNMENTS

In this section of Chapter 2, you'll find a quick guide to preparing and delivering your first speech. By following each of these steps, you should be able to pull together a workable speech and deliver it on the appointed day. Refer to your assignment description or ask your instructor which of these steps you will be responsible for, and emphasize them in your preparation. If you'd like to know more about any of these steps, use the following table to find the corresponding chapter where each step is discussed in more detail.

If you want to know more about	Go to
analyzing your audience	Ch. 5
selecting a topic for your speech	Ch. 6, pp. 166–71
determining your speech's rhetorical purpose	Ch. 6, pp. 172–73
creating a thesis statement	Ch. 6, pp. 179–83
determining your main points	Ch. 9, pp. 255–58
developing supporting materials	Chs. 7–8
organizing the body of your speech	Ch. 9, pp. 258–69
outlining the body of your speech	Ch. 11
organizing and outlining the introduction and conclusion	Ch. 10
incorporating transitions	Ch. 9, pp. 269–71; Ch. 11, p. 314
considering word choice	Ch. 12
considering presentation aids	Ch. 14
practicing your speech	Ch. 13, pp. 372–73
delivering your speech	Ch. 13
mediated presentations	Ch. 15

Analyze Your Audience

Speeches should always be given for the benefit of the audience—whether to inform, persuade, or mark a special occasion. **Audience analysis** is the process of learning about an audience's interests and backgrounds in order to create a speech that meets their needs. It is important to learn about the audience members (or make educated guesses) before you select a topic and choose the ideas you will use to develop your topic.

At this early point in the course, you may not be able to conduct a detailed, formal analysis of your audience. However, you probably have spoken with classmates and learned about their interests and backgrounds. You also may have heard them share information during class (for example, perhaps your instructor had students introduce one another during the first week of class). In addition, you and the other students will likely have shared experiences in class and at your college or university. Use your knowledge of these shared experiences to anticipate your listeners' attitudes and interests.

If you feel you need to do more to analyze your audience, here are some questions you could ask several classmates:

- Are there popular sports teams, activities, and traditions on campus? Unpopular experiences such as scarce parking or difficulty in signing up for required classes?
- Are students active in community service? Are there organizations or classes on campus that promote community service?
- Are many of our classmates first-year students? Seniors? Do most of them live on campus or commute? Are most working to finance their education?
- What are the cultural backgrounds of the people taking this class?

Jot down responses to these questions, as well as your own thoughts about topics that may interest your classmates.

Select Your Topic

Your **topic** is the subject you will address in your speech. The topic for your first speech will depend on the assignment your instructor has given you. Typical assignments include informing the class about an interesting issue you studied in another course, telling the class about a pet peeve, or sharing a cultural tradition with your audience.

To choose a topic, list as many possibilities as you can, and then use your audience analysis to select one that you think would most appeal to your listeners and also appeal to you. When you personally care about the topic, you'll invest more time in preparing and practicing the speech.

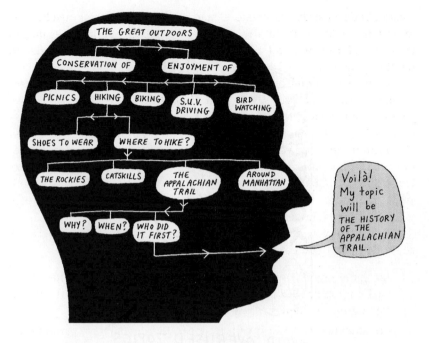

You'll also convey your interest in the topic while delivering your speech, which will further engage your audience.

Make sure to avoid overused topics—such as the drinking age, steroids in sports, abortion, or the "art" of making a perfect peanut butter and jelly sandwich. Every instructor has a list of "reruns" that she or he would prefer not to watch again. If you choose a topic that is often presented in student speeches (for example, the death penalty or legalization of marijuana), you must make sure to take a fresh perspective or approach. If you have any doubts whatsoever whether your topic is appropriate, be sure to check with your instructor.

Finally, consider ways to narrow your topic. Most topics are too broad to cover in a five- or ten-minute presentation. For example, you would run out of time long before you could discuss everything there is to know about your major, culture, or favorite sport. Select one or more *aspects* of your topic that you think will most interest your audience and that you can also cover in the available time for your speech. For example, instead of trying to describe your entire culture, you might focus your topic on how your family or neighborhood celebrates a particular holiday.

AVOID OVERUSED TOPICS

Determine Your Speech's Rhetorical Purpose

Every speech must have a **rhetorical purpose**—a primary goal for the speech. For example, do you want to help listeners broaden their understanding of your topic? Persuade your audience to support a cause? Mark a special occasion? Inspire audience members and move them emotionally? Speeches typically have one of the following objectives:

- *Informing:* Increasing your audience's understanding or awareness of your subject

- *Persuading:* Trying to influence your audience's beliefs or actions with respect to your subject

- *Marking a special occasion:* Commemorating events, such as graduations, memorial services, weddings, awards ceremonies, and holidays

The rhetorical purpose you choose focuses the content of your speech. This is because each idea you develop must support the purpose

you've selected. For classroom speeches, your instructor may specify a rhetorical purpose. If he or she does not, determine the purpose yourself. How? Decide whether you want your audience members to understand, believe, feel, or do something in particular about your topic after they listen to your speech. For instance, one student who was concerned about a regional drought wanted audience members to practice water conservation techniques in the residence halls.

Create a Thesis Statement

After you've selected your topic and identified your rhetorical purpose, draft a thesis statement for your speech. The **thesis statement** (sometimes called the *central idea* or *topic statement*) is a single sentence that sums up your speech's main message and reflects your narrowed topic and rhetorical purpose. Basically, the thesis statement should convey your speech's bottom line, enabling audience members to understand the essence of your overall speech message. Here are some examples of thesis statements:

- "New Year celebrations in my culture include three unique traditions."
- "You should try a vegan diet for one week."
- "There are several humorous aspects of online shopping."

Determine Your Main Points

Main points are the major ideas you will emphasize in your presentation. By calling attention to these points, you help your audience understand and remember the most important ideas from your speech. When speakers fail to do so, their listeners have difficulty following and retaining a speech's message.

To determine main points, begin by making a list of ideas you might like to cover. These ideas can come from what you already know and from research you do about your topic. Then select main points by considering which ideas would be most interesting to your audience and best help listeners obtain a deeper understanding of your topic.

Each main point you select must also support your thesis statement. Otherwise, your audience may conclude that you're straying off course and may lose interest or become confused.

> ▶ To practice with organizing main points, try Video Activity 2.1, "Previews, Transitions, and Summaries."

Develop Supporting Materials

Once you've selected your main points, develop **supporting materials**— information that bolsters and fleshes out the claims made in each of those points. There are several types of supporting materials, including examples, definitions, testimony, statistics, narratives, and analogies. You can generate supporting materials internally by brainstorming and externally by conducting research.

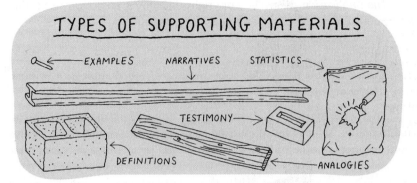

Brainstorming is the process of quickly listing every idea that comes to mind, without evaluating its merits, in order to develop a substantial list of ideas. To brainstorm potential supporting materials, ask yourself questions such as "What do I know about my topic?" and "What do I think is most important or interesting about this topic?" List all the responses to these questions that come to mind. Your goal is to create a diverse list of many possible ideas, not to make a final decision about which ones you will use.

Research is the process of gathering information from libraries, quality online sources, and interviews with authorities on your topic. Through research, you obtain information from experts that will enhance your understanding of the topic and strengthen your speech's credibility. Even if your instructor requires less research for your first speech than for later assignments, you should still do a little research to answer any questions you have about your topic area.

As you research, be sure to save a copy of any useful material you unearth. Also keep track of the **bibliographic information** for the sources of your information, noting the following items so that you can incorporate them into your outline and your speech:

- *The author:* The writer or sponsoring organization of a book, an article, or an online entry
- *The author's credentials on the subject:* Her or his job title, relevant education or job experience, or academic or institutional affiliation
- *The name of the source:* The title of a book, the title of an article and the name of the periodical or newspaper it ran in, or the name of a person you interviewed

- *The publication date:* The copyright date for a book you used, the publication date of a periodical or newspaper you researched, the date you accessed a Web site, or the date you conducted an interview
- *The page(s)* on which you found relevant information in a printed source or the URL of an online source

After brainstorming and researching supporting materials for your main points, select the supporting materials that would most interest your listeners and help them grasp what you're saying about your topic.

Organize and Outline the Body of Your Speech

A speech should be well organized, meaning that your ideas are structured in a way that enables the audience to follow your message easily. To organize your speech, draft an **outline**. Your outline contains the text of your speech in complete sentences or briefer phrases (depending on what your instructor prefers).

A speech outline has three major parts—the introduction, the body, and the conclusion. The **body** is the core of your speech and is where you present your main message about your topic. For this reason, we recommend outlining the body of your speech before outlining the introduction, even though the body follows the introduction when you actually deliver the speech.

To create a full-sentence outline for the body of your speech, first express each of the main points you've selected as a single sentence

ALWAYS BUILD THE BODY FIRST—IT'S THE CORE OF YOUR SPEECH (AND YOUR SNOWMAN)

that states a key idea you're planning to emphasize. Then number each main point with a roman numeral. It is common to have between two and five main points, although your instructor may ask you to develop a single main point in your first speech.

Next, create subpoints from the supporting materials you have gathered through brainstorming and research. **Subpoints** explain, prove, or expand on your main points. In your outline, indicate each subpoint with a capital letter, and indent each under its corresponding main point.

An important principle of outlining is **subordination**. Each main point must relate to your specific purpose, and each subpoint must relate to the main point that it supports. If you include additional supporting material under any subpoint (a sub-subpoint, so to speak), it must relate to that subpoint. Here's a generic example of how subordination might look in a typical outline:

I. Main Point 1
   A. Subpoint
   B. Subpoint
      1. Sub-subpoint
      2. Sub-subpoint
II. Main Point 2

Outline Your Introduction and Conclusion

The **introduction** to your speech serves several vital purposes, each of which is the basis for one major section of the introduction, as shown in the following list (your instructor may require a specific combination or order of these elements):

I. *Attention-getter.* Start your speech with a brief story, quotation, striking fact or statistic, or humorous incident that grabs listeners' attention while also hinting at what your speech will cover.

II. *Thesis statement.* In a single sentence, convey the topic and purpose of your speech.

III. *Show the audience what's in it for them.* In one or two sentences, summarize why audience members should listen to your speech. Will you provide information they need to know? Information they will want to share with friends and family?

IV. *Establish your credibility.* To show that you are a believable source of information on your topic, indicate any relevant expertise, experience, or education that you have.

V. *Preview your main points.* To help the audience understand where you will be going in your speech, list each main point using no more than one sentence per point.

The **conclusion** of your speech summarizes what you have said and leaves the audience with a memorable impression of your presentation. There are two main parts to a conclusion:

I. *Summary of your main points.* Briefly recap the major points you made during your speech.

II. *Clincher.* End with a closing sentence or paragraph that leaves your audience with a vivid memory of your speech. A clincher may be related to the introduction (for example, supplying a happy ending to a story you began in the attention-getter), or it may consist of a statement or quotation that characterizes the content of your speech.

Incorporate Transitions

After you've outlined the body, introduction, and conclusion, you will want to create transitions to connect the parts of your speech. A **transition** is a sentence that indicates you are moving from one idea to another. Transitions are especially helpful in the following places:

- Between the introduction and your first main point
- Between each main point
- Between the final main point and the conclusion

Here are some examples of transitions:

- "First, let's talk about . . ." (*transition from introduction to first main point*)
- "Now that we've considered . . . , let's move on to . . ." (*transition between two main points*)
- "This completes our discussion of . . ." (*transition from final main point to conclusion*)

Consider Your Word Choice

Reread your entire outline, this time carefully considering the language you will use to express your ideas. Effective **word choice** (or **diction**) can help make your speech much more memorable and engaging for listeners. When preparing your speech, select words that your audience will understand, use precise terms to express your ideas, and choose language that makes your speech come alive. Focus on simplifying your sentences (remember, audience members cannot reread parts of your speech if they become confused). Finally, be sure to avoid biased language that may hurt others or damage your credibility.

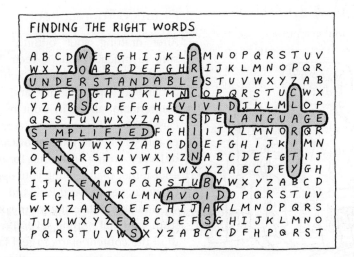

FINDING THE RIGHT WORDS

Consider Presentation Aids

A **presentation aid** is anything beyond the speech itself that your audience members can see or hear that helps them understand and remember your message. Traditional aids include actual objects or models (for example, a physical model of a DNA molecule), video and audio recordings (such as a short clip of several birds and their calls), drawings, photographs, charts, maps, and graphs. PowerPoint presentations or other electronic slide shows are also common aids.

Each presentation aid must support the point that you are developing. For example, if you want your audience to appreciate the differences between birdcalls, an audio recording that clearly demonstrates those differences would be entirely relevant. Also take care that audio aids are loud and clear and that visual aids are uncluttered and large enough for your audience to see from all points in the room.

Practice Your Speech

After drafting your outline, make sure to practice your speech. With practice, you'll feel more confident about your presentation—and more comfortable talking in front of your classmates. This comfort level will enable you to use **extemporaneous delivery**—using only notes for reference rather than reading your speech to the audience word-for-word.

Practice delivering your speech from your full outline several times, until the content starts to feel familiar. Then condense your outline into a set of briefer notes. This will be

the outline you'll use when actually presenting your speech, and it will help you deliver your speech in a more conversational way, explaining the main points and subpoints in your own words, without reading word-for-word. Place your speaking outline on index cards or 8½ in. × 11 in. paper, using large type so that it will be easy to glance down and find your place while you are presenting. You may refer to your notes when you need to refresh your memory, but you should usually be looking at the audience.

Instead of delivering your speech face-to-face, your assignment may call for a **mediated presentation**. This means that your speech will be transmitted through a mechanical or electronic medium. When practicing a mediated speech, be sure to practice with the recording technology and camera operator you will use on the day of the speech. Play your practice speech back to see how your speech will appear to the viewers, and make adjustments if needed.

> ▶ To see an example of a mediated presentation, try Video Activity 2.2, "Lui, Preventing Cyberbullying."

Deliver Your Speech

The moment has come: you're watching a classmate wrap up her speech, and you're next in line. As you approach the lectern and start delivering your speech, keep the following guidelines in mind:

- *Project your voice.* Speak loudly and slowly enough that your audience can easily hear what you are saying.
- *Maintain an even rate of speaking.* Many speakers tend to rush through a speech, particularly if they are nervous. Speak at a rate that enables you to pronounce the words clearly, allowing the audience to follow your speech.
- *Convey interest in your topic.* Maintain energy and variety in your speaking voice so that you build audience enthusiasm for your speech.
- *Maintain eye contact.* Try to make eye contact with people in each section of the room during the course of your presentation.

Each speech you deliver is a learning experience. Your instructor (and perhaps your classmates) will offer feedback after your presentation. Use these suggestions to prepare future speeches; you'll soon see your public speaking skills improve.

> ▶ To analyze an example of student delivery in a classroom speech, try Video Activity 2.3, "Gentz, My Hero, Marilyn Hamilton."

OVERCOMING SPEECH ANXIETY

As you begin to prepare for your first speech, you may experience some nervousness about speaking in front of an audience. If so, you're not alone. Although the claim that people fear public speaking more than death may be an urban legend, almost everyone—from college students to the public at large—feels nervous about speaking before an audience.[9] The symptoms of **speech anxiety**—the worry or fear that some people experience before giving a talk (also called **stage fright**)—can take a wide variety of forms. Some people experience the stereotypical sensation of "butterflies in the stomach," as well as sweaty palms and a dry mouth. Others endure nausea, hyperventilation, and downright panic.

A little nervousness actually can be a good thing when you're giving a speech: it helps focus your attention. But in its extreme form, speech anxiety can prevent you from speaking clearly or keeping your train of thought while delivering your presentation. Although speech anxiety is quite common, you *can* learn to manage it. As one seasoned public speaker put it, "You may not be able to get rid of the butterflies, but you can at least get them flying in formation." You are already taking an

important first step by participating in a public speaking course. Research indicates that students in such classes become more self-assured and experience less apprehension about speaking as the term progresses.[10]

The following strategies can help you combat speech anxiety and build confidence in your public speaking skills.

Prepare Early and Follow a Plan

One of the best ways to build confidence in your ability to deliver a successful speech is to get to work soon after you receive an assignment and follow an organized plan to craft and practice your speech. Resist the temptation to procrastinate: speech apprehension is associated with inadequate preparation.[11] Conversely, high anxiety can be reduced by good preparation.[12] When a speaker gets down to business and makes progress on a speech, he or she will feel less anxious.[13] The point is clear: select a topic as soon as possible, and draft an outline well in advance.

After you have an outline, you can take other steps to improve your speech and build confidence. One helpful suggestion is to get your instructor's feedback on your outline. This feedback—perhaps in the form of comments on your outline or a list of the standards she or he uses for grading—will help you improve your speech and reduce the stress of not knowing how it will be evaluated.[14]

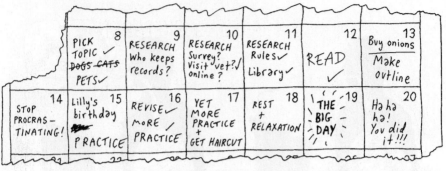

8	9	10	11	12	13
PICK TOPIC ✓ ~~DOGS CATS~~ PETS✓	RESEARCH Who keeps records?	RESEARCH Survey? Visit vet?✓ online? ✓	RESEARCH Rules✓ Library✓	READ ✓	Buy onions ——— Make outline
14 STOP PROCRAS- TINATING!	**15** Lilly's birthday ~~~ PRACTICE	**16** REVISE✓ MORE ✓ PRACTICE	**17** YET MORE PRACTICE + GET HAIRCUT	**18** REST + RELAXATION	**19** ' ' THE BIG DAY	**20** Ha ha ha! You did it!!!

EARLY PREPARATION IS KEY

You also can gain confidence by practicing your speech. One study found that when students delivered their speech three times before a small group of classmates, they experienced a reduction in speech anxiety.[15] If it is not practical to practice with a group of classmates, you can present your speech to friends and family. If you follow this plan—beginning right away, asking for feedback, and practicing—you will be on the right track to building confidence.

Imagined interactions are another form of practice. During this process, a speaker mentally practices delivering a speech to the audience, presenting the content of the message and picturing a positive interaction with the audience (such as applause).[16] Research has found that practice using imagined interactions before speaking reduces the number and length of silent pauses during a presentation and strengthens the speaker's assessment of his or her performance.[17]

Take Care of Yourself

Be sure to get a good night's sleep before a speech. Avoid excessive sugar and caffeinated beverages the morning of your presentation: these will make you more jittery. If you don't feel like eating much on the day of your speech, consume a light meal before you deliver your presentation. Then reward yourself with a favorite feast when it's all over.

Also, budget your time in the days leading up to your speech. It's hard to get sufficient sleep, prepare nutritious meals, and practice your presentation if you have to work six hours, study for a test, and write a ten-page paper the day before you deliver your speech. Having too much to do in too little time intensifies anxiety. To avoid this scenario, look at the syllabi for all your courses early in the semester to see when major assignments are due. Consider other commitments as well, such as job, family, and community responsibilities. Then plan your time so that the days leading up to your speech are as relaxed as possible.

Visualize Success

Researchers have found that a simple activity reduces anxiety for public speaking students—visualizing success.[18] With **visualization**, you imagine yourself scoring a resounding success, such as concluding your speech and winning enthusiastic applause from an appreciative audience. Make your visualization as specific as possible. For example, imagine yourself striding confidently to the front of the room. Contemplate speaking to the audience in the same way you would converse with a

friend—natural and relaxed. Picture the audience nodding in agreement with a key point, smiling when an idea hits home, and laughing at your jokes. Listen to the thundering applause as you wrap up your speech. The power of positive thinking is no mere cliché. When you visualize success, you can ease your anxiety—if not eradicate it entirely.

Use Relaxation Techniques

When you're suffering from speech anxiety, your muscles tense up, and your mind swarms with negative thoughts. You know you should relax. But who can chill out on command? **Relaxation strategies**—techniques that reduce muscle tension and negative thoughts—can help. For many people, exercise is a powerful relaxation strategy. It helps you expend nervous energy, and it leaves you feeling relaxed and limber on the day of your presentation. It's also renowned for clearing your mind. But exercising doesn't necessarily mean heading for the nearest gym to lift weights or taking a Pilates class. All you have to do is practice tightening and releasing your muscles—wherever you are at the moment. Breathe in as you tighten a group of muscles, and then exhale as you release the tension. Consider progressing from your neck muscles down to your feet. You can use this and other relaxation techniques even as you're waiting to deliver your speech.

Volunteer to Speak First

Many public speakers experience more anxiety shortly before their presentation than during the actual speech.[19] As anxious speakers

SPEECH CHOICES

A CASE STUDY: *MIA*

Let's take a look at how Mia began her speech preparation process.

Early in the semester, Mia's teacher assigned an informative speech in her public speaking class. It would require a full-sentence outline, presentation aids, supporting materials that appeal to different learning styles, and at least four credible research sources. Mia felt stressed: with the speech and outline due in four weeks, there was a lot of work to be done! Mia's first speech in class—a three-minute speech about a hero in her community—had gone pretty well, and she'd gotten a B. But she'd felt nervous in front of the class and knew that her presentation had been a bit choppy and disorganized. This time, Mia wanted to do even better.

To prepare, Mia reviewed the steps of speech preparation and created a schedule for accomplishing each stage. She gave herself a couple of days to relax and made no plans on the day before an exam or major assignment for another class. But she planned to spend time on her speech most other days and leave enough time to practice after her outline was complete. Mia also took note of her instructor's office hours, just in case she had questions along the way.

Mia wanted to select her topic early so she could get started on preparation. She made a list of possible topics on the night she received the assignment. The next day, she stopped in the library to do some research on additional possibilities. Whenever Mia felt a pang of anxiety about the assignment, she thought positively and visualized a successful performance. She also scheduled one more item—a home-cooked meal at her aunt's as a reward after she presented the speech.

YOUR TURN:
What will be your first steps when you receive your next speech assignment?

For more questions and activities for this case study, please go to LaunchPad at macmillanhighered.com/speakup4e.

think about their upcoming presentation, it is also possible for them to exaggerate the risk that their speech will not succeed or that the audience will be critical when their nervousness shows.[20] If this describes you and you're going to be one of several speakers in a

SPEECH CHOICES

A CASE STUDY: JACOB

Let's consider how Jacob used his time after receiving a persuasive speech assignment.

Jacob was not thrilled when the instructor passed out a persuasive-speech assignment. He needed to prepare an eight-minute original speech about a serious problem in his local community, supported by credible research and organized using Monroe's Motivated Sequence. (You'll read about this organizational pattern in Chapter 17.) His two previous presentations had not gone well, and the last thing he needed was another speech assignment. Jacob had one advantage—he was comfortable speaking in front of a class. Unfortunately, this self-confidence led him to believe that he would be able to present a high-quality speech without much preparation.

Jacob's instructor had invited students to come by the office and discuss their ideas for a topic. But instead of going, Jacob figured that he could check with one of his roommates who had taken public speaking last year and see if he might have an idea.

Confident that he would come through at the last minute, Jacob thought little about his speech during the two weeks after he received the assignment. Once he went to the library to do some research but got distracted by an art exhibit on the second floor. He had a paper due in another course two days before the speech was due and then a midterm exam in a third class the following day. He tried to repress thoughts of all three assignments. Why get stressed out now when there were two weeks to go?

YOUR TURN:
What problems do you think Jacob might have if he waits until the last minute to prepare?

For more questions and activities for this case study, please go to LaunchPad at macmillanhighered.com/speakup4e.

class or program, ask to speak first—or as early as possible in the lineup. That way, you'll have less time to work up a debilitating level of worry.

Never Defeat Yourself

It is easy to become your own worst critic while giving a speech. If audience members are yawning or frowning, such feedback can increase

your speech anxiety.[21] Do not fall into the trap of making negative judgments as you speak. There is a good chance that a frowning classmate is trying to remember where he left his keys or worrying about an upcoming math test.

Even if you do make a serious mistake during your speech, do not give up. Your classmates will be hoping you recover and finish strong. We have seen one student's outline disappear when her iPad crashed midspeech, another remain silent for two minutes while putting a jumbled pile of note cards in the right order, and a third watch his dog (a visual aid) have an "accident" as the speech concluded. In these situations, the first postspeech comment from an audience member has consistently been a supportive statement about the speaker's effort to recover.

CHAPTER REVIEW

> **Preparation and perseverance are the keys to a successful speech.**

The most successful presentations in history, such as Martin Luther King Jr.'s "I Have a Dream" speech, usually derive from careful thought, planning, and preparation. Both beginning and more experienced speakers should remember this lesson: even a first-time speaker can give a much stronger presentation by taking a bit of extra time and effort.

In this chapter, we emphasized the importance of preparing for public speaking. First, we introduced the five classical canons of rhetoric, a set of guidelines that continue to inform the way many speech instructors teach speech preparation today.

Next, we presented a step-by-step process for preparing your first speech. It's important to note that speech development is a craft comprising a set of specific skills that you can master. The nine main steps are analyzing the audience; selecting a topic; determining the rhetorical purpose; creating a thesis statement; determining your main points; developing supporting materials; organizing and outlining the body, introduction, conclusion, and transitions; considering word choice and presentation aids; and practicing and delivering the speech. By making good choices at each step of the speech preparation process, you improve your chances of delivering a successful presentation.

In this chapter, we also outlined some basic techniques to help you overcome your speech anxiety by emphasizing that you can channel your nervousness to help you become a better speaker. To help you "get the butterflies flying in formation," we suggest that you prepare early and follow a plan. Strive to take care of yourself by balancing responsibilities with personal needs. To build a positive outlook, try visualizing success, using relaxation techniques, and volunteering to speak first. And when you are speaking, stay positive: don't be your own worst critic.

 LaunchPad
macmillan learning

LaunchPad for *Speak Up* offers videos and encourages self-assessment through adaptive quizzing. Go to **macmillanhighered.com/speakup4e** to get access to:

✓ **LearningCurve**
Adaptive Quizzes

 Video clips that help you understand public speaking concepts

Key Terms

classical canon of rhetoric *38*
invention *38*
arrangement *39*
style *39*
memory *39*
delivery *39*
audience analysis *41*
topic *42*
rhetorical purpose *44*
thesis statement *45*
main point *46*
supporting material *46*
brainstorming *47*
research *47*
bibliographic information *47*

outline *48*
body *48*
subpoint *49*
subordination *49*
◉ introduction *49*
◉ conclusion *50*
◉ transition *50*
word choice (diction) *51*
◉ presentation aid *52*
extemporaneous delivery *52*
mediated presentation *53*
speech anxiety (stage fright) *54*
imagined interaction *56*
visualization *57*
relaxation strategy *58*

Review Questions

1. What are three common mistakes that inexperienced speakers make when preparing a speech?
2. Name and define each of the five classical canons of rhetoric.
3. What is audience analysis, and what are three questions you may want to answer about your audience?
4. Explain what is meant by rhetorical purpose. What are the three basic rhetorical purposes that speeches can serve?
5. What is a thesis statement, and how does it differ from a speech topic?
6. What are supporting materials, and how do they help a speaker develop main points?
7. Define *main points* and *subpoints*, and explain the principle of subordination.
8. What are presentation aids, and how can a speaker make sure they support her or his message?
9. What is extemporaneous delivery, and why is it generally the best approach for speakers?
10. List three guidelines for effective delivery.

11. Name and explain five techniques that can help you overcome speech anxiety.

Critical Thinking Questions

1. How would you analyze your public speaking classmates as an audience? Consider their backgrounds and interests. What are some of their shared experiences? How could you use this information to adapt a speech to your classmates?

2. How would the research and supporting materials you might use in a persuasive speech differ from those you might use in a special-occasion speech?

3. When you see a speaker who is obviously feeling nervous, how can you as an audience member help put him or her at ease? Can thinking about your experience as an audience member help you feel less nervous as a speaker?

Activities

1. In small groups, look at each of the steps involved in preparing a speech (pp. 40–53). Discuss which classical canons of rhetoric are applied during each step.

2. In small groups, prepare a skit in which a speaker uses at least three different techniques for reducing speech anxiety. Then present your skit to the entire class. Have other class members try to identify the techniques that each group is using.

3. ⊙ Video Activity 2.4: "Garza, How to Buy a Guitar." Watch Richard Garza's speech, and analyze how he has followed the different steps involved in preparing a speech. How does Garza relate his speech to the audience? Indicate his thesis and main points? Use supporting materials (including presentation aids)? What has he done to develop his introduction and conclusion? How well does he follow this chapter's advice about delivering a speech? Is there any advice in this chapter that Garza did not adopt? What could he have done differently?

4. Think back on any awards programs you like to watch (for example, the Oscars, Grammys, ESPYs, or Video Music Awards) and the ways

in which different winners approach their acceptance speeches. Is it obvious when a winner has prepared a speech beforehand? Is it obvious when she or he has not? Have any speakers made comments that you thought were inappropriate for that type of event?

5. Prepare a one- to two-minute talk on any topic of interest. Then break into small groups, and listen to each group member's presentation. After each speech, discuss what you liked about the speaker's content and delivery.

Study Plan

_____

_____

_____

_____

_____

_____

_____

_____

_____

_____

_____

_____

_____

_____

_____

_____

SPEECH ETHICS

3

All of us face difficult choices throughout our lives. For example, imagine that your romantic partner recently modeled a new, expensive sweater, saying, "I just love this fabric. What do you think? Do I look good in this?" You find the sweater downright hideous, but you know from experience that if you answer honestly, you will hurt your loved one's feelings and perhaps even start a fight. Yet you also feel uncomfortable telling a lie. So you hesitate, wondering what exactly to say. These kinds of ethical quandaries are not limited to what you say: they also can arise when you mislead people by painting a false picture of something.

Consider Alex, a recent college graduate who works in the marketing division of a software company. He makes a good salary for a new graduate, but his hours are long, and his job is challenging. His boss travels a great deal for business and stays in touch with Alex and others in his division by using Skype. Because of conflicting calendars, the boss schedules a meeting via Skype with Alex early on a weekday morning. He asks Alex to give him and a colleague a short oral report on his progress in marketing to a potential client. Because he knew that his boss would be out of town, Alex had planned to work from home that morning and then attend an afternoon Major League Baseball game.

When Alex sets up his laptop to begin his Skype session, he is wearing a suit jacket and tie (which are the clothes he usually wears to work). Beneath the laptop and the table, however, he is still in his boxers and slippers. After Alex gives his report, his boss compliments him both on his presentation and on the fact he is in the office and at work so early. Alex, who is at home, does not correct his boss's misperception and instead responds with a smile and a shrug: "Work, work, work!" Here, Alex has not overtly deceived his boss in his presentation, but he has misled and misdirected him, by both his appearance and his nonanswer. Alex rationalizes this, believing that if he gets his work done, it shouldn't matter if he is in the office. He neglects to consider, however, how his boss would feel if he learned he had been deceived.

The scenario with your romantic partner's sweater and the story about Alex demonstrate the difficulty posed by ethical dilemmas—situations in which the right decision isn't immediately clear.

In public speaking, **ethics**—rules and values that a group defines to guide conduct and distinguish between right and wrong—come into play during every stage of the process. For example, as you research and write your speech, you make decisions about what information you'll include and how that information will influence your audience. As you deliver your speech, you have to make choices about language, tone of voice, and the ways that those aspects of your presentation will affect your listeners. In this chapter, we examine the responsibilities of both speakers and their audiences.

CODES OF ETHICS: ABSOLUTE, SITUATIONAL, AND CULTURALLY RELATIVE

How do people make ethical choices? Some adopt a code of behavior that they commit to using consistently. These individuals are demonstrating **ethical absolutism**—the belief that people should exhibit the same behavior in all situations. For instance, you would be using ethical absolutism if you decided to tell your romantic partner how you really felt about the sweater. In this case, your code of ethics might contain a principle saying, "People should always tell the truth, even if doing so hurts loved ones."

Other people use **situational ethics**—a shifting code that suggests that ethics can vary depending on the situation at hand. For example, a student would (inappropriately) use situational ethics if she decided that under extenuating circumstances (say, a lack of time), it would be OK for her to plagiarize "just this once."

Whether you tend to see ethical decisions in absolute or situational terms, there are some generalizations that apply in most situations. For example, most societies believe that it's more ethical to tell the truth than to lie. In the context of public speaking, most people believe that lying is wrong. They see it as an ethical violation and in some circumstances a possible violation of the law.

Yet some of these same individuals might think little or nothing of intentionally exaggerating their qualifications during a job interview—especially if they believe that "everybody does it and gets away with it." Thus, many people use a blend of approaches to making ethics-related choices. In truth, most people are not strictly absolutists. Even those who generally follow a strict ethical code may sometimes face dilemmas

that compel them to engage in situational ethics, and all of us face such situations at some point in our lives.

In this book, we do not presume to tell you what your ethical system must be; we do insist, however, that you always strive to make the most ethical choice. To help you with such choices, in this chapter we expose you to the kinds of communication-related ethical dilemmas that speakers and audience members sometimes face, and we also explore behaviors most people consider unethical. As you'll discover, one guiding principle that can help you make ethical choices is that of respect for other people—the old adage of treating others the same way you would want to be treated, as well as avoiding treating them in ways you would *not* want to be treated. For instance, if you would resent a public speaker who had withheld important information in order to persuade you to take a particular action, you shouldn't exhibit that same behavior in your own speeches.

Ethics also can vary across societies, making them **culturally rela-tive**.[1] For example, in some cultures, people believe that knowledge is owned collectively rather than by individuals. In cultures with strong oral and narrative traditions, for example, stories are passed from one genera-tion to another and are shared as general knowledge. Within such a system, people don't consider working together or paraphrasing without attribution to be cheating or any other form of unethical behavior. By contrast, when discussing ethics in this book, we reflect a Western cultural perspective, which holds that individuals *do* own the knowledge they create. This perspective informs the academic guidelines and honor codes that are explicitly stated by most colleges and universities in the United States. Indeed, you often will find these guidelines cited in your instructors' syllabi. Thus, we require proper citation and attribution of sources for all speeches.

As you read on, consider your own approach to making ethical decisions while developing and delivering presentations. What are your beliefs regarding proper behavior in general and in public speaking in particular? Do you always honor these beliefs strictly, or do you do so only in certain situations? To help you answer these questions, let's consider some of the ethical issues you may confront. These include communicating truthfully, crediting others' work, using sound reasoning, and behaving ethically when you're listening to someone else's speech. Although making ethical choices in public speaking situations can sometimes be difficult, this chapter helps you develop a responsible system for doing so. The key word here is *responsibility*. Whenever you give a speech, you wield power—over what your listeners think, how they feel, and what actions they end up taking—and are thus responsible for your audience's well-being. The following sections offer guidelines for shouldering that responsibility by exhibiting ethically responsible behavior in public speaking.

LEGAL SPEECH VS. ETHICAL SPEECH

As we connect ethics and public speaking, it is worth observing that many people in the United States often confuse (sometimes intentionally) **ethical speech** with **legally protected speech**. Although these two concepts sometimes overlap—that is, what you say is both legal and ethically responsible to your audience—they are most definitely *not* the same. Ethical speech refers to incorporating ethical decision making into your public speaking process *and* into what you ultimately say. It means that you follow guidelines for telling the truth and avoid misleading an audience—because such actions are ethical and *the right thing to do*.

Focusing on legally protected speech, by contrast, refers to using the law as your boundary for what you may say *and* how you say it. Thus, with this approach, you would make decisions about telling the truth or withholding information based on whether there is a legal requirement to take a certain action or a legal consequence for violating the rules. When you rely on legal guidelines for acceptable speech, your

LEGAL

ORGANIC JUICE*

NOT REALLY THAT

INGREDIENTS: WATER, HIGH FRUCTOSE CORN SYRUP, CALCIUM LACTATE, ASCORBIC ACID, *5% ORGANIC JUICE, NATURAL FLAVOR, EXTRACTED ORANGE JUICE CONCENTRATE, CITRIC ACID.

ETHICAL

ORGANIC JUICE

REALLY!

INGREDIENTS:

100% ORGANIC JUICE

decision-making calculus has nothing to do with ethics: it is driven only by what is technically within the legal rules. If you use legal protection as your guiding principle for speaking, you can technically stay within the bounds of what is lawful but still speak unethically.

It's vital to note that far more types of speech are technically legal than are strictly ethical. In the United States, the First Amendment to the U.S. Constitution mandates "freedom of speech," and this freedom allows for a vast range of legally protected statements. In fact, there are relatively few exceptions, and these typically are handled in narrow terms such as slander (intentional falsehood about another person), fighting words (words meant to provoke a violent response), and obscenity (hard-core, sexually explicit expression). Political speech—expression that relates to political discourse—is the most legally protected and privileged form of expression under the First Amendment, sometimes to a surprising degree. Political campaign speeches are one of our wonderful traditions of civic engagement for public speaking. In 2015, Donald Trump announced his candidacy for the 2016 presidential race in the United States with a fiery speech that included remarks on immigration. His speech specifically targeted unlawful illegal immigrants from Mexico, about whom he made insulting and incendiary remarks.[2]

As political speech, Trump's incendiary, insulting comments were protected by the Constitution, but that did not make his speech ethically responsible. Not suprisingly, his comments caused a backlash against him, including a decision by Spanish-language television giant Univision to sever all business ties with Trump business interests—including the broadcast of Trump's Miss Universe pageant.[3]

Make sure that you understand the distinction between ethical and legal speech when crafting your own presentations. When you consider ethics, you are doing more than just what is legally required: you are doing what is morally correct for your situation.

COMMUNICATING TRUTHFULLY

The most basic ethical guideline for public speaking is this: *tell your audience the truth.* How do you feel when someone has lied to you or intentionally misled you? If you're like most people, you resent it and feel manipulated. Audience members who discover that a speaker has deceived them seldom believe anything that person said—and they rarely do what he or she asked of them. They also remember being lied to. A known liar will have trouble ever convincing future listeners of his or her credibility or trustworthiness.

That being said, the words *truth* and *truthfully* are fairly subjective and elude precise definition. It is easier to describe truth in public speaking by examining what is *not* truth.

Lying

Public speakers who lie are intentionally seeking to deceive their audience. Why do they lie? Some fear what their listeners would do if they knew the truth; they don't trust their audience to react in a supportive or understanding way. Consider an older student giving a speech on gun safety who fabricated his identity as a military veteran. Although he was an experienced hunter and certified in the safe handling of firearms, he lied because he thought it would give him more credibility. Yet his audience might well have accepted his suggestions anyway; after all, hunting experience and a certification course are worthy credentials. By lying about his background, he risked losing his listeners' trust if they ever learned of his deception.

Half-Truths

When a speaker reveals only part of the truth and then mixes it with a lie, she or he is telling a **half-truth**. In practice, a half-truth has the same damaging impact as a lie: it deceives the audience. Take the example of a corporate manager required to explain to the board of directors why her company recently lost several top executives. In her presentation, she said that many of the departing executives had accepted positions at other companies or simply elected to take early retirement—normal occurrences

in business. Although the first part was true, the second part was a half-truth. The two executives who chose to retire early did so as part of a legal settlement related to accusations of accounting malpractice.

False Inference

When a speaker presents information that leads listeners to an incorrect conclusion, that speaker has caused a **false inference**. Speakers who commit this ethical breach intentionally drop hints designed to make their audience believe something that isn't true. For example, in a presentation titled "UFOs, Extraterrestrials, and the Supernatural," a student described a series of events that occurred in a midwestern town—an increase in the number of babies with birth defects, a rise in the rate of kidnapping, and a jump in the amount of farmland seized by the federal government. This student did not say outright that there was a government conspiracy to conceal the presence of aliens and unidentified flying objects (UFOs), but he clearly intended his audience to draw this inference. In reality, the increase in birth defects amounted to exactly

FALSE INFERENCE

one—from six to seven. The rising kidnapping rate was actually a state-wide statistic, caused by a change in laws about divorce and child custody. And the government seizure of land had happened—but only for the construction of a highway overpass. The speaker had unethically arranged his facts in a way that could make his audience conclude that the government was trying to conceal the presence of aliens, *X-Files*–style.

False inferences also can occur accidentally, as when a speaker gathers insufficient data and therefore unknowingly presents an incomplete understanding of the speech topic to the audience. Creating accidental false inferences isn't unethical, but it prevents you from conveying accurate information to your audience, thus damaging the effectiveness of your speech. To avoid causing an accidental *or* a deliberate false inference, avoid overgeneralized claims based on statistical findings, and always explain to your audience what the statistics mean and how they were derived.

Taking evidence out of context is another form of false inference. Here, the speaker shares a source's data or statements without explaining how they relate to the original situation. The speaker uses these facts or words *selectively* to support an argument. For example, in a speech about the propensity of pit bulls to attack people, one student quoted an animal-behavior expert out of context to imply a genetic predisposition toward attack: "[T]here is an observable tendency in the genetic makeup of pit bulls to viciously attack humans." The student did *not* explain to her audience that the quotation came from a longer statement that clearly defies this view:

> Some have argued that there is an observable tendency in the genetic makeup of pit bulls to viciously attack humans. But surely this is not the case. Although it is true that *some* pit bulls have attacked *some* humans, there is no research to definitively prove a genetic tendency to attack humans. More study of this is needed.

Philosophers—and cheating romantic partners—have long argued about whether keeping silent about something is the same thing as lying about it. Thus, **omission** is another source of false inference. Here, presenters mislead the audience not by what they say but by what they leave unsaid. For example, in a presentation about on-campus drug use, a student government representative was asked about the extent of drug use and abuse in her campus dormitory. In response, she merely smiled and moved on to another question. Her silence and body language implied that there was no drug problem in her dormitory, but in fact, her dorm had the worst record for on-campus substance abuse. Similarly, the story about Alex presenting a report on Skype and not correcting his employer's perception about *where he was working* (at home, just before heading out to a baseball game) was also misleading. If silence about a topic will mislead your audience and you are aware of this likelihood, but you withhold information anyway, then you have acted unethically through omission. Such actions suggest that you view your listeners as consumers of information and take an unethical and cynical caveat emptor (let the buyer beware) approach to public speaking.

To communicate truthfully and therefore ethically, never lie, never tell half-truths, and never cause false inferences—whether by taking evidence out of context or by omitting pertinent information. There are always alternatives. For example, if you fear that the truth may weaken your argument, then you need to do further research and perhaps take a closer look at your stance. Still, remember that there are at least two sides to every issue, as well as multiple solutions and perspectives to consider. If you fear what the audience might think if they knew the

"... ~~Some have argued that~~ there is an observable tendency in the genetic makeup of pit bulls to viciously attack humans. ~~But surely that is not the case. Although it is true that some pit bulls have attacked some humans, there is no research to definitely prove a genetic tendency to attack humans.~~ More ~~study of this is needed...~~"

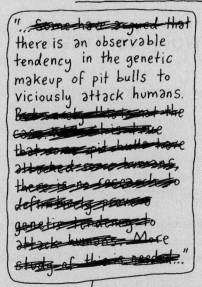

"... Some have argued that there is an observable tendency in the genetic makeup of pit bulls to viciously attack humans. But surely this is not the case. Although it is true that *some* pit bulls have attacked *some* humans, there is no research to definitively prove a genetic tendency to attack humans. More study of this is needed..."

truth, consider the opposite: how will they react if they learn you have deceived them? In most situations, listeners will react to a lie much more negatively than to an unwelcome truth.

ACKNOWLEDGING THE WORK OF OTHERS

Researching a speech topic exposes you to a wealth of interesting facts, information, and ideas—many of which you will want to include in your presentation. But finding these materials also raises some questions: Should you include a particular piece of information in your presentation? If so, how should you use it? And how will you acknowledge its source?

> ▶ **To watch examples of how to acknowledge the work of others, try Video Activity 3.1, "Citing Sources (Statistics and Testimony)."**

Listeners—and especially speech instructors—want speakers to demonstrate their own ideas and thought process during a presentation. At the same time, all of us recognize that most speeches can be enhanced by research and examples from outside sources. The question is, how should you reconcile these objectives? To do so, you must use materials that demonstrate your own ideas and also ethically incorporate and acknowledge the original ideas of others. This approach is honest for you and fair to your listeners and sources.

Imagine coming across an article or a published essay addressing the same topic as your speech. Maybe you admire the way the author worded his prose. Would it be a problem to incorporate a few lines from the article word-for-word without citing the quotations? What about taking a preponderance of the ideas from the publication, rewording them, but not attributing them to the author? Would that be unethical? The answer to these questions is an unequivocal yes!

Presenting another person's words or ideas as if they were your own is called **plagiarism**, and it is always unethical. Plagiarism is "the deliberate and knowing presentation of another person's original ideas or creative expressions as one's own."[4] If you plagiarize, you mislead your audience by misrepresenting the source of the material you've used. Unfortunately, plagiarism is increasingly common at colleges and universities—and much of that owes to the rise of the Internet.[5] Students may feel that plagiarism is a lesser evil than other kinds of cheating and use rationales to excuse it ("I don't have time," "No will one find out").[6] However, these are still just excuses for unethical behavior. When you plagiarize, you are stealing the ideas and words of another person—a crime most colleges and universities consider worthy of expulsion.

Although plagiarism is wrong, people sometimes have difficulty discerning the line between plagiarism and appropriate use of researched material. To illustrate why, let's consider plagiarism in two contexts—quoting from a source and paraphrasing the work of others.

Quoting from a Source

Suppose a student named Larissa was planning a speech about the history of drive-in movie theaters. She had drawn her inspiration from a magazine article she saw in an airport while traveling home from school for the holidays. She thought the topic was unusual enough to make an interesting presentation, and her instructor agreed and approved her choice.

When trying to research the topic, however, Larissa could find little or no material beyond the magazine article she had found in the airport. Panic set in as the day for her in-class speech approached. In desperation, Larissa decided that no one in her class at the University of Michigan–Ann Arbor would know about the article because it had been published in *Nevada Horizons*, a magazine sold only in the greater Las Vegas area. Rationalizing her actions, she used nearly all of the article verbatim as her speech.

It turned out that the magazine article had appeared simultaneously in several different publications, including a large national newspaper where Larissa's instructor had read it. Larissa earned an F in the class and was suspended from school.

Clearly, what Larissa did constituted plagiarism. But what if she had taken only one-third, one-half, or even just a few lines of the story and represented the material as her own? Would any of these scenarios still constitute plagiarism? Yes. Whether she lifted five pages or one page or only a single sentence, she still would be stealing the original author's words and ideas. By analogy, a shop owner won't care whether you stole one or two eggs or an entire dozen. Either way, you stole.

Plagiarism is particularly common among students who research their speech topics online. The temptation to lift and use text from a Web site can be overwhelming, but doing so without attribution is stealing. Students face the related danger of unintentional plagiarism when they copy a quotation from a source and paste it into their notes without writing down the citation information. When they return to their notes later, they may not remember that they had copied and pasted the material as opposed to writing it themselves.

Most of the direct quotations you use in a speech will be short—a line or two or a short paragraph. To avoid plagiarism, you must attribute the quote to its source. How should you cite the source? If Larissa had just used several quotes from the magazine article, she might have attributed the material in the following way:

> As Roberta Gonzales wrote in the June 19 issue of *Nevada Horizons* (D4), "The growth and popularity of drive-in theaters tracked with the affordability of automobiles for a larger and younger population of drivers."

The first part of this sentence is the attribution, which includes the page number. In delivering your speech, it's OK not to cite the page numbers of all your sources. However, we strongly suggest that you document a complete citation on your speech outline or text. That way, anyone (including your instructor) who wants to check your facts can easily do so. Before preparing your speech, make sure to check with your instructor to find out if he or she has additional expectations for proper attribution.

▶ To see an example of citing sources, watch **Video Activity 3.2, "Citing Someone Else's Idea."**

Paraphrasing the Work of Others

Suppose Larissa never lifted the text from the magazine article verbatim. Instead, she used **paraphrasing**—restating the original author's ideas in her own words. Would this constitute plagiarism?

This is where the rules defining plagiarism are a bit less clear. Is it stealing if you use your own words but not necessarily your own ideas? Your teachers will not expect you to be an authority on every speech topic you address; you *will* have to research your subject matter. This may cause you to wonder, "How could it be plagiarism if I'm paraphrasing someone else's words or ideas? After all, these are *my* words!"

Students at the college level regularly struggle with this challenge. To resolve the dilemma, consider this simple rule of thumb: if you're using most or all of the original material, simply rearranged and restated in your own words, you're still taking another person's ideas and presenting them as your own. This isn't the same as directly copying without attribution, but it is wrong on several fronts. For one thing, you're not generating your own ideas and opinions about your topic—so you're not meeting your instructor's expectations. For another, you're being unfair to the person whose ideas you're presenting as your own.

The safest bet is always to acknowledge the original source of any material you use in your speech, whether you are directly quoting or paraphrasing. For example, if Larissa had paraphrased some ideas from the magazine article, she could have mentioned the author and source of her material in the following way:

According to Roberta Gonzales, writing in the June 19 issue of *Nevada Horizons* on page D4, drive-in theaters tended to grow in popularity with Americans who were increasingly able to afford and enjoy the freedom of automobiles. This was especially true of younger drivers, who yearned for freedom of mobility and a common place to meet and socialize outside the scrutiny of Mom and Dad.

Common Knowledge

There are limited situations—known as common knowledge—in which you can use information from a source without giving a direct citation. **Common knowledge** information is widely known and disseminated in many sources. For example, you may not need to cite the fact that France presented the Statue of Liberty to the United States in 1886, but you might need to cite a source if you wanted to give statistics, such as the statue's

SPEECH CHOICES

A CASE STUDY: *MIA*

Let's check in with Mia to see how she is dealing with developing her topic and its significance in a way that is truthful.

Mia was excited by her new speech idea. It involved two timely topics—smartphone applications (apps) and refugees—that she knew would interest students. As she began researching, Mia came across one article about refugees who were using smartphones to access social media sites—especially Facebook—so they could communicate with relatives in other countries. Mia was now tempted to frame her story about smartphones by connecting it to social media. But this article was the only one she could find that had that focus. All others seemed to be about using smartphones for GPS or for doing research on supplies and conditions. Mia wanted to focus on Facebook because most students in her class used it. But if she did, she might be misrepresenting its significance for her topic.

After wrestling with this topic, Mia remembered that a family in her church had recently sponsored a family of refugees. She contacted the family and was able to conduct a brief interview with the daughter, who was her age. This woman confirmed that social media had been instrumental in helping them make contact with their host family at the church. Mia decided she would use this evidence honestly to illustrate how social media was important to refugees. Instead of unethically overclaiming its significance, she merely listed it as one of the factors and considered the family's story as she prepared her speech.

YOUR TURN:
Have you ever exaggerated the significance of one point you were making because it made your story better or your speech more appealing?

For more questions and activities for this case study, please go to LaunchPad at macmillanhighered.com/speakup4e.

total weight (125 tons), the weight of the statue's concrete foundation (27,000 tons), or the distance the statue's torch sways in the wind (5 inches).[7] Be sure to check with your instructor on guidelines for common knowledge. But remember: when in doubt, include the citation.

USING SOUND REASONING

Every public speaker has a responsibility to provide well-reasoned support for his or her points. **Fallacious reasoning** is faulty (and thus unsound) reasoning, in which the link between a claim and its supporting

SPEECH CHOICES

A CASE STUDY: *JACOB*

Let's look in on Jacob and see how and if he is identifying the work of other people in his speech.

After the satisfaction of picking a topic—student athletes should be paid—Jacob realized that besides being a current college football fan, he didn't know a lot about it. To make matters worse, his speech instructor required students to submit an early progress report that listed their possible arguments and provided at least five sources for their claims. Jacob decided to begin his research online by typing the search terms "paying college athletes." This led to more than 290,000 results. Without doing more reading, he simply copied some of the titles, dates, authors, and publishing sources of the first five articles that had come up.

This still left the matter of his arguments. One of the search results was a video from the HBO show *Last Week Tonight with John Oliver*. Jacob watched the whole twenty-one-minute broadcast. The show brought up two arguments: athletes don't get an education at their schools because they're encouraged to take "easy" majors, and athletes may not learn much from their coaches as role models. To make this last point, Oliver's program featured a dizzying array of coaches yelling and swearing at their athletes. Jacob decided to use both arguments. Without citing his source, he used exact quotations from experts and planned to use some of the video of the coaches as a visual aid for his speech. In so doing, it didn't occur to him that he was using someone else's material and passing it off as his own.

YOUR TURN:
How might Jacob have made use of this material from the John Oliver show in an ethical way?

For more questions and activities for this case study, please go to LaunchPad at macmillanhighered.com/speakup4e.

material is weak. Unfortunately, fallacious reasoning is all too common in speeches, even if it's often unintentional. When public speakers *intentionally* misuse logic to deceive their audience, their actions are profoundly unethical. Four common ways in which a speaker might misuse logic include the following:

- **Hasty generalization:** Making a claim about all members of a group from information based on a limited part of the group
- ***Post hoc* fallacy:** Wrongly identifying the cause of one event as the event that immediately preceded it

- ***Ad hominem* (personal attack) fallacy:** Attempting to weaken someone's argument by making unsubstantiated claims about her or his character
- ***Ad populum* (bandwagon) fallacy:** Believing that an argument is true simply because other people believe it

We will discuss these and other logical fallacies in more depth in Chapter 18, Methods of Persuasion.

BEING AN ETHICAL LISTENER

So far, we've focused our discussion of ethics on speakers' responsibilities. But audience members also have a responsibility to demonstrate ethical behavior. The qualities that characterize what we call an **ethical audience** include courtesy, open-mindedness, and a willingness to hold a speaker accountable for his or her statements. When you're listening to someone who's giving a speech, consider the following guidelines for exhibiting ethical behavior.

Show Courtesy

The old adage about treating others as you'd like to be treated applies just as much in public speaking as in all other areas of life. When someone else is delivering a presentation, extend the same courtesy you

would appreciate if you were speaking. Courteous behavior includes focusing your attention on the speaker as soon as she or he begins, and stopping any activities that may distract you or the speaker (working on a class assignment, texting your friends, chatting with your neighbor). Show the speaker that you are actively paying attention.

Demonstrate an Open Mind

Avoid prejudging the speech or speaker. Even if you have a strongly held belief on the topic or you dislike the speaker, look for parts of the message—or aspects of the speaker—that signal common ground. Consider the fact that you might hear something that changes your mind or that broadens your perspective on the speech topic.

Hold the Speaker Accountable

Prejudging a speech or speaker is clearly unethical. But mindlessly swallowing what the person says in his or her presentation can be equally damaging. To avoid this, you need to hold the presenter accountable for his or her claims. How can you do so? If time is available at the end of the speech, ask questions that prompt the speaker to explain or defend statements you think require additional evidence. If your instructor allows time for a longer exchange, don't hesitate to honestly (and respectfully) express your response to the speech. Convey questions and opinions

politely, focus on the content of the speech itself, and scrupulously avoid attacking the speaker's character. For example, say, "Can you tell us more about how you arrived at those figures?" rather than, "You obviously didn't care enough to do a thorough job in your research." In offering feedback to the speaker on his or her presentation, frame your comments or suggestions constructively—that is, in ways that can help the person build his or her public speaking skills. Avoid destructive feedback, which diminishes the presenter and denigrates his or her speech.

CHAPTER REVIEW

"Strive to be an ethical public speaker."

As you saw with the scenario of being truthful with a romantic partner about your opinion of an expensive new sweater or the story of Alex and his misleading appearance on Skype at the beginning of this chapter, public speaking can present numerous ethical challenges—dilemmas that make it difficult to determine what constitutes right and wrong behavior. In this chapter, we focused on those challenges, from both speakers' and listeners' perspectives. First, we discussed the different codes of ethics, including ethical absolutism, situational ethics, and cultural relativity. We then examined the differences between legal and ethical speech. We showed how people can be unethical in public speaking, mainly through lying, using half-truths, and causing false inferences. We also discussed the ethical ways to acknowledge the work of others (quoting from a source, paraphrasing, and using common knowledge). We touched on using sound reasoning, which we discuss in more depth in Chapter 18. Finally, we shared how to be an ethical listener: show courtesy, demonstrate an open mind, and hold the speaker accountable.

 LaunchPad
macmillan learning

LaunchPad for *Speak Up* offers videos and encourages self-assessment through adaptive quizzing. Go to **macmillanhighered.com/speakup4e** to get access to:

✓ **LearningCurve**
Adaptive Quizzes

 Video clips that help you understand public speaking concepts

Key Terms

ethics *68*

ethical absolutism *68*

situational ethics *69*

culturally relative *70*

ethical speech *71*

legally protected speech *71*

half-truth *73*

false inference *74*

taking evidence out of context *75*

omission *76*

plagiarism *78*

◎ paraphrasing *81*

common knowledge *82*

fallacious reasoning *83*

hasty generalization *84*

post hoc fallacy *84*

ad hominem (personal attack)
  fallacy *85*

ad populum (bandwagon) fallacy *85*

ethical audience *85*

Review Questions

1. Define *ethics*, and explain the difference between ethical absolutism and situational ethics.

2. What ethical responsibilities does the speaker have in a public speaking situation?

3. What rules govern legally protected speech? How do they differ from the rules governing ethical speech? Which category is broader, and why?

4. Describe three ways in which a speaker can present untruthful information.

5. Name and describe the different types of false inferences covered in this chapter.

6. Define *plagiarism*, and explain the importance of properly citing your sources.

7. How is a paraphrase different from a quote? How are they similar?

8. What are the ethical responsibilities of the audience in a public speaking situation?

Critical Thinking Questions

1. As an audience member, have you ever felt that a speaker was intentionally misleading you? What gave you this feeling? How might you have verified her or his facts?

2. How does the failure to properly acknowledge a source in a speech affect the speaker's credibility?

3. ▨ The illustration on page 69 poses the ethical dilemma that arises when someone who loves or trusts you asks your opinion about something that may be personal to him or her and the truth may be uncomfortable for this person to hear. How would you handle an ethical dilemma like this? What is more important—keeping this person happy or telling the truth?

4. Name a practice on your campus that is legal but not necessarily ethical. Why do you think students engage in this practice, and what would you say to a friend who is considering it?

Activities

1. As indicated earlier in this chapter, the approach to ethics can vary by individual and culture. Consider your family's cultural background: what examples might you provide that show some variance of opinion about ethics and communication? For example, how do members of your family feel about exaggerations or little white lies—as opposed to big lies? Do they tolerate the former and reject the latter? Do they think they are all unacceptable—or all unavoidable? Where do you stand on these questions?

2. Review your school's policies on plagiarism. How clear is the definition of *plagiarism*? Do you think the guidelines provide clear rules for citing others' work? What is the punishment for stealing someone else's words or ideas? Based on this information and what you've learned in this chapter, where would you draw the line between plagiarizing material for a speech and using the material as inspiration for what you write?

3. Listen to a few of the twentieth century's greatest speeches (you can find most of them at AmericanRhetoric.com). Do they all stand up to ethical scrutiny? Does the Internet—which has multiple Web sites devoted to fact-checking in real time—make modern public figures more or less careful about what they say?

4

LISTENING SKILLS

"Listening is a vital skill in public speaking and beyond."

Jason was psyched. While preparing an informative speech on the ways young people use the Internet, he focused on the popularity of Twitter. An active Twitter user, Jason found the topic fascinating and looked forward to developing the speech. To learn more about the habits of other students using Twitter, he conducted six face-to-face interviews with classmates from his speech course. Jason felt pleased with the amount of information his classmates shared during the interviews, but when he later reviewed his interview notes, he realized they were a bit sparse.

With time running out, Jason finished developing his presentation using the few insights he could pull from his notes. On the day of his speech, Jason proudly presented his claims about young people's use of Twitter—basically, that they too often reposted content from other platforms (like news sites and blogs) instead of using it as an independent medium. As he spoke, he felt confident and comfortable talking in front of his class. All that changed, however, during the question-and-answer period following the speech. Judging from the questions his classmates threw at him, few—if any—agreed with his observations about student Twitter users. In fact, they argued that he had it exactly backwards: those who engaged only in the kind of activity he described were easy to recognize as new to Twitter—and often were perceived as not having a lot to say. Feeling confused and blindsided, Jason wondered where he'd gone wrong.

Jason's unpleasant experience reveals the importance of listening in public speaking. Unfortunately for him, he missed two major opportunities to listen. First, when he was interviewing his classmates, he failed to pay enough attention to take comprehensive notes. This lack of attention was confirmed later, when he couldn't recall details from the interviews. Second, Jason failed to listen to his audience as he was delivering his speech. If he had focused on his classmates while he was talking, he may have detected both auditory and visual signs that they disagreed with his claims (eye rolls, head shakes, and muttered comments such as "Seriously?"). By not listening carefully while researching *and* delivering his speech, Jason never connected with his audience members and lost credibility with them.

As Jason's story reveals, listening is a vital skill for public speakers at all stages of the speech preparation process. Yet many novice speakers find this idea surprising. After all, it's the *audience* who has to listen, right? To be sure, audiences can be good listeners by respectfully and carefully attending to the speaker's message, but speakers have many opportunities to practice good listening skills while preparing and delivering a presentation. Think about it: You interview people to research your speech. You practice your presentation in front of trusted friends or family members and listen to their feedback. And you deliver your speech, paying attention to your audience's responses to decide whether you need to adjust your voice, volume, pacing, or some other aspect of your delivery. By failing to listen at any of these stages, you risk ignoring important information that you need to present the most effective speech possible.

If you're not particularly skilled at listening, you're not alone: many people have a similar difficulty. Yet you *can* learn how to strengthen your listening skills, and this chapter offers helpful guidelines. In the pages that follow, we explore the importance of listening in public speaking, examine the process of listening, and then consider the causes behind ineffective listening behaviors. We also offer suggestions for effective listening that you can put into practice as both a speaker and an audience member.

Who needs to demonstrate good listening here?

A: THE AUDIENCE?   B: THE SPEAKER?   C: BOTH?

THE LISTENING PROCESS

It's crucial for speakers *and* audience members to understand the listening process. How you listen as a speaker—while both preparing and delivering a speech—can have a powerful effect on the quality of your presentation and your ability to connect with your audience. How you listen as an audience member can strongly affect your ability to absorb the information the speaker is imparting to you. Equally important, improving your listening skills as both a speaker and an audience member will help you interpret and use more of what you hear from others in a wide variety of situations—not just in your public speaking course.

For example, consider the usefulness of listening within the field of civic engagement. Suppose that later in life you marry and start a family—but just as your child is approaching the age of five, you are informed by your pediatrician that your daughter has been diagnosed with autism. There are a range of things that can be done for her, but in the meantime, you are disheartened to learn that your local school district does not have special programs or instruction for children with autism spectrum disorders. You are not alone in coping with and dealing with this problem, and thus you decide that you should organize with other parents of children with special needs. Good listening will help you identify which school board members are likely to be sympathetic to your demands for more services when you make a presentation at the school board meeting. It also will help you be more likely to sense any confusion or disagreement among your audience members and adapt your delivery as needed to win their attention and support.

To understand the listening process, we'll start with the specific differences between listening and hearing.

Listening vs. Hearing

Listening and hearing are two different activities, and research affirms the importance of listening—versus merely hearing—for both public speakers and their audiences. Several studies have suggested that when people hear without actually listening, they can miss virtually all the content of oral messages (imagine the droning adult voices in Charles Schulz's *Peanuts* cartoons).[1] **Hearing** means merely receiving messages in a passive way. **Listening,** on the other hand, means actively paying attention to what you're hearing; it involves both processing the message to decide on its meaning and retaining what you've heard and understood.

To further explain this distinction, let's briefly consider how both science and communication researchers define listening and hearing. Cognitive scientists—those who study the mind—consider listening to be a conscious mental process that includes the following components:[2]

- Selection (attention, perception)
- Organization (interpretation)
- Integration (storage recall)

Communication researchers define listening in a slightly different manner— with terms that describe listening as a step in the communication process:

- Sensing
- Interpreting
- Evaluating
- Responding[3]

Both cognitive scientists and communication researchers agree that hearing is a passive, physical activity—the act of sound waves reverberating against the eardrums, triggering messages that are sent to the brain.[4] Although listening is possible after hearing begins, listening is an altogether more complicated process.[5] Take the acts of watching television versus reading a book. Whereas watching TV is a passive activity (like hearing),[6] reading is a learned activity that requires information processing (like listening).[7]

In the following section, we further discuss listening. For the purposes of this book, we focus on two main aspects of listening—processing and retaining.

Processing What You've Heard

When you engage in **processing**, you actively think about a message you're receiving from someone else—not only the words but also the nonverbal cues. For example, suppose you're a small-business owner who's meeting with Jeff—a salesperson for eLogic, a business-software developer. You want to decide whether eLogic's software for tracking and

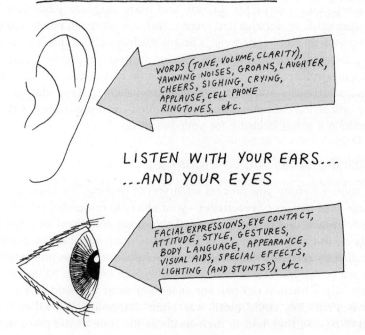

ADAPTING TO THE AUDIENCE

WORDS (TONE, VOLUME, CLARITY), YAWNING NOISES, GROANS, LAUGHTER, CHEERS, SIGHING, CRYING, APPLAUSE, CELL PHONE RINGTONES, etc.

LISTEN WITH YOUR EARS...
...AND YOUR EYES

FACIAL EXPRESSIONS, EYE CONTACT, ATTITUDE, STYLE, GESTURES, BODY LANGUAGE, APPEARANCE, VISUAL AIDS, SPECIAL EFFECTS, LIGHTING (AND STUNTS?), etc.

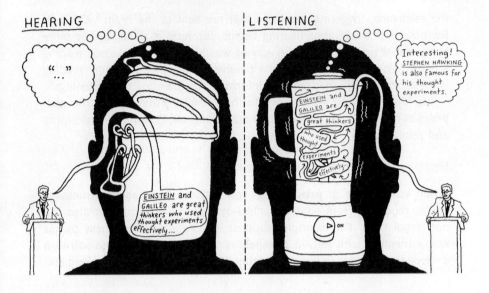

fulfilling orders is right for your business. As Jeff describes the product, you consider the implications of what he is saying, how using the software will affect your bottom line, and whether Jeff represents a reputable company. You observe his attitude and body language (confident and knowledgeable or nervous and inept?). You may jot down notes. You then mull over a series of questions: "Can my business afford this investment? Will I need to provide extensive training to help my workers learn the new software? Are there other programs that can deliver similar advantages but are easier and cheaper to use?" By weighing these matters—that is, by processing the information in your mind—you stand a better chance of making a smart decision for your business.

Retaining What You've Processed

The more carefully you process what you're hearing, the more you will engage your powers of **retention**—your ability to remember what you've heard. In fact, one of the authors of this textbook joined in a ten-year study of listening patterns and found that poor retention of a speech was directly related to audience attentiveness during the presentation.[8] This study also found that individuals with poor attention habits remembered only a fraction (25 percent or less) of what was said in a speech. Worse, what they *could* recall was often inaccurate or confused with something else they had in their heads at the time of the presentation.

Among people who fail to process what they're hearing, the ability to accurately recall what was heard decays just three to six hours after the original communication.

The study also revealed a recurring pattern of attentiveness—called "the attentiveness curve"—in people who did not listen well. At the beginning of a presentation, poor listeners tended to pay little attention. Their attention quickly improved as the presentation continued (perhaps because they realized they *should* have been paying attention), just as quickly fell to a low level, and finally rebounded near the end of the speech. Clearly, their sporadic levels of attention made it much harder for these listeners to process messages; it is no wonder, then, that they retained very little.

To further see the connection between processing and retention, consider your own listening behavior as a student. How much information do you retain if you pay little attention to your instructors in class? If you take notes during lectures, how accurate are they? How much do you remember from lectures in which you did not process what you were hearing? There's

THE ATTENTIVENESS CURVE

ATTENTIVENESS

TIME OF SPEECH

no doubt about it: the more carefully you process messages, the more likely you'll remember what you heard—and retain it accurately.

In the next section, we analyze listening behavior further by examining the different types of listening styles.

Listening Styles

Research shows that the different ways people listen can be categorized into specific styles. In general, most people usually default to a specific style out of habit[9] and are reluctant to switch from the style of listening they usually use,[10] even if doing so might make them better at receiving and retaining information. In fact, it appears that most people default to a traditional style of listening out of habit.[11] The best listeners, however, often will modify or alter their listening behavior depending on the context or situation.[12] If you are able to recognize these styles and adapt them to certain situations, this can help maximize your listening behavior as both a speaker and an audience member. As a speaker, you can recognize the style your audience might be using and adapt your message and delivery to best connect with them. As an audience member, you can change your listening style based on your situation in order to maximize your listening skills.

Learning about the different listening styles—*action-oriented listening, content-oriented listening, people-oriented listening,* and *time-oriented listening*[13]—is the first step to using them to your advantage. Let's consider each of these in turn.

- **Action-oriented listening.** People who use this style of listening usually focus on immediately getting to the meaning of a message and determining what response is required. These listeners indicate a preference for messages that are direct, concise, and error-free. Conversely, these listeners are easily frustrated by those who ramble or take a while to get to the point.

- **Content-oriented listening.** In contrast to action-oriented listeners, content-oriented listeners favor depth and complexity of information and messages. They are willing to spend more time listening, pay careful attention to what's being said, and enjoy discussing and thinking about the message afterwards.

- **People-oriented listening.** Like content-oriented listeners, people-oriented listeners are willing to invest time and attention in communications, yet they are differentiated by their interest in being supportive of friends and strengthening relationships. These listeners notice the mood and body language of speakers and express more empathy toward them.

- **Time-oriented listening.** The major identifying element of this listening style is time—or more precisely, a concern with managing time. These listeners see time as a precious resource to be conserved and protected. Thus, they can exhibit impatience and rush interactions.[14]

Did you recognize any of these styles as your default? Using one or two of them more often doesn't mean you can't embrace other styles

LISTENING STYLES

and use them in appropriate contexts. Do you have a friend with personal problems who needs someone to talk to? Most likely, a people-oriented approach is best. Did a fellow student ask you to critique an oral reports she plans to deliver in class? You should consider a content-oriented approach. But what if she asks you to critique the report when you have your own looming deadline? In that case, you would probably take a time-oriented approach, explaining your time constraints and setting reasonable expectations about what you can listen to and deliver.

THE CULPRITS BEHIND POOR LISTENING

Although recognizing and using the right listening style is a big step in the right direction, you will likely still face listening challenges, both as a speaker and as an audience member. Some of the causes behind poor listening include such behaviors as *unprocessed note taking, nonlistening, interruptive listening, agenda-driven listening, argumentative listening,* and *nervous listening*. Later in this chapter we also discuss defeated listening and superficial listening. In the following sections, we offer the challenges along with tips to help you overcome them.

Unprocessed Note Taking

Ben is a former National Football League (NFL) center and now is working for a large national bank. As a business-development officer, he sells the bank's financial products to wealthy clients. This is his first job after a career in sports, and Ben is aware that a primary reason he was hired was his professional football experience. His manager thinks this background might open doors for him. Ben is very conscientious about keeping an accurate record of what he discusses with each prospective client. When prospects speak in their initial meetings, Ben takes copious notes—often without even looking up. Later, however, Ben finds that he recalls very little of these meetings and has a hard time distinguishing one prospective client from another. Why? Ben is taking in the information, but he is not processing it.

Note taking can be a useful tool at various stages of the speechmaking process—from writing notes while interviewing an expert during the research phase to jotting down key ideas when you're an audience member. However, note taking can become a problem if you engage in **unprocessed note taking**—copying the speaker's words verbatim without considering what you're writing down. Unprocessed note takers physically hear words, but they don't listen—that is, actively process and retain them. Instead, the words enter their consciousness and just as quickly exit, deposited in their notebooks or on their laptops—sometimes in incomprehensible form. Unprocessed note takers usually have trouble remembering what was said in an interview, a lecture, or a speech. They also miss opportunities to ask clarifying questions or to comment in informed, thoughtful ways. When you're taking notes, be sure to focus fully on your interviewee or speaker, processing what she or he is saying and writing down the most important points.

Nonlistening

People who engage in **nonlistening** simply do not pay attention to what they're hearing. For example, if you're overly interested in your own questions during an interview, you won't be attuned to what the interviewee has to say in response. In a lecture, you are likely to engage in nonlistening if you are focused more on your own thoughts about the subject than on what the speaker has to say. Not surprisingly, nonlistening prevents you from processing another person's message—and therefore keeps you from retaining it. If you feel distracted when interviewing a source, giving a speech, or listening to a speech, take a moment to calm your mind and redirect your energy to listening. Remind yourself of the importance of listening in this situation: it could be to learn new information, strengthen existing knowledge, or even get a good grade!

Interruptive Listening

With **interruptive listening**, one person consistently interrupts another. You may have seen or heard instances of interruptive audience members, voicing their opinions or blurting out questions before the speaker is ready to entertain them. Speakers also can be interruptive listeners. For example, a speaker might call on an audience member who raises his hand, but

instead of listening to his question, the speaker cuts him off midsentence and finishes the question for him. Speakers who do this are likely to miss certain aspects of the question or comment. Worse, they often come across as rude and arrogant, thus losing the respect of their audience.

Be sure not to interrupt when listening to others: let them get their thoughts out fully before responding (if you are asked to respond). If you are the speaker dealing with an interruptive listener, tell the audience you'll be happy to answer more questions at the end of the speech.

Agenda-Driven Listening

Public speakers who focus solely on the mechanics of their presentation may demonstrate **agenda-driven listening**. This listening challenge applies primarily to a speaker giving a presentation who also has to accommodate questions and comments from audience members. For example, this speaker might ignore raised hands from the audience or "listen" to questions while scanning her notes. Or she might provide monosyllabic and overly brief responses—revealing that she's not really listening to her audience. Not surprisingly, this behavior can annoy audience members and damage the speaker's credibility. This type of speaking is especially common with speakers who are anxious: they may be focusing so strongly on their task that they fail to notice their audience.

To avoid this problem, make sure you are constantly analyzing your audience to confirm that they are keeping up with and understanding your speech (see Chapter 5 for more on audience analysis). Happily, this also may help to quell any nerves because you'll be taking the focus off yourself and putting it on your audience.

Argumentative Listening

People who feel in conflict with the individuals they are listening to may display **argumentative listening**, or selective listening—listening to only as much as they need to in order to fuel their own arguments. Argumentative listening also can afflict speakers who feel personally attacked by audience members during question-and-answer sessions. Because these speakers focus more on their irritation than the actual question, they may listen to only part of what a questioner has asked and so can't respond in a thoughtful, informed way. This hurts their credibility.

Speakers also can fall victim to argumentative listening during an interview if they disagree with the interviewee's opinions or ideas. Here, they may again focus more on their own views and miss out on everything the other person has to say.

If you find yourself speaking to or interviewing people whose statements you disagree with, remind yourself to listen first before making judgments. If you ever speak to an argumentative or hostile group, you

ARGUMENTATIVE LISTENING

may need to address their potential disagreement—a process we discuss in Chapter 5 (p. 145). If you are the one who disagrees while listening to a speaker, try to keep an open mind—at least through the end of his or her speech!

Nervous Listening

People who fall victim to **nervous listening** feel compelled to talk through silences because they're uncomfortable with conversational lapses or pauses. If an interview subject takes a long time to answer a question, a nervous listener might blurt out more questions and comments, stopping the interview subject from answering fully and leading to incomplete research. As a speaker, imagine giving a speech introduction in which you ask a provocative question in an attempt to engage the audience. If no one in the room responds to your question, you might get thrown off and feel compelled to say something—anything—to get the speech moving again. You might fill in the silence with an awkward comment ("Tough crowd!"), only to see confused or annoyed looks on your listeners' faces.

Nervous listening—in any context—can damage your ability to gather and interpret information you need to deliver an effective speech. If you feel twinges of nervousness, collect yourself and wait a few beats before continuing. Remember that pauses are normal and can even be used to stress the importance of what you're saying through a thoughtful choice of words (see Chapter 13, pp. 383–84).

BECOMING A BETTER LISTENER

Along with overcoming specific culprits of poor listening, you also can improve your general listening skills by focusing on **interactive listening**, which includes *filtering out distractions, focusing on the speaker(s)*, and *showing that you are paying attention*. These behaviors help improve both processing and retaining, in turn making you a more effective listener.

Filter Out Distractions

There are potentially countless distractions in any speaking situation, both external and internal. *External distractions*, or **external noise**, include street noise, a flashy visual aid left up during an entire presentation, or chattering audience members. *Internal distractions*, often referred to as **internal noise**, are any thoughts that make it hard for you to concentrate—such as worrying about how well you're doing in class or pondering aspects of your personal life. If you are an audience member, filtering out distractions means avoiding nonlistening activities, such as gazing around the room or surfing online. As a speaker, filtering out distractions during presentations or question-and-answer sessions means focusing on reactions or questions from audience members rather than looking ahead to your next point. When conducting interview research, this means focusing on your current question and the interviewee's response rather than thinking about your next question or an unrelated topic.

ONE LISTENER EXPERIENCING INTERNAL NOISE

Focus on the Speaker

In any listening situation, keep your mind on what the speaker is saying, not on what you may be about to hear or what you're going to say next. Ask yourself, "What does this statement that I've just heard mean? Do I agree or disagree with it? Do I have questions or comments of my own about it—or even a different point of view? How might other people think or feel about this comment or issue?"

Show That You Are Listening

As a responsible listener, you can use a combination of nonverbal and verbal cues to show that you are listening. Look at the other person while he or she is speaking *and* as you are responding. Indicate nonverbally—perhaps with alert posture and a smile or nod of your head—that you are paying attention.

When the opportunity presents itself, you can also verbally communicate that you are listening. As an audience member, you can ask thoughtful questions during a question-and-answer session or even applaud appropriately at a rousing portion of the speech. As a speaker, paraphrase

questions asked by audience members to show that you understand and to allow them to correct any misinterpretation. And in interview situations, maintain eye contact and be ready to move into new lines of questioning based on your interviewee's responses.

MAXIMIZING YOUR AUDIENCE'S LISTENING

Despite your best efforts, you occasionally may find yourself delivering a speech to audience members who do not listen well. For example, while doing **audience surveillance**—paying attention to an audience's nonverbal and verbal responses while giving a speech—you may notice some audience members who *act* as if they are listening but who you can tell (perhaps by their expression or lack of eye contact) are not. The good news is that there are several strategies you can use to help your audience members listen more effectively to your speech. In this section, we outline several steps that you, as a speaker, can take to both anticipate and deal with audience listening challenges.

HAMMER HOME YOUR MAIN MESSAGE AT THE BEGINNING AND AT THE END

Anticipate Ineffective Listening before Your Speech

Advance preparation is key to ensuring that your audience will truly listen to your message. Be sure to consider your audience's needs as well as outside factors, and plan your speech accordingly.

Consider Your Listeners' Attention and Energy Levels. People listening to a speech at 8:30 on a Monday morning will likely have a limited attention span. Many may be tired from the weekend and may not have adjusted to the new week. Therefore, avoid delivering a long speech with no audience interaction during times like this. Instead, give a concise presentation and allot time for active listener participation.

Assess Your Audience's Knowledge and Abilities. If your audience members know little about the subject of your speech, they may become confused when faced with unknown jargon or many technical details. To avoid that, explain concepts and define key terms. Also, consider any barriers to understanding, such as whether everyone in your audience has a similar capacity with the English language or whether anyone has problems with hearing. Then adjust your word choice or volume level as needed.

Front- and Back-Load Your Main Message. Listeners tend to pay the most attention just after the beginning of a speech and just before the end. For this reason, plan your speech ahead of time in the following way: front-load your main message (that is, present it early in your speech), and then use your conclusion to give listeners another opportunity to process and retain your message.

Use Presentation Aids Strategically.

Presentation aids can help you capture audience attention and thereby encourage listening. There-fore, plan to space these aids throughout your speech to maintain interest. Also, don't incorporate a given presenta-tion aid until you want your audience to see or hear it. When you are finished with it, put it away outside your lis-teners' view or hearing range.

DEALING WITH ARGUMENTATIVE LISTENERS

Encourage Active Listening during Your Speech

When you are ready to give your speech, be sure to pay attention to what you see among your audience. Practice audience surveillance, pay particular attention to if and how they are listening to you, and be prepared to make adjustments as you go.

Tailor Your Delivery. As you deliver your speech, pay attention to factors you can control that affect your audience's ability to listen—voice, volume, fluency, projection, rate, and timing. Speaking too quietly can inhibit listening, as can poor fluency, fast delivery, or excessive pausing. Be sure to maintain eye contact with your audience, and avoid making obtrusive gestures (such as pointing at the audience) or turning your back on the group while adjusting a visual aid.

Watch Out for Argumentative Listeners. As discussed earlier in this chapter, argumentative listeners will attend to only as much of your presentation as they need to build up their own case against it. To improve your chances of keeping their attention, acknowledge their viewpoints early in your speech (for example, "I know that some of you may not think that having tattoos will affect your careers"), and repeatedly press your main message throughout the presentation.

Watch Out for Defeated Listeners. Defeated listening occurs when listeners feel overwhelmed by your message and find it too difficult

to follow. Speakers who deliver technical or detailed presentations may find this a particular challenge. Defeated listeners may avoid eye contact or work on something else while you speak.

You can prevent defeated listening by pausing occasionally during your speech to ask the audience questions—such as whether they understand your last point or if they can think of an example or application of what you have just said. By doing so, you can test their comprehension while assessing whether they are really following along. If you cannot engage them here, back up and repeat your message, using simpler language and different examples.

Watch Out for Superficial Listeners. Audience members who pretend to pay attention but who are in fact distracted by internal or external noise (such as wandering thoughts, cell phones, or conversation) are engaged in **superficial listening**. To prevent it, request that people turn off cell phones and resist checking for messages on handheld devices or laptops during the presentation. Also, be sure to use direct eye contact with people who you sense are listening superficially (they will pay more attention if they see that you are watching them), and go ahead and ask them questions—or invite them to ask you some.

LISTENING WHEN YOU ARE IN THE AUDIENCE

When you're an audience member, listening not only helps you retain the speaker's message but also enables you to provide the speaker with an informed **speech critique**—written or oral feedback offered after a presentation. Critiquing is an essential component of public speaking classes because it helps speakers learn from their experiences. Your instructor will likely specify what you should cover in a critique. The following can give you additional guidance:

- *Take notes*. While listening to a presentation, jot down your thoughts about the speaker's delivery and message. By recording your impressions as you form them, you'll be able to access your thoughts when it comes time to offer your critique.

- *Identify main points*. As you take notes, begin to distinguish the speaker's main points—the two or three most important ideas the speaker wants you to remember (often called "takeaways" or the "take-home message"). Most speakers preview their main points in the introduction, signal them in the body with transitions, and restate them during the conclusion.

- *Consider the speech's objectives*. To provide **constructive criticism**—feedback a speaker can use to improve her or his skills—strive to understand what the presenter is trying to accomplish. Identify the speech's general rhetorical purpose—to inform, persuade, or mark a special occasion—as well as its specific purpose. Next, evaluate how well the speaker achieves her or his goal.

- *Support your feedback with examples*. Instead of offering overly general comments ("good eye contact" or "work on your organization"), be sure to provide specific details ("You made eye contact with people on every side of the room" or "You had a good preview, but I found the organization of your main points difficult to follow"). Specific comments help speakers know which behaviors to do more of during their next speech and which to avoid.

- *Be ethical*. Be courteous in your critique, and treat the speaker the same way you hope and expect to be treated when it's your turn to receive feedback. During the speech, avoid prejudging the speaker or topic, and think critically about the message you're hearing. Finally, make sure you hold the speaker accountable for her or his words. If you are offended by or disagree with something in the speech, tell the person while providing your critique. Do so courteously, however, and avoid making your comment sound like a personal attack. Explain why you disagree, and offer examples.

CHAPTER REVIEW

> Listening is a vital skill in public speaking and beyond.

In this chapter, we discussed a major contrast—hearing noises, sounds, and words versus listening to them. *Hearing* refers to passively receiving these stimuli; *listening* refers to how one processes and understands them. This is particularly relevant to public speaking because both speakers and audience members must develop good listening skills to effectively convey and understand information. Good listening is not limited to words or even sound. By paying attention to an audience's responses, a speaker can tell if he or she needs to adjust tone of voice, rate of speech, or some other aspect of his or her delivery.

We further explored how the listening process works, how information is retained, what the types of listening styles are, how individuals may listen differently in different contexts, what causes ineffective listening, and how to improve your listening skills both as a speaker and as an audience member. Listening is vital not only for developing and delivering a successful speech but also for observing and critiquing a presentation, and happily it is a skill that can be learned. To make the transition from hearing to listening, a person must process the message, coming to her or his own conclusions, and then retain or remember the message.

There are a host of culprits that lead to unsuccessful listening, including unprocessed note taking, nonlistening, interruptive listening, agenda-driven listening, argumentative listening, and nervous listening. Techniques for better listening include filtering out distractions, focusing on the speaker, and showing that you are listening. As a speaker, you can anticipate ineffective listening before your speech and plan accordingly, and you can maximize listening during your speech by tailoring your message and watching out for argumentative, defeated, and superficial listeners.

As an audience member, make sure to take notes and identify the speaker's main points. When giving feedback, offer constructive criticism by considering the speech's objectives, supporting your feedback with examples, and keeping appropriate ethical guidelines in mind.

LaunchPad
macmillan learning

LaunchPad for *Speak Up* offers videos and encourages self-assessment through adaptive quizzing. Go to **macmillanhighered.com/speakup4e** to get access to:

✓ **LearningCurve**
   Adaptive Quizzes

 Video clips that help you understand
   public speaking concepts

Key Terms

hearing *94*
listening *94*
processing *95*
retention *96*
action-oriented listening *98*
content-oriented listening *98*
people-oriented listening *98*
time-oriented listening *99*
unprocessed note taking *101*
nonlistening *102*
interruptive listening *102*

agenda-driven listening *103*
argumentative listening *104*
nervous listening *105*
interactive listening *106*
external noise *106*
internal noise *106*
audience surveillance *108*
defeated listening *110*
superficial listening *111*
speech critique *112*
constructive criticism *112*

Review Questions

1. What is listening? How does it differ from hearing?

2. What are the various *styles of listening* identified in this chapter? How are they different from one another?

3. Identify and describe at least one internal and one external barrier to effective listening.

4. What two steps make up the listening process? Explain each one.

5. Detail four of the six culprits behind poor listening.

6. What is interactive listening? Describe three methods for improving your listening skills through interactive listening.

7. Explain four ways you can prepare in advance to enhance the way your audience listens to your speech.

8. As a speaker, what do you need to look for to determine if your audience is listening? If audience members are not listening, how can you reengage them?

9. Explain three guidelines for listening when you are in the audience.

Critical Thinking Questions

1. Reflect on your own listening skills. How well do you process information as you listen? How well do you retain a speaker's message? What are some techniques you can employ to improve each of these?

2. Give three reasons why our culture might negatively affect our ability to listen. How can we counteract each of these?

3. ◪ Consider the attentiveness curve presented on page 97. Do you recognize this pattern in your own behavior during lectures? How can you combat the pattern as both an audience member and a student? As a speaker, how might your knowledge of this pattern influence the way you choose to organize and deliver your speech?

4. How would you distinguish the ways you can anticipate ineffective listening before you speak from the techniques you might use to deal with ineffective listening once you are speaking?

5. How can good listening skills help you give a constructive critique to a classmate?

Activities

1. Test your listening skills by going to either Youtube or Netflix and watching a monologue from a late-night talk show. After viewing it once, write down a summary of the monologue. Then watch it again with your summary in hand, and see how much you remembered. Try the same activity with a cooking program. If you try both variations on this activity, are the outcomes any different? If so, what is different, and why?

2. For five or ten minutes in class, try viewing your public speaking instructor as a speaker trying to keep an audience (the class) engaged in effective listening. How could your instructor be more effective in encouraging effective listening? How does your instructor encourage good listening?

3. ◪ Look at the illustration on page 111 that shows how to deal with superficial listeners. Think of what the speaker might have said to encourage audience members to turn off their cell phones for the speech. In your opinion, would a direct approach work best, or is the promise of speech content worth their attention? Write your own speech bubble above the illustration.

AUDIENCE ANALYSIS

5

"Let the audience drive your message." Helena and Matt were newlyweds, fresh out of college, who decided to become organic farmers. After searching for land they could use, they were fortunate to find an agriculture park on rural land owned by the water district for a nearby city. For two years, they farmed their acres, growing some eighty different types of organic vegetables and fruit. They sold their produce to restaurants and farmers' markets and also to low-income families in a small town near their farm. One day they learned that the water district had decided to expand a parking lot for its workers on land next to the ag park. It would wipe out most of Helena and Matt's farmland and would threaten other farmers' land as well.

Representatives of the water district held a public meeting to discuss the new parking lot. Helena and Matt encouraged other farmers to attend the meeting, hoping to convince the representatives of the district that the plan should be halted or altered. At the meeting, Helena noticed that many local residents had come to sit in the audience. She also noted two reporters from the region's two largest newspapers were present.

After she and Matt consulted with each other, they each took to the podium to address the water district officials, but they used different messages intended for two separate audiences. Helena spoke at length about how important organic farming was to the local area—how local restaurants benefited and how low-income families (including many in the audience) received healthy and affordable vegetables and fruit because of farms like hers. Matt then spoke about how senseless it was to destroy valuable and precious farmland (the soil at the ag park was unique and rich) and replace it with a parking lot—especially when other spaces for such a lot were available. When Matt spoke, he looked directly at the reporters—and then paraphrased the lyrics to an old Joni Mitchell song: "Don't it always seem to go that you don't know what you got 'til it's gone? You pave paradise, to put up a parking lot!"

When they finished, many local residents stood in line to speak—and all echoed or repeated what Helena and Matt had said. No one spoke to support the parking lot idea. The next day, news stories in both papers reported the meeting and the controversy. Both led with headlines about "Paving Paradise to Put Up a Parking Lot." After local negative feedback and two stories that made the district plan appear foolish, the water district announced it would build a parking lot elsewhere.

As you can see by this (true-life) example, speakers who tailor their message to their listeners create enormous value for their audience *and* themselves, in some of the following ways:

- Listeners become much more interested in and attentive to the speech.
- They experience positive feelings toward the speaker when he or she has made an effort to understand listener concerns.

A WELL-TAILORED EXCUSE (ALMOST)

Sorry, but I have to ask for an extension.

Why?

Well... er... My dog was sick, and I had to rush him to the vet...

What was wrong with him?

Well... when they opened him up in surgery, they found his stomach full of homework...

TAILOR YOUR MESSAGE TO LISTENERS

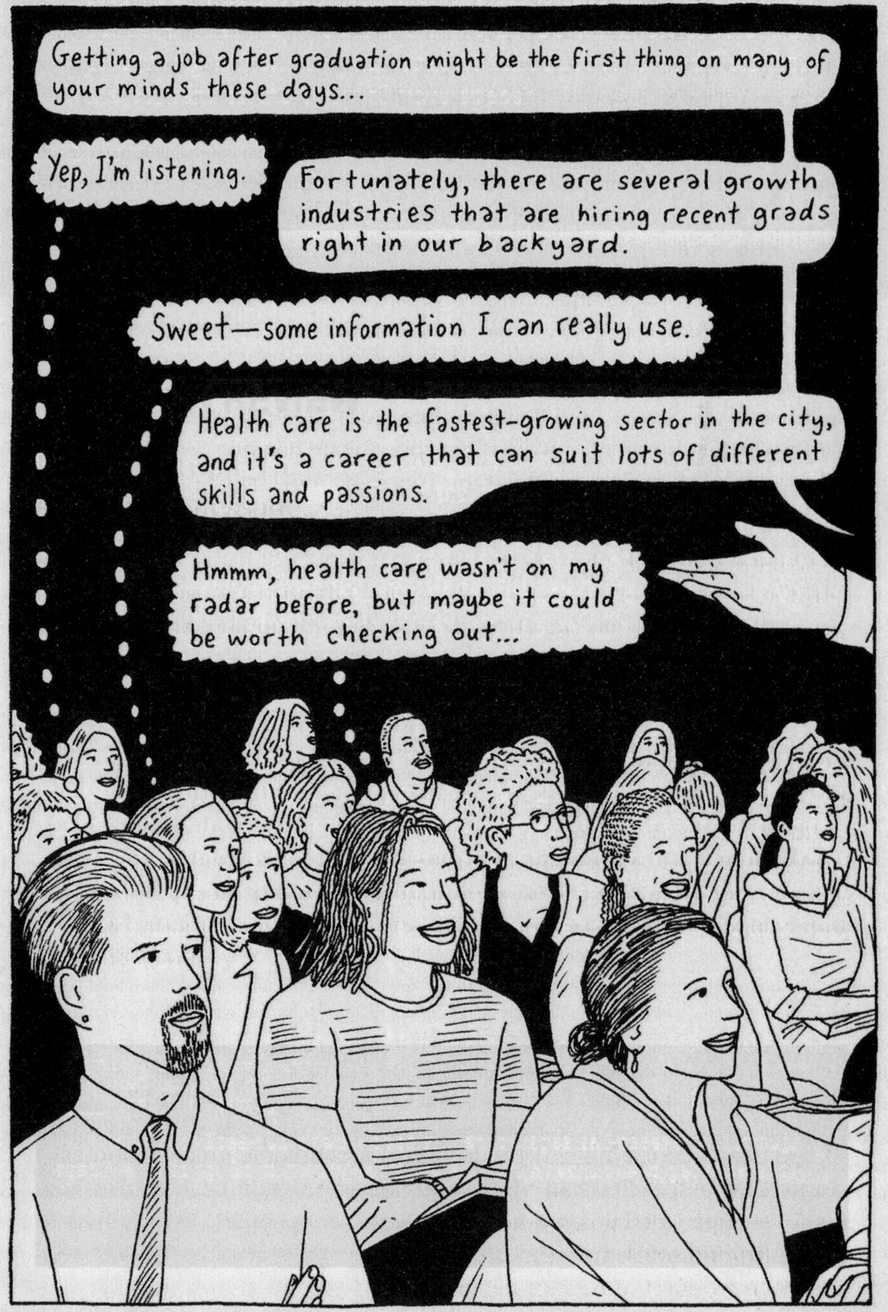

- They open their minds to the speech message because it targets their specific needs, interests, and values.
- They are also more open to being persuaded by a message that appears to be tailored for them and their specific interests.

Of all the things Helena and Matt did right, the most important was to analyze their audience—recognizing that the residents and the reporters were their real audiences and that, by motivating and persuading them, they could increase the likelihood of persuading the water district to change its plans. Audience analysis is used in more than just public speaking. Even in everyday conversation, we continually shape our messages as we focus on the people we're talking to. It's not surprising that this skill is highly important in the context of public speaking. To learn about your audience before developing your speech, you will need to gather various kinds of information about your listeners.

In this chapter, we organize the types of information you will need to gather into the following categories—situational characteristics, demographics, common ground, prior exposure, and audience disposition. We also provide some tips for gathering these details, as well as suggestions for what to do if you discover halfway through a speech that you've misread your audience.

UNDERSTANDING SITUATIONAL CHARACTERISTICS

Situational characteristics are factors in a specific speech setting that you can observe or discover *before* you give the speech. They include audience *size, time, location* (*forum*), and *audience mobility*.

Size

Audience size refers to the number of people who will be present for your speech. In a classroom setting, the size of your audience will be obvious. But in the world beyond school, this information may not be so apparent. For example, if the leader of a charitable organization asks you to give a speech at an awards dinner, you would need to ask how many people will be attending: Seven to ten people? Twenty-five to thirty? Three hundred? A thousand?

SIZE MATTERS

When it comes to speech presentations and audience, *size matters*. In other words, the number of audience members affects how you'll craft *and* deliver your message. The smaller the group, the greater the opportunity for you to interact with your audience—for example, through question-and-answer sessions.[1] With small audiences, you also can communicate a more detailed and specific message because you're tailoring it to the needs of just a few people. Conversely, the larger the audience, the less opportunity you have for interaction. You'll have to work harder to anticipate your listeners' questions and craft a more generally accessible message.

Consider the example of Jeanine, a marketing representative for a software company. Jeanine's boss asked her to visit several cities and deliver big and elaborate sales presentations—what the boss described as "dog and pony shows"—for a revolutionary new software product designed to create striking visual online advertisements. Up to that point, Jeanine had presented the product only to groups of five to seven people in intimate boardroom settings. In contrast, the dog and pony shows would be in large hotel ballrooms, and her audiences would range from three hundred to five hundred prospective customers.

As she prepared for the first presentation, Jeanine realized that unlike her previous experiences, she simply would not be able to answer every audience member's question as it cropped up; if she did, she'd never get through the presentation. Nor would she have time for a lengthy question-and-answer period. With this in mind, she decided to incorporate some of the more likely audience questions into her presentation.

Jeanine also realized that among audience members, there would be a wide range of computer know-how. As a result, she decided to cover technical issues by "teaching to the middle." Rather than pitching her speech to the few listeners who would be extremely computer savvy or slowing down things for the few who would know very little about technology, she focused her content for the large group in the middle. That way, she could feel confident that her talk would be accessible to the largest portion of her audience.

Time

Time is an important aspect of any presentation you deliver, in terms of both the time allotted for the speech and your listeners' own time rhythms in the day. Thus, you will want to consider two aspects of timing—*presentation time* and *body clock*.

Presentation time is the length of time you have to deliver your speech. Is it one minute? Five minutes? Twenty minutes? As long as you wish? The answer should shape how you prepare and deliver your presentation.

For example, when your presentation time is short, you have to make tough choices about what to include and what to leave out. Remember, though, that television ads—some of the most powerful, persuasive messages we see—are just fifteen to thirty seconds long, yet they convey extensive information and can strongly influence an audience's behavior. To exert the greatest effect in a very short speech, carefully reduce your message to something your audience can quickly digest.

If your presentation time is relatively long, you'll have more opportunity to develop your main points, but you'll also be more at risk of digressing—or veering away from your central message. With long speeches, concentrate on sticking closely to your main message. That way, you'll keep your audience members (and yourself) focused.

Body clock—also known as **chronemics**—refers to the time of day or day of the week when your audience members will be listening to your presentation. If you have a choice about when to give your class presentation, which days and times would you select? Which would you avoid?

If you sought to avoid speaking on a Monday morning, you'd be making a wise choice. Many students are still mentally rooted in the weekend and will have difficulty focusing on your speech. Similar distractions abound for people close to lunchtime, at the end of the day, or at the end of the week.

Nevertheless, you can still deliver an effective speech at such times. For example, you might include more humor or anecdotal references to engage your audience. Or with your teacher's approval, you might open by asking direct questions of some audience members, which would heighten their attentiveness. Finally, you could simply shorten your speech to match your audience's attention span.

One of the authors of this book was once invited to give a presentation to a group of lawyers at 3:00 p.m. on a Tuesday. The twenty-five-minute speech about effective negotiating strategies was part of an all-day conference. Unfortunately, the conference schedule lagged, and the presenter realized that he would have to speak much later, at 4:30 that afternoon. Because his listeners' attention span would be minimal at that time, he quickly reframed the speech—five minutes of simple tips plus a quick question-and-answer period. Invigorated by the concise and lively presentation, the lawyers were fully engaged and asked spirited questions at the conclusion of the speech.

Location

Location, also known as **forum**, is the setting where your audience will listen to your speech. Speech locations vary widely—from classrooms and auditoriums to conference rooms and outdoor venues. Each type strongly influences how you deliver your speech.

Consider the following true story. Loren, a high school junior, was running for student-body president. Each candidate had to deliver a campaign speech at an afternoon rally. The location of the rally was the recently completed high school quadrangle (quad), a sunken plaza built about eight feet below the foundations of four surrounding brick buildings. This design produced some rather spectacular acoustics when sound within the plaza was projected against the brick buildings.

Loren spoke first at the rally. Concerned that the huge crowd would not be able to hear him, he had decided to speak with a microphone. What he hadn't realized was that the plaza design would amplify his voice anyway. When he spoke into the microphone, the sound was so loud that his listeners grimaced and covered their ears. Because of his inattention to location, Loren's speech was literally too painful to hear!

NOT TAKING FORUM INTO ACCOUNT

Loren failed to consider the acoustics of his speech location. In addition to acoustical problems, locations can present other challenges, such as availability of audiovisual equipment (are there electrical outlets for your presentation aids, or should you bring handheld visual aids?), lines of sight (will your listeners be able to see your visual aids?), and lighting (is it adequate?).

How can you anticipate and address location challenges? Go to the place where you'll deliver your speech. Stand there and imagine yourself giving the presentation. Now position yourself where the audience will be, and imagine listening to the speech. Will all your listeners be able to see and hear you?

If Loren had taken stock of the forum for his speech ahead of time, he probably wouldn't have elected to use a microphone. Given the size of the forum, he also might have decided to walk from behind the podium and make himself more accessible to his audience so that listeners could hear *and* see him better.

Mobility

Different speech settings may have different implications for your audience's mobility—the degree to which listeners move around during a speech. For example, if you're giving a presentation in a classroom, lecture hall, or conference room, you will likely have a **stationary audience**, meaning that listeners will be relatively motionless (sitting or standing) and captive as you're talking. If you are delivering a presentation at an

TAKING FORUM INTO ACCOUNT

exhibitor's booth at a sales conference, on a town common, or on a city sidewalk, you'll probably have a **mobile audience**—listeners will be strolling by, stopping for a moment to listen to you, or drifting off to get on with their day.

If you're making a presentation in a college classroom, you know that you will have a stationary audience because your listeners are captive; their grades depend in part on their class attendance and participation. Don't fall into the trap, though, of taking a stationary audience for granted. Surely you have experienced lecturers who do exactly that; knowing that their audience must remain present, they assume they don't have to work as hard to capture the audience's attention. Veteran teachers know they need to work to keep a lively, interested class.

Capturing the attention of a mobile audience is clearly more challenging than capturing that of a stationary one. To do so, take a hint from the salespeople who make their livings at conventions and county fairs selling everything from rugs and hot tubs to produce and kitchenware. These vendors contend with an entirely mobile audience, so they must draw an audience's attention quickly and magnetically. For example, a seasoned vendor might try to sell a fruit and vegetable knife by arranging colorful, precut fruit in pleasing shapes, such as a flower or a windmill. She also might make the speech interactive by stopping passersby and encouraging them to "test-drive the knife, have some fruit, watch a little slice and dice!" You can adapt these effective techniques to your own presentations by offering fun (and

maybe edible!) visual aids and making your presentation interactive—either by inviting audience members to come over or by asking invitational questions that fit with your overall message. (Just make sure the questions are appropriate to the speech setting and aren't invasive or personal.)

INCORPORATING DEMOGRAPHICS

In addition to considering situational characteristics, you also need to take demographics into account. **Demographics**—a term that's originally from the world of public relations and marketing—refers to certain characteristics of your listeners.[2] For example, demographics can include *age, gender composition, sexual orientation, race and ethnicity, religious orientation, socioeconomic background*, and *political affiliation*.[3] By assessing your audience members' demographics, you can better anticipate their beliefs about your topic, their willingness to listen to your message, and their likely responses. In this section, we examine demographic characteristics you should consider while developing and delivering a presentation.

Age

Age can affect how audience members respond to your message. For example, a presentation on safe snowboarding would not likely interest most retired persons. But it may hold great appeal for athletic students in their late teens and early twenties.

Naturally, when you're speaking to a large group of diverse listeners, their ages may vary considerably. How can you consider age when targeting these varied listeners? Try tailoring your supporting materials (such as examples and quotations) to the needs of different age groups within your audience. For instance, older listeners may not understand references to the popular musical groups or late-night comedy shows that younger people tend to appreciate. And younger listeners might not understand references to classic film stars like Greta Garbo or Cary Grant or even early rock stars such as Elvis Presley. For younger listeners, you also might try to avoid referring to events that took place before they were born unless you place the events in context for them. When speaking to an audience of mixed ages, be sure to either add some context to your references or use references that would appeal to a wide range of listeners.

> ⊙ To see an example of a speaker appealing to a younger audience, try Video Activity 5.1, "Poplin, The Importance of Community Service and Civic Engagement."

Gender Composition

The **gender composition** of your audience—*mixed* (male and female) or *single gender* (all female or all male)—affects how your listeners will respond to your speech. Some stories, illustrations, or examples might resonate better with one gender grouping than another.

Car sellers, for example, pay close attention to differences in buying patterns between genders. In recent years, marketers in the automotive industry observed that more women were buying cars and that sales pitches aimed at men did not work effectively when applied to female customers. Minh, a former student of ours and an automotive salesperson, told a story that shed light on this development. In Minh's experience, effectively selling Volvo station wagons to men and women required two very different approaches.[4] To appeal to men, Minh emphasized the cars' turbocharged engines, high-performance tires, and special detailing. To capture women's interest, he stressed features related to safety, reliability, and fuel economy. Although Minh aimed the same broad message

at all shoppers—"You'll want to buy this wonderful car"—he tailored the specifics of the message to each gender.

Although consideration of gender is a valid component of audience analysis, you must never assume you know about an individual audience member's views based on gender. The views of countless men and women cut against the grain of traditional ideas of **gender stereotypes**—oversimplified and often distorted views of what it means to be male or female. Likewise, ethical speakers never resort to **sexist language**, or language with a bias for or against a given gender.

> To watch a speaker who could use more gender-inclusive language, try Video Activity 5.2, "Singh, The Importance of Playing Sports Has Grown over Time."

Sexual Orientation

Another demographic characteristic that has become increasingly important to consider and acknowledge is the **sexual orientation** of your audience members. This can include straight men and women as well as lesbian, gay, bisexual, transgender, and queer or questioning individuals—or LGBTQ for short. In spite of the 2015 U.S. Supreme Court decision[5] concerning marriage equality (a victory for the LGBTQ community), there has been controversy surrounding questions of status and legal protection for members of the LGBTQ community. Not everyone in the country feels

comfortable with or accepting of people whose sexual orientation is different from his or her own.

Given this environment, some might object to acknowledging the LGBTQ demographic, but we strongly believe that acknowledging members of the LGBTQ community is not only a smart and strategic move for a speaker but also an ethical responsibility. Statistics vary, but estimates suggest that gay or lesbian people (only two parts of the LGBTQ designation) account for up to 10 percent of our population and that those who identify as transgendered may be as much as 3 percent.[6] Because speakers have a responsibility to all members of their audiences—not simply those in the dominant majority—ignoring LGBTQ listeners means excluding and potentially alienating a substantial portion of an audience from the discussion.

Acknowledging a difference in sexual orientation can be accomplished both overtly and passively, depending on what is appropriate for your speech and your situation. Open and overt acknowledgment of these differences might be accomplished by including examples or illustrations that reference LGBTQs as well as straight people. For example, a speech on conflict in relationships might include examples of gay or lesbian couples in the same breath as examples of heterosexual couples. Likewise, a speech that deals with parenting could include the story of two fathers raising a child, along with examples featuring a mother and father or a single parent.

You can offer passive acknowledgment of the LGBTQ community (and do so sensitively) through inclusive word choice when referencing sexual or relational orientation. For example, instead of speaking only of "married couples" or "a wife searching for a husband" (or vice versa), you might refer to "loving partners" or "individuals looking for a long-term

commitment." Inclusive word choice invites everyone in the audience to share in the speech while avoiding language that privileges one form of sexual orientation over another.

Race and Ethnicity

In the United States today, the population is far more racially and ethnically diverse than in previous eras. With this increased diversity, your audience members are likely to come from a wide variety of racial and ethnic origins. In preparing and delivering your speech, you need to be sensitive to your listeners' diverse backgrounds and speak to their varied interests. At the same time, however, you must not generalize about particular races or ethnicities. For example, all Americans of white European descent don't necessarily feel the same way about affirmative action. Neither do all Americans of African descent.

Still, **race**—common heritage based on genetically shared physical characteristics of people in a group—*can* affect how listeners respond to a speaker's message. This is especially true in situations in which racial issues are sensitive, affecting people throughout their lives.

Ethnicity—cultural background that is usually associated with shared religion, national origin, and language—is another important demographic aspect to consider because it can shape beliefs, attitudes, and values of audience members. A student named Gunther learned this lesson the hard way. Gunther gave a presentation to members of his campus's student-run Middle Eastern Society and spoke to an audience he was told consisted of students who had fled from Iraq shortly after the U.S. invasion in 2003. Attempting to show courtesy, Gunther addressed his listeners as "Iraqis."

Only later did Gunther learn that his audience had been made up of Assyrians who had been living in Iraq. Although Assyria no longer exists as an independent nation, there are millions of people who continue to identify themselves as Assyrian. They speak a common language, share religious beliefs, and have their own distinctive traditions and customs. Although many of the Assyrians in Gunther's audience realized his mislabeling of them as Iraqis was unintentional, they still took offense at being categorized with a group with whom they did not identify. They (rightly) concluded that Gunther hadn't cared enough to find out about their actual backgrounds. Offended and annoyed, many didn't bother to listen to much of Gunther's presentation.

Religious Orientation

Religious orientation—a person's set of religious beliefs—is another demographic characteristic that can influence how people respond to your speech. In the United States alone, there are as many as 2,300 religious identifications—including Baha'is, Buddhists, Christians, Confucians, Hindus, Jews, Muslims, and Zoroastrians, to name just a few.

For some people, religious orientation strongly shapes their views on a wide range of issues—including but not limited to gay marriage, abortion, and men's and women's roles in family life and society. Moreover, some of the larger religions have numerous subdivisions, whose adherents possess conflicting beliefs about specific issues. For example, Anglicans and Roman Catholics share common elements in the celebration of the Eucharist, but they are widely divided over such issues as allegiance to the papacy and the admission of women into the priesthood. Likewise, Reform and Orthodox Jews differ in their dietary laws and in their interpretations of the Torah. Thus, like any other demographic characteristic, religious orientation does not preordain (pardon the pun) an audience's reaction to a given message, yet it can still exert great influence. Presenters who craft their speeches accordingly stand a better chance of connecting with their listeners.

One particularly enduring example of this approach is the late pope John Paul II's address to the state of Israel at the Yad Vashem Holocaust memorial in March 2000. The pope knew that many Jews believed that his predecessors had been indifferent to Jewish suffering during the Holocaust. Demonstrating his sensitivity to their feelings, the pope repeatedly used Old Testament passages to describe suffering and awareness of human evil. In addition, he condemned all the hatred, acts of persecution, and displays of anti-Semitism directed at Jews by Christians throughout time.

The current pope, Francis, has continued John Paul II's example and taken many steps further toward improving relations between Christians and the worldwide Jewish community. Welcoming a Jewish delegation to Rome in 2015 to commemorate the fiftieth anniversary of the *Nostra aetate*, the declaration promulgated by Paul VI that led to improved relations between Jews and Catholics, Francis declared in his address to the public at St. Peter's Square: "Yes to the rediscovery of the Jewish roots of Christianity. No to anti-Semitism."[7]

Socioeconomic Background

Related to but distinct from questions surrounding demographic characteristics such as race, religion, and political affiliation are those that concern the social and economic background of an audience member or group. **Socioeconomic status** is a measure of where individuals stand in relation to other people in terms of financial resources, education, and occupation. As a speaker, it's important to consider your audience's socioeconomic status and how it might influence their individual and collective concerns. For example, in the 2012 presidential election, both Barack Obama and Mitt Romney recognized that middle-class voters would largely decide the election and often tailored their messages specifically to them.[8] But four years later, as candidates prepared for the 2016 race, the term *middle class* seemed to have disappeared from their

speeches.[9] One possibility suggests that the term *middle class* used to be associated with homeownership, a job, children's college funds, and maybe money for retirement—accessible parts of the American dream. But after what has been called the Great Recession (which began at the end of the first decade of the twenty-first century), being a member of the middle class is now associated with a lower standard of living, difficulties in finding jobs without special technical training, and houses lost to bank repossessions. The number of people within this group has grown substantially, and now the term tends to remind people who identify as middle class of their financial plight. Instead of using the term *middle class*, presidential candidates in their speech rhetoric took to referring to middle-income people as "the millions of people who aren't rich" (Marco Rubio), "working families" (Bernie Sanders), or "hardworking men and women across America" (Ted Cruz).

Financial Resources. It is likely that the experiences of people who come from wealth and privilege will be different from those who are poor and have fewer resources and options. For this reason, a person who has always been financially comfortable may have very different concerns than a person who is struggling financially. A speech extolling the benefits of using online coupon sites like Groupon and Living Social, for example, might be of more interest to a lower-income group than it is to an affluent group. Conversely, a speech on stock market investing might fail to capture the attention of students with little or no money to invest.

Negotiating your path through assumptions about socioeconomic status can be tricky business: labels like *rich*, *poor*, and *middle class* are relative terms that carry little real meaning. You can, however, analyze your audience to get an idea of their collective economic status. For example, for a speech focused on whether it was ethical and appropriate for regents of the state university system to increase student tuition, Eleanor considered the following facts: many of her classmates had attended community colleges before transferring to the four-year state university; the majority worked to pay for all or part of their tuition; and due to work obligations, a large portion attended class part-time and would need five or six years to graduate. Eleanor concluded that these aspects of her audience's background would undoubtedly affect their attitudes about the cost of education and what they would be willing to spend.

Education and Occupation. Your audience's level of education and occupation also can influence their reaction to your speech. For example, suppose many of your listeners are already familiar—through formal education or life experience—with the facts you plan to present in your speech. If you're aware of this familiarity beforehand, you'll know that you won't have to provide extensive background information in your speech. But if your audience is unlikely to have had exposure to your topic through formal schooling or life experience, you'll need to provide more explanation and examples to help them understand your presentation.

Consider the story of Roy, a civil engineer responsible for civic projects, such as building new bridges and highways. To get approval for his projects, Roy often made presentations about zoning issues to a civilian commission. While doing careful analysis of his audience's educational backgrounds, Roy realized that the commission members actually knew very little about the necessary zoning issues. They lacked formal training in zoning, and because they served only brief two-year terms, no one ever served long enough to acquire extensive knowledge about the relevant issues. Roy therefore kept his speeches simple, explaining or avoiding technical terms. To help his listeners decide how to vote, he explained how issues currently before them compared with issues on which they had voted in the past.

Listeners who lack background in your subject might also benefit from presentation aids that clarify the points you're making. Carefully repeating

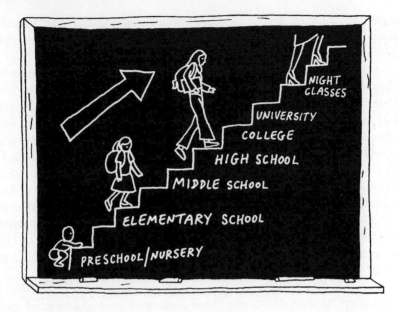

your main points also can help your audience members understand your presentation by giving them time to absorb and process the information.

Political Affiliation

In some respects, **political affiliation**—a person's political beliefs and positions—is the most difficult of the demographic characteristics to pin down. Traditional labels like *liberal* or *conservative* and *Republican* or *Democrat* elude specific meaning and are so broad as to be relatively useless in predicting a person's views on every issue. *Conservative*, for example, may refer to *fiscal conservatism* (belief in balanced budgets and reduced taxes), *law-and-order conservatism* (belief in the need for a stronger criminal justice system), *defense conservatism* (belief in the necessity for a strong defense and military preparedness), or *social conservatism* (positions on controversial social issues, like abortion or the right to die, often informed by religious perspectives). Members of your audience who identify themselves as conservative won't all necessarily hold the same beliefs about each of these dimensions of conservatism. Likewise, membership in a political party does not guarantee that someone will vote for a specific candidate or respond to a speaker's message in a predictable manner.

Nevertheless, knowing your listeners' political orientation—as well as their views on specific political issues—can help you determine how

to craft your speech. In a highly polarized political climate, attention to your listeners' political orientation becomes especially crucial to making a successful presentation.

Putting the Demographic Pieces Together

Great public speakers use their knowledge of their listeners' demographic characteristics to understand the people they are addressing—and to make their messages more effective. Every audience is unique; by iden- tifying characteristics that many of your listeners share, you gain insights into how they might respond to your message. You can then incorporate these insights as you develop your speech and frame your message for the audience.

For example, Jackie, a middle-aged doctor, was asked to give two speeches on safe-sex practices—one to a group of teens in a runaway shelter and another to a group of middle-income parents at a school. Jackie knew she would need to craft her message differently for each audience. Because she knew the teens would be suspicious of authority figures, she avoided calling attention to the age difference between her- self and her listeners. In contrast, when Jackie gave her speech to the group of parents, she made reference to her age and her own role as a mother.

PUTTING THE PIECES TOGETHER FOR MY SPEECH
TO THE COLLEGE ACTIVISM TASK FORCE

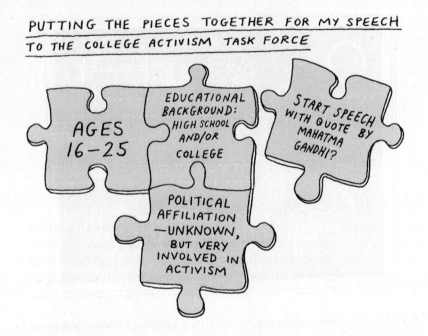

AGES 16–25

EDUCATIONAL BACKGROUND: HIGH SCHOOL AND/OR COLLEGE

START SPEECH WITH QUOTE BY MAHATMA GANDHI?

POLITICAL AFFILIATION —UNKNOWN, BUT VERY INVOLVED IN ACTIVISM

Using demographics is also important in more complex situations—such as when you're trying to make a persuasive case to audiences with opposing views. For example, a city council member named Ignacio was campaigning for his proposal to continue funding a pension program for retired city workers *while also* scaling back benefits for newly hired, younger city employees. When speaking to an older audience of retired

workers, Ignacio acknowledged that the city had to honor its thirty-year-old promise to provide for their pensions—especially because he knew that many of these individuals grew up in a time when employers took care of their employees for life. In exchange for honoring the city's commitment, he asked them to consider increasing their contributions to their health care. When Ignacio spoke to younger workers, he established common ground by acknowledging that he, too, felt the burden of paying for older retirees' pensions—but that in keeping this promise to older workers, they could trust him to keep his word regarding future policies.

SEEKING COMMON GROUND

Another way to analyze your audience is to look for **common ground**—beliefs, values, and experiences that you share with your listeners.[10] Consider Jay, a student at a commuter school who gave a persuasive presentation to convince his listeners to use mass transit instead of driving to school. Like many of his listeners, Jay had spent his first year of college driving to school every day—getting caught in traffic, having trouble finding parking, and arriving late for classes. As he presented his arguments, Jay shared his own experiences with driving because he knew that many of his listeners faced these same challenges. By establishing this common ground, Jay gained credibility with his listeners.

In some cases, you can communicate your perception of common ground nonverbally. For example, a candidate for national political office may don a cowboy hat while delivering a speech to voters in Texas or

a sports cap from a local team. Of course, merely putting on a hat doesn't necessarily mean you share actual common ground with your audience. Use this technique only if you feel a genuine sense of shared identity with your listeners, and then reinforce that authenticity by referring to common ground during your speech.

> Ⓒ For an example of verbally asserting common ground, see how this speaker uses the word "we" in the first minute of her speech: "Kim, The Non-monetary Uses of Gold" in Video Activity 5.3.

IDENTIFYING PRIOR EXPOSURE

Do you remember getting a lecture from your parents or teachers that you had heard before—and finding yourself completely unconvinced because their points were not persuasive the first time? Or perhaps you've heard a sales pitch or an ad slogan that seemed lame initially and only more so every subsequent time? This can be a problem for public speakers, too—as a student named Henry discovered while giving a required persuasive speech in an advanced speech class. This speech critiqued the existence of climate change. In making his speech, Henry picked up where he had left off in an earlier informative speech explaining how people uncritically accepted what they heard from television news media. In the original speech, Henry had used climate change as one of the examples of "stories that television media push on people"—and he added that climate change was a myth. At this point in the speech, people had showed that they were critical (rolling their eyes and smirking), but Henry had failed to notice. When he received compliments for his speech delivery, he took that as a sign that his audience had agreed with his message. When Henry revisited the issue in his persuasive speech, he repeated the same criticisms of climate change—and was later surprised to learn that the audience disagreed with him. Henry's mistake was *not* in taking an unpopular position about climate change but in ignoring the audience's reaction to what he had said the first time and simply repeating those arguments for the same audience.

Analyzing your audience also includes gauging listeners' **prior exposure**[11]—the extent to which they have already heard your message. The degree of this prior exposure should guide you either to include particular points in your speech or to craft something entirely new. How can you determine whether your audience has had prior exposure to

POOR ASSESSMENT OF PRIOR EXPOSURE

your topic—and then use that information to shape your presentation? Ask yourself the following questions:

Has My Audience Heard This Message Before?
If your answer is no, your listeners have had zero prior exposure and will have no pre-conceived notions about or positions on your message. You can craft your message as you want, but you may have to explain all relevant issues and concepts in basic terms. If your answer is yes, your audience has had prior exposure. Move on to the second question.

Has My Audience Responded Positively to the Message?
If the goal of an earlier speech on your same topic was persuasion, consider whether audience members actually engaged in the actions or adopted the beliefs the speaker advocated. If the purpose of that earlier speech was to inform, determine whether audience members became interested in the subject and understood the information the speaker presented.

If you answer yes—meaning your audience responded positively to the message in the past—then use the new speech to reinforce the previous message, add any pertinent new information, and motivate your audience to take action (if you are giving a persuasive speech).

If you answer no—meaning your audience did not respond positively to the message in the past—then avoid the approach used in the previous presentation. Now proceed to the third question.

Why Did the Previous Message Fail?
Assess what went wrong the last time your audience heard the message. Then use the resulting insights

to tailor a more successful approach. In the case of Henry's speech, he would have benefited from asking his classmates why they disagreed with his position in his first speech. Perhaps he would have discovered that some of them questioned his knowledge of science, some of them knew about climate change only from what they had heard on television, and some may have found him a bit arrogant. Knowing the answers to this question would have given Henry other options for his second speech.

Additionally, if your audience has had a major change in perspective since the previous presentation, consider whether you need to adjust your message to accommodate listeners' new viewpoints. For example, during the 2008 presidential campaign, Barack Obama pushed for universal health care coverage. Given his win, Democrats assumed that support for the new president would translate into ongoing backing of the health care bill. However, in late 2009, many members of Congress found themselves confronted by angry constituents who were not amenable to the bill.

What happened? Democrats had failed to ask themselves whether anything had changed for voters since their prior exposure to the message. And something had changed—namely, people's economic situation and job security, due to the 2008 economic crash. Many were concerned about growing deficits and increases in taxes and government spending. As the economic slump continued, voters on both sides of the issue worried about the cost and effectiveness of an expensive federal health care program. Both the Democratic Party and President Obama realized they needed to recalibrate their message to show the necessity of affordable health care access in the face of economic uncertainty. Due to their updated message, they were able to rally support for the Affordable Care Act, which passed in 2010.

IDENTIFYING AUDIENCE DISPOSITION

Finally, complete your audience analysis by assessing listeners' **disposition**—their likely attitude toward your message. In most situations, audiences can be divided into three groups—*sympathetic*, *hostile*, and *neutral*.

A **sympathetic audience** already agrees with your message or holds you in high personal esteem and will therefore respond favorably to your speech. For example, imagine that you are giving a speech advocating the controversial and hot-button issue of gun control to an audience made up of American Medical Association (AMA) members—in this case, surgeons who work in emergency departments, often on victims of gun violence. More than likely, you will have found a sympathetic audience.

In contrast, a **hostile audience** opposes your message or you personally and therefore will resist listening to your speech. Imagine, for example, that you are giving the same speech advocating gun control, but this time you are a speaker at a convention of the National Rifle Association (NRA). The audience in this instance would likely be hostile to your message because the NRA strongly opposes restrictions on gun ownership.

A third type of audience is the **neutral audience**, which has neither negative nor positive opinions about you or your message. Listeners may be neutral for several reasons. Some may be apathetic and simply not interested in you or your ideas. Others may be very interested in hearing you talk but lack strong feelings about your topic. The key thing to remember about neutral audiences is that depending on how you deliver your speech, they can tip toward supporting your message or opposing it. To extend the earlier example, imagine that you are now giving the same speech on gun control to the American Bar Association (ABA), an organization for lawyers. The membership of this association has mixed attitudes about gun control and would likely be considered a neutral audience.

As with the other elements of audience analysis, gauging your listeners' disposition can help you figure out how to craft your speech. For example, suppose you'll be facing a uniformly hostile audience. In this case, you should probably define realistic goals for your speech. Although you may not be able to persuade your listeners to follow a course of action you recommend, you might succeed in getting them to reevaluate their opposition to your message or to you personally. Thus, seek incremental or small changes, as opposed to a complete turnaround in attitudes.

An excellent example of this is when the late senator Edward (Ted) Kennedy was invited to speak in October 1983 at Liberty Baptist College, a conservative Christian school established by the Reverend Jerry Falwell. Kennedy, a well-known liberal lawmaker, agreed to speak at the school, even though he knew he would face a hostile audience. For his speech, Kennedy addressed the emotionally charged subject of separating church and state. His speech, titled "Truth and Tolerance in America," focused on the appropriate place for religion in discourse about politics. In a speech that at times found common ground with Baptists and Falwell

himself, Kennedy carefully but clearly encouraged religious groups to enter political discourse where moral and ethical questions were concerned. He also suggested they avoid name-calling or disparaging those who disagreed. It is unlikely Kennedy convinced many in the audience to change their minds about contentious issues like abortion—but he did gain the audience's respect for working to find some commonality with them.[12] Indeed, after Kennedy's speech, a bond of sorts between Kennedy and Falwell was established, and it remained to the end of their lives.[13]

If you're addressing a sympathetic audience, you don't need to bother investing a lot of time and energy in trying to convince listeners that your ideas have merit or that you're a credible speaker. Instead, push for more commitment: rather than simply asking your audience members to agree with you, urge them to act on your message.

If you'll be facing a neutral audience, determine whether your listeners' neutrality stems from apathy, disinterest, or a lack of firm conviction about you or the issue at hand. Then figure out how to overcome these forces of neutrality and get your listeners to support you—not oppose you.

Note, though, that many audiences don't fit neatly into just one dispositional group. In most cases, some listeners in a particular audience will be hostile, others sympathetic, and still others neutral. You'll need to tread carefully to deliver the most effective speech possible. If

most of the people in your audience are
neutral, some are sympathetic, and the
remaining few are hostile and very vocal,
what should you do? Expend just enough
effort to silence the hostile listeners, make
an equally modest effort to motivate your
sympathetic listeners to act on your message, and devote the lion's share of your
energy to reaching your neutral listeners—
and persuading them to take your side.

GATHERING INFORMATION ABOUT YOUR AUDIENCE

Thus far, this chapter has reviewed the types of information you will need
to analyze your audience. Here we examine three techniques you can
use to obtain that information—*surveying*, *interviewing*, and *observing*.

Surveying Your Audience

A **survey** is a set of written questions that you ask your audience to
answer in advance of your speech. Surveys allow you to ask your future
audience members direct questions about topics related to your speech.
If the audience is small—let's say thirty or fewer—try to survey all of them.
If it is larger, you may want to survey a smaller, representative sample.

Three general types of questions typically appear in a survey—fixed-
response, scaled, and open-ended.

A **fixed-response question**—such as a true/false, multiple-choice,
or select-all-that-apply question—gives your respondents a set of specific
answers to choose from. Fixed-response questions are useful for gaining
concrete insights into an audience's experience with or views on a topic.
For example, imagine that Megan, a student, wanted to give an informative speech on why visiting the dentist is a good idea (partially to convince herself!). She could ask fixed-response questions to find out if
audience members have any experience with dental care or even to learn
about potential for common ground because some audience members
could also be nervous about dentist visits.

A **scaled question** measures the intensity of feelings on a given
issue by offering a range of fixed responses. The ranges vary. They can

take the form of a numerical scale (for example, from one to ten for lowest to highest) or a list of options (including "strongly agree," "agree," "neutral," "disagree," or "strongly disagree").

Determining the intensity of your audience's feelings about a topic can help you determine their prior exposure and disposition. For her speech on visiting the dentist, Megan sought to discover the extent to which pain influenced people's attitudes about visiting the dentist. If her classmates were very frightened by the prospect of pain, she could focus her points on advances in dental anesthesia and new teeth-cleaning technologies that lessen uncomfortable scraping.

An **open-ended question** invites respondents to write an answer of their choosing, rather than offering a limited set of responses. For such a question, Megan might ask respondents to describe any problems they have had with dentists.

Open-ended questions can help you identify issues you might not have otherwise considered or covered in your other questions. If Megan thus wanted to know the range of dental problems her audience members had experienced, she could best find out through an open-ended question.

Open-ended questions also allow respondents to communicate in their own words. With fixed-response questions, it's possible that none of the options accurately describe the views of a specific audience member; open-ended questions allow each person to state an individual, nuanced answer.

Interviewing Your Audience

In addition to distributing surveys, you may want to **interview** audience members. Ideally, you will do so in person, but you also can conduct interviews over the phone or even via e-mail or instant message. Interviews allow you to interact through conversation, in which you learn facts and hear stories you couldn't have gotten through a survey. Interviews also allow you to get to know members of your audience before you speak. This can serve as a great icebreaker, especially if you don't know the people you will be addressing. Finally, you may find it more practical to interview a few audience members than to distribute a survey to a large group.

If you use interviews, carefully consider your interview subjects. Often, it's easiest to talk to audience members you already know. Also, if you are presenting to a professional group with a leader, it would be logical to interview him or her. And if your audience has diverse backgrounds and interests, be sure to interview a range of audience members.

Megan Dambrowski's <u>DENTAL SURVEY</u>

1. Have you ever been a patient at a dentist's office?

YES ☐   NO ☐

2. In the past, why have you gone to the dentist? (CIRCLE AS MANY AS NECESSARY)

A: REGULAR CHECK-UP   B: SPECIFIC PROCEDURE (e.g., cleaning)
C: SPECIFIC PROBLEM (e.g., cracked filling)

3. Have you ever been given an anesthetic at a dentist's office?   YES ☐   NO ☐

4. Please respond to the following statement by circling the answer that best reflects your feelings:

"I am nervous about visiting the dentist."

STRONGLY AGREE ——————— I am terrified of the dentist.
AGREE ——————— I get nervous when I visit the dentist.
NEUTRAL ——————— I am neither nervous nor excited.
DISAGREE ——————— I don't mind going to the dentist.
STRONGLY DISAGREE — Whoopee, it's time to go to the dentist!

5. When you are going to have dental treatment, how important is it to you that you experience no pain? PLEASE ANSWER ON A SCALE OF 1 TO 10, WITH "1" REPRESENTING "NOT IMPORTANT AT ALL" AND "10" REPRESENTING "VERY IMPORTANT."

1   2   3   4   5   6   7   8   9   10

6. Describe any problems you may have had during recent visits to the dentist (e.g., pain, discomfort).

_____

_____

_____

THANKS   *Megan*

When conducting interviews, ask the same sorts of fixed-response, scaled, and open-ended questions that are used in surveys. It is often a good idea to use fixed-response or scaled questions to get an overall impression of your interviewee's views on a topic and then ask open-ended questions to gain more insight. During your interview, make sure to put your listening skills into practice by paying attention and always being respectful. Make sure to observe the following: prepare your questions ahead of time, show up at the interview location as scheduled, observe appropriate grooming habits, and be friendly. Also, make sure to thank your subject with a card or e-mail after the interview is over; after all, she or he is helping you out with your presentation!

Considering and Observing Your Audience

Surveys and interviews are two effective methods of obtaining information about your audience. But you may not always have the chance to communicate with audience members before you speak. If this is the case, you will need to rely on less direct methods to learn about your audience. Ask yourself why your audience will be attending the speech. If your talk will occur during a class, you already know several things: you have a captive audience, your status as a student provides you with obvious common ground, and you share some background with

SPEECH CHOICES

A CASE STUDY: *MIA*

Let's check back with Mia and see how she is integrating audience analysis into her speech preparation.

Over the first two days of speeches from other students, Mia noticed something interesting. Several students mentioned they were first-generation Americans, meaning that they were the children of immigrant parents. Mia decided to interview some of these classmates to find out how long ago their families had come to the United States and under what conditions. She was interested to know what challenges they had faced in coming here and what resources they used to overcome them. Although their parents' journeys to America had preceded smartphones, the challenges they had to overcome were not all that different. Mia decided she would catalogue these challenges and how the families had solved them—and then show how a smartphone could be used to solve these challenges today.

Moreover, aware that every student in her class had a smartphone, Mia decided to interview five more audience members and ask them what apps or functions on their smartphones they used the most. Mia made careful notes of these functions (such as getting the weather, viewing maps, using social media) and began thinking about how this might compare with the ways refugees might use smartphones. In addition to helping her think about how to structure her speech, this also allowed her to create common ground with her audience: audience members would be more likely to understand and appreciate her speech because she was tying it to their own lives.

YOUR TURN:
How did Mia use audience analysis to improve her speech? How might you use audience analysis to improve yours?

For more questions and activities for this case study, please go to LaunchPad at macmillanhighered.com/speakup4e.

your audience in the academic discipline of the course. If you are a member of the College Republicans and are asked to participate in a debate at the College Democrats club, you would likely find a hostile audience. Those attending would be there voluntarily and would thus be free to leave at any time. Nevertheless, politics would be a major interest to your audience, and the fact that both you and your audience participate in political clubs on campus would give you some common ground.

Finally, consider seeking out literature about your audience members. If they belong to an organization, they may have pamphlets or brochures that they distribute, or there may be articles (online or published), Web sites, or even books written about them.

SITUATIONAL AUDIENCE ANALYSIS

Occasionally in your speaking experience, you may find that you have done everything you are supposed to do in terms of tailoring your presentation to your expected audience, only to arrive at the venue to discover that the audience you are facing is not quite the audience you expected. At other times, you may notice that the audience does not seem to be following along while you are delivering a message or that listeners seem to disagree strongly with your main points. The following suggestions will help you analyze the audience *in the moment*—a skill known as **situational audience analysis**.

If the audience ends up being different from the one you expected, avoid communicating your surprise: audience members will likely interpret your comments as a signal that you are not prepared. Take a quick look at your outline, and check whether the examples you have chosen make sense with this new audience. If the audience is smaller than you expected, consider jettisoning a portion of your outline and making time for questions and answers. Also, quickly consider whether your

SPEECH CHOICES

A CASE STUDY: *JACOB*

Let's see how Jacob is using audience analysis in his speech preparation.

Jacob had a bad habit of arriving to class late. He tried to get there on time, but for some reason (late bus, delicious breakfast sandwich, etc.) he just couldn't manage it. This meant that he was rarely there when his teacher took attendance. If he had been, he might have noticed that the names the teacher called in his class were mostly those of women. In fact, out of his class of thirty-two students, twenty were women. He might have observed this fact during the rest of class, but between taking notes and surfing the web on his laptop, he didn't notice. Furthermore, six of the twenty women in his class were in fact college athletes: two were basketball players, one was a volleyball player, one was a hockey player, and two were swimmers.

As he built his speech, Jacob divided the different seasonal sports between "revenue-producing sports" and "the rest," which were paid for by the dollars generated by the revenue-producing sports. It didn't cross his mind that many of the women in his audience might interpret the phrase "revenue-producing sports" as code for men's basketball and football—and that it might imply that women's sports couldn't generate revenue or fan interest. Worse, he failed to use examples that included women's sports as he described how college athletes were exploited. Audience analysis should ideally include all the audience—or at least most. With twenty women out of thirty-two students in the class, Jacob was ignoring more than 60 percent of his audience!

YOUR TURN:

Has there ever been a time you've failed to use audience analysis to address your entire audience? What did you learn that you could apply to the future?

For more questions and activities for this case study, please go to LaunchPad at macmillanhighered.com/speakup4e.

assumptions about common ground, prior exposure, or disposition of audience still apply. If not, you may need to verbally add more background or explanation than you had expected. Finally, consider your presentation aids. Do they make sense for the new audience configuration? Because it would be difficult to create new visual aids at this point, you may decide to get rid of some if the new audience is already informed about the topic. Or you may want to provide more explanation for certain aids if the new audience is less informed.

Because communication is a transaction between you and your audience, your audience will be sending you messages during your delivery as well. What if you are delivering your speech and your audience seems confused, lost, or hostile? Try to read the mood of your audience members, and adjust your delivery appropriately. If listeners seem confused, slow down, leave out some of the specifics or technical concepts, and instead explain a few of your points in more detail. Humor might also lighten the mood and get listeners on your side. If listeners seem bored or unengaged, consider inviting audience questions or spicing up your delivery by adding enthusiasm and varying your tone of voice—either approach will allow you to increase audience interest.

You may notice from your listeners' body language, gestures, or even voices that they are opposed to your position. In this situation, you can always flash a sincere smile or use a comforting tone of voice. You may want to reconsider common ground with the audience and your audience's prior exposure to your message. If you can see another element of common ground you share with audience members, you may wish to incorporate that into your speech. Likewise, if the new audience seems to have less prior exposure to your message than you anticipated, you may want to discard some of the points from your outline. If there is more prior exposure—coupled with a slightly more hostile disposition—emphasize points of common ground even more strongly.

CHAPTER REVIEW

“Let the audience drive your message.”

In this chapter, we shared five ways to analyze your audience: assess situational characteristics, consider demographics, identify common ground, gauge prior exposure, and anticipate your audience's disposition. We suggested ways of gathering information on these elements of audience analysis, such as surveying, interviewing, and observing your audience. Finally, we explained that exceptional speakers analyze their audience while they're preparing a speech *and* while they're delivering it, if necessary to retain their audience's attention and support (situational audience analysis).

Given the fact that audience-driven presentations are consistently the most effective, we strongly encourage you to analyze your audience in advance of your presentation and to use that analysis as a tool to shape your main points, supporting material, and even delivery (including time and visual aids). It is important to recognize, however, that audience analysis is an ongoing process—a process worth reexamining as you develop your topic and message and hone the final product into a speech. You may even be faced with a slightly different audience than you expected on the day of your delivery. Don't be afraid to alter your speech if assumptions you made about the audience are no longer accurate. Being flexible and open will help you craft and deliver a message that is targeted to the specific audience you address.

 LaunchPad
macmillan learning

LaunchPad for *Speak Up* offers videos and encourages self-assessment through adaptive quizzing. Go to **macmillanhighered.com/speakup4e** to get access to:

✓ **LearningCurve**
Adaptive Quizzes

▶ **Video clips that help you understand public speaking concepts**

Key Terms

situational characteristics *120*
audience size *120*
presentation time *123*
body clock (chronemics) *124*
location (forum) *125*
stationary audience *126*
mobile audience *127*
 demographics *128*
age *130*
gender composition *130*
gender stereotype *131*
sexist language *131*
sexual orientation *131*
race *133*
ethnicity *133*

religious orientation *134*
socioeconomic status *135*
political affiliation *138*
common ground *141*
prior exposure *142*
disposition *144*
sympathetic audience *144*
hostile audience *145*
neutral audience *145*
survey *147*
fixed-response question *147*
scaled question *147*
open-ended question *148*
interview *148*
situational audience analysis *152*

Review Questions

1. Describe the following situational characteristics as they relate to audiences: size, time, location, and mobility.

2. Explain what demographics are, and note seven demographic characteristics that a speaker can consider when analyzing an audience.

3. What areas of common ground can a speaker focus on when addressing a diverse audience?

4. Define *prior exposure*, and explain why it is important.

5. Identify and describe three types of audiences in terms of audience disposition.

6. Name and describe three tools a speaker can use to gather information about his or her audience.

7. Explain the nature of situational audience analysis.

Critical Thinking Questions

1. After reading this chapter, answer this question: is there ever an occasion when it may be better to make a general speech message you can apply identically in any audience situation?

2. Based on what was suggested about prior exposure in this text, can you think of a reason to repeat a message that previously failed with an audience? When would it make sense to repeat a message or argument that hadn't worked the first time?

3. If your classmates are to be your primary audience for your speech, how can you use class time to perform informal audience analysis? How might the timing of your speeches (both day of week and time of day) over the course of the semester affect your knowledge of your audience?

4. What kinds of situational adjustments do you make in everyday conversation? How can you apply these strategies to a speech?

Activities

1. In 2015, Ben Carson, a retired neurosurgeon turned presidential candidate for the Republican nomination, appeared to take a page

out of front-runner Donald Trump's playbook. (Trump had made headlines with his controversial remarks about Mexicans who came into the United States illegally, as well his comments about fellow GOP candidate Carly Fiorina's physical appearance.) Carson said in an interview: "I would not advocate that we put a Muslim in charge of this nation." When his comments later drew criticism that he was showing insensitivity to many American voters in his audience who might also happen to be Muslim, Carson dismissed the claims, saying the media was twisting his words. Pretend that you were advising Carson—and he told you that he had intended his comments to refer only to extremists. How would you advise him to rephrase his original quotation in a way that did not appear to diminish or insult a religion?

2. Make a list of the demographic groups to which you belong. Some of these demographic groups will include age, gender composition, sexual orientation, race and ethnicity, religious orientation, socioeconomic background, and political affiliation. If a speaker were to address you based on only one of these demographic characteristics, how would you react?

3. Take a good look at the other people in your public speaking class: they will be your audience for many if not all of your in-class presentations. Using some of the tools for audience analysis in this chapter, assess the ways that members of your audience are alike (what characteristics do they share?) and the ways that they are different. What do you think they may have in common with you and you with them?

Study Plan

_____

_____

_____

_____

_____

_____

SELECTING YOUR TOPIC

6

"Use your topic to focus the message."

Early in the semester, Sara received the first major assignment for her public speaking class: "Prepare a speech on a topic of interest to you and your audience." Feeling panicked, Sara thought, "How on earth am I supposed to pick a topic?" While numerous possibilities floated through her mind, she wondered how she could make the best choice. The course had barely started, and already she felt overwhelmed.

But when Sara thought more about her situation, she realized that in a sense, she actually chose topics many times every day. When she wanted to start a conversation with a friend, a family member, or the student standing behind her in a long line at the bookstore, she needed to figure out what to talk about. In these situations, she tried to select subjects that interested both her and the other person. Usually these topics led to satisfying conversations.

With this in mind, Sara considered several topics for her speech. She knew what topics interested her, and most of them centered on emergency management—the process of preparing for and coping with disasters. The previous term, she'd interned for a state emergency management agency specializing in natural disasters. Her first idea was a speech about the community hazard-vulnerability analysis she had helped create, but this topic seemed technical and complex. Because Sara was planning on a career in emergency management, she considered speaking about potential jobs in this field (first responders, social service managers). But her classmates had diverse majors and career plans, and so they wouldn't necessarily be interested in this topic.

Sara changed gears and tried to think of related topics that would interest both her and her audience. Because her school was located in a region that recently sustained major flooding, she thought her classmates might wonder how they could best prepare for and deal with a future flood. Sara decided this topic would be perfect: she knew it well, and it would be relevant and helpful to her audience.

Sara's experience shows that even if you are initially unsure about what sort of topic to choose for your speech, you can find something interesting if you put your mind to it. In this chapter, we present a process for selecting and refining your topic—including developing a list of

possibilities, choosing the most promising one from the list, and narrowing that topic so that it meets your speech's objectives and can be covered in the allotted time.

DEVELOPING A SET OF POTENTIAL TOPICS

Possible speech topics are as varied as human experience. For example, your topic could be lighthearted or serious, address ancient history or current events, or relate to professional interests or a recreational activity—and that's just the beginning. Here are some topics we've seen students select over the past several years:

artificial lung research	Iditarod dogsled race
birthright trips	life on other planets
Cleopatra	my dog Max
college e-sports teams	neonatal technology
concussion prevention	Ozark trail
driving for Uber	Peruvian civilizations
good bacteria	social music platforms
Great Wall of China	volunteering in an election
helicopter parents	wardrobes of the future
Hmong weddings	zebras

Often, it is the speaker's responsibility to select a topic, although in some instances you may be assigned a topic by your instructor, by your employer, or by those who have invited you to speak. When you are called on to choose your own topic, there is a process you should follow to select the best topic for your speech. The first step is to develop a diverse set of possibilities using the following strategies—*research, brainstorming, word association,* and *mind mapping.* Each of these strategies encourages **divergent thinking**, meaning that your mind generates diverse and creative ideas.[1]

Research

Research is often an effective way to begin your topic selection process. General newsmagazines, newspapers, and Web sites are great sources for subjects because they include articles on current events, science, geography and culture, famous people, and the arts. These resources can provide ideas for topics that are new to most audience members or can offer new perspectives on topic areas that may already be familiar to the audience. This can help you avoid repeating a message that many of your classmates have already heard. For example, you might read about new research suggesting that sleep enhances your memory.[2] This focus would provide a new twist on the more general topic of sleep or the overdone topic of sleep cycles.

Many libraries keep recent print periodicals and newspapers in easily accessible locations, and you often can find their online versions on the Internet or through online library portals. You also can browse more broadly for topics online, but beware! As we note in Chapter 3, it is not ethical to plagiarize a speech. If these sites contain links to actual speeches, do not copy all or part of a speech (or use it after changing some of the words) and represent it as your own work.

The ideas you generate through research serve not only as potential speech topics themselves but also as starting points for other topic selection strategies, including *brainstorming, word association,* and *mind mapping.*

Brainstorming

When **brainstorming**, you list every idea that comes to mind without evaluating its merits. Your goal is to develop a sizable list of topics quickly; later, you will consider which one would be best. Do not censor any idea at this point in time: just let your thoughts flow.

To brainstorm, consider your interests and experiences, issues you care about, organizations you belong to, people you admire, events you find significant, places you have been, and lessons about life you have found important. Think about favorites in each of these categories. For example, what is your favorite use of spare time? The most interesting course you have ever taken? The best organization you've ever belonged to? By focusing on questions like these, you will soon build up a strong list of potential topics.

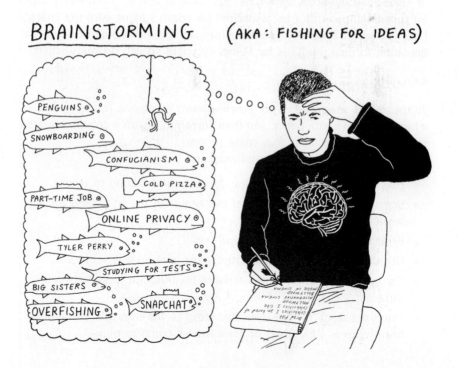

Word Association

Another strategy for generating ideas is **word association**. Start by listing one potential topic (as you do when brainstorming). Then write whatever comes to mind when you think about that first idea. The second idea may suggest yet a third one, and so on. Write each new thought next to the previous idea. Word association (as well as mind mapping, which we discuss next) enables your mind to function somewhat like a search engine. Your brain is your database, and when you write down a word or phrase, your mind "searches" for other terms that you associate with the original idea. If you use word association for every topic idea you generated while brainstorming, your set of options will grow even more.

If you have done research for topic ideas, a current news story may also suggest a variety of topics through word association. For example, a story about wildfires could result in the following topic sequence—firefighters, fire prevention, smoke detectors, lie detectors. With this technique, even a topic that would not be a good choice may lead you to an appropriate one. Consider what Mike, a public speaking student, experienced. His assignment was to deliver a speech on "a tip for college success." One of Mike's starting-point ideas was "my football coach," an unlikely topic for this assignment. But he associated his coach's name with the coach's favorite saying: "Success comes when preparation meets opportunity." That quotation formed the basis for Mike's excellent speech on study habits.

Mind Mapping

To use **mind mapping**, write down a word or phrase in the middle of a large piece of blank paper, and then surround it with words and images representing other ideas that come to you.

Here are some tips for mind mapping:[3]

- Use images (sketches, doodles, symbols) in addition to words.
- Start with a word or sketch at the center of the page, and then work outward.
- Print rather than write in script.
- Use colors to indicate associations and make ideas stand out.
- Use arrows or other visual devices to illustrate links between different ideas.
- Don't get stuck on one concept. Move to different places on your mind map as new ideas or associations come to mind.

WORD ASSOCIATION

THIS IS MIND MAPPING

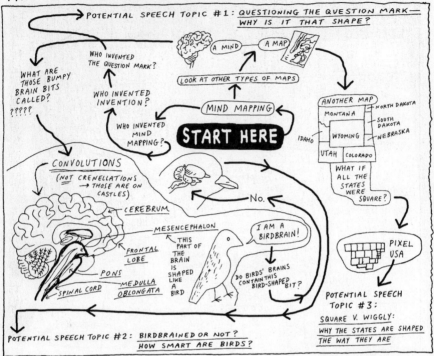

- Jot down ideas as they occur, wherever they fit on the paper.
- Be creative, and have fun with the experience.

The use of multiple colors, pictures, and symbols to create a mind map stimulates your thinking process.[4] You use both sides of your brain and generate more—and more creative—topic ideas.

SELECTING THE BEST TOPIC

You've generated a list of topics through one or more of the techniques described so far. Now you need to select the best one. To make your choice, *consider the assignment, your audience, your knowledge and interests*, and *the context of your speech*. And after you have selected a topic, stick with it. The following guidelines will help you pick the one best topic from the list of possibilities you've generated.

CONSIDER THE ASSIGNMENT

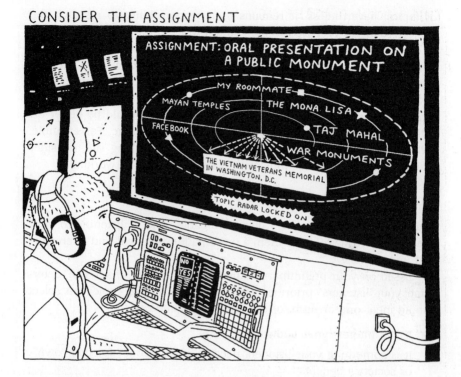

Consider the Assignment

As a student of public speaking, it's important that you select a topic that meets your instructor's criteria for the assignment. For example, in most classroom speeches, your instructor will require references to research. In such cases, you need to make sure that appropriate research sources are available for the topic you select. A humorous speech about your experiences as a food server, horror stories about your former roommates, or a demonstration of how you make your favorite fruit salad probably would fail to meet your instructor's criteria for the assignment.

In some cases, a specific topic might be assigned. For example, a history instructor may require an oral report on ancient China, or an agriculture professor may assign a debate on water policy. On the job, your manager may ask you to develop an online sales presentation on a new product. Alternatively, you may be asked to speak face-to-face to a small group of concerned citizens about a proposed new housing development on agricultural lands. In life, you do not always get a choice of topics; nevertheless, it remains your responsibility to research the subject well and prepare an interesting presentation for the audience.

Even if you have some latitude in choosing a topic, your instructor may have a list of topics that should be avoided. Certain topics crop up in public speaking classes every semester, such as capital punishment, abortion, the drinking age, steroids in sports, and marijuana. Rather than selecting an obvious and overused topic, you would be better off trying to *get ahead of the curve* when choosing a topic. For example, rather than talking about an existing social networking site, consider researching how new technology will change social networking.

Consider Your Audience

Your audience members will devote valuable time to listening to your speech. In return, you owe them a presentation they will find interesting and important.

Based on your preliminary audience analysis (see Chapter 5), determine your listeners' priorities and backgrounds. The topic you select should meet one or more of the following criteria:

- It will interest your audience.
- It is something your listeners need to know about—for their own or society's benefit.
- It will likely inspire, entertain, or emotionally move your audience.

Consider Your Knowledge and Interests

Among all the potential topics you've accumulated, which ones are you most interested in and knowledgeable about? When you choose a topic you're familiar with and passionate about, you'll give a more fluent and enthusiastic presentation. One of our students captivated his audience with a speech on Legos (even though his classmates had not played with toys for years) because his enthusiasm for the subject was so infectious. Conversely, a student who appeared totally uninterested in her topic of job interviews failed to connect with her listeners, even though the subject was highly relevant to them.

Your listeners are also more likely to believe your claims if they know you have experience with the subject area. One student discovered firsthand the perils of selecting a topic she knew little about. Although she had no children or child-care experience, she chose to talk about why day-care centers are better than in-home day-care providers. Because of her inexperience, she made some assumptions that didn't line up with the experiences of several parents in the class, and she based her cost figures on national averages, which differed markedly from local child-care costs. She also maintained (without providing proof) that in-home day-care providers typically have no background in child development. Because her claims were inconsistent with the experiences of class members who had children, she had to defer to these more knowledgeable classmates during the question-and-answer session. By the time she sat down, she had lost most of her credibility on this topic.

Finally, by selecting a topic you're familiar with, you streamline the research process. You can focus on researching information that supplements the facts you already know rather than gathering general background information.

> ⓞ To see an example of a student who has chosen a topic she is passionate about, try Video Activity 6.1, "Humanity 4 Haitian Development."

Consider the Speech Context

The **context** of your speech is the occasion, surrounding environment, and situation in which you will deliver your presentation. These factors often make one topic choice better than another.

For example, if you are asked to speak at an awards banquet for a campus organization to which you belong, the audience will expect an upbeat speech on a topic related to that organization. A speech on a more serious idea, such as the need for changes in higher education, would be better saved for a less celebratory occasion.

Situational characteristics—such as the physical setting of your speech, the time of day, and audience size and mobility—also should influence your topic choice. For instance, suppose you need to play an audio snippet to effectively present a certain topic you care about. You would not choose that topic if you will be giving your speech in a large, noisy location, where listeners would have difficulty hearing the clip. You should also keep this in mind if you are in an online class and your speech is going to be recorded for later viewing by your classmates. As we discuss in Chapter 15, there are special consider-ations to take into account when your audience will not be physically present.

Outside of the classroom, speakers also must consider the context when selecting a speech topic. Consider the challenge faced by fashion designer and research fellow Suzanne Lee when she was asked to give "the talk of her life" at a TED (Technology, Entertainment, Design) con-ference. She selected a cutting-edge topic—Grow Your Own Clothes—but because she knew that few of the creative thinkers in her audience would be fashion or biology experts, she tailored her speech for a general audience. Rather than discussing the technical aspects of fab-ric farming from bacteria and microbes, she gave a basic step-by-step overview. She also supplemented her speech with compelling photos, animation, and videos. Her audience left with a new understanding of and appreciation for a topic that—until the speech—they hadn't known existed.

Choose a Topic and Stick with It

After you've selected an appropriate topic from your list of possibilities, stick with it. In our experience, students who agonize over their topic selection for days or waver back and forth between several possibilities lose valuable speech preparation time.

An analysis of more than one thousand speech diaries kept by public speaking students revealed one consistent difference between strong speeches and weaker ones—the topic selection process. The more suc-cessful speakers carefully considered their topic choice but chose a topic promptly and then stayed with it, investing the bulk of their time in preparation. The less successful speakers spent days trying to settle on an acceptable topic.[5]

REFINING YOUR TOPIC

After you have selected a topic, you must refine it by first *deciding on your rhetorical purpose,* or how you want your speech to affect your audience. Then you can *narrow your topic* to achieve that effect.

Decide Your Rhetorical Purpose

Your intended effect on the audience constitutes your **rhetorical purpose**. In a public speaking class, your purpose often will be assigned for each speech. Outside the classroom, your purpose may be assigned (for example, by your employer) or dictated by the context of a special occasion (such as a wedding, memorial service, or roast). For other speeches, the choice of purpose will be left to you. The scenario that follows shows how one public speaking student went about deciding her rhetorical purpose.

Amber's instructor allowed his students to select their own topic and purpose for their first speech. Amber chose her major, theater arts, as her topic. She then considered a variety of purposes:

- *Informing.* When your purpose is **informative**, the message is educational, and your objective is to increase the audience's understanding or awareness of your subject. For example, Amber could tell her audience about the courses taken by theater arts majors.

INFORMATIVE

PERSUASIVE

MARK A SPECIAL OCCASION

- *Persuading.* When your purpose is **persuasive**, you seek to convince audience members to consider or adopt a new position, strengthen an existing belief, or take a particular action. For instance, Amber might try to persuade her audience to attend a play put on by the theater arts department.

- *Marking a special occasion.* When your purpose is **marking a special occasion**, you seek to honor that occasion by entertaining, inspiring, or emotionally moving your audience. For example, Amber could amuse her audience by roasting her favorite director or move listeners by presenting a tribute to a favorite drama professor who would be retiring soon.

Each of these options could result in a speech that relates to theater arts on campus in some way. However, the rhetorical purpose of each would be different—to inform, to persuade, or to mark a special occasion. Therefore, each would have a different effect on Amber's audience.

Narrow Your Topic

After you've determined your rhetorical purpose, think about which aspects of your topic you want to cover in your speech: in other words, how will you narrow your topic so that you fulfill your rhetorical purpose? You can't cover all aspects of the topic in a single speech, so you need to decide which aspects to focus on.

Narrowing your topic is vital for several reasons. First, it allows you to fit your speech into the available time. Whether you are speaking in a classroom or in your community, it is inconsiderate to take more than the time allocated for your presentation. Audiences may stop listening if you exceed the time limit. Also, resist any urge to speak fast or to cover each idea sketchily in order to say everything you had planned. Audiences don't respond well to those tactics.

Second, narrowing your topic helps you focus your speech. This is an especially important step for new speakers, who often select overly broad topics. When giving a speech on a specific sport, such as cricket, a novice speaker might try to cover the equipment required, the rules, the techniques for playing well, and maybe even the sport's history—way too much for the speaker to cover adequately or for listeners to remember.

BROAD TOPIC:

NARROWER TOPIC:

NARROWED TOPIC:

Conversely, one of the best sports speeches we ever heard succeeded because the speaker effectively narrowed the topic of tennis. She focused her informative speech on four interesting professional tennis personalities. The points she covered—such as the classic 1973 "Battle of the Sexes" match between Billie Jean King and Bobby Riggs—truly captivated her audience. Even listeners who were not tennis fans or had not yet been born when that match took place enjoyed and remembered the speech.

How should you narrow your topic? Many of the techniques you used to select your topic also can help you narrow it.

Remember Your Audience. Ask yourself whether the aspects of your topic will be interesting or important to your listeners. Kendra, a student who wanted to deliver a speech about figure skating, surveyed her classmates and found that few were interested in learning how to skate. However, most of the class planned to watch the Winter Olympics on television. Kendra narrowed her topic with the Olympics viewers in mind, choosing to explain in her speech how listeners could score the skating events while watching at home.

Draw on Your Interests and Expertise. Your special expertise or unique perspective on an aspect of your subject area can help you narrow the topic. Consider Cesar, a student who attended elementary and secondary schools in both Mexico and the United States. He selected high-stakes testing (tests for which failure has serious consequences, such as the inability to graduate or be promoted) as his speech topic and narrowed that topic based on his own educational experiences. He compared tests that students in the United States take with those that students in Mexico must take. His listeners were interested to learn that some of the same controversies surrounding testing in the United States have also emerged in Mexico.

SPEAKING ABOUT YOUR INTERESTS AND EXPERTISE

Review Your Rhetorical Purpose. Try to narrow your topic to an aspect appropriate for your rhetorical purpose. For example, suppose you wanted to give a speech about sleep. A focus on sleep disorders and sleep science could make an appropriate informative topic. A speech extolling the benefits of getting eight hours of sleep a night could be an emphasis for a persuasive speech. And a speech honoring the director of your university's sleep research center would make a great special-occasion speech.

Evaluate the Situation. You also can use situational characteristics to help narrow your topic. For example, one student, Michelle, was interested in entomology (the study of insects), so she chose bugs as her topic. Initially, she considered narrowing her topic to the use of insects to determine time of death of murder victims. But she rejected that idea when she remembered that she would be delivering her speech shortly after lunch—when listeners might be especially squeamish. Instead, she (wisely) narrowed her topic to interesting facts about bees, including how they make honey—a perfect after-lunch focus.

If your speech is going to be presented in a mediated context, the technology that you use can influence the direction of your speech. Consider an agricultural researcher who was used to relying on audience interactions when speaking in her local area about strategies for reducing

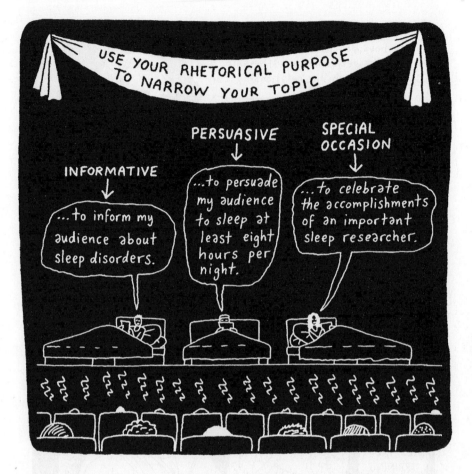

pesticide use. Her employer asked her to record her presentation so it could be viewed at remote locations, which would make interactions impossible and therefore required a change in her approach. In the weeks before she recorded the speech, she emailed company customers in those locations and asked them what agricultural pests are most problematic in their region so she could revise her message to focus on their concerns.

> ▶ To see a student giving a speech about a topic that should be narrowed, try Video Activity 6.2, "Overused Topic (Needs Improvement)."

DRAFTING YOUR SPECIFIC PURPOSE

After you've identified your rhetorical purpose and narrowed your topic, your next step is to determine your **specific purpose**—the objective of your speech—and express it in a concise phrase.

To write your specific purpose, start with a phrase expressing your rhetorical purpose ("to inform," "to persuade," or "to mark a special

CORRAL YOUR IDEAS TO FIT THE SPECIFIC PURPOSE

occasion"), and then add language indicating what you want to accomplish in your speech. Some good examples follow:

- "To inform my audience about the events at a Portuguese festa"
- "To persuade my audience to drink milk produced by our state's dairy farms"
- "To honor the leaders who organized our summer mission trip to Cuba"

You can use your specific purpose to guide which ideas you should develop in your speech. When selecting ideas, choose those that help you accomplish your specific purpose, and exclude those that are not relevant. Thus, like the sideline on a football field, your specific purpose indicates which ideas are "out of bounds" given your speech's objective.

DRAFTING YOUR THESIS STATEMENT

After you have determined your specific purpose, create your **thesis statement**—a single sentence that captures the overall message you want to convey in your speech. This statement conveys the "bottom line" of your speech—the ultimate message that all the points in your speech

YOUR THESIS STATEMENT MUST BE ONE SENTENCE

{WRONG}

The dog ate my homework, then my special fella broke up with me, then my grandmother died and I had to go to the funeral. After that my computer crashed and my car broke down on the way here and then the doctor called and said I had iron-poor blood. For all these reasons, I should not be penalized for turning in this assignment late.

{CORRECT}

Due to unforeseen and serious circumstances, I should not be penalized for turning in this assignment late.

support. As long as your audience members can remember your thesis statement, they should be able to recall the essence of your speech.

In this book, we use the term *thesis* to mean the main position of any type of speech. Some speech instructors may prefer using the term *thesis statement* when a speaker is advocating a position in a persuasive speech and the term *topic statement* when a speaker intends to inform or mark a special occasion. Your instructor will let you know if he or she prefers this alternative usage.

Here are some examples of thesis statements:

- "Advances in robotics will change the job market in the next twenty years."
- "There are many opportunities for service in nonprofit organizations in our community."
- "A weeklong meatless diet can show you the path to a healthier lifestyle."

SPEECH CHOICES

A CASE STUDY: *MIA*

Let's check back in with Mia to see how she's handling topic selection.

Shortly after receiving the assignment, Mia went to the library to begin selecting a topic for her informative speech. She looked at recent newspapers and magazines, and a couple of topics caught her attention, including refugees who were relocating to her community and advances in three-dimensional (3-D) printing. Mia used word association and came up with more topics that came to mind when she considered her favorite sport (soccer), her career interest (sports medicine), and her favorite activities (doing family history research and volunteering with an animal rescue organization).

After generating a list of more than twenty topics, Mia needed to select the best one. The three choices that stood out to her the most were refugees, researching family history, and sending an expedition to Mars. She decided to save the Mars topic for a persuasive speech and did more research on the remaining two topics. She was surprised to find that many families had traveled hundreds of miles from the Middle East to European nations on foot and in small boats. This fascinated her because it was not unlike her own ancestors' migration across Europe years ago. But would this interest her audience?

After she found an article about how twenty-first-century refugees use smartphones during their migration, Mia had an "aha" moment. Her classmates loved technology and many were addicted to their smartphones. The creativity of emigrants with their phones and the way they used various apps would definitely pull in her audience. And this would narrow her topic to fit the available time. So Mia formulated a thesis: "Smartphones are central to the success of emigrants' journeys." Her next steps would be more detailed audience analysis and research, but that night, she and her best friend went out for ice cream.

YOUR TURN:
Which of Mia's strategies would you use to select a speech topic?

For more questions and activities for this case study, please go to LaunchPad at macmillanhighered.com/speakup4e.

SPEECH CHOICES

A CASE STUDY: *JACOB*

Let's see what's happening with Jacob as he decides what his topic should be.

Two weeks after Jacob's instructor assigned the persuasive speech, Jacob still had not started the assignment. Before the next class, his instructor asked students if they had selected a topic for their persuasive speech. Several students had ideas, and she helped them formulate a topic that would work well as a persuasive speech. Jacob didn't have any ideas yet, but he did make a note to himself to find a topic.

That evening, Jacob and his roommates watched a football game while they ate dinner. He asked them if they had any ideas for a speech topic. One roommate said, "Last year, I did a speech on whether student athletes should be paid. That's a cool topic." Jacob thought about it for a minute. If he and his roommates were interested in college football, surely his class would like it, too. Would this topic be easy to research? He googled "should student athletes be paid pros and cons." Yes! There were over 94,000 results. One was an article in *The Onion*, one of Jacob's favorite Web sites. It must be a sign. "You've got this," thought Jacob.

YOUR TURN:
Based on Jacob's experiences, what are some pitfalls you should avoid when picking your topic?

For more questions and activities for this case study, please go to LaunchPad at macmillanhighered.com/speakup4e.

- "Today we honor the Missouri Veterinary Medical Teaching Hospital's greyhound blood-donor program."

Here are some guidelines for ensuring that your thesis statement conveys your purpose and topic to the audience efficiently and accurately:

- *Keep it to one sentence.* Make sure that your thesis consists of a single sentence that states the bottom line of your speech.

- *Express your intentions.* Ensure that your thesis clearly conveys what you hope your audience will know, do, or feel after listening to your speech. Listeners can better follow your message if they know what to expect.

- *Be consistent with your specific purpose.* Because your specific purpose guides how you research and prepare your speech, make sure your thesis communicates the same idea as your specific purpose. That way, you'll avoid the all-too-common problem of presenting a thesis in your speech introduction that differs from the content of the body of your speech.

> ⊙ **To compare two thesis statements on the same topic, try Video Activity 6.3, "Thesis Statement" and "Thesis Statement: Needs Focus (Needs Improvement)."**

CHAPTER REVIEW

Use your topic to focus the message.

As Sara's story revealed, selecting a topic for your speech can seem overwhelming at first. But the systematic approach described in this chapter can help you move past any feelings of frustration or confusion. First, develop a set of potential topics based on the results of research, brainstorming, word association, and mind mapping. Select the best topic based on an understanding of the assignment, your audience, your knowledge and interests, and the context of your speech. Then refine your topic by determining your rhetorical purpose and narrowing your topic to the most relevant aspects, given the time available for your speech. To draft your specific purpose, express your rhetorical purpose, and decide what you'd like to accomplish in your speech. Finally, hone in on your specific purpose by creating your thesis statement—a single sentence that captures your overall message and what you'd like your speech to convey.

 LaunchPad
macmillan learning

LaunchPad for *Speak Up* offers videos and encourages self-assessment through adaptive quizzing. Go to **macmillanhighered.com/speakup4e** to get access to:

✔ **LearningCurve**
Adaptive Quizzes

⊙ **Video clips that help you understand public speaking concepts**

Key Terms

Review Questions

1. Name and describe four techniques for generating speech topics.
2. Name four basic considerations speakers should keep in mind when choosing a topic.
3. Explain how you can narrow a speech topic by considering your rhetorical purpose.
4. Define the specific purpose of a speech.
5. Define the thesis of a speech.
6. Name and explain three guidelines for drafting a thesis statement.

Critical Thinking Questions

1. How do the topics you generate from an initial word in mind mapping or word association differ from the results you would get if you put that same term into a search engine? What are the benefits of writing possible topics on paper and drawing on your own thoughts, ideas, and knowledge? What are the benefits of accessing the nearly endless topics available on the Internet?
2. Why is it ethical to search for speech topics on the Internet but unethical to use as your own all or part of a speech that you found on the Internet?
3. What role should audience analysis, discussed in Chapter 5, play in selecting a topic for a speech?
4. Based on what you know about students in your class, what would be a good specific purpose for an informative speech? For a persuasive speech?

5. How would your topic selection differ if you were delivering a speech to a club or team to which you belong rather than to students in a public speaking class?

Activities

1. Working in small groups, brainstorm a list of potential speech topics. Then decide which topics would be most interesting to the group and which would be less interesting. Have group members explain why they decided that certain topics would be more interesting than others.

2. Divide into small groups. Have each group use one topic generation process (brainstorming, word association, or mind mapping) to create a list of potential topics. Have each group share with the class the topics they listed. Discuss how different processes can result in different topic ideas.

3. Discuss potential topics with other students in your public speaking class. Which topics are already familiar to students? Which topics are likely to be familiar to your instructor? For the topics that are familiar, discuss ways they could be narrowed to present new and original perspectives to the audience.

4. Read through the op-ed page in a national newspaper or the commentary in a newsmagazine. How successful are the topics in catching your interest? How do you think columnists come up with their topics? Are they always about current events?

5. ⊙ Video Activity 6.4: "Gentz, My Hero, Marilyn Hamilton." Watch Lillian Gentz's speech. What do you believe her rhetorical purpose is? How did she narrow her topic? If you were going to deliver a speech about a hero in your life, what main points would you emphasize? Why?

Study Plan

_____

_____

_____

RESEARCHING YOUR SPEECH

7

"It is not a fact until you prove it to the audience." One afternoon, Katie, Mandeep, and Sherri were strolling by their local courthouse after lunch when they noticed a police officer shooting at crows sitting on top of the building. They were appalled and soon called the police department to complain. The police chief explained that this practice was warranted because the crows were a public nuisance: they were noisy and annoying, they left droppings that posed a health risk, and they made it impossible to keep the courthouse steps clean. The crows had to go, the chief said, and other solutions (such as catching and releasing) were just too expensive.

Unconvinced by this explanation, the three students decided to take action. They gathered dozens of signatures on petitions and presented them to city officials, who invited them to speak about the subject at a city council meeting. The police chief also would attend to present her side of the issue.

The students knew that this was their one chance to prove their case and that they had to be prepared to respond to the police chief's claims. To that end, they decided to find out whether the crows indeed constituted a health hazard, whether other towns had found alternatives to shooting them, and how effective and costly these alternatives were.

In other words, these students set out to *research* their presentation so that they could convince the city council to end the practice of shooting crows. When you research well, your speeches can have the same effect. In Chapter 7, we begin with a discussion of why research is a vital step in speech preparation, and then we cover how you can set up a research plan. Next, we consider how to evaluate the credibility of your research sources, followed by an explanation of how to best conduct research using library sources, online materials, and interviews. Finally, we discuss how to present the information you have researched in your speech.

RESEARCH IS ESSENTIAL

Why should you learn how to research well and then use those skills to prepare your speech? The advantages are many. Research skills help you develop a quality speech, convince your audience, impress your instructor, and be effective in the workplace after you graduate.

One main benefit is that you gain a broader understanding of your topic. This knowledge will give you more choices when you decide which main ideas to include in your speech and how you can best develop them. Not only will you gain deeper knowledge, but you also may discover new insights or determine that some of your existing beliefs on the topic are incorrect.

A second benefit is gaining audience agreement. Research enables you to gather **evidence**—information from credible sources that you can use to support your claims. If audience members are uncertain about a point you are making (or if they outright disagree with you), evidence may convince them to accept that point.[1] If they accept that the source of your evidence is trustworthy and better informed than they are, they will be more likely to agree with your claim, even if they would not accept your opinion alone.

Evidence also strengthens your own credibility with the audience. When you present evidence in your speech, it shows that you have prepared and learned about the topic. This makes audience members more likely to believe what you say.[2]

A third benefit is demonstrating college-level skills to your instructor. He or she will appreciate a speech that is backed by **academic research**. This means that the claims you make in your presentation are supported

by experts who have education and experience in your topic area and whose work has been reviewed by other authorities in the field. Finding such sources requires more advanced research skills than might have been required earlier in your educational career. It will not suffice to go with the first three or four sources that you happen to come across. In academic speaking and writing, you are sharing *knowledge* with your audience. This means that you must research enough credible sources to be confident that the facts you present are accurate.

> ▶ **To see an example of someone providing evidence in her speech, try Video Activity 7.1, "Roth, Emergency in the Emergency Room."**

CREDIBLE EVIDENCE CONVINCES AUDIENCES

A fourth benefit is that research skills are increasingly important in the workplace. In business, more and more decisions are made based on "data-based analytics" rather than on "gut instinct."[3] Research shows that data-driven decisions improve productivity.[4] Thus, they are increasingly being used to resolve questions in such diverse fields as education, medicine, agriculture, and the military. In your career, if you are able to support the claims you make with evidence, you will be more convincing and contribute to your organization's success.

RESEARCH WORKS BEST WHEN YOU HAVE A PLAN

Skilled researchers develop a strategy for finding and keeping track of the information they need. Gaining experience, they improve on that strategy throughout their lifetime, particularly as new technologies change the nature of research. The following steps will help you formulate a **research plan**—a strategy for finding and keeping track of information to use in your speech. It's important to put this plan into action quickly, as almost three-fourths of college students report that procrastination harms their research efforts.[5]

Inventory Your Research Needs

Begin by determining your **research objectives**—the goals you need to accomplish with your research. Your knowledge of the topic will influence your goals. If you don't know a lot about the subject, begin with general research to learn more about the basics. On the other hand, if you know your topic well (for example, you already have a good idea of your thesis and even some of your main points), you might want to use research to learn more about specific aspects of your topic. When determining which aspects of your topic to research further, consider your rhetorical purpose and your instructor's research requirements. Finally, before moving ahead with your research, make a list of the subject matter you need to research and the questions you need to answer. This will help you stay focused on your research objectives.

Find the Sources You Need

After you have determined your research objectives, consider where you can find the information you need. The library is a great resource when you research your speech. If you have access to people with expertise on your topic, you also may want to set up an interview or two. Although the Internet can be a useful source of information, there are risks in using online sources. Therefore, it's always advisable to use Internet research as a supplemental resource rather than the focus of your efforts.

We strongly recommend that you discuss your topic with a **research librarian**. These librarians are career professionals who are hired to assist students and faculty with their research. They are experts at tracking down hard-to-find information and thus can be amazingly helpful

RESEARCH WORKS BEST WHEN YOU HAVE A PLAN

and knowledgeable about the resources available on your topic. Studies suggest that students may think that librarians are not there to help students or that their main job is to direct people to the correct location.[6] Nothing could be farther from the truth! Their job is to help you find the best resources, and you can count on them to assist you in discovering the most useful and credible sources.

You also will need to consider what types of sources best meet your research needs. In this section, we discuss the benefits of different library resources, including books, journal articles, newspapers, government documents, and reference works. You also may want to research high-quality Internet sources or conduct interviews if experts on your topic are available.

Use library indexes (often available on the library's Web site) to develop a list of sources to research. Library indexes usually are organized by **keyword**—a word or term related to your topic, including a synonym of the word. If you do not find what you are looking for under the keywords you have chosen, be persistent. Try using broader, narrower, or related terms until you find useful sources.

TYPES OF KEYWORDS FOR SEARCHES

SUBJECT: "IDENTITY THEFT"

BROAD TERM:	NARROW TERM:	SYNONYM:
"fraud"	"Dumpster diving"	"identity fraud"

Keep Track of Your Sources

One of the most important (and unappreciated) steps in the speech preparation process is maintaining complete and accurate records of your research sources. When you prepare your speech outline, your instructor will expect you to properly cite the sources of all the research you will use in your presentation. If you have lost track of the sources of your evidence or have incomplete citations, it will be very difficult to go back and find this information later. Furthermore, if you cannot cite the source of a piece of information, you cannot use that material in your speech.

Therefore, it is essential that you find and keep full citations for all research sources you may use in your speech. The **citation** contains information about the source author and the location of your evidence:

MAINTAIN ACCURATE RECORDS OF YOUR SOURCES

it's the academic equivalent of a map to your source. When a source is cited properly, it should be easy for another person to find the original source, whether it is in the library or online. Your instructor will have a citation format that you need to follow; be sure you know what information is required so you can make note of it immediately. Typically, the following information is needed:

- Name of the author and her or his credentials
- Title of the article or book chapter if the work appears in a newspaper, a periodical, an anthology, or online
- Source (name of the book, magazine, or newspaper)
- Date of the publication
- Volume number (for periodicals)
- Publisher and city of publication (for books)
- Page number where the evidence appears
- URL for Internet sources

Many computer-based library indexes now allow you to **export** the citations for your research sources by cutting and pasting the citation into a Word file. This is a very efficient way to keep track of source citations. If you are not sure how to do this, check with a research librarian.

You also need a reliable system for matching each citation to the evidence you obtain. However you choose to keep a copy of your evidence (note cards, downloads, photocopies), be sure that you also immediately record the evidence's citation information. One of the most common mistakes our students make is to assume that the URL that appears on the page when Internet evidence is printed out is sufficient for a citation. Please note: it is *not* sufficient! In this case, you also need to find and record the name of the author of the information, his or her credentials, and the date of the information.

EVALUATING A SOURCE'S CREDIBILITY

No matter where you gather evidence for your speech (library, Internet, or interviews), you must ensure that each is a **credible source**—one that can be reasonably trusted to be accurate and objective. When you use the most credible sources possible, you can be confident that the facts you present are valid, and your audience will be more likely to accept your claims.[7]

To evaluate the credibility of a given source, examine four distinguishing characteristics—*expertise*, *objectivity*, *observational capacity*, and *recency*.

Expertise

Expertise is the possession of knowledge necessary to offer reliable facts or opinions about the topic in question. An expert source has education, experience, and a solid reputation in her or his field. For example, a nutrition professor would likely have expertise on the topic of whether eating red meat is healthy, and a seasoned backpacker would have expertise on how to prepare for a long hiking trip. Likewise, you can look for expertise in printed or online sources by

WHO WOULD YOU GO TO FOR MEDICAL ADVICE?

Don't worry, it's definitely NOT skin cancer.

Don't worry, it's definitely NOT skin cancer.

evaluating whether the authors or sponsoring organizations are established and well-informed in the areas about which they are writing.

Objectivity

Sources who demonstrate **objectivity** have no bias—prejudice or partisanship—that would prevent them from making an impartial judgment on your speech's topic. People can be biased for several reasons. Some have economic self-interest, or the desire to make money, so they may slant facts or explanations to make certain alternatives seem more attractive. Others may need to please superiors—for example, a government worker who defends poorly conceived government policies. Still others have what's called ego investment: they're so wrapped up in a pet theory or cause that they lose their ability to evaluate it with an open mind.

Needless to say, you should avoid evidence from biased sources. If you use it, audience members will be unlikely to accept the point you are trying to prove.[8] Furthermore, you can't be confident that you have met your ethical duty to present truthful facts to the audience.

OBSERVATIONAL CAPACITY: MORE AND LESS

Observational Capacity

People who have **observational capacity** are able to witness a situation for themselves. For example, a person who was in Nepal to analyze the effects of the 2015 earthquake or was in Syria and witnessed the civil war would have more credibility than those who watched these events unfold on television. Sources with training and experience also make more credible observers. Thus, a person with expertise in child development would learn more by watching children respond to a violent video game than would a member of the general public.

Recency

Credible sources are also characterized by **recency**, or timeliness. Generally, because many aspects of life change constantly, newer evidence is more reliable than older evidence. For instance, when the Ebola virus epidemic first broke out in West Africa, September 2014 estimates indicated that there could be over a million cases by January 2015.[9] Fortunately, a number of successful practices were instituted to limit the spread of the virus, and the actual number of cases by March 2015 was closer to 35,000.[10] In general, if you have a choice between pieces of evidence from two equally credible sources and one is more current, you should select the more recent evidence.

Of course, some evidence is classic and endures to this day. For example, although the teachings of Confucius are ancient, they command more respect today than the precepts of many contemporary philosophers. And the ideas of Machiavelli are still pertinent to the subject of international relations, even though they are almost five hundred years old. To decide whether evidence is outdated, ask yourself, "Has the claim made by my source become doubtful or false because of changing circumstances since the claim was made?"

> ⊙ To view someone citing sources and to assess the sources' credibility, try Video Activity 7.2, "Citing Sources (Statistics and Testimony)."

With these criteria for source credibility in mind, let's now look closely at three major strategies for researching your speech—*using a library*, *searching the Internet*, and *interviewing experts in your topic*.

CONDUCTING LIBRARY RESEARCH

Libraries remain one of the best resources for researching your speech. Despite the Internet's increasing popularity as a research tool, the library still offers convenient access to the broadest range of *credible* sources. In addition, libraries allow you access to strong evidence and credible sources that are not available on Web sites. And last but not least, no search engine has been able to match the experience and expertise of professional librarians in guiding you to the best material on your topic.

Libraries house a wealth of information sources, including books, periodicals, newspapers, reference works, and government documents, along with powerful digital resources and databases that you might not be able to access otherwise. For students who are new to college, the sheer size of the library can be challenging. In one study, college freshmen encountered libraries with collections averaging nine times the size of their high school library. There were differences in the arrangement of materials and the resources for finding articles.[11] But as you gain experience and take advantage of the skills of the library staff, you can become a skilled library researcher.

Books

Books are one of the best systems that humans have ever developed for storing and conveying information. They have important advantages as information sources and often are the best place to start your research. Because books have been the primary tools for sharing and storing ideas throughout human history (for example, a surviving part of the Egyptian *Book of the Dead*, written on papyrus, dates from the sixteenth century BCE), many of today's books contain thousands of years of accumulated human knowledge. In addition, many books are written by people with extensive expertise in their subject—although, of course, you should always check each author's credentials using the four criteria described earlier.

Books are longer than most other information resources and thus are likely to provide more in-depth information on your topic. Books typically offer *synthetic* thinking on your topic because authors combine information from diverse sources along with their own ideas and critical judgments. Additionally, most books—especially scholarly books—are vetted before publication. Both the publisher and other experts in the field may review and edit content to ensure a book's credibility.

To find books related to your topic, start by searching your library's electronic catalog by subject. Such catalogs are usually available online, allowing remote access; you also can search online catalogs by author name and book title. After entering your search terms, you'll see a list of links specifying relevant book titles. By clicking on these links, you can find bibliographic information as well as details on where in the library the books are located and whether certain titles have been checked out or are available in the stacks.

Another way to check books out from the library is to use your digital e-reader. After you log into the library's site and check out the e-book remotely, it should appear in your e-reader's list and remain there for the checkout period. Checking out e-books combines the quality of book evidence with the ease of an online search.

Finally, here's a tip followed by some expert library users. After you find some books on your topic in a library's catalog, go into the library

stacks, and locate the books you have identified. But don't just pull the books you found and leave; instead, browse through some of the books *nearby*. Because libraries organize nonfiction books by topic—usually using the Library of Congress or Dewey Decimal system—the nearby books are likely to have similar coverage and touch on some different but related areas. These nearby books might point you to aspects of your topic you haven't yet considered.

Periodicals

A **periodical** is a publication that appears at regular intervals—for example, weekly, monthly, quarterly, or annually. These publications include scholarly journals and news and topical-interest magazines. Often, the most credible information on your speech topic will come from articles in scholarly journals, generally written by people with expertise on a subject. Articles in such journals are subjected to **peer review**—that is, an editor decides to publish only articles that are approved by other experts in the field and that meet the publication's other requirements. In contrast, newsmagazines are particularly helpful for speeches on current events.

The following strategies will help you locate appropriate periodicals.

Consult General Periodical Indexes. General periodical indexes list articles on a wide variety of topics. Traditionally, these resources were available in bound volumes. Now most college and public libraries have subscriptions to online indexes.

Online indexes are particularly helpful because they often include a **full-text source** for each entry—a link to the complete text of the article in question. When they do not provide the full text, indexes often supply an **abstract**, or a summary of the article's contents. The abstract can help you assess whether the article would be useful for your speech. These indexes also provide other helpful utilities, such as the proper citation formats for the articles you find. Representative examples of online indexes that can be used to research a wide variety of speech topics include the following:

- *Academic Search Complete.* Over 13,000 journals indexed, including over 8,800 full-text journals (7,700 peer reviewed). Also provides access to over 60,000 videos. Covers a wide variety of academic disciplines.

ONLINE INDEXES OFFER THE BEST OF BOTH WORLDS: THE QUALITY OF LIBRARY MATERIALS AND THE SPEED OF THE INTERNET.

- *JSTOR* (journal storage). Archive of over 2,000 scholarly journals in arts, humanities, social sciences, and science. Allows full-text searches and provides scanned articles. Now includes e-books.
- *LexisNexis Academic.* Full-text documents from over 15,000 sources, including print, broadcast, and online media. Emphasis on news, business, and legal topics.

Use Specialized Periodical Indexes. Specialized periodical indexes focus on specific subject areas and are increasingly available online. Library Web sites often list available indexes and provide you with a link. These resources are available for a wide range of topics, as can be seen by the following sample list: *AGRICOLA* (agriculture), *Art Full Text*, *Communication and Mass Media Complete*, *Criminal Justice Abstracts*, *Gender Watch*, *Historical Abstracts*, *MEDLINE* (medical journals), *PsycArticles*, and *Science Online*.

Ask Your Reference Librarian for Help. Although you may consider research a solitary activity, reference librarians can be a great asset. As we mentioned earlier, these trained professionals can help you track down a book or periodical or even order it for you through interlibrary loan if it's not immediately available. Don't be afraid to ask them for help.

Newspapers

Newspapers are another useful source, especially when you need very current information. Many college libraries have indexes for articles published in major national newspapers, such as the *Christian Science Monitor, New York Times, Wall Street Journal, and Washington Post.* University libraries often offer access to full-text articles from newspapers that restrict content to subscribers. Your library also may have indexes for your local newspaper and papers from large cities in your region. Most newspapers now have Web sites, and some are exclusively online (for example, the *Seattle Post Intelligencer* and the *Christian Science Monitor*'s daily newspaper). Many of these sites allow you to search for articles. This can be particularly helpful if you want to focus on news from a specific region—for example, coverage of the auto industry in Detroit newspapers. *Editorials on File* reprints editorials from newspapers across

NEWSPAPERS:
ACCESSIBLE IN MANY FORMS

the United States and Canada that offer diverse perspectives on current issues.

General newspaper indexes include *LexisNexis Academic*, the *National Newspaper Index (Gale Group)*, *NewsBank*, and *ProQuest Newsstand*. Many such indexes provide links to full-text articles. More specialized indexes, such as the *Alternative Press Index* and *Ethnic NewsWatch*, also cover a wide variety of newspapers.

Reference Works

A **reference work** is a compilation of background information on major topic areas. Reference works are helpful for doing exploratory research on your subject area or discovering a specific fact (such as the number of people with Internet access worldwide or the capital of Kazakhstan), as opposed to in-depth information. Reference works are increasingly available in both printed and online form in your library.

There are several major categories of reference works. Most include general works that cover a comprehensive range of topics as well as specialized works that focus on a single subject (for example, philosophy or art) in more detail. **Encyclopedias** offer relatively brief entries that provide background information on a wide range of alphabetized topics. **Dictionaries** offer definitions, pronunciation guides, and sometimes etymologies for words, and **quotation books** offer famous or notable quotations on a variety of subjects. **Atlases** provide maps, charts, and tables relating to different geographic regions. Finally, **yearbooks**—such as the *Statistical Abstract of the United States*—are updated annually and contain statistics and other facts about social, political, and economic topics.

Government Documents

If your topic relates to government activities, laws, or regulations, government documents can provide useful information for your speech. Document authors may be experts, but beware of documents motivated by political objectives. To find government documents, use the following resources:

- *Catalog of U.S. Government Publications* (catalog.gpo.gov/F) provides citations to federal publications, congressional hearings, and committee reports. It includes records for over 500,000 publications, a number of which can be accessed online. Congressional hearings can be particularly good research sources because they generally are held before major federal legislation is adopted, and experts on both sides of the issue are likely to testify.

- *FDsys—Federal Digital System* (www.gpo.gov/fdsys) contains links to congressional hearings and reports as well as the *Congressional Record*, which covers all debates in the U.S. House of Representatives and the U.S. Senate. Legislators often add news articles, reports, and other documentation to the *Record*. *FDsys* also includes links to U.S. Supreme Court opinions, oral arguments before the Court, and opinions of lower federal courts, as well as information issued by the executive branch of the federal government.

- *CQ Electronic Library* (available through many college libraries) features information from *Congressional Quarterly*, which provides nonpartisan reporting on Congress and politics. *CQ Weekly* provides information about bills pending in Congress and articles about major issues confronting the federal government, whereas *CQ Researcher Online* provides extended reports on major news issues.

USING THE INTERNET

The Internet has become the go-to research option for many college students. Although 95 percent of college students researching online use search engines, only 9 percent report using the library more than the Internet when searching for information.[12] These research habits can be hazardous to the typical student's academic progress; in fact, a study found that higher grades are associated with more frequent use of the library.[13]

Whereas libraries emphasize quality research sources, searching the Web can be a bit like sending an untrained dog out to retrieve the morning newspaper. He might come back with the paper, but he could just as easily end up digging up your flower bed or eating a neighbor's chicken. In other words, you can't always be certain that your search will generate the information you need. By understanding both the *benefits* and the *limitations* of Internet research, you can get the most from this tool.

Benefits of Internet Research

Internet research allows you convenient access to information on nearly any topic without leaving your desk. Even better, many libraries offer access to full-text periodical and newspaper indexes from remote locations. Such indexes are among the most useful available online, and we recommend that you focus on them when the convenience of researching from your own computer is important.

The Internet also offers speed—enabling you to track down a news report or a research finding almost instantly, from anywhere in the

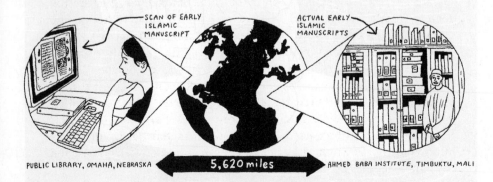

SCAN OF EARLY ISLAMIC MANUSCRIPT

ACTUAL EARLY ISLAMIC MANUSCRIPTS

PUBLIC LIBRARY, OMAHA, NEBRASKA   5,620 miles   AHMED BABA INSTITUTE, TIMBUKTU, MALI

world. Finally, this research tool puts an immense volume of information at your fingertips. A decade ago, University of California at Berkeley researchers estimated that the World Wide Web contained about 170 *trillion* bytes of information, which is seventeen times the size of the print collections in the Library of Congress.[14] In 2015, there were over 875 million Web sites in existence.[15] With careful searching online, you may be able to find quality information that simply does not exist in your own library.

Disadvantages of Internet Research

Despite the Web's vastness, most of the world's knowledge is still contained in printed works. Authorities in many fields publish their works primarily in books and scholarly journals. Many of these works are copyrighted, so they won't likely be available on Web sites that a typical online search engine will lead you to. And if they are available, you may need to pay a fee to access them.

Moreover, you can't assume that information you find online is credible, because most of it is not vetted in the same way that books and periodicals are. There are literally millions of Web sites created by individuals, advocacy groups, clubs, and businesses that may contain incorrect or biased information.[16] As anyone with a Tumblr, Facebook page, or Twitter feed knows, it's a snap for anyone to publish as much and as often as desired in the online world. Although expert review is essential in academic research, Internet information frequently is posted without any professional review.[17]

As a consequence, many of the Internet sources found by students do not have the quality that is expected by their instructors. Professor Wendy Lerner Lym of Austin Community College compares Internet research to fast food: sources can be quickly obtained, but they are not good for your academic health.[18] Research has confirmed the low quality of many sources found on the Web. For example, a team headed by Professor Chuanfu Chen of Wuhan University, China, recently evaluated 2,814 Web pages found through keyword searches on Google, Yahoo!, and AltaVista on such topics as genetically modified foods. The researchers concluded that 11 percent of the Web sites were very weak and 45 percent were weak. Only 11 percent were rated as excellent or good.[19] Research also has discovered inconsistencies in the quality of online information relating to healthy diets, health information for patients, and developmental disabilities.[20]

Some students have been taught to evaluate the quality of a Web site by assessing the **top-level domain** of its URL (Uniform Resource Locator)—the designation at the end of a Web address that indicates the site sponsor's affiliation. For instance, *.com* was assumed to designate a commercial business, *.org* an organization, and *.net* a network. However, this is not a sufficient guideline to judge credibility because Web sites have long been given the choice to register as .com, .org, or .net without restriction.[21] And as of 2013, organizations that can afford the $185,000 application fee may create their own top-level domain.[22] Any entity with a product or an idea to sell can strategically choose the term it will use. App developers can request a variety of labels, including .app, .cloud, and .unicorn.[23]

Furthermore, a Web site's name does not necessarily indicate its credibility. For example, a site such as TobaccoTruths.org may look like

DANGERS OF INTERNET RESEARCH

it was created by research scientists with impeccable credentials, but it could have actually been created by public relations specialists funded by the tobacco industry; similarly, a professional, polished design offers no guarantee of a site's credibility.

Evaluating the Credibility of Online Sources

Evaluating the credibility of Web sites can be particularly difficult. Many sites fail to identify authors or the dates of publication, and even sites that indicate authorship may provide no information on authors' credentials. And of course, many articles are posted online without expert reviewing or editing.

Thus, it's essential that you develop guidelines for evaluating the credibility of all sites you're considering using. For example, if a Web site provides the name but not the qualifications of an author, research that author further—either online or in periodical indexes such as *Academic Search Complete*—to see if he or she has published in scholarly journals. For online documents that don't indicate an author, try to

determine what organization sponsored the site, and then assess that organization's credibility through further research.

How can you learn about a sponsoring organization? Robert Berkman, a faculty member of the graduate media-studies program at the New School University, suggests reviewing the organization's stated purpose to gain insight into its objectivity or bias. Also research the credentials of any listed directors or board members of the organization. Consider whether they may have any political or economic interest that compromises their objectivity.[24]

The Virtual Chase, a Web site established to teach legal professionals about online research, offers the following additional guidelines for assessing the credibility of Internet information:[25]

- *How credible are the Web sites linked to and from the site?* If the linked sites are credible, the site in question is more likely to be credible.

- *Does another credible source provide information similar to that found on the site you're evaluating?* If so, that's a good sign of credibility.

- *Does the site weigh arguments for both sides of an issue?* If so, this suggests objectivity—a key criteria for credibility.

- *Is there advertising on the site?* If so, evaluate whether the site's creator(s) may have an economic incentive to offer content that pleases the advertiser.

- *Is the site's word choice professional?* A source is more likely to be suspect when it uses biased language (see Chapter 12) or denigrates those with opposing viewpoints.

If it is not apparent that a Web site meets the criteria for credibility as an evidence source (expertise, objectivity, observational capacity, and recency), do not use that site.

Credibility of Social Media

Increasingly, online information is found on **participatory (or social) media**, in which people both create and access information. However, the lack of review taking place before information is posted makes it difficult to assess the credibility of these sites.[26] Thus, you should proceed with caution before using this evidence in your speech.

Wikipedia, a site on which any user can modify the content, is the most popular example of this media. Some studies have suggested that this site is a credible source of factual information, with similar error rates to other reference works.[27] Nevertheless, you should be very careful about using *Wikipedia* as an evidence source. As a 2011 study found,

Wikipedia "suffers less from inaccuracies than omissions," reflecting "the limited expertise and interests of contributors."[28] Another study concluded that *Wikipedia* is not a neutral source of information; as a "socially produced" work, it "reflects the viewpoints, interests, and emphases of the people who use it."[29]

Ironically, a May 2013 *Wikipedia* entry on "Wikipedia: Academic Use" provides useful advice. The Wiki page questions the credibility of the site and cautions against its use as a source in academic work. While stating that *Wikipedia* and other reference works can be used to gain background information at the start of your research, it cautions that books, articles, and other sources will provide better research.[30]

Searching the World Wide Web

You've likely used **search engines**—specialized online programs that continually visit Web pages and index what is found there. When you enter a search term, the engine searches millions of Web pages to find the best matches for the term.[31] Results are sorted in an effort to make them more useful. Some engines organize the results by listing them according to specific criteria—such as how frequently your search term is used, how often a search term of more than one word occurs together, or whether a search term appears in the title or near the top of a page.[32] Other engines list sites based on how many other sites link to them. But beware: a search engine may prioritize sponsored sites. If so, carefully consider the sponsor's credibility. You also may want to try more than one search engine.

Which search engine is best for you? Try several, and compare their features and functionality. You also can check online for reviews of engines that highlight key features and provide updates as more features become available. In the United States, the most frequently used search engine is Google, followed by Bing and Yahoo![33]

How can you improve the quality of your search? Here are a few suggestions:

- *Use quotation marks around key phrases.* If you are researching a proposed tax on soft drinks, searching for "soda tax" will focus your results on the proposed tax rather than sites dealing with soda or taxes more generally.

- *Use precise search terms.* For example, if you want to search for the health effects of a soda tax, search for "soda tax" and "health effects." Use the same process to focus your search on economic effects or the constitutionality of such a tax.

- *Use **advanced search** features.* These features allow you to limit your search by date, language, country, or file format. You also can prioritize your search terms based on where they occur in the Web page. The safe-search feature avoids sites with pornographic or explicit content.

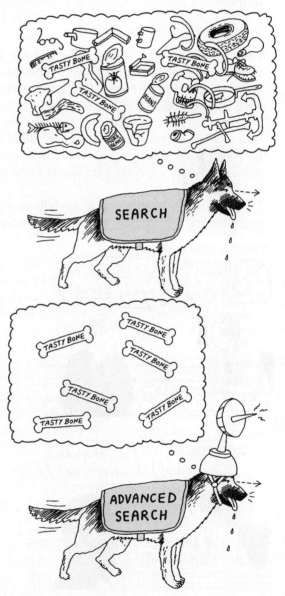

- *Use scholarly search features.* Search engines such as Google Scholar and Microsoft Academic Search limit their results to information from scholarly sources. Some search results include full-text articles, but don't be surprised if only the citation is available. Tip: If there is a fee to access an article, copy down the citation. Your college librarian can probably help you access the article for free.

INTERVIEWING SOURCES

You also can learn about your topic by interviewing people with expertise on your topic. Here are some tips for getting the most out of your interviews.

Prepare for Your Interview

First, determine what you want to find out through an interview. Are there any questions you are having difficulty answering through library and Internet research? Are there any individuals who, if interviewed, would add credibility to your speech?

Next, decide whom to interview. The person you talk with should be an expert on your subject. If your school has a department focused on your subject, ask the chair or another knowledgeable person to recommend faculty members who would make good interview subjects for your speech.

Off-campus sources—such as high-ranking members of political organizations, government agencies, businesses, nonprofit entities, and community groups or clubs—also can prove useful. Many of these individuals are "people persons" who will appreciate the opportunity to talk about their areas of expertise. If the person whom you would like to interview is too busy, he or she may give you a lead about another expert you might interview.

Students who have not researched their speech in advance sometimes rely on friends, family members, or neighbors for interviews because they can be found at the last minute. Although these sources may be able to provide lay testimony on some topics, they generally are not the type of credible research sources that instructors will expect. Check with your instructor in advance before using this type of interview to obtain evidence.

Set Up Your Interview

If possible, contact potential interview subjects in person. (It's far easier for busy people to say no to an interview request via e-mail or over the telephone than face-to-face.) Identify yourself, explain that you're preparing a speech, and describe what you hope to learn from the interview. You will need to be willing to accommodate the interviewee's schedule.

Plan Your Interview Questions

After you have set up your interview, decide what you want to ask the person you will interview. Prepare focused questions that he or she is in a unique position to answer, rather than general questions you could easily address through your own research.

In Chapter 5, we discussed fixed-response and open-ended questions. Frame each question based on the information you need. If you want the interviewee to elaborate or provide examples, use open-ended questions that require more than a yes or no response. For example, you might ask a journalist "How does the growth of online media affect your profession?" You also might plan to ask the interviewee a candid question that you think he or she would prefer to avoid. If you do, be sure to phrase the question professionally. Coming across as needlessly confrontational will put your interviewee on the defensive and may cause him or her to clam up.

Conduct the Interview

Arrive on time for your interview, and dress professionally unless the occasion warrants different attire (for example, an interview on a farm). When you arrive, greet your interviewee and introduce yourself if you have not already met.

Keep the following considerations in mind during the interview:

- *Explain the purpose of your interview.* Be sure the subject understands that you are gathering information for use in a classroom speech, and ask for permission to use his or her responses in your speech.

- *Start with friendly, easy-to-answer questions.* Straightforward questions allow you to establish rapport before you pose more difficult questions. If the interviewee has a limited amount of time, however, move on to your most important questions quickly.

- *Take notes.* Be sure to jot down the words and phrases your interviewee uses.

- *Stay focused.* If the interviewee digresses, politely steer the discussion back to the topic.

- *Maintain eye contact.* Although you occasionally may need to look down to read your questions or to take notes, keep the interview conversational and relaxed through frequent eye contact.

- *Be open to new information.* If new and valuable ideas come up, don't feel forced to stick to your planned questions. Feel free to deviate from them to explore the new information.

- *Listen carefully.* To ensure you're hearing your subject's actual answers, paraphrase key responses back to the person.

- *Record the interview if your subject gives permission.* Secretly recording an interview is a serious breach of ethics.

In addition to traditional face-to-face meetings, people are increasingly using new voice-over-Internet-protocol (VoIP) technologies, such as Skype and Google Hangout, for interviews. These can allow you to chat with experts in remote locations. Before conducting such an interview, review the tips in Chapter 15.

Evaluate Your Notes

Immediately after the interview, check your notes to see whether you wrote down all the responses you may want to use in your speech. If you did not get everything in your notes, write down the person's answers while the interview is still fresh in your mind. If you cannot remember an answer accurately, contact the interviewee to clarify his or her response rather than guessing. You need to be sure you are quoting or paraphrasing accurately in your speech. And no matter what, send a thank-you note to the person.

PRESENTING EVIDENCE IN YOUR SPEECHES

You have finished researching and selected credible evidence to use in your speech. Good work! You are well on the way to earning the benefits of a well-researched speech, but another essential job remains. You need to cite your research correctly in your speech and directly quote or paraphrase your source's ideas. Let's take a look at how this is done in a manner that makes it clear to the instructor and audience that you are presenting evidence accurately.

Clearly Cite Your Source

When you use information in your speech that you have gained from your research, you have an ethical obligation to *attribute* that information to the author. This means that you state the author's name, her or his qualifications, the source where you found the information, and the date (see an example from a speech on family farms on p. 219). The audience needs to understand that you are citing evidence. It is not enough that you have the citation on a works cited page of an outline that you submit to your instructor. Audience members need to understand that you are citing evidence at the time that you are presenting it orally in your speech.

Present the Information Accurately

After you cite your evidence, the next step is presenting the information. You have an ethical obligation to present the author's ideas accurately. This is accomplished either through direct quotation or paraphrasing.

When you use a **direct quotation**, you present his or her ideas word-for-word. Any time you use the author's exact words (even a short phrase), you put them in quotation marks in your notes and in any written outline or copy of your speech that you submit to your instructor. (See the illustration on p. 218.) If you leave out quotation marks when using information word-for-word, you are representing that the wording choice is your own and not the author's. This is unethical and is likely to be a violation of your college's policy on cheating and plagiarism.

When you cite your source with a direct quotation, use the claim-source-support order. Begin by stating the point you are making. Next, fully cite your source, presenting the author, his or her credentials, the

PARAPHRASING AND QUOTING SOURCES

ORIGINAL QUOTATION:

Look, no hands!

"This utopian notion of roads and future travel will be far from the truth, however, if driverless car manufacturers don't address some of the security fundamentals. The risk is that if security isn't tackled now, we will see hackers sending people to wrong locations, 'spam traffic jams,' valuable goods diverted for theft, and accidents due to deliberate collisions."

DIRECT QUOTATION (QUOTE AUTHOR WORD-FOR-WORD AND USE QUOTATION MARKS):

"The risk is that if security isn't tackled now, we will see hackers sending people to wrong locations..."

APPROVED

PARAPHRASE (REWRITE USING YOUR OWN WORDS):

Hackers will be able to direct cars to incorrect destinations unless there is a plan to protect computer systems in driverless cars.

APPROVED

PARAPHRASE PLUS QUOTATION MARKS WHEN USING AUTHOR'S PHRASE:

Hackers will be able to create "spam traffic jams" unless there is a plan for driverless car computer security.

APPROVED

PLAGIARISM (USING TOO MANY OF THE AUTHOR'S WORDS WITHOUT QUOTATION MARKS):

The danger is that if auto security isn't tackled soon, we will see hackers sending drivers to wrong locations.

DANGER

SPEECH CHOICES

A CASE STUDY: *MIA*

Let's find out how Mia went about researching her speech.

Mia started her research in the library. Before going, she brainstormed some search terms such as emigrants, refugees, and smartphones. After she reached the library, Mia discovered a challenge. Her topic was so current that few scholarly sources were available yet. She did find some recent articles in traditional print newspapers and news-magazines. Mia read them to get a feel for her topic, being sure to save each one along with a full citation.

Next, Mia turned her attention to online sources. A search on Google quickly led her to a number of online articles on her topic. The good news was that these articles were all recent—within the last six months. But she could not be sure of their credibility. So she checked the credentials of the authors. Fortunately, most had earned degrees at leading journalism schools, and many had published articles in well-known newspapers and magazines. Mia also re-searched the credibility of Web sites she wanted to use.

YOUR TURN:
For your next speech topic, what resources would best help you find credible sources?

After locating twelve articles from sources she found credible, Mia lettered them from A to L and made sure she had a full citation for each. Then she read each one carefully and took notes on cards in or-der to make it easy to cite the sources when outlining her speech.

For more questions and activities for this case study, please go to LaunchPad at macmillanhighered.com/speakup4e.

publication, and the date. Finally, quote or paraphrase the evidence. See the following example:

> Family farms are thriving. [*claim*] An example is provided by Chrystia Freeland, global editor-at-large for Reuters News Agency, in the July/August 2012 issue of the *Atlantic* [*source*]: "Urbanites may picture farmers as hip heritage-pig breeders returning to the land, or a struggling rural underclass waging a doomed battle to hang on to their patrimony as agribusiness moves in. But these stereotypes are misleading. In 2010, of all the farms in the United States with at least $1 million in revenues, 88% were family farms." [*evidence*]

SPEECH CHOICES

A CASE STUDY: JACOB

Now let's see how Jacob did research for his persuasive speech.

Jacob's opportunity to use the *Last Week Tonight with John Oliver* video was limited because he did not keep track of the sources in the show who had provided information he might have used. Therefore, he had to do some more research. A quick search on Google turned up an article entitled "Twenty-One Reasons Why Student Athletes Are Employees and Should Be Allowed to Unionize." This article looked like a winner because Jacob needed only about three main points. The author of the article said that he wrote about legal issues in sports, fantasy sports, and online gaming. Had Jacob done more research, he would have discovered that this author was a law professor, which would have added to his credibility.

Jacob was a big fan of the Kentucky Wildcats college basketball team, and he wanted to use Anthony Davis as an example of an athlete who could have stayed in college if athletes were paid, rather than leaving for the NBA after one season. He looked up Davis's rookie salary and his statistics. Because his plan was to pay athletes in profit-generating sports, not "non-revenue" sports, he looked up attendance figures for different sports teams at his college.

The day before he was scheduled to give his speech, Jacob decided he might need another source. Although his instructor said that students' research should come from scholarly sources, he decided to interview one of his roommates, who had played on the football team for his first year before injuring his knee. Who would know more about the topic than an actual student athlete? "Yeah, athletes should be paid," his roommate said. "Going to practice and playing games feels like a full-time job. We fill up the stadium, and they make millions of dollars. The scholarships are so low that you always run out of money before the end of the month."

YOUR TURN:

What are some of the risks you take when you rely on a roommate's opinion rather than a more credible evidence source?

For more questions and activities for this case study, and to see a ⊙ video clip from Jacob's speech on research and evidence, please go to LaunchPad at macmillanhighered.com/speakup4e.

When you **paraphrase**, you restate the author's information in your own words. To paraphrase ethically, you must be sure that the words are your own instead of the author's. A good technique for paraphrasing is to read the author's words and make sure you understand the idea. Then put the source aside, and write down the idea without looking at the author's words. *Do not* use your word processor to cut and paste the author's words and then change a few terms. In our experience, this practice often gets students in trouble for plagiarism because they end up using words that are mostly the author's. If you discover that you are using sentences or even phrases that the author used, then those words must be placed in quotation marks.

It is also essential to paraphrase accurately. The words you use must correctly represent the author's intent. It is unethical to present evidence using **power wording**—that is, to reword evidence in a way that better supports your claim but misrepresents the source's point of view.

Ⓒ **To watch someone giving a direct quotation in a speech, try Video Activity 7.3, "Citing Sources (Statistics)."**

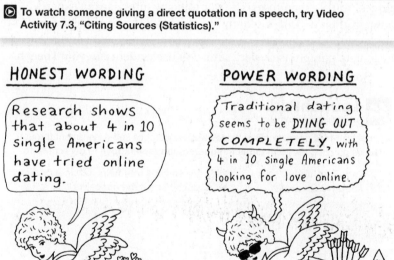

CHAPTER REVIEW

> **It is not a fact until you prove it to the audience.**

From the story about Katie, Mandeep, and Sherri's activism against police officers shooting crows on their local courthouse building, it's clear that providing evidence for the claims in your speech can help make your presentation more convincing and make you more credible as a speaker. To create your research plan, take the following steps: inventory your research needs, find the sources you need, and be sure to keep track of your sources. To evaluate a source's credibility, consider the author's expertise, objectivity, and observational capacity, as well as the source's recency. When conducting library research, vary your focus among books, periodicals, newspapers, reference works, and government documents. Although many students use the Internet for research, there are both advantages and disadvantages to this, and you need to carefully evaluate the credibility of online sources. You also can research your topic by interviewing experts. When you've gathered your research, be sure to present evidence in claim-source-support order, cite your sources completely, and use direct quotes or accurate paraphrases every time you use evidence in your speech.

 LaunchPad
macmillan learning

LaunchPad for *Speak Up* offers videos and encourages self-assessment through adaptive quizzing. Go to **macmillanhighered.com/speakup4e** to get access to:

✓ **LearningCurve Adaptive Quizzes**

▶ **Video clips that help you understand public speaking concepts**

Key Terms

 evidence *188*
academic research *188*
research plan *191*
research objectives *191*
research librarian *191*
keyword *192*
 citation *193*

export (citations) *194*
credible source *195*
expertise *195*
objectivity *196*
observational capacity *197*
recency *197*
periodical *200*

Review Questions

1. What are two key benefits of doing research for your speech?

2. Explain the three main steps involved in creating a research plan.

3. Why is it important to copy down complete citation information for a source at the time you obtain it?

4. What four key characteristics determine a source's credibility?

5. What advantages do libraries offer over the Internet?

6. Describe the advantages and disadvantages of Internet research.

7. Explain the steps involved in conducting a useful interview.

8. What is the proper way to present evidence in a speech?

Critical Thinking Questions

1. How do peer review, vetting, and editing affect the quality of information presented in a book or journal? How can you determine whether information you find online has been through these processes?

2. How can you determine the credibility of information presented on a Web site? Are there any red flags that immediately make you question a site's integrity? What characteristics are likely to make you trust an Internet source?

3. Imagine you have been assigned to speak on a controversial topic. How would you go about choosing potential interviewees? What kinds of questions would you ask your interviewees? How would you use the information gleaned in interviews to bolster your thesis ethically?

4. Go to the *Wikipedia* entry for a subject you might like to discuss in a speech. Identify claims that are made without any supporting footnote or citation. How can you determine whether the author of these comments is credible? Next, identify claims that are supported by a footnote or citation. What would you need to do to determine whether the sources for these claims are credible?

Activities

1. Divide into groups. Working individually, select a topic of interest, and jot down the steps you would follow in a research plan. Then share your research plan with the group. After each plan is presented, have the other group members provide additional suggestions for how the topic might be researched effectively.

2. Working in groups, make a list of several potential speech topics. Then create a composite character for a person who would be a credible source on that topic. What is this source's educational background? Occupation? Reputation in the field? Observational capacity?

3. Working in groups, brainstorm potential speech topics. Then, discuss search terms you might use when researching each topic. In your discussion, be sure to consider synonyms, broader terms, and narrower terms that could be used on each topic.

4. Suppose you are considering whether to purchase the next-generation Apple iPod. In groups, discuss and rank the credibility of the following sources of information about this product: (a) a friend who has purchased the product, (b) a sales representative at the Apple Store, (c) an article by the technology editor of your local newspaper, (d) an instructor in the music department at your college, (e) a Web site that ranks portable media players.

5. ▶ Video Activity 7.4: "Kruckenberg, John Kanzius and the Quest to Cure Cancer." Watch David Kruckenberg's speech. Identify the evidence sources he uses. Evaluate the credibility of each source based on the criteria of expertise, objectivity, observational capacity, and recency.

6. Go to the campus library and locate a book on a topic you are considering for a speech. Then try the process discussed on pages 199 to 200 to find other books on your topic. Did you find additional useful information in these books?

7. Use an index for scholarly sources, such as *Academic Search Premier* or *JSTOR*, to find three articles on a topic you are considering for a speech. Then find three Web sites that cover that topic. Compare the credibility of the authors of the scholarly sources with that of the online sources. Also compare the content of the information at the three sources.

8. ◪ Review the chapter-opening illustration, which depicts how Katie, Mandeep, and Sherri used research to strengthen their presentation to local officials. Then consider a problem in your community that you might discuss at a public meeting, and decide how you could use evidence to strengthen your case. Create your own illustration of that scenario using the chapter-opening illustration as a model. (Stick figures are fine if you are not a natural artist).

Study Plan

_____

_____

_____

_____

_____

_____

_____

_____

_____

_____

8

USING SUPPORTING
MATERIALS FOR YOUR SPEECH

"The sum of the parts determines the success of the whole speech."

Graciela was a member of her college's varsity tennis team, so for her informative speech topic, she chose to focus on Title IX—the federal law prohibiting sex discrimination by educational institutions that receive federal aid. As she began her research, one of the first things she discovered was that there are three ways a school can demonstrate compliance with Title IX. Graciela's first feeling was relief: the assignment called for an eight- to ten-minute speech, and it would take at least six to explain the ways a college could comply. She was more than halfway done!

Then Graciela reconsidered. Of all the points she could make about this important and sometimes controversial law, would the details about compliance be the most interesting and noteworthy aspects to share with her audience? She decided to do more research about how Title IX issues were handled at her college. She found a tremendous amount of material—articles in the school newspaper about the effects of Title IX when it was first applied on campus, stories from athletes about their experiences on the college's first women's teams, and even a copy of the program from the first women's tennis tournament ever held on campus.

Now Graciela had ideas and evidence that would be much more relevant and interesting to her classmates. By going the extra mile to find engaging support, she had the materials she needed to back up her main points soundly.

As we note in Chapter 2 and throughout the book, every speech offers a limited number of main points. **Supporting materials** are the different types of information you use to develop and support your main points. You discover these materials as you research your speech; they then become the building blocks you use to construct a successful speech.

Selecting the best supporting materials for your main points is a key step in the speech preparation process, similar to choosing the right mix of ingredients for a special meal you'll be preparing. In an outstanding speech, the supporting materials fit together to help your listeners better understand your message, to capture their interest, and to convince them that you've done your research and are informed about your topic.

Consider a class in which you learned a lot about a subject, a political argument you found persuasive, or a movie that kept you glued to your seat for hours. Chances are good that the teacher used understandable language and examples that clarified the concepts and made the subject seem relevant. The person making the political argument likely offered convincing proof of his or her claims and touched your emotions in a way that you remembered at the voting booth. And the movie probably combined an interesting story with memorable characters and an exciting plot. With the right supporting materials, you can craft a speech that has an equally strong impact on your audience.

In this chapter, we show you why supporting materials are important, what supporting materials you can use, and how to present supporting materials effectively.

WHY USE SUPPORTING MATERIALS?

Supporting materials strengthen your speech in many ways. They build audience interest in your topic, enhance audience understanding of your ideas, and help audience members remember your presentation. In addition, they convince the audience that your points have merit and breathe life into your speech.

SELECT SUPPORTING MATERIALS THAT RELATE TO THE AUDIENCE

Building Audience Interest

If you want audience members to actively listen to your speech—and ignore everything else going on—you must motivate them to focus on what you're saying. By selecting supporting materials that appeal to your listeners' interests, you sweeten the odds that they will pay attention to you. For example, suppose you are developing a speech on cooking with locally grown products. Your supporting materials should focus on ingredients that are available at farmers' markets in your region—citrus or tropical fruits in Florida, avocados in California, or summer squash in Michigan. It also would be important to choose foods your fellow college students can afford.

By including supporting materials that surprise audience members, make them laugh, or touch their emotions, you increase the chances that they will listen to what you are saying.

Enhancing Audience Understanding

If you're presenting information that's new to your listeners, they may have difficulty understanding it. The key to strengthening understanding is to anticipate the reasons that an idea may be difficult for audience

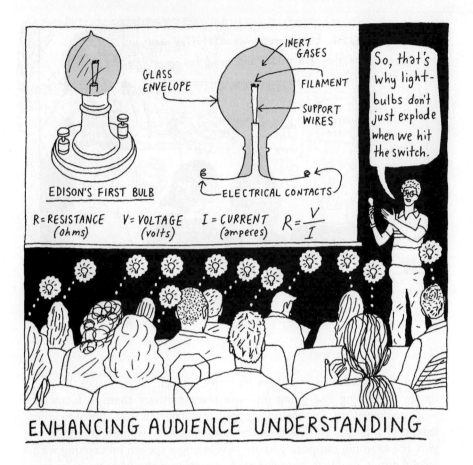

ENHANCING AUDIENCE UNDERSTANDING

members to grasp and to select supporting materials that will help them comprehend.[1]

For instance, let's say you're preparing a speech on string theory for an audience of mostly liberal-arts students. In this case, definitions could help your audience members understand the meaning of technical terms such as *superstring*. And brief, accessible examples could help them grasp the basic concepts behind your topic and help them form mental images of a superstring.

Strengthening Audience Memory

An important goal of any speech is to make a lasting impression on your audience. If listeners applaud your presentation but a week later can

remember hardly anything you said, your speech will have limited effect. To help audience members remember your presentation, you need to give them "hooks" that aid in the process. How does this work? A comparison to the fastener Velcro can be used. Velcro contains tiny hooks on one side and loops on the other; when the sides are compressed, many of the hooks are caught in the loops, and they become attached.[2] Now imagine that a human brain has many millions of loops; the more hooks you can provide for an idea, the better the chance that an idea will "stick" in the minds of your audience members.[3]

Supporting materials provide hooks for the ideas you present. If you merely tell the audience that the Inca culture used groups of strings and knots called *khipu* (key-poo) to keep records,[4] listeners may quickly forget what *khipu* are and how they were used. But suppose you follow up on that statement by showing the audience the word and having them pronounce it with you. Next, you explain that *khipu* means "knot" in the Inca language and that the strings are made from cotton or alpaca wool. Finally, you show a picture of a *khipu* and explain how the knots are positioned to store information. Now you have given the audience several hooks to help them remember what *khipu* are and how they were used.

Winning Audience Agreement

You can't expect your listeners to unthinkingly embrace all the claims you make in your speech. Rather, audience members may be skeptical

of a point if they've never heard it before, if it strikes them as counter-intuitive, or if it contradicts their worldview. To show that a claim is probably true, you need to provide supporting data that offer a good reason for accepting the claim. (This pattern of reasoning, first described by British logician Stephen Toulmin, is called the *Toulmin model of argument*.)[5] To do this, you might quote an expert, present a demonstration, or provide examples to illustrate the claim. For example, in a speech asking for volunteers for a local Special Olympics competition, you might combine a study documenting the link between athlete participation and subsequent employment and the narrative of a former Special Olympics swimmer who is now in the workforce. If your audience accepts the link between the supporting materials and your claim, there is a good chance they will agree with your point.

Evoking Audience Emotion

Factual information greatly enhances any speech. However, you'll capture more of your audience members' attention and interest if you also touch their emotions. For example, an effective speaker may use humor to warm up her listeners or give them a mental break from a slew of sobering statistics. The right supporting materials can also stimulate listeners' empathy, anger, or commitment.

TYPES OF SUPPORTING MATERIALS

There are many types of supporting materials from which to choose to develop your main points. Here, we take a closer look at some of the more common types—*examples, definitions, testimony, statistics, narratives,* and *analogies.*

Examples

An **example** is a sample or an instance that supports or illustrates a general claim. In everyday conversation, you probably use examples frequently. To illustrate, suppose you tell a friend that parking is difficult on your campus, pointing out that you couldn't find a spot three times last week and your roommate drove around for thirty minutes the other day to find a space. In this case, you are using examples to support your claim that parking is difficult.

A **brief example** is a short instance (usually a single sentence) used to support or illustrate your claim. A set of three or four brief examples often can be used to great effect. The following excerpt shows how such examples can be used to support the claim that Americans' privacy is at risk:

- A survey of 381 university admissions officials found that about three in ten had checked an applicant's social media pages and found material that harmed a candidate's chance for admission.[6]

- There is a growing trend in the corporate world to search social media to track behaviors of current employees and learn more about prospective workers.[7]

EXAMPLES OF THREATS TO PRIVACY

- Cities are increasingly investing in software that analyzes citywide surveillance videos and reports anything it deems "suspicious or abnormal behavior." Sales of this technology are expected to reach $3.2 billion by 2016.[8]

You also can use an **extended example** to illustrate a point. An extended example provides many details about the instance being used, giving your audience a deeper and richer picture of your point. The following extended example describes a new threat to privacy from smart televisions:

> A firestorm was created when it was reported that smart televisions could track private talks in the home. After the manufacturer warned customers that technology enabling vocal commands to their televisions could also record and send private speech to a third party, there was an outcry on social media. One activist compared the company policy to a depiction of a telescreen that could track conversations in the novel *1984*.[9]

Definitions

When you introduce new information to audience members, you might use terms unfamiliar to them. If you don't take time to define these terms, your listeners may have difficulty understanding your message, which can leave them feeling frustrated.

For example, suppose you're preparing an informative speech on the Persian empire, and you want to explain that the Persians practiced a religion called Zoroastrianism. This term will probably be new to your audience, so you'll need to define it. There are several different types of definitions you could use:

- A **dictionary definition** provides the meaning of a term as presented in a dictionary. You might use a general dictionary (such as Merriam-Webster) or, if available, a specialized dictionary for your topic. For example, "According to *Cambridge Dictionaries Online*, Zoroastrianism is 'a religion which developed in ancient Iran, and is based on the idea that there is a continuous fight between a god who represents good and one who represents evil.'"[10]

- An **expert definition** comes from a person who is a credible source of information on your topic. For example, "According to Mary Boyce, professor of Iranian studies at the University of London, Zoroastrians believe that 'there is a supreme God who is the creator; that an evil power exists which is opposed to him, and not under his control.'"[11]

- An **etymological definition** explains the linguistic origin of the term. This type of definition is appropriate when the origin is interesting or will help the audience understand the term. For example, "Zoroastrianism has been so named in the West because its prophet, Zarathustra, was known to the ancient Greeks as Zoroaster.[12] Zoroastrians believe that Ahura Mazda (God) revealed the truth through Zarathustra."

- A **functional definition** explains how something is used or what it does. For instance, a speaker might define Zoroastrianism in terms of how it is practiced by its followers: "According to the Ontario Consultants on Religious Tolerance, Zoroastrian worship 'includes prayers and symbolic ceremonies.' Rituals 'are conducted before a sacred fire. . . . [Practitioners] regard fire as a symbol of their God.'"[13]

Testimony

Testimony consists of information provided by other people. Typically, you will find testimony from the sources you research at the library and online or through interviews.

Expert testimony consists of statements made by credible sources who have professional or other in-depth knowledge of a topic. As with any source, you must carefully assess any expert testimony and be sure that expert sources have specialized knowledge of the topic, objectivity, and observational capacity. Testimony from expert sources is likely to increase audience members' acceptance of your claims. Thus, you should try to use expert testimony when you are asserting claims the audience may not accept.

A second type of testimony is **lay testimony**, which consists of statements made by persons with no special expertise in the subject they are discussing. Because they lack expertise, lay sources generally should not be used to prove factual claims in a speech. This type of testimony is *not* a substitute for evidence. For example, testimony from laypersons would not credibly prove that a low-carbohydrate diet improves people's health or predict the effect of expanded offshore oil drilling on the U.S. economy. However, lay testimony can help you show how a typical person has been affected by your topic. Thus, you could quote lay sources to explain their particular experiences with a low-carbohydrate diet or to discuss how they were affected by high gas prices.

Ⓒ **To see an example of a speaker who uses testimony in her speech, try Video Activity 8.1, "Royzpal, Litter."**

Statistics

A **statistic** is a piece of information presented in numerical form. Statistics can help you quantify points you're making in your speech and help your audience understand how often certain types of situations occur. Whereas supporting materials such as examples or anecdotes help the audience understand a single instance, statistics can help you show the big picture regarding multiple instances or instances over time of the situation you are discussing.

For example, in a speech on the rising costs of a college education, you might present an example of a single student who struggled to pay more than $1,200 for books and supplies in 2015. Then you could use statistics to argue that this cost is typical: "The College Board reports that the average cost of books and other course materials at four-year public colleges in 2014–15 was $1,225."[14]

Although useful, statistics also have disadvantages. Specifically, as your use of statistics increases, so does the chance that your audience members will perceive your topic as overly complicated.[15] A long string of statistics may also bore or confuse your listeners if they're struggling to figure out what "all those numbers" mean. To present statistics in a

way that helps your audience understand the information and remain interested in your speech, apply the following guidelines:

- *Limit the number of statistics you present.* Of all the possible statistics you could offer your audience, select three or four of the best ones.
- *Use visual aids to explain your statistics.* For example, you could use a bar graph to illustrate increases in textbook costs, tuition, and overall cost of living over the past eighteen years.
- *Establish context.* Explain what the statistics imply for your listeners. For instance, "What does a 6.5 percent annual increase mean? The average cost for tuition, books, supplies, and room and board at a public four-year college is now over $20,000. At this rate of increase, the cost will rise to over $27,000 in five years."

> ▶ To view a speaker using statistics, try Video Activity 8.2, "Citing Sources (Statistics and Facts)."

Narratives

A **narrative** is an anecdote (a brief story) or a somewhat longer account that can be used to support your main points. Narratives stimulate your listeners' interest because humans (by our nature) love a good story.[16]

THIS IS A NARRATIVE

Once upon a time, drawings of people having ideas in comic strips looked like this:——→

It's not really clear what I'm doing. Am I having an idea or just doing a funny little dance ?!?

But then, in 1879, Thomas Edison invented something:

I call it a **LIGHT-BULB!**

These "lightbulbs" made comic strip artists so happy. Now they could make it instantly obvious that someone in a drawing was having an idea:

However, the comic strip artists didn't just get to live happily ever after, as now, in the 21st century, people are beginning to have differently shaped ideas:

Here is an example of a medium-length anecdote presented in a speech about a fledgling Uber service for air travel:

> Before she took a dreaded long drive on a congested highway from the Bay Area to Lake Tahoe, Sarah Buhr received an email about "UberX for small planes." A few days later, she was in the air in a tiny private airplane with a pilot who loved to fly but needed a passenger to help share the cost of fuel.[17]

In a speech on the construction of the thousand-mile Alaska-Canadian highway during World War II, a presenter used the following longer narrative to show how the project not only built a highway but also contributed to civil rights:

> Three African American regiments were sent to the mountains of northern Canada to work on the highway. They faced hostile conditions as well as prejudice and doubts about their ability. Working nonstop for three days and using the headlights of trucks when it got dark, these soldiers cut down trees, built trestles, and worked chest-deep in the icy water to build a bridge across the Sikanni Chief River. The unit earned a reputation for its ability to rapidly build strong bridges in the worst of environments, helping "pave" the way for desegregation of the armed forces in 1948. The highway has been called "the road to civil rights."[18]

Stories like these are great for capturing audience attention or for illustrating a point. Consider incorporating such stories as attention-getters or when you want to show how concepts play out in the real world. And you can always use a quick anecdote—lasting no more than five or ten seconds—to reenergize an audience after tackling complex or technical material.

Narratives and anecdotes are like lay testimony in that they can effectively build audience interest or illustrate a concept; however, anecdotal evidence is no substitute for credible proof. Stories about a relative who smoked two packs of cigarettes a day and lived to ninety-eight or a roommate who partied every night and still maintained a 3.8 grade-point average do not prove that such behaviors are safe for the population as a whole.

Analogies

An **analogy** is a comparison based on similarities between two phenomena—one that's familiar to the audience and one that is less familiar. Analogies can be **literal**, meaning that two entities in the same category are compared. For example, a speaker might compare the careers of Diana Ross (lead singer of the Supremes in the 1960s and a solo star in the 1970s) and Beyoncé, or the wind energy policies of Germany and the United States. Analogies also can be **figurative**, which means that although the two entities are not in the same category, the characteristics of one (which is familiar to the audience) can help the audience understand the characteristics of another (which is unfamiliar). This type of comparison helps listeners use their existing knowledge to absorb new information.[19]

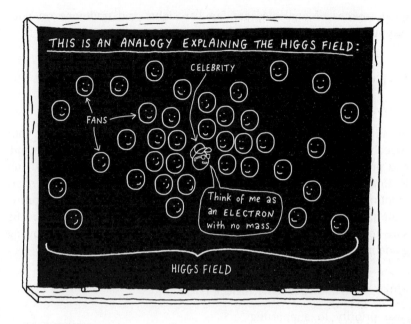

Here's how Dean Lee, a physicist from North Carolina State University, used an analogy during a talk at the North Carolina Museum of Natural Sciences. He was discussing recent research at the Large Hadron Collider in Europe that provided evidence of the existence of the Higgs field (and the Higgs boson, often referred to as the "God particle" in the media). In the paraphrased text that follows, Lee explained what this field does:

> The Higgs field gives mass to other particles. Without the Higgs field, an electron would have no mass. Think of a celebrity as an electron with no mass. He or she walks through a crowded room and is suddenly surrounded by fans who want his or her autograph. The celebrity has effectively formed a crowd with a lot of mass. That is sort of what the Higgs field is doing. It surrounds particles and gives them mass.[20]

When you are preparing a speech, one effective approach is to provide analogies that draw on concepts you've heard in your classmates' speeches. That way, you'll know that your audience members will understand the concepts you're using, and you'll demonstrate goodwill to show that you have learned from your classmates' presentations. Additional good sources of analogies are familiar sights and traditions on your campus or aspects of college life that your listeners can all relate to.

GUIDELINES FOR USING SUPPORTING MATERIALS

Recall that supporting materials serve a variety of purposes in your speech—building audience interest, helping the audience understand, and proving facts to the audience. In the Internet era, it is not difficult to find enormous quantities of information on your topic in a short amount of time. It is not as easy, however, to select the best supporting materials out of all the information you have found. How can you be sure to select the most effective supporting materials? The following guidelines can help.

Choose the Most Credible Proof

Give priority to supporting materials that are backed by credible evidence. Whether you are relying on examples, testimony, statistics, or other types of support, these materials will be most effective when they are proven. For example, in a speech on the hazards of texting while driving, the statement that the average "eyes-off-the-road time" for sending a text message is equivalent to "traveling the length of a football field at 55 miles per hour without looking at the roadway" is a compelling analogy. But it will be a much more believable one if you identify the author of the study—the Virginia Tech

Transportation Institute.[21] If you merely assert this fact without proof or attribute it to a Web site of uncertain authorship, the analogy will be much less convincing.

Use a Variety of Supporting Materials

In the previous section, you learned about a number of different types of supporting materials. To get the best results, you should use a variety of these materials to support your main points. If you use the same type of supporting material over and over, your effectiveness will be reduced as fatigue sets in with your audience.

For instance, one funny personal example might pull listeners into your speech, a well-chosen analogy can help your audience understand a key point, and a startling statistic can convince audience members that a problem you're describing is serious. By contrast, a speech that uses mainly one type of support—whether personal examples, analogies, or statistics—will quickly lose listeners' interest.

Appeal to Different Learning Styles

Select supporting materials that appeal to different audience members' learning styles. *Active learners* learn best by "doing something active"

LEARNING STYLES

with the material that is being presented, and *reflective learners* "prefer to think about it."[22] *Visual learners*, by contrast, tend to "remember best what they see," whereas *verbal learners* tend to "get more out of words—written and spoken explanations."[23]

To appeal to this range of learning styles, use a combination of supporting materials throughout your speech. For instance, to clarify a point for verbal learners, you could use a spoken definition along with a vivid analogy; to appeal to visual learners, you also could incorporate visual aids (see Chapter 14). One landmark study found that

SPEECH CHOICES

A CASE STUDY: MIA

Let's take a look at Mia's selection of supporting materials.

Over the next three days, Mia read and took notes on the articles she'd found. She was fascinated by the number of different and creative ways that emigrants used smartphones. Although Mia counted at least twenty different uses of smartphones, she realized she couldn't fit them all into her speech. Rather than rushing through a long list, she would have to select several uses and develop them.

Mia's research materials gave her a variety of different supporting materials. She could use emigrants' lay testimony to provide examples, brief anecdotes, and narratives, which she knew would be compelling to her audience. Mia also could use expert testimony to support broader claims about smartphone use. Because most of the class was familiar with smartphone apps, she could use analogies to make points about apps used by emigrants, along with functional definitions to explain some of the apps and sites. Mia decided to limit the use of statistics and be sure to round them off so they would not be overwhelming.

Finally, Mia wanted to appeal to different learning styles. Several pictures that she found could be used to supplement verbal explanations. These images would reinforce the message in a memorable way and provide additional proof for the claims she was making. She thought about having students use their own smartphones to search for apps that emigrants might use but decided against it because there would be too much downtime while students fiddled with their phones. She would use rhetorical questions to help students visualize how they might need to use apps.

YOUR TURN:
What are some other supporting materials that Mia might have considered for her speech?

For more questions and activities for this case study, and to see two video clips from Mia's speech on supporting materials, please go to LaunchPad at macmillanhighered.com/speakup4e.

students retained 26 percent of what they heard and 30 percent of what they saw, but those totals increased to 50 percent for information they heard *and* saw.[24] If you are delivering a **multimedia presentation** (with various forms of supporting materials, such as video clips, PowerPoint slides, and illustrations), audience members will be more likely to grasp the material if you combine words and

SPEECH CHOICES

A CASE STUDY: *JACOB*

And let's check out which supporting materials Jacob is using in his speech.

After doing some research, Jacob was ready to start preparing his speech. He wanted to start with the example of his favorite basketball player, Anthony Davis. He also had examples to show how much time student athletes devote to their sports and how colleges take advantage of their players. In addition, Jacob had discovered a number of statistics that he could use as supporting materials. These figures would show what a good player Davis was, the average attendance figures for different teams on campus, the money colleges make from their athletic teams, and the appropriate salary for college athletes.

YOUR TURN:

Jacob is using many statistics in his speech. How should he present them effectively?

Finally, Jacob had lay testimony in the form of his roommate's opinion about paying athletes. Unfortunately, he didn't speak with any athletes on women's teams.

For more questions and activities for this case study, and to see a ▶ video clip from Jacob's speech on selecting and presenting supporting materials, please go to LaunchPad at macmillanhighered.com/speakup4e.

---

images.[25] And finally, asking thought-provoking questions or providing opportunities for audience members to think about a concept can help reflective learners.

How does this work in practice? To appeal to diverse learning styles in a speech on abstract art, for example, you might begin by defining abstract art and comparing it to other related art forms, such as nineteenth-century African masks and traditional Japanese prints. You then might present a few pictures of abstract art pieces (perhaps alongside some nonabstract pieces) and then ask the question, "Which pieces are examples of abstract art?" (See Chapter 10 for a discussion of rhetorical questions.)

To combine a verbal and visual explanation, take the example of a speech about business models for food trucks. You could show a video clip of a truck on a busy day while explaining how the truck is operating efficiently.

To appeal to active learners, you can give audience members a chance to do something with your supporting materials. For instance, after using a narrative to help her listeners understand how bees fly, one student invited audience members to manipulate their arms to simulate the motion of bees' wings.

Avoid Long Lists

People usually find it difficult to understand and remember long strings of facts, examples, or statistics, especially when they are not presented with any elaboration. Consider this excerpt from a speech entitled "My Hometown":

> There are great restaurants in my town. You can get Chinese food, Italian food, Mexican food, and Ethiopian food. There are lots of places to go. You can go to the lake, the amusement park, the movies, or the ballgame. If you like to exercise, try our running trails, swimming pools, and bicycling paths.

If this speaker followed this pattern for five minutes or more, his presentation would quickly become tedious and forgettable.

To avoid this scenario, select a smaller number of supporting materials (most should take between fifteen and thirty seconds to present), and focus on the materials that *best* develop your main points. The "My Hometown" speech could have been more effective if the speaker had concentrated on the most noteworthy aspects of the town and expanded on them. By focusing on a notable hometown restaurant, for instance, the speaker could use examples, testimony, and analogies to help audience members see themselves dining in that restaurant and tasting the food.

Consider Your Audience

Your audience members' knowledge and interests can be useful in helping you choose the best possible supporting materials. For example, suppose you want to persuade your listeners to volunteer for community service. If your audience consists of future teachers, you might offer examples and narratives about service opportunities with young children. Or if many of your listeners enjoy outdoor activities, your supporting materials could relate more to environmental service.

> ▶ To see an example of supporting materials and decide if they were adapted to the audience, try Video Activity 8.3, "Examples (Humorous)."

Respect the Available Time

Select supporting materials that you can comfortably fit into the time you have available for your speech. For a five- to ten-minute speech, for instance, you wouldn't have time to use supporting materials that each take one minute or more to present—no matter how interesting and relevant they might be. To illustrate, suppose your employer asked you to prepare a ten-minute podcast about best practices in urban agriculture. You might be tempted to include a four-minute narrative about how you came to be involved in this field, but this would take up almost half of your speaking time and cut into the available time for explaining best practices. You would need to find a different, shorter narrative that would help viewers to understand these methods.

CHAPTER REVIEW

 The sum of the parts determines the success of the whole speech. As the story about Graciela's speech on Title IX illustrates at the beginning of this chapter, the right supporting materials can help you build listeners' interest in your presentation, enhance audience understanding of your topic, strengthen the likelihood that audience members will remember your speech, convince your audience that your claims have merit, and breathe life into your speech by touching on audience emotions. To choose the best supporting materials, you can start by understanding the many forms they take—such as examples, definitions, testimony, statistics, narratives, and analogies. You then can apply important guidelines, such as choosing the most credible proof, using a variety of supporting materials, appealing to different learning styles, avoiding long lists of information, considering your audience's knowledge and interests, and ensuring that your supporting materials don't consume too much of the time available for your presentation.

LaunchPad
macmillan learning

LaunchPad for *Speak Up* offers videos and encourages self-assessment through adaptive quizzing. Go to **macmillanhighered.com/speakup4e** to get access to:

✔ **LearningCurve Adaptive Quizzes**

 Video clips that help you understand public speaking concepts

---

Key Terms

supporting material *228*
example *233*
  brief example *233*
  extended example *234*
  dictionary definition *235*
  expert definition *235*
  etymological definition *235*
  functional definition *236*
testimony *236*

expert testimony *236*
lay testimony *236*
statistic *237*
narrative *238*
analogy *240*
  literal analogy *240*
  figurative analogy *240*
  multimedia presentation *245*

249

Review Questions

1. Name five purposes for using supporting materials.
2. Name and define the six types of supporting materials.
3. Explain why it is important to select supporting materials that are backed by credible evidence.
4. Identify four or more guidelines for using supporting materials in a speech.
5. Define four different learning styles.

Critical Thinking Questions

1. What are a speaker's ethical obligations when presenting statistical information? How could failing to provide solid context for statistics mislead audiences?
2. Narratives and anecdotes often are used to evoke an emotional response. What other types of supporting materials might tap audience members' emotions? Could expert testimony support an emotional appeal? Could statistics generate an emotional response?
3. Think of a time when one of your instructors explained a subject effectively. What supporting materials did he or she use to help the class understand the topic? What supporting materials did he or she use to build interest in the subject?
4. Think of a topic that you understand well but that is likely to be new to many of your classmates. How could you use a figurative analogy to explain some aspect of that topic to your audience?

Activities

1. Working in groups, select a speech topic, and then have each group member select a different type of supporting material for the topic. Next, have each member provide an example of the supporting material that could be used in a speech on the selected topic.
2. Working in groups of up to five students, select a potential speech topic. Then have each group member choose a different purpose for supporting materials (such as building audience interest or strengthening audience memory) and select an example of a

supporting material that would help achieve that purpose. Discuss whether each supporting material chosen would be likely to achieve its purpose.

3. ⊙ **Video Activity 8.4: "Kim, The Nonmonetary Uses of Gold."** Identify the types of supporting materials Kim uses to develop her ideas. How well does she follow the guidelines for using supporting materials that are discussed in this chapter?

4. ▟ Review the illustration on page 241 ("This is an analogy explaining the Higgs field"). Select any speech topic of interest to you, and think of an analogy you could use as supporting material. Draw your own illustration of that analogy.

5. Review the evidence sources cited within this chapter, and then look at the endnotes for this chapter in the back of the book. What types of sources did the authors use to back up the points they raise? What kinds of supporting materials are included in this chapter that do not require citations to research? Would the chapter work as well if only one or the other type of supporting material were presented?

6. Review a newsmagazine article or another source that presents statistics to support the points it makes. How well do the statistics support the author's thesis? Does the author provide appropriate context for the statistics?

Study Plan

_____

_____

_____

_____

_____

_____

_____

_____

9

ORGANIZING YOUR SPEECH

"Good organization makes the message clear."

Carly stood at the lectern and began her speech. After trying to build audience interest by telling a joke about a leading fashion magazine, Carly revealed that her speech would be about magazines targeted to women and girls. She then launched into her topic. Showing her listeners several magazine advertisements featuring gaunt models, Carly explained how listeners could help friends struggling with anorexia or bulimia. One of the ads was for cosmetics, and Carly presented evidence supporting the claim that the testing of cosmetics harms animals. Carly also showed several magazine articles with titles she considered inane—such as "Are You Ready for Neon Hair?" and "How Much of a Katniss Are You?" She then contrasted these articles with pieces from more serious magazines.

Carly concluded her speech with a plea for audience members to cancel their subscriptions to women's magazines. Then she sat down, feeling confident that she had scored a success with her audience. When they evaluated her speech, however, many classmates said they'd had trouble following her presentation. Some admitted that they'd found her ideas downright confusing. Surprised and upset by the feedback, Carly didn't realize that she had made an all-too-common mistake—failing to organize her speech clearly.

Carly's story reveals the importance of organization in developing a successful speech. When you organize your ideas clearly, you help audience members see how the different ideas in your presentation fit together, which allows them to better comprehend your message.[1] They know what to listen for because your organization provides cues to indicate the main ideas. And they don't have to devote their mental energy to figuring out what your main points are and how all the details in your speech relate to those points.

Good organization is particularly important in oral communication because listeners don't have the luxury of reviewing printed information to understand your message. By contrast, those who are reading a printed message—whether online or in a book or magazine—can go back and reread the text if they're confused. Thus, when giving a speech, you must take special care to help the audience follow your ideas.

When you organize your speech clearly, you also enhance your credibility. Effective organization shows that you have taken the time to prepare your talk.[2]

Organizing a speech is not merely a matter of applying an arbitrary set of rules. Rather, a well-organized presentation imposes order on the set of points you present in your speech by showing the relationship *between* ideas. Thus, the organizational pattern you select can communicate important information to the audience: What are the most important ideas? Why

do you believe that each idea has merit? What evidence are you providing to back up your claims?

In this chapter, we focus on organizing the **body** of your speech—the part where you present your main points and support them with examples, narratives, testimony, and other materials. To organize a speech effectively, you must learn to group your ideas into a sequence your audience can easily follow. In the following pages, we explore ways to select your main points and structure your supporting materials. We also examine common patterns for arranging main points and present some organizing language you can use to make your speech structure clear to your audience.

SELECTING YOUR MAIN POINTS

The body of your speech should be structured around your **main points**—those few ideas that are most important for your listeners to remember. The body also contains **supporting points**—materials designed to prove or substantiate your main points. A speech body organized around main points and their corresponding supporting points helps listeners make sense out of the details of your presentation. By contrast, if you present randomly ordered ideas about your topic (as Carly did), your audience will have trouble determining what is most important and understanding the information you're presenting. Even a five-minute speech requires careful organization because it can contain fifty or more sentences.

How should you select your main points? The following guidelines can help.

Consider Your Purpose

Make sure that every main point you select relates to the specific purpose of your speech. For example, consider the following two sets of main points for a speech to the campus community with the following specific purpose—to persuade your college to adopt a plan to minimize food insecurity.

FIRST SET OF MAIN POINTS

I. The elements of a healthy diet
II. Symptoms of malnutrition
III. Our college should adopt a food insecurity plan.

SECOND SET OF MAIN POINTS

I. Many students on our campus experience malnutrition.
II. Rising costs of tuition and living expenses are depleting students' food budgets.
III. Our college should establish a food pantry and offer students emergency meal cards for the campus dining hall.

Which set of main points would be a better option? In the first set, main points I and II do not relate to the specific purpose but provide general background information about malnutrition and healthy diets. Only main point III relates to the specific purpose. Conversely, in the second set, each main point relates to the specific purpose: the first demonstrates the problem of malnutrition on campus, the second discusses the causes of the problem, and the third presents steps the college can take to reduce the problem. Given this contrast, the second set of main points would be a better alternative.

Take Your Audience into Account

Out of the many relevant main points you might use to develop your topic, which ones will prove *most* interesting to your audience? Which ones will provide your listeners with the information that is most useful to *them*?

Consider the following two sets of main points for a speech on backpacking tips:

FIRST SET OF MAIN POINTS

  I. Choosing the right backpack
  II. Remembering the essential equipment
  III. Packing your backpack strategically

SECOND SET OF MAIN POINTS

  I. Coping with extreme elevation changes
  II. Selecting light, nutritious food for weeklong trips
  III. Choosing optimal equipment for subzero temperatures

Both sets of main points contain information that fits the topic of "backpacking tips." Thus, they fit the first guideline for main points: they relate to the specific purpose of the speech. However, the question of which set is better depends on the audience. The first set contains basic information that would be appropriate for novice backpackers. The second set contains information that would be more useful for experienced backpackers who are contemplating challenging trips.

Select an Appropriate Number of Main Points

In most situations, effective speeches present two to five main points. In our experience, student speeches typically contain three main points. However, there is no rule that you must have three. You also may have two, four, or five main points if that number gives you the most logical organization of ideas.

Most audiences have trouble remembering more than five points. Also, it is unlikely that you will have enough time to develop that many points. Here are a few suggestions for whittling down your main points to a manageable number:

- See whether any of your main points are related. Can two or more main points be combined into a single broader category?

- Review your audience analysis. Are there points that can be excluded because they are less likely to resonate with your audience?

- Evaluate which points are the most important to developing your topic or thesis. Exclude the point(s) that are less essential.

CHOOSING THE APPROPRIATE NUMBER OF MAIN POINTS

If you find that you have only one main point, consider making that point into the topic or thesis of your speech. Then organize the information you plan to use to support that point into two to five key ideas, which will become your main points.

ORGANIZING YOUR SUPPORTING MATERIALS

After you select your main points, you need to develop (explain and prove) each one with supporting materials. Supporting materials enable your audience to understand your main points and help prove why you think those main points are valid. In Chapter 8, we discussed a number of different types of supporting materials that you can use, such as examples, definitions, and statistics. Now we consider how you can organize these supporting materials to help audience members follow your speech.

Subordination and Coordination

The principle of subordination is the key to a well-organized speech. Using **subordination** means creating a hierarchy of points and their supporting materials in your speech. Thus, main points are the most important (or highest) level of subordination, and supporting materials used to develop a main point (called **subpoints**) are subordinate to that main point. (There should be at least two subpoints to support each main point.) In the same way, materials that support subpoints are called **sub-subpoints**, and these sub-subpoints are subordinate to their corresponding subpoint. A well-organized speech also features **coordination**. Each main point is coordinate with other main points—that is, they are at the same level of significance— just as subpoints are coordinate with other subpoints, and so on.

Sound confusing? It isn't, really. To see how subordination and coordination work, compare the subpoints (indicated by capital letters) supporting each main point (signaled by roman numerals) in the following outline for an informative speech on filmmaking in India:

    I. Culture plays an important role in Indian filmmaking.
       A. Indian moviemakers developed a style of their own by the 1950s, based on the teachings of *Natya Shastra* (Science of Theater), a thousand-year-old Hindu book. Entertainment was to embody nine essences—love, hate, sorrow, disgust, joy, compassion, pity, pride, and courage.[3]
       B. According to Professor Murthy and colleagues in journalism and mass communication at Tezpur University, "The common core areas that one should know to understand and interpret Indian

cinema are as follows: (1) celebrated epics . . . , (2) classical dance traditions . . . , and (3) the traditional folk theaters."[4]

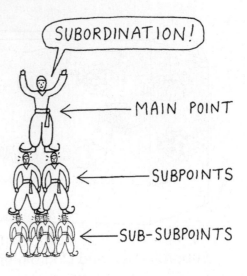

II. There are differences between Indian-made films and films made in the United States.
  A. In India, films need not follow the linear, scripted story line that is popular in Western movies. Of any hundred films made in India, about three will have scripts prepared in advance, according to screenwriter Anjum Rajabali.[5]
  B. New York University anthropology professor Tejaswini Ganti notes that as Bollywood was becoming an internationally acknowledged brand, lip-synched songs were a staple of Hindi films. Over time, the use of music has remained important, but lip-synched songs are no longer essential for a film to draw a large audience.[6]

Notice that both subpoints for main point I pertain to the subject of the main point—the role of culture in Indian filmmaking. These subpoints are *subordinate* to main point I. Next, consider main point II. Subpoint IIA supports the main point, but subpoint IIB does not because it fails to explain why U.S.-made and Indian-made films are different. Instead, it discusses a development in Hindi films (use of music) and offers no contrast with American movies. Because subpoint IIB is not relevant to the idea that U.S.- and Indian-made films are different, it is not subordinate. Therefore, the speaker should not include it under main point II.

▶ To practice identifying main points and subpoints, try Video Activity 9.1, "Without Liberty and Justice for All."

A, B, AND C ARE SUBPOINTS

I. Leonardo da Vinci's art had many impacts.

   A. Leonardo's artistic technique was unprecedented.

   B. Leonardo's technique influenced future artists.

   C. Leonardo's art has generated many controversies.

1, 2, AND 3 ARE SUB-SUBPOINTS

   C. Leonardo's art has generated many controversies.

      1. Who was the model for the *Mona Lisa*?

      2. Who is to the right of Jesus in *The Last Supper*?

      3. Is the *Vitruvian Man* a geometrical algorithm?

WHEN A SUBPOINT DOESN'T FIT

When a Subpoint Doesn't Fit

In developing a speech, you may discover that some of the supporting materials you researched do not relate to any of the main points you selected. Nevertheless, you believe that these materials would improve your speech. What should you do?

One option is to reword one or more main points to encompass the additional information. In the first example that follows, the main point is that healthy eating is essential for college students. Note in this example how subpoint B focuses on getting exercise, not on healthy eating. Thus, it does not relate to the main point. In the second example, the speaker has rewritten the main point to make both subpoints subordinate.

FIRST EXAMPLE

    I. Healthy eating is essential for college students.
        A. Limiting fried foods, whole milk, and sweetened drinks helps you avoid the "freshman fifteen."
        B. Participating in intramural sports and walking to campus help you stay fit.

SECOND EXAMPLE

I. A *healthy lifestyle* is essential for college students.
  A. Limiting fried foods, whole milk, and sweetened drinks helps you avoid the "freshman fifteen."
  B. Participating in intramural sports and walking to campus help you stay fit.

A second option is to create an additional main point to include the supporting material in question. If you use this option, be sure you have enough supporting materials to develop the new main point. Also, be sure the new main point relates to your topic or thesis statement.

ARRANGING YOUR MAIN POINTS

After you have settled on your main points, you'll need to decide the order in which they will be arranged. To do so, first familiarize yourself with the common patterns of organization, and then select the pattern that best suits your speech. In this section, we take a closer look at these patterns—*spatial, chronological (temporal), causal, comparison,* and *categorical (topical)*.

Spatial Pattern

In a **spatial pattern**, the main points represent important aspects of your topic that can be thought of as adjacent to one another in location or geography. This approach is effective with speech topics that can be broken down into specific parts that relate to each other spatially. You take the audience from one part to the next—much as a museum guide ushers a group from exhibit to exhibit or as an anatomy professor chooses to lecture about the parts of the human skeleton from head to toe.

For example, a geologist might use a spatial pattern to discuss seismic zones in the continental United States:

I. The Ramapo Fault goes through New York, New Jersey, and Pennsylvania.
II. The New Madrid earthquake region includes eight states in the central United States.
III. The Wasatch Fault runs just west of the Rockies.
IV. The West Coast has both the Cascadia subduction zone and the San Andreas Fault.

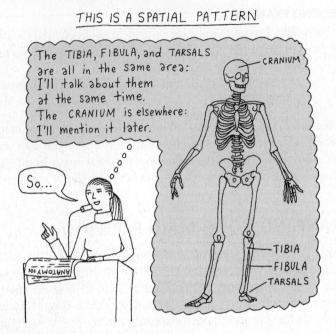

Chronological (Temporal) Pattern

In a **chronological (temporal) pattern**, you present the information in time-based sequence, from beginning to end. Each main point covers a particular point in the chronology. If you are discussing a subject that follows a sequence, such as a historical event or a process, this pattern can help your audience keep track of what you are saying. For instance, a speech discussing the decline and rebound of bald eagles in the lower forty-eight states could use a chronological pattern:

    I. In 1963, the bald eagle had nearly disappeared from the lower forty-eight states.

   II. In 1972, the harmful pesticide DDT was banned in the United States.

  III. During the next twenty years, governments and individual citizens took steps to protect bald eagles.

  IV. In 2007, bald eagles were taken off the list of endangered species.

Causal Pattern

If your speech is explaining a cause-and-effect relationship, a **causal pattern** will help your audience understand the link between particular events and their outcomes. There are two ways to organize main points

when you use this pattern. First, if several major causes exist for the situation or phenomenon you are discussing, each main point can cover one of the causes. For example, in a speech about causes of fashion trends,[7] a speaker could use the following main points:

I.   Major news events influence fashion choices.
II. Styles displayed in popular culture become fashionable.
III. Economic conditions affect clothing trends.
IV. Technological innovation creates new fashion options.

Second, if there is a chain of events between cause and effect, each main point can become one link in the chain from cause to effect. So to explain why e-commerce has grown in significance, you might use the following chain of causation:

I.   Internet use has grown rapidly in the past twenty years.
II. Businesses took advantage of this new channel of communication by marketing products online.
III. Consumers have increasingly chosen to shop online because of the convenience.

Comparison Pattern

A **comparison pattern** organizes the speech around major similarities and differences between two events, objects, or situations. Each main point discusses an important similarity or difference. This pattern can help your audience learn about a new subject by comparing or contrasting it to a subject with which they are familiar. To illustrate, you might compare recent scientific discoveries about planets outside our solar system (exoplanets)[8] with certain characteristics of our own solar system:

I. Like our sun, most other stars have planets.
II. Our planets orbit one sun, but many exoplanets orbit two "suns."
III. Our planets have remained in similar orbits, whereas many exoplanets' orbits have significantly changed.
IV. Our planets tend to be smaller than the exoplanets scientists have discovered.

Categorical (Topical) Pattern

Another option for organization is a **categorical (topical) pattern**. This pattern is effective when you have a diverse set of main points

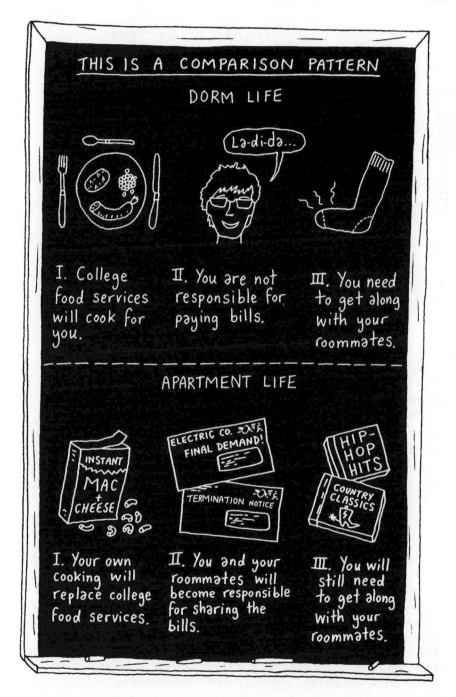

to support the thesis of your speech. Each main point emphasizes an important aspect of your topic that you want the audience to understand.

For example, Jodie was presenting an after-dinner speech poking fun at the practice of holiday gift giving. She used a categorical pattern as follows:

   I. Gift wrap and gift bags generate four million tons of waste.
   II. Holiday shopping is a major source of anxiety.
   III. Half of all Americans admit to regifting.
   IV. Charitable donations are a worthwhile alternative to gift buying.

> ▶ To see an example of one type of organizational pattern in a speech, try Video Activity 9.2, "Singh, The Importance of Playing Sports Has Grown over Time."

Persuasive Speech Patterns

When your rhetorical purpose is persuasion, there are a number of organizational patterns that can help you convince your audience. We elaborate on these formats in Chapter 17, Persuasive Speaking.

USING ORGANIZING WORDS AND SENTENCES

As the person who has developed your speech, you will know what your main points are, when you are moving from one point to the next, and what part of the speech you are delivering at any point in time. However, without assistance from you, your audience members will have difficulty keeping track of your organization. To see how difficult this task is, watch a speech with two or three classmates, and have each person try to outline the speaker's main points. Unless the speech is very well organized, chances are good that you will each have different perceptions of what the main points were.

To make the structure of your speech easy for audience members to follow, you need to insert organizing words, phrases, and sentences throughout your presentation. These words, phrases, and sentences offer the audience clear signals that will help them identify your main points and navigate your supporting information. The primary types of organizing language include *transitions, signposts, internal previews,* and *internal summaries.*

Transitions

A **transition** is a sentence that indicates you are moving from one part of your speech to the next. The words in a transition should indicate that one thought is finished and a new idea is coming. The following are examples of transitions from an informative speech on Joan of Arc:

- Now that *we have seen* how Joan of Arc prevailed at Orléans, *let's take a look* at her efforts to free Paris.

THERE ARE TWO PARTS TO A TRANSITION

JUST LAUNCHING INTO A NEW IDEA WITHOUT GETTING CLOSURE ON THE OLD ONE CAN BE CONFUSING AND ISN'T REALLY A TRANSITION.

Ugh, why's it not moving?

OLD IDEA

NEW IDEA ⟶ Let me describe how to safely tow a trailer.

PART ONE: REFERENCE THE PREVIOUS IDEA. | PART TWO: INTRODUCE THE NEW IDEA.

Now that you have learned how to install a hitch to a vehicle, | let me describe how to safely tow a trailer.

- *You have learned* about Joan of Arc's military strategies; *next* we will consider the effects of her spiritual beliefs.

Note how these transitions both introduce a new point and signal the end of the previous point. Students often have trouble creating transitions that achieve both of these tasks, as shown by the following failed attempts:

- What happened when Joan of Arc attempted to free Paris?
- Joan of Arc's military strategies were influenced by her spiritual beliefs.

Neither of these sentences would make a good transition. The first one asks a question pertaining to the main point to follow (the campaign to retake Paris), but it does not help the audience see that the speaker has finished discussing Joan's efforts at Orléans. The second sentence includes two different ideas, but it does not use any words to signal that the one idea is finished and a new main point is about to begin.

> ⊙ To practice developing transitions, try Video Activity 9.3, "Patterns of Arrangement: Causal."

Signposts

A **signpost** is a word or phrase within a sentence that helps your audience understand your speech's structure. Signposts in a speech serve the same function as their counterparts on a road. Highway signs tell drivers what direction they're traveling in and how the roads are organized. In a similar vein, speech signposts inform audiences about the direction and organization of a presentation.

SPEECH CHOICES

A CASE STUDY: *MIA*

Now that Mia has chosen her supporting materials,
let's see how she organized them into main points.

After gathering her supporting materials, Mia spent the next few
days studying for a midterm exam for another class. Because she
was on schedule for her speech preparation, she could take some
time to relax, so she went to a movie with friends. The next day, Mia selected her
main points. She wrote a brief description of each of the supporting materials that
she was considering on a sticky note and then sorted these notes into categories.
She ended up with ten different categories—which seemed like too many! Mia
noted that several categories (such as using apps to calculate currency exchange,
find lodging, and plan the next day's route) could be combined into one main point
about using smartphones for taking care of daily needs on emigrants' journeys.
Two other categories (limiting reliance on traffickers and surviving crises at sea)
could fit under one main point on coping with danger. Other supporting materials
fit under the general idea that a large number of emigrants rely on smartphones
and consider them essential to their journey. Several other supporting materials fit
into a potential main point about how smartphones help emigrants after they reach
their final destination. She decided to leave this main point out because it did not
relate to her specific purpose—emigrants' use of smartphones *during their journey*.

Next, Mia considered the organizational pattern and order of main points
in her speech. She selected a topical pattern because her main points did
not really proceed in a chronological manner or fit a
spatial pattern. Mia decided that her first main point
would show the audience that many emigrants do
consider smartphones essential. Then she would
explain their uses for daily needs. She would end
with the use of smartphones to deal with dangerous situations, which included some of her most
compelling material.

YOUR TURN:
How would you advise
Mia to organize her
supporting materials
if she wanted to use a
chronological pattern?

For more questions and activities for this case study, please go to LaunchPad
at macmillanhighered.com/speakup4e.

You can use signposts to show that you are at a specific place in
your speech (for example, "to preview my main ideas," "my third point
is," or "in summary"). You also can use signposts to indicate that you

SPEECH CHOICES

A CASE STUDY: *JACOB*
Here's how Jacob went about organizing his ideas.

Jacob needed to get going: he was presenting in two days. The speech was supposed to be at least a thousand words, and Jacob was determined to make that mark. He began by writing his introduction, telling the story of his favorite basketball player, Anthony Davis, who left college after one year to play professional basketball. Next, Jacob wrote down the opinion of his roommate, the former football player, to support the claim that scholarships did not provide student athletes with enough money. These two points took almost three hundred words. He was on his way!

YOUR TURN:
How did Jacob's procrastination limit his ability to construct a strong speech?

Jacob cut and pasted several chunks of information from the article he found on Google, and he made it to six hundred words. Jacob then added his own opinions about why students on revenue-producing sports teams deserved to be paid a salary, supported by statistics. Finally, he added his plan. He had over one thousand words! Time to call it a day.

For more questions and activities for this case study, and to see ⊙ video clips from Jacob's speech on presenting and developing main points, speech organization, and the "solution" main point, please go to LaunchPad at macmillanhighered.com/speakup4e.

are about to cite research ("according to") or to indicate that a key point is coming ("if you remember one idea from this speech, I hope it's that . . ."). In addition, signposts help your audience understand the structure of your subpoints. For example, in a persuasive speech advocating education reform, you might have a main point on the causes of poor student performance. You then could write your subpoints with signposts, as follows:

- *One cause* of poor student performance is inadequate funding of public schools.
- *Another cause* is educators' low expectations for students.
- *An additional cause* is that athletics receive higher priority than do academics.

Internal Previews and Internal Summaries

In crafting your speech, you may have selected a main point or subpoint that needs several different points of support or requires considerable detail to develop. To help the audience follow your explanation of a complex point, you may want to use an **internal preview**—a short list of the ideas that will follow. Or to help the audience remember a particularly detailed point, you might use an **internal summary**—a quick review of what you just said in your point.

For example, in an informative speech on test strategies, suppose that one of your main points covers test preparation. You might state your main point followed by an *internal preview*, as shown here:

Test taking requires good planning and healthy living. *The four steps for test preparation that I will cover are as follows: plan your study time in advance, follow your study schedule, get a good night's sleep, and eat a healthy breakfast.*

In a speech on limiting student loan debt, you might follow a main point on possible solutions with an *internal summary*:

To review my proposed solutions: First, never use loans for nonessential items such as dorm furniture. Second, limit total borrowing to your expected first-year salary. Finally, use federal loans, which have a fixed interest rate, whenever possible.[9]

CHAPTER REVIEW

> **"Good organization makes the message clear."**

In this chapter, we focused on the importance of a well-organized speech and presented strategies for organizing the body of your speech. Good organization helps your audience understand your message and enhances your credibility as a speaker. Remember the following principles when you organize the body of your speech: With your purpose and audience in mind, select an appropriate number of main points. Organize your supporting materials to back up each main point. Arrange your main points in a pattern that will best convey your ideas to the audience. Finally, use organizing words and sentences to help the audience keep track of where you are in a speech.

 LaunchPad
macmillan learning

LaunchPad for *Speak Up* offers videos and encourages self-assessment through adaptive quizzing. Go to **macmillanhighered.com/speakup4e** to get access to:

✓ **LearningCurve**
  Adaptive Quizzes

▶ **Video clips that help you understand public speaking concepts**

Key Terms

body *255*
◉ main point *255*
  supporting point *255*
  subordination *259*
  subpoint *259*
  sub-subpoint *259*
  coordination *259*
◉ spatial pattern *263*
◉ chronological (temporal) pattern *264*

◉ causal pattern *264*
  comparison pattern *266*
◉ categorical (topical) pattern *266*
◉ transition *269*
  signpost *271*
  internal preview *274*
  internal summary *274*

Review Questions

1. What three main factors should a speaker consider when selecting her or his main points?

2. Explain the importance of subordination and coordination when organizing supporting materials.

3. Name and describe five organizational patterns that you can use to arrange the main points of your speech.

4. Describe transitions, signposts, and internal previews and summaries, and explain how these types of organizing language help speakers indicate the structure of their speech to the audience.

Critical Thinking Questions

1. In what ways does organizing a speech resemble organizing a piece of written work? How does it differ? Are there any organizational tools that a writer can use that a speaker cannot? Does a speaker have any options that a writer does not?

2. Which kinds of organizational patterns do you think are most common in public speaking? Is there one kind of pattern that you think can work for almost any speech?

3. Select a speech from a Web site such as AmericanRhetoric.com or Gifts of Speech (gos.sbc.edu). How could you revise the main points or add organizing language to make the speech's structure more apparent to the audience?

4. In the illustration on page 269, the speaker dons a large hat whenever he makes a main point. Although this is clearly an exaggeration, might a speaker use nonverbal cues or presentation aids to help the audience navigate his or her speech? Would such tools work if the speech itself did not make proper use of organizing language?

Activities

1. Consider Carly's speech about women's magazines, described at the beginning of the chapter. If you were to reorganize her speech, how would you do it?

2. Working in groups, select three organizational patterns, and choose a topic area. For each pattern you have chosen, write the

title (in one sentence) of three to five main points on your topic that fit that pattern.

3. ✒ Review the comparison pattern illustration on page 267. Then think of three points of comparison between being a student in college and high school. Illustrate each point of comparison (stick figures are all right).

4. ⊙ **Video Activity 9.4: "List, Gender-Based Responses in Sports Chat Rooms."** From Amanda List's informative speech on gender and sports chat rooms, can you identify what her main points are? Does she use transitions, signposts, or other organizational devices to clarify the structure of her speech? How could she use the advice presented in this chapter to improve her organization?

5. ✒ Consider the newscaster illustration on page 274. With that image in mind, watch a broadcast of a nightly newscast, and jot down the different types of transitions, internal previews, and internal summaries that are used by the news anchor. What purpose do they serve? Would you use the same tools in a speech? Why or why not?

Study Plan

_____

_____

_____

_____

_____

_____

_____

_____

_____

_____

_____

INTRODUCTIONS AND CONCLUSIONS

10

❝Strong introductions create audience interest; strong conclusions create lasting impressions.❞

You've finally had time to break away from your schoolwork and see the latest James Bond movie. You're sitting in the theater, munching popcorn as the curtains open, the lights dim, and the film's opening sequence starts to roll. Every element of that sequence—the music, the visuals, the credits for the movie's title and cast—conveys information about the film and heightens your desire to see more.

For the next two hours, you're transported into an exciting world. And at the end of the movie, you're left with the lasting sense that you've had a great time. The final close-ups of Bond's face, the swelling of the classic James Bond theme, and the sweeping views of gorgeous scenery as the camera pans back: all of these elements combine to conclude your experience on a satisfying note.

Just as a movie's opening and closing elements powerfully influence the quality of your theater experience, your speech's introduction and conclusion play crucial roles in your audience's reception of your message. An effective introduction builds audience interest, orients audience members to the speech, and establishes your credibility as a speaker, and a strong conclusion leaves audience members with an enduring impression of your speech.

After planning the body of your speech, your next step is to prepare the introduction and conclusion. Although these elements are shorter than the body, they're just as crucial. After all, you won't get your message across unless your audience is eager to listen. You also want your audience to remember your presentation long after it ends—so they can put the information you've imparted to them into action. In this chapter, we show you how to craft memorable beginnings and endings to your presentations.

INTRODUCING YOUR SPEECH

In public speaking, as in many other situations in life, first impressions are vital. Your introduction creates a first impression of you as a speaker *and* of your message. For as long as people have discussed speechmaking, scholars have recognized the importance of the introduction: Cicero included the introduction as one of six essential parts of a speech,[1] and contemporary scholars note that the introduction is a key opportunity for the speaker to build a bond with the audience.[2]

A good introduction thus accomplishes a number of important purposes:

- Gains your audience's attention
- Signals your thesis
- Shows the relevance of the topic for your audience
- Establishes your credibility
- Previews your main points

Your introduction must accomplish all this in a brief period of time. For example, in a five- to ten-minute speech, the introduction should take no more than one minute. With these kinds of time constraints, there's no doubt about it: your introduction needs to be efficient *and* effective. Let's look more closely at each of the objectives your introduction must achieve.

Gain Your Audience's Attention

Begin your speech with an **attention-getter**—material intended to capture the audience's interest at the start of a speech. People listening to a presentation may have other things on their minds (for example, a problem at home, a distracting sound coming from the next room, or worries about an upcoming test or paper). You need to help your listeners redirect their focus from these other matters to you and your message. Otherwise, they won't absorb or remember the information you convey in your speech.

How do you craft an effective attention-getter? The following guidelines can help.

Tell a Story or an Anecdote. Most people love a good story, so opening with one can be a compelling yet comfortable way to begin your speech. If you start your speech with a story, be sure it relates to your message, takes up an appropriate amount of time, and comes across as believable. Avoid making up a story to open your speech unless you note that you are offering a hypothetical example.

Here is how one student used an anecdote to begin a speech about reforming the No Child Left Behind education law:

The May 2, 2005, issue of *Time* magazine reported that in the Utah War of 1857 to 1858, President James Buchanan sent thousands of federal troops into the territory to install a non-Mormon governor. The people of Utah did not respond well. They spooked the federal livestock, burned federal wagons, and incinerated over 300,000 tons of military provisions. Nearly 150 years later, the Utah legislature sent another message to Washington by becoming the first state to pass a bill that gives schools options for ignoring the No Child Left Behind Act.

Notice how the anecdote about Utah in the 1850s grabs the audience's attention by relating a dramatic historical incident in vivid language and startling detail. The story also relates to the speech's topic because in both cases, the state of Utah rebels against a federal mandate.

Offer a Striking or Provocative Statement.

A compelling fact or idea pertaining to your topic can immediately pull the audience into your speech. For example, you might present a surprising statistic or make an ironic statement to defy your listeners' expectations about what they'll hear during your speech. This approach works only if you present a fact or an idea that's new, ironic, or counterintuitive to your audience. You also are likely to be more effective if you incorporate dynamic language into your striking or provocative statement.

Consider Václav Havel, a playwright and dissident who became the first popularly elected president of Czechoslovakia in more than forty years. From 1948 until 1989, Czechoslovakia was under the rule of corrupt, authoritarian Communist leaders, and after the Soviet Union and its allies invaded the country in 1968, Havel's works were banned. He

was arrested many times in the 1970s and 1980s and was a leader of the 1989 nonviolent Velvet Revolution. On January 1, 1990, in his first presidential address to the Czech people, Havel offered a striking statement that differentiated him from his unelected predecessors, who had controlled the Czech media and propagandized the government's achievements:

> My dear fellow citizens, for forty years on this day you heard from my predecessors the same thing in a number of variations: how our country is flourishing, how many millions of tons of steel we produce, how happy we all are, how we trust our government, and what bright prospects lie ahead of us. I assume you did not propose me for this office so that I, too, should lie to you.[3]

Build Suspense. Consider increasing audience curiosity and anticipation before you reveal your topic. For example, "What will be one of the biggest problems in the next ten years?" or "One of the most exotic vacation spots in the world is unknown to 98 percent of American tourists." Here's how one student built curiosity in the introduction of his speech:

> There is a growing problem on our campus. Affected students find it difficult to wake up and get to class. They may experience threats to their academic performance, physical health, and mental health, too. The problem is bingeing. I'm not referring to binge eating or drinking, although these are serious problems. If you've ever stayed up all night watching *Game of Thrones*, *The Walking Dead*, or *Orange Is the New Black*, you know what I am talking about.

This student then proceeded to document the risks of excessive binge watching and offered tips for controlling the time students spend viewing their favorite shows.

Let Listeners Know You're One of Them. Consider highlighting similarities or shared interests between you and the audience. When listeners believe that a speaker is like them, they tend to see him or her as more credible—something that encourages them to pay close attention to the speech. However, to make this type of attention-getter effective, be sure to assert *genuine* common ground. Otherwise, you won't win your audience's confidence.

Here's how one student highlighted common ground in a speech about the resources available on the U.S. Department of Agriculture's ChooseMyPlate Web site:

> When I surveyed our class, I discovered that over 70 percent of you agreed with this statement: "I try to eat a healthy diet." Like many of you, I have been on a diet more than once, and I do my best to eat my fruits and vegetables. I would like to share one of the best resources that I have found—the U.S. Department of Agriculture's ChooseMyPlate Web site. This site shows how to select healthy meals from fruits, vegetables, grains, protein, and dairy products, and it includes a variety of tools to help you achieve your nutrition and fitness goals.[4]

Use Humor. Most people enjoy jokes, amusing stories, or other humorous references. A funny or playful attention-getter can be a great way to gain audience interest, break the ice, and enhance your credibility. However, not all humor is created equal. If you begin a speech with humor, the material should relate to your topic. Also, consider your audience members, and choose material they will find funny. Don't tell jokes or stories that may offend some or all of your listeners.

Also note that using humor as your attention-getter can be a high-risk, high-reward approach. If the audience appreciates a joke, your credibility is liable to increase, you'll feel especially confident, and your speech will be off to a great start. For example, here is how an informative speaker began her speech about scientific skepticism regarding extrasensory perception (ESP):

If you have ESP, raise your hand, and tell the audience what this speech will be about.

If you have trouble telling jokes or remembering punch lines, you may find that a relevant anecdote from your own life is a better source of humor. At one time or another, most people have told a funny story about something that has happened to them. This more personal approach may help you feel more relaxed and conversational.

Ask a Rhetorical Question. A **rhetorical question**—one that you want listeners to answer in their heads—can capture audience members' attention because it gets them thinking about your speech topic. For example, to introduce a speech about the Winter Olympics, you could ask, "What's the first sport that comes to mind when you think about the Winter Olympics?" Make sure your rhetorical question addresses something of interest to your audience. And avoid asking overly general questions ("What would you like to learn about winter sports?"). Your listeners won't find them as interesting as more focused queries.

Here is how a speaker could use a rhetorical question to gain audience attention in a speech about digilantism,[5] or vigilante behaviors on the Internet:

> Imagine that a photo of the back of your car (showing the license plate number, your bumper stickers, and a rather large dent) driving past a visible street sign appeared on a social media forum in your community. Below it was this caption—"40 mph in a school zone." You are confident that you have never gone over the speed limit on that street. How would you feel?

Provide a Quotation. A stimulating quotation that illuminates your topic can make an effective attention-getter—especially if you're quoting someone your audience likes and respects or if the quotation is thought provoking or counterintuitive. For example, in a speech about the credibility of *Wikipedia*, you might quote a related joke from Stephen Colbert about the site: "It's the first place I go when I'm looking for knowledge, or when I want to create some."[6]

You also can quote an expert in the field as an attention-getter. Consider the beginning of a speech on the need for college students to improve their sleep patterns:

> According to Dr. LeAnne Forquer and her colleagues in the Central Michigan University psychology department, "Adolescents and young adults, including college students, appear to be one of the most sleep-deprived groups in the United States. Individuals in this group require about 9 hours of sleep each night; however, most receive only 7 to 8 hours. This sleep deprivation can have detrimental effects on performance, including driving and academics."[7]

▶ **To see an example of an attention-getter in a speech on housing policy, try Video Activity 10.1: "Anecdote (Personal) in an Informative Introduction."**

Signal Your Thesis

After you've riveted your listeners' attention, your next step is to indicate the thesis of your speech. You can use your topic statement for this purpose. Recall from Chapter 6 that your thesis statement is the single sentence that expresses the aspect of the topic you will be emphasizing in your speech: your thesis conveys the speech's "bottom line." Providing this statement early in the speech answers a question that is in the minds of many audience members—"What will this speech be about?" It also helps listeners to focus on your message rather than use their mental energy figuring out what your speech topic might be.

Your thesis statement should clearly convey your topic and purpose in delivering the presentation, further preparing your audience members to listen. It also should be specific and include a signpost that makes it clear that your attention-getter is finished and you are now revealing your topic. Consider the following example:

ATTENTION-GETTER

I. The tallest mountain in North America. Grizzly bears eating berries just ten feet from the road. Clean, fresh air that you will not find in "the lower forty-eight."

TWO POSSIBLE THESIS STATEMENTS

II. *Vague thesis statement:* All these features can be found in a pristine wilderness environment.

II. *Specific thesis statement:*
You can find all these features in Denali National Park, Alaska, and I hope to convince you to visit Denali.

Notice that the specific thesis statement clarifies that the subject of the speech is Denali and that the presenter's purpose is to persuade his audience to go there.

Show Your Audience What's in It for Them

After you have revealed your thesis, you need to generate audience interest and motivate active listening. Our former colleague Dr. Gail Sorenson referred to this as "What's in it for me?" or WIIFM ("whiff-em"). Through WIIFM, you clarify why your message is relevant to and important for your listeners.

To accomplish this goal, provide one sentence or a short paragraph that indicates why the audience should take an interest in your topic. Instead of going on and

VAGUE THESIS STATEMENT

SPECIFIC THESIS STATEMENT

on, give listeners just enough to whet their appetite. You'll go into more detail in the body of your speech, where you'll show how the ideas or suggestions in your presentation will benefit listeners.

Following are some examples of effective WIIFM statements:

- The dangerous practice drunkorexia—or eating little food during the day to offset calories consumed by drinking in the evening—is not just a problem on somebody else's campus. The director of our health center reports that this is a growing concern at our college.

- I doubt that many of you have lost sleep over the state budget deficit. It did not make my "Top Ten Worries" list, either. But

WHAT'S IN IT FOR ME?

when I found out that our tuition had increased by 27 percent this year as one means of making up the shortfall, I started to worry. And you should, too.

- Today we will consider the history of the 1846 war between the United States and Mexico from a Mexican perspective. This will provide an alternative to the romanticized version many of us were taught in our high school history classes.

- My survey showed that 77 percent of this class believes they are spending too much time on school and work at the expense of their social lives. So instead of focusing on academics today, let's take a brief look at the art of asking someone out on a date.

Establish Your Credibility

Your audience members now know what they'll get out of listening to your speech. Next, you need to answer the question, "Why should we listen to *you*? What makes you a credible source on this topic?"

How do you build credibility? You do it the same way that your sources of evidence do—by showing that you have relevant experience and education and that you've thoroughly researched the subject area

of your speech. You gain even more credibility when your listeners see you as trustworthy and perceive that you have their best interests at heart.

To establish credibility, explain how you have gained knowledge about your topic. In one or two sentences, emphasize your most relevant credentials (resist the urge to recite your entire résumé or life history!), making sure to adopt a modest, nonsuperior tone.

A student speaker named Alexandra established her credibility in an informative speech about judging competitive ice skating by emphasizing her own relevant experience. Alexandra was especially qualified to speak on the subject because she won nearly one hundred awards during her skating career and also served as a judge at several prestigious skating events in her home state. She could have chosen to discuss her many accomplishments in the sport, but she chose to establish her credibility in this clear, concise, and unpretentious way:

> I have been active in the sport of ice skating since I was six years old and have won my fair share of events. I still love skating, so after retiring from competition, I became certified as a judge and have judged at many competitions during the past two years.

With this information, Alexandra left no doubt in her listeners' minds that she was a good source of information on ice skating. She also held their interest by summarizing her experience without providing excessive detail about specific awards or competitions, which would have meant little to them.

Preview Your Main Points

A **preview** is a brief statement of the main points you will be developing in the body of your speech. It lets your audience members know what main ideas to expect and helps them visualize the structure of your speech—the sequence of ideas you'll present. Your preview should consist of no more than one sentence per main point.

To differentiate the main points in your preview, include *signposts* (for example, *first*, *next*, and *finally*) to help your audience grasp the structure of your speech. Also, avoid the use of *and* or other connecting words while previewing a single main point.

Consider the two previews on the next page, which Alexandra might use in her speech about judging competitive ice skating.

WEAKER PREVIEW

The rules of judging and the ways you can judge, along with the many controversies about Olympic judges, are all interesting aspects of judging competitive skating.

STRONGER PREVIEW

Today we'll look at *three major topics* about judging competitive ice skating: *first*, we'll look at rules for judging a skating event; *then*, I'll share some tips you can use to score the performances yourself; and *finally*, I'll discuss some of the judging controversies that have occurred at past Olympics.

Both of these previews offer information about the main points to be developed. However, the first preview is much less explicit than the second. It mentions the three points Alexandra plans to cover but runs them together in a single clause. This doesn't help the audience understand the structure of the speech. This preview also contains no hints indicating that Alexandra is previewing her main points. This statement could just as easily be an attempt to connect with the audience. By contrast, the strong second preview clearly signals the speech structure, making it easy for Alexandra's audience to recognize the main points and the sequence in which she will cover them.

> ▶ To watch a preview in a speech about groundbreaking cancer treatments, try Video Activity 10.2, "Attention-Getter, Support, Creative Preview."

CONCLUDING YOUR SPEECH

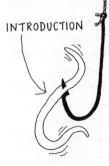

INTRODUCTION

Your introduction helps you set the stage for your speech, and your conclusion serves another equally important purpose: it helps you sum up the message you developed in the body of your speech and leave a memorable impression with your audience members. Don't use the conclusion to develop new ideas about your topic or further expand on points you've just made. Instead, use it to highlight content you have already presented. A good conclusion generally takes one minute or less (few sins of a speaker are worse than saying "in conclusion" and then continuing to

speak for several more minutes). Your conclusion should start with a *transition, summarize
your main points*, and *finish with a memorable clincher*. We examine each of these
elements in this section.

Transition to Your Conclusion

After presenting your final main point,
insert some transitional language that signals you're ready to wrap up your presen-
tation. For example, a persuasive speech encouraging students to participate
in a campus food drive might offer this transition to the conclusion:

> Today *we have seen* how important it is for every member of this
> class to participate in our annual campus food drive.

In this example, the use of the phrase *we have seen* signals that you're
finished with the main part of your speech and ready to move on to the
next part. Here's another example of a transition into the conclusion:

> I hope *you have learned more* about the first cultures to inhabit
> the Americas.

Summarize Your Main Points

The first part of your conclusion is a **summary**, a brief review of your main
points. The summary is similar to the preview of your main points that you
offered in your introduction, except that here you are reminding the audience of what you already said instead of telling them what ideas you'll be
presenting. You may summarize in a single compound sentence that covers
each main point, or you may restate each main point in a complete sentence. In either case, your goal is to remind the audience of your main ideas
one last time. An effective summary helps listeners remember your message
by enabling them to put your speech together in their own minds.

Be sure that your summary includes each main point from your speech.
That way, you'll break the speech down into manageable sections for your
audience members and remind them of the presentation's structure.

Here is how Alexandra might summarize her main points during the
conclusion of her speech about judging competitive ice skating:

DON'T REGURGITATE YOUR WHOLE SPEECH... SUMMARIZE IT WITH QUICK BULLET POINTS

This afternoon *we have covered* three major topics about judging competitive ice skating. First, we considered the main rules for judging ice skating. Then, we considered some tips for you to use if you want to score at home. Finally, we considered controversies in the judging at past Olympics.

Note how Alexandra made a clear reference to each main point and used the past tense to help the audience recognize that she was reviewing her points rather than developing new material.

Finish with a Memorable Clincher

Finish your conclusion with a **clincher**—something that leaves a lasting impression of your speech in your listeners' minds. After your speech ends, audience members will have countless demands on their time and attention. To make your presentation memorable, select and word your clincher carefully.

The clincher should take only about thirty seconds in a five- to ten-minute speech. Rock musicians have been known to smash their guitars at the end of a show to leave a lasting impression. We would not recommend such mayhem in a speech, but there are a number of less destructive strategies you can use to make your speech memorable. Following are several ways to craft a good clincher.

Tie Your Clincher to the Introduction.

If you began your speech with a compelling anecdote or example, consider extending it in your clincher. One speech asking audience members to serve as volunteer tutors began with the story of Hector, a twelve-year-old at risk of dropping out of school because he had fallen behind. The presenter effectively touched again on Hector's story in her clincher:

> Remember Hector, the boy who was on the verge of dropping out in sixth grade? Ana, a student at this university, became his tutor and role model. Today, Hector has a B average in high school and has applied to several colleges. There are many more Hectors in our local schools, and your help as a tutor will make sure that there is a happy ending to their stories, too.

End with a Striking Sentence or Phrase.

There may be a single sentence or phrase that effectively sums up your speech. Advertisers and political campaign managers often use this technique because the words are easy to remember. For example, an advertiser refers to a product as "the one," or a campaign manager describes his candidate as possessing "the right stuff for the job." We do not recommend ending your speech with a trivial phrase or a catchy tune. However, do consider using memorable, relevant phrasing to conclude your speech.

SPEECH CHOICES

A CASE STUDY: MIA

With her main points organized, it was time for Mia to plan her introduction and conclusion.

After Mia organized the body of her speech with main points and supporting materials, she budgeted some time the next day to draft her introduction and conclusion. She considered several different options for her attention-getter. This was an important decision if she wanted to pull her audience into the speech. She thought about using a quotation from an emigrant about the importance of smartphones or possibly an anecdote about how an emigrant had used a smartphone. In the end, she decided to ask a rhetorical question that would encourage audience members to think about what they might need if they were emigrating from a war-torn country.

Mia already had drafted her thesis, so next she considered how to connect the topic to the audience. She knew that a number of her classmates' families had their own stories of emigration and that they were regularly on their smartphones, so she decided to use this combination. Then she considered her own credibility, emphasizing the research she had done to prepare for the speech. Finally, she drafted a clear preview of her three main points.

For her conclusion, Mia began with a summary of each main point. She then thought about tying her attention-getter and clincher together by asking listeners another rhetorical question after they had heard about the usefulness of smartphones. But she had an even more dramatic story of an emigrant, Mohamed, who was with other emigrants on a boat that lost its engine in the Mediterranean. Mohamed used his smartphone to find his latitude and longitude coordinates and texted them to his cousin in Hawaii, leading to his rescue. The narrative could be combined with a visual aid showing the actual text exchanges between Mohamed and his cousin. This would be a memorable way to end her presentation!

YOUR TURN:
Which type of attention-getter would best build your classmates' interest in a speech?

For more questions and activities for this case study, and to see ▶ video clips showing the introduction and conclusion from Mia's speech, please go to LaunchPad at macmillanhighered.com/speakup4e.

A speech about Hmong history effectively concluded with a theme that had been evident in each main point:

The word *Hmong* means "free." And no matter what continent we are living on, that is what we will always be—a free people.

SPEECH CHOICES

A CASE STUDY: *JACOB*

And this is how Jacob planned his introduction and conclusion.

Jacob knew he wanted to begin with the story of his favorite basketball player. For a minute, he wondered if Anthony Davis was actually a good example for his speech: Davis had signed a multimillion-dollar pro contract, far more than any proposed salary for college players. But, no. He had a plan, and he was sticking to it.

Jacob still needed to add to his introduction. He knew that his instructor was always talking about citing research sources. So as part of his introduction, Jacob listed his research sources. This would give him credibility and, he believed, spare him the need to cite sources as he used them in his speech.

Jacob didn't feel a need to write a conclusion, now that he had over one thousand words. He'd come up with something when he delivered his speech. An off-the-cuff ending probably would make it more exciting, anyway.

YOUR TURN:
What risks did Jacob take when he decided not to draft a conclusion?

For more questions and activities for this case study, and to see a ▶ video clip showing the introduction from Jacob's speech, please go to LaunchPad at macmillanhighered.com/speakup4e.

Also, consider Manal al-Sharif, a Saudi women's rights activist who was jailed after posting a YouTube video showing her driving a car. (Women are forbidden to drive in Saudi Arabia.) She used the following clincher in a speech to the Oslo Freedom Forum:

> The struggle is not about driving a car. It is about being in the driver's seat of our destiny.[8]

Highlight Your Thesis. Rather than summing up your speech with a single key sentence, you may decide to use a few lines to reinforce the heart of your message. Consider an example from Sally Ride, the first American woman in space (she was awarded a posthumous Presidential Medal of Freedom in 2013). After ending her career as an astronaut, Dr. Ride became a dedicated advocate for improving math and science education for kids. Here is how she concluded her speech "Shoot for the Stars":

FINISH WITH A MEMORABLE CLINCHER

When I was a little girl, I always dreamed of flying in space. And amazingly enough (I still cannot believe it to this day), that dream came true for me. Now it is up to all of us to ensure that this generation of students in school today has access to a high-quality education so the boys and the girls can build the foundation that will enable them to reach for the stars and achieve their dreams too.[9]

Conclude with an Emotional Message. Recall a speech or presentation that ended by appealing to your emotions. If you're like most people, that speech affected you more than a speech that used only cold hard facts. Often, a clincher that delivers an emotional charge makes a speech particularly memorable—especially in a persuasive or commemorative presentation. For example, one student concluded a tribute to a beloved pet in the following way:

My mind flooded with memories—finding him as a tiny kitten and nursing him to health with my own hands. He became my best friend. I let him go lovingly, with the same arms that held him fast as a baby. Good-bye, my friend. I'll never forget you.

End with a Story or an Anecdote. A story that illustrates the message of your speech can make an effective clincher. Consider the following anecdote about Albert Einstein that a student used as her clincher in a speech advocating greater efforts to raise students' self-esteem and prevent them from dropping out:

> Over one hundred years ago, there was a boy who was considered "backward" by his teachers. They said the boy was mentally slow and adrift forever in his foolish dreams. His father said that when he asked the headmaster what profession his son should adopt, he was told, "It doesn't matter; he'll never make a success of anything."[10]
>
> Who was that hopeless student? Believe it or not, his name was Albert Einstein.
>
> We must never give up on the mind of a child. Educators must convince every student that he or she is valued and capable of learning. Even one dropout is unacceptable.

> ▶ To see an example of a clincher in a speech about college instructors, try Video Activity 10.3, "Clincher: Evokes Response."

CHAPTER REVIEW

> Strong introductions create audience interest; strong conclusions create lasting impressions.

In this chapter, we provided ideas for crafting effective introductions and conclusions for your speeches. We noted that a good introduction has several purposes—including capturing your audience's attention, indicating your thesis, conveying the importance of your topic for audience members, establishing your credibility, and previewing your main points.

We also showed that an effective conclusion transitions smoothly from the body of your speech, helps your audience remember your main points, and enables you to leave a lasting impression on listeners. There are many strategies to choose from in developing your introduction and conclusion, so you have room to be creative. By tailoring these elements of your speech to your audience and allotting the right amount of time to each, you stand an excellent chance of delivering an effective presentation.

 LaunchPad
macmillan learning

LaunchPad for *Speak Up* offers videos and encourages self-assessment through adaptive quizzing. Go to **macmillanhighered.com/speakup4e** to get access to:

 **LearningCurve
Adaptive Quizzes**

 **Video clips that help you understand
public speaking concepts**

Key Terms

attention-getter *281*   summary *294*
rhetorical question *286*   clincher *295*
preview *292*

Review Questions

1. Briefly explain the five major functions of a good introduction.
2. Describe seven specific strategies you can use to create an attention-getting introduction.
3. What three steps must you take to develop a solid conclusion?
4. Offer five types of memorable clinchers.

Critical Thinking Questions

1. Why is it important to offer an attention-getting introduction in a speech? In what kinds of public speaking situations do you think it might be preferable to present a less dramatic or entertaining opener?

2. How can you effectively use audience analysis to determine whether humor would be a good attention-getting strategy and whether a particular joke will work or fall flat?

3. What happens if you fail to present a solid conclusion to your speech?

Activities

1. Working in groups, select a potential speech topic. Then have each group member select a different attention-gaining strategy and use that strategy to develop an attention-getter. Share your attention-getter with other group members.

2. Imagine that you are about to give a speech to a group of total strangers you know little about. How would you use your introduction to establish credibility? How would this differ from the way you would establish credibility to a group you had something in common with—for example, students at your college, members of your religious faith, or people who participate in the same sport or activity that you do?

3. Working in groups, select a potential speech topic that is relevant at your campus. Then discuss how you could show each of the following audiences "what's in it for them": students who work while attending school, student athletes, students who are active in extracurricular activities, students with children.

4. ✐ Review the illustration "Finish with a Memorable Clincher" and the accompanying text on page 299. Imagine you are presenting a speech on a problem of concern in your community. Indicate what your topic would be, and develop your own memorable clincher, using astronaut Sally Ride's speech as an example.

5. ▶ **Video Activity 10.4: "Full Introduction: Attention-Getter, Thesis, and Preview" and "Full Conclusion."** Watch the introduction and conclusion to Cameron's speech analyzing a quotation by Confucius. Which parts of an introduction does he include (attention-getter, thesis, connection with the audience, credibility, preview)? Does his conclusion include a summary and a clincher? Evaluate the quality of his introduction and conclusion. Is there anything you would add or change?

Study Plan

_____

_____

_____

_____

_____

_____

_____

_____

_____

_____

_____

_____

_____

_____

_____

_____

_____

_____

_____

_____

_____

OUTLINING IS USEFUL (AND FUN)

11

OUTLINING YOUR SPEECH

"A good outline strengthens organization and preparation." Veenu, the mother of two young children, was active in her kids' education and had been elected to the School Site Council twice. She was pleased with the teachers and classes at her children's school, but at the end of the school year, a problem loomed. Her first-grader was assigned to a new combination second- and third-grade class for September. She did not think that her daughter would thrive when mixed in with older students. Other parents also were concerned about the combination class.

Administrators scheduled several School Site Council meetings to discuss combination classes. Most parents at these meetings spoke ineffectively, expressing their outrage, complaining that their own child was mistreated, but presenting few useful ideas that could help the council make improvements. It was a relief when their speaking time was up. Veenu did not want to be one of those parents and was determined to make a difference.

Veenu talked to teachers and parents involved with combination classes at other schools in her city. Based on these conversations, she decided to focus on three main points—the problems students experienced in combination classes, the challenges teachers faced in these classes, and ideas for how her school could provide support for the students and teachers who were assigned to these classes. She wrote down these three main points and under each one listed the ideas she could use to support that point. Then she practiced her speech to become familiar with the material and make it fit into the available time. After she knew her speech well, she wrote brief notes on her tablet that she could refer to if needed.

Veenu's speech was a success. She knew the material well and was able to look at audience members while speaking. She expressed her main ideas clearly, and the School Site Council adopted several of her suggestions for the combination class.

Veenu's use of **outlining**—organizing the content of her speech into a structured form—played a big role in her success. Outlines can help you plan and organize a successful speech, too. They can help you lay out the sequence and hierarchy of your ideas so that you can see if your speech flows logically and covers the subject matter adequately. You also can use an outline to practice your delivery and then present your speech with confidence and flair. In most speech situations, an outline can help you further polish your skills. Even seasoned presenters find outlining highly useful!

The key function of *all* outlines is to show the hierarchy of the ideas in your speech—your main points and the material that supports each main point. By using alphanumeric headings (beginning with roman numerals for main points and moving through capital letters, arabic numerals, and so on) and indentation, you can present all of your points and show how your points are supported by evidence. This system makes outlines different from manuscripts and essays, which are organized paragraph by paragraph. In this chapter, we discuss the creation of two types of outlining—a working outline and a speaking outline.

TWO STAGES OF OUTLINING

Imagine that you're about to set off on a car trip to a place you've never been before. Unless you have GPS and can type in the address of your destination, there are two steps you probably would take before you begin. First, you'd likely consult a Web site like Google Maps to assess

THIS IS AN OUTLINE

I. How an outline helps speakers organize their thinking

    A. Shows relationships between ideas

        1. SHOWS IDEAS IN THE ORDER OF PRESENTATION

        2. SHOWS WHICH IDEAS ARE MOST IMPORTANT

II. How outlines can improve presentations

THIS IS A MANUSCRIPT, NOT AN OUTLINE

Today I will discuss the major ways that outlines are especially important tools for public speakers. First, outlines show relationships between ideas by showing ideas in their presentation order and showing which ideas are the most important.

307

where you need to go, how you might get there, and how long it would take. You'd study the route, commit the general picture to memory, and figure out any tricky portions. Second, you might print out a brief set of directions that summarize the information from the map ("Take this highway to that exit, turn right at this street," and so on) so that you could glance at the printout while driving.

In much the same way as you'd take these two steps to ensure a safe journey, many speech instructors suggest taking two steps when outlining your speech. In fact, many instructors require two versions of your outline for each presentation. The first is usually known as a *working outline*, which functions as a road map to help you prepare your speech. The second is known as a *speaking outline*, which, like a brief set of directions, provides you with quick and easy-to-follow notes you can refer to without really "taking your eyes off the road"—or, in this case, your audience.

In this section, we take a look at these two types of outlines, each of which represents an important step in the development of your presentation. But it's essential for you to check with your instructor about his or her requirements for outlining in your speech course. Individual instructors have different philosophies about creating outlines, so be sure to follow your instructor's requirements.

The Working Outline

A **working outline** (also referred to as a *detailed* or *preparation outline*) is a long outline that you use to craft your speech. A working outline should include all elements of your entire speech—from attention-getter to clincher—with each idea written down in full sentences or detailed phrases (depending on your instructor's preference). If you were to wake up with laryngitis on the day of your presentation, another classmate should be able to use your working outline to deliver your speech.

A working outline offers many benefits, both for you and for your instructor. Because it is detailed and formatted in a way that shows the hierarchy of ideas, it helps you assess the content and organization of your speech, ensure that your thesis and main points are well supported, and create smooth transitions between (and connections among) all the points and evidence you present. Because your instructor might wish to review your working outline to evaluate your preparation effort, it should show that you have included all required components, cited research sources properly, developed your ideas in sufficient detail, and organized all of your information thoughtfully. Finally, your working outline can serve as a reference when you *begin* to practice your speech, helping you become familiar with the content. After you've become more comfortable with the material, you're ready to transition to a speaking outline.

The Speaking Outline

A **speaking outline** is a short outline that expresses your ideas in brief phrases, key words, or abbreviations rather than in complete sentences or detailed phrases. You will use this outline when you actually deliver your speech. Like the brief set of driving directions we talked about earlier, this brief outline (often written on note cards rather than manuscript paper) provides quick notes that you refer to, rather than read, as you deliver your speech.

FULL SENTENCE:

The study showed that even a large spider, on a good day, makes only 1.5 mg of silk.

The purpose of a speaking outline is to facilitate **extemporaneous delivery**. As we discuss in both Chapter 2 and Chapter 13, extemporaneous delivery requires that you speak with limited notes—not recite from memory or read word-for-word from a manuscript. Your limited notes are a reminder of what idea comes next, but when you trust yourself to deliver the details more spontaneously, your speech feels fresh and conversational.

DETAILED PHRASE:

Study—large spider on good day makes 1.5 mg silk

BRIEF PHRASE / KEY WORD:

Study: Best = 1.5 mg silk

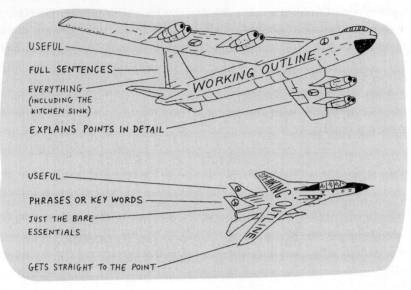

USEFUL

FULL SENTENCES

EVERYTHING
(INCLUDING THE
KITCHEN SINK)

EXPLAINS POINTS IN DETAIL

WORKING OUTLINE

USEFUL

PHRASES OR KEY WORDS

JUST THE BARE
ESSENTIALS

GETS STRAIGHT TO THE POINT

SPEAKING OUTLINE

CREATING YOUR WORKING OUTLINE

A working outline consists of three main sections—the introduction, the body, and the conclusion of your speech. (Most instructors will recommend that you outline the body of your speech first and then go back to outline the introduction and conclusion.) As you create your working outline, label each of these three parts ("Introduction," "Body," and "Conclusion") in bold so that you can more easily see the speech's structure.

Outlining the Body of Your Speech

You can think of the **body** of your speech as representing the "meat" of your presentation. In the body, you'll present your main points and supporting materials (such as examples, stories, statistics, and testimony from experts). The body thus contains most of the content of your speech. Follow the practices listed in this section to outline the body of your speech effectively.

Use proper labeling and indentation. Start each main point at the left margin of your working outline, and indicate each new main point with a roman numeral. Indent each of your subpoints, and label them with capital letters. If you develop a subpoint further with two or more supporting ideas, indicate each of these sub-subpoints with arabic numerals, and indent the sub-subpoints another step beneath the subpoint they

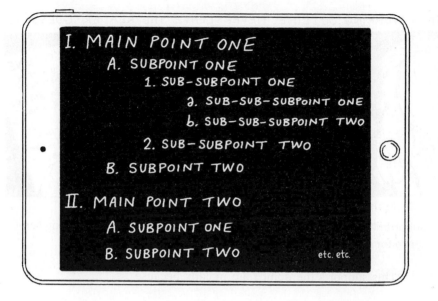

support. Typically, you'll want to include between two and four subpoints for each main point and the same number of sub-subpoints for each subpoint. (In a proper outline, support can never stand alone. You must *always* include a minimum of two subpoints supporting each main point and two sub-subpoints supporting each subpoint.)

Use full sentences or detailed phrases. In your working outline, you should express your main ideas, subpoints, and sub-subpoints in complete sentences or detailed phrases (each instructor will have his or her own preference for the level of detail required). As noted earlier, your working outline should be detailed enough that another person could deliver your speech from it. Furthermore, your instructor is likely to require you to turn in a copy of your working outline. If it is too brief, he or she may misinterpret the points you want to make or, even worse, conclude that you haven't put enough effort into preparing your speech.

Check for subordination. In a well-organized speech, supporting materials show **subordination** to their corresponding main points. Thus, be careful that each subpoint is relevant to the main point it's supposed to support and that each sub-subpoint relates to its corresponding subpoint. How can you tell whether your supporting materials show appropriate

IN A WORKING OUTLINE, NEVER LEAVE THE READER GUESSING

subordination to their corresponding point? Complete the following sentence for each of your supporting materials:

"This supports the point I am making because . . ."

If you can't come up with a logical way to complete this sentence, you may need to reexamine your supporting materials and find ways to make them more clearly relevant. For example, you might want to move a subpoint to a place in your outline where the idea fits better. Or you may decide to reword a main point or subpoint so that the supporting material more clearly explains or expands the idea it is meant to support. Finally, you could consider developing a supporting example or explanation into a main point.

SUBORDINATION

Include full information for citations, quotations, and other evidence. When you use evidence to support a claim, you need to include in your working outline all the information about the source of your **evidence**—the author, her or his qualifications, the source publication or Web page, and the date of publication. And if you are quoting a source, be sure to present the information word-for-word and enclose the information in quotation marks to indicate that you are using someone else's words.

For example, here's how you would outline evidence for a commemorative speech about Cammi Granato, one of the first two women elected to the Hockey Hall of Fame and a two-time U.S. team captain at the Winter Olympics. In this case, the evidence is used as subpoint A, which supports a main point about Granato's influence on young female hockey players:

    I. Cammi Granato is a role model for young girls.

       A. The Olympic gold medal was a catalyst. According to Barbara Ann Williams, a skating coach in the National Hockey League, in *Positive Power*, 2014, after the U.S. women's team defeated Canada in the 1998 gold medal game, "little girls were now able

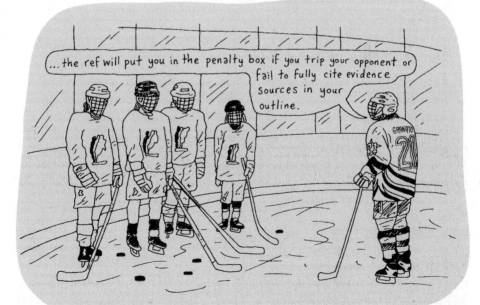

to turn on their TV's and see Cammi Granato, captain of the U.S. team, on Nike commercials with other famous athletes. These women had become our dream team and were the catalyst for the continued rise of interest in our sport."

Insert transitions. As discussed in earlier chapters, a **transition** is a sentence that indicates you are moving from one part of your speech to another. Using transitions helps you keep on track and makes it easier for listeners to follow along. At minimum, include transitions

- between the introduction and the body,
- when you move from one main point to the next, and
- between the body and the conclusion.

In your outline, indicate a transition by labeling it and placing it in brackets, as shown in the following example:

> [TRANSITION We have considered the physical skills needed to become a Navy Seal; next, let's turn our attention to mental abilities.]

> ◎ To see the use of transitions and signposts in a speech, try Video Activity 11.1, "Roth, Emergency in the Emergency Room."

Outlining Your Introduction

After you've outlined the body of your speech, turn to outlining the **introduction**. In Chapter 10, we identify the five purposes of an introduction—gaining your audience's attention, signaling your thesis, showing the relevance of your topic for your audience, establishing your credibility, and previewing your main points. Each of these purposes provides the basis for one part of your introduction. When you have prepared them, insert each one into your working outline. The introduction should include the following elements:

INTRODUCTION

   I. Attention-getter
  II. Thesis statement
 III. Relevance of topic for audience
 IV. Speaker's credibility
  V. Preview of main points

In your working outline, each of these five elements should be expressed in complete sentences or detailed phrases so that a reader would know what you were planning to say for each part.

Outlining Your Conclusion

After you've finished outlining your introduction, do the same for the **conclusion** of your speech. Just as the introduction grabs your listeners' attention, your conclusion should end your speech on a strong note. Start by outlining the two parts of the conclusion we discuss in Chapter 10—a summary of your main points and a clincher. When you have prepared these two parts, write them in your outline as roman numerals I and II. In your working outline, the conclusion should include the following elements (with each part expressed in complete sentences or detailed phrases):

CONCLUSION
    I. Summary of main points
    II. Clincher

> ▶ To identify the elements of an introduction and conclusion, try Video Activity 11.2, "Without Liberty and Justice for All."

Creating a List of Works Cited

Your instructor may require you to include a **list of works cited**—a list of the sources you cited in your speech—at the end of your outline. Your list should *not* include sources you discovered during your research but did not quote or otherwise use in your speech. Some colleges consider including unused sources in your references to be academic dishonesty and will take strict disciplinary action against students who commit this kind of wrongdoing.

If a list of works cited is required, include a full citation for each source you used in your speech. Your instructor probably will require you to use a particular style for documenting sources. The three most common documentation styles are those recommended by the American Psychological Association (APA), the Modern Language Association (MLA), and the *Chicago Manual of Style* (*CMS*). Regardless of which style you use, make sure to follow your instructor's requirements for the works cited.

A list of works cited is *not* a substitute for the proper citation and quotation of evidence in your outline or speech. Even if you include this list at the end of your working outline, it remains your ethical obligation to attribute all information that comes from research sources. Each time such information is used in your outline or speech, you must identify the source.

Inserting the Title, Specific Purpose, and Thesis

Some instructors also may ask you to write the title, specific purpose, and thesis of your speech at the top of your working outline to guide the development of your main and supporting points. If your professor has requested this information, indicate the title of your speech, and type or write it out in relatively large or bold type. Indicate your speech's specific purpose and thesis at the left margin, as shown in the following example from a speech on phantom energy.

THE HIDDEN COSTS OF PHANTOM ENERGY

SPECIFIC PURPOSE	To inform my audience about the nature and effects of phantom energy
THESIS	Many household devices consume phantom energy, wasting power and costing you money.

A SAMPLE WORKING OUTLINE

Josh Betancur of Santiago Canyon College developed a speech titled "Invisibility: Science Fiction No More!" In his presentation, he informed the audience about recent scientific developments in the field of invisibility. In this section, we show the full-sentence working outline of his speech, with updated evidence, along with annotations highlighting key concepts covered in this chapter.

INVISIBILITY: SCIENCE FICTION NO MORE!

SPECIFIC PURPOSE	To inform my audience about advances in the science of invisibility
THESIS	Invisibility science is making great progress.

BOGUS BIBLIOGRAPHIES = BIG TROUBLE

• Anecdote from comic book for attention-getter

INTRODUCTION •

I. After surviving a cosmic storm, comic book heroine Susan Storm was amazed that she was still alive and even more amazed that she had gained the power to become the Invisible Woman. By creating a force field, she could bend the light waves around her so that she could not be seen. This may sound like science fiction, which it is—for now.

II. Today we will take a look at advances in the science of invisibility.

III. These developments have the potential to affect every aspect of our lives—from aesthetics, architecture, and entertainment to the military, telecommunications, and transportation. •

• Introduction includes the five components—attention-getter, thesis, relevance to audience, credibility, and preview

IV. After conducting library research and interviews with professors on campus, I have been amazed to learn about the process of invisibility.

V. To understand this exciting new use of technology, it is necessary to first consider the physical science of invisibility, then review experiments attempting to render objects invisible, and finally have a better look (so to speak) at the tremendous effects that this technology could have on our lives in the future.

• Transition from introduction to body

[TRANSITION   Let's begin by considering what it takes to make an object invisible.] •

BODY

I. Invisibility requires transporting light around an object.

A. Fiction writers have depended on magical properties. •

• Subpoints and sub-subpoints are indented properly.

1. In Greek mythology, the Cyclops gave Hades an invisibility helmet to give him an advantage when battling the Titans.

2. British science fiction writer H. G. Wells wrote of a magic elixir that a person could drink to become invisible.

3. J. K. Rowling imagined an invisibility cloak for Harry Potter.

B. Rather than focusing on science fiction, researchers have focused on scientific principles.
  1. Visibility depends on light. In a personal
      interview on February 10, 2007, Profes-
      sor Craig Rutan, physics chair at Santiago
      Canyon College, explained that to make
      something appear invisible, you must find
      a way to transport light around the object.
      For example, for the blackboard in this
      room to be visible, light must travel toward
      it. If something blocks that light, the board
      will become invisible. •   • Full citation
  2. This effect explains how you see a mirage   of research
      on a hot summer road. In the November 2006   sources
      issue of *Discover*, Duke University physicists
      David Smith and Dave Schurig note that
      "when light rays from the sky hit the hot, thin
      air just above the surface of the asphalt, they
      bend. . . . Rays once headed from the sky to
      the ground are redirected to your eye, mak-
      ing the road shimmer like water. In effect, the
      mirage is cloaking the (now invisible) road
      behind an image of the blue sky."

[TRANSITION   Now that we know what is required for
          invisibility, we'll take a look at scientific
          efforts to make objects invisible.]

II. Invisibility research is progressing well. •   • Experiments
  A. Research began with microwaves.   presented in
    1. According to senior editor Josie Glausiusz   chronological
        in *Discover*, November 2006, the Duke   order
        physicists used microwaves instead of light
        waves because they have a "substantially
        longer wavelength, which makes the cloak-
        ing effect considerably easier to achieve."
    2. The same source indicates that the physicists
        used specially created metamaterials that
        "possess an ability, not found in nature, to
        bend light at extreme angles." They placed
        rings of these materials around a small

cylindrical object and were able to "bend microwaves to flow around the cylinder like water flowing around a pebble in a stream." •

• Use quotation marks when quoting a source word-for-word.

[SHOW VISUAL AID OF THIS PROCESS]

B. More recent trials have cloaked objects from visible light.

1. Lynn Yarris of the Berkeley Lab Communications Department reported new findings in "Making 3D Objects Disappear," September 17, 2015. A Berkeley research team headed by Professor Xiang Zhang created an ultra-thin "skin cloak" with a width of 80 nanometers (about 3 millionths of an inch). The cloak was placed around a tiny three-dimensional object, and when light was focused on the object, "the light reflected off the skin cloak was identical to light reflected off a flat mirror, making the object underneath it invisible."

• Note where presentation aids will be used.

[SHOW VIDEO OF INVISIBILITY CLOAK WORKING] •

2. In *Science*, September 18, 2015, Professor Xingjie Ni and colleagues on the Berkeley research team note that "the cloak can also conceal objects with sharp features like abrupt edges and peaks." They add that if the cloak is "designed correctly, both the container and the objects inside the container will become invisible."

C. How long will it take until an invisibility cloak that can shield larger objects from sight becomes feasible? According to *National Geographic News*, November 20, 2008, Ulf Leonhardt, a visiting professor at the National University of Singapore, states that "it's a question of the will and the money put into this field."

• Transition shows movement from one main point to the next

[TRANSITION   We have seen how scientific research is proceeding. Next, let's consider how invisibility technology could affect our lives in ways that we can now only imagine.] •

III. Invisibility technology has many practical applications.
   A. First, an invisibility cloak can improve our visual environment. Ian Sample, science correspondent for the *Guardian*, wrote on March 18, 2010, that "some scientists believe cloaking materials could be used to hide unsightly buildings or high-security facilities." •
   B. Second, invisibility technology can save energy. According to the Helmholtz Association of German Research Centers, in "Invisibility Cloak Might Enhance Efficiency of Solar Cells," October 1, 2015, "Modules that are presently mounted on roofs convert just one-fifth of the light into electricity." Scientists at the Karlsruhe Institute of Technology are working on "optical invisibility cloaks" to "guide sunlight around objects that cast a shadow on the solar panel."
   C. Third, satellite connections may become more efficient. Jim Kerstetter, senior

• The words *first, second, third,* and *finally* signpost the four applications.

editor for *CNET News*, wrote an August 21, 2012, article on the *CNET News* site about Intellectual Ventures, a company that has received funding from investors that include Bill Gates. The company has patented metamaterials technology that would eliminate the need for the heavy and expensive equipment planes that now are used to stay connected with satellites. The technology, about the size of a laptop, could even be used to create a "personal satellite hot spot."

D. Finally, invisibility research is being extended to shields that protect us from other types of waves. Adam Piore, contributing editor for *Discover* magazine, wrote in the July–August 2012 issue that scientists are exploring how sound waves can be cloaked to reduce noise pollution, how seismic waves can be cloaked to protect buildings, and how ocean waves can be deflected from ships.

• Transition from body to conclusion

[TRANSITION   Today we have ventured into the unseen world of invisibility.] •

CONCLUSION

• Efficient summary of main points

I. First, we examined the science of invisibility. Second, we looked at current research into the process of making objects invisible. Finally, we looked at the tremendous effects that this new technology could have on all our lives. •

II. Now, you may not be able to run out tomorrow and purchase an invisibility cloak, but in the not-too-distant future, research into invisibility will benefit diverse fields, including national defense, medicine, and communications. Furthermore, individuals like Susan Storm, with her Invisible Woman identity, may no longer just be comic book characters. •

• Clincher ties conclusion back to introduction

Works Cited

Glausiusz, J. "How to Build an Invisibility Cloak." *Discover* 46 (November 2006): 54.

Helmholtz Association of German Research Centers. "Invisibility Cloak Might Enhance Efficiency of Solar Cells." October 2, 2015. https://www.kit.edu/kit/english/pi_2015 110_invisibility -cloak-might-enhance-efficiency-of-solar-cells.php.

Kerstetter, J. "Remember Invisibility Cloak Tech? It's Useful for Talking to Satellites." *CNET News*, August 21, 2012. http:// news.cnet.com/8301-11386_3-57497129-76/remember -invisibility-cloak-tech-its-useful-for-talking-to-satellites.

Lovett, R. A. "Invisibility Cloak 'Feasible Now.'" *National Geographic News*, November 20, 2008. http://news .nationalgeographic.com/news/2008/11/081120-invisibility -cloak.html.

Ni, X., Z. J. Wong, M. Mrejen, Y. Wang, and X. Zhang. "An Ultrathin Invisibility Skin Cloak for Visible Light." *Science* 349 (September 18, 2015): 1310.

Piore, A. "How to Make Anything Disappear." *Discover* 33 (July–August 2012): 70.

Rutan, C. Personal interview, February 10, 2007.

Sample, I. "Cloaking Device Makes Objects Invisible—to Infrared Light, Anyway." *Guardian*, March 18, 2010. http://www .guardian.co.uk/ science/2010/mar/18/cloaking-device -objects-invisible-infrared.

Yarris, L. "Making 3D Objects Disappear: Berkeley Lab Research- ers Create Ultrathin Invisibility Cloak." September 17, 2015. http://vcresearch.berkeley.edu/news/making-3d objects -disappear-berkeley-lab-researchers-create-ultrathin -invisibility-cloak.

• Full citation of sources in list of works cited (check with your instructor about his or her preferred citation format)

CREATING YOUR SPEAKING OUTLINE

As noted earlier, your speaking outline is a brief version of your long work- ing outline. Essentially, it is a set of notes that help you to deliver your speech extemporaneously. By limiting these notes to brief phrases, key words, and abbreviations, you prevent yourself from reading the speech word-for-word and allow yourself to improvise by choosing fresh words as you speak. The speaking outline provides useful reminders of your main and supporting points.

To deliver the most effective extemporaneous presentation possible, you'll need to transform your working outline into a speaking outline. You may want to prepare the speaking outline *after* you've practiced your speech several times with your working outline and become thoroughly familiar with the ideas in your presentation. Then you can use the speaking outline for your final practice sessions and for delivering your speech.

Formatting Your Speaking Outline

Prepare your speaking outline on 5 in. × 7 in. note cards or on standard $8\frac{1}{2}$ in. × 11 in. paper. Keep your points brief, using only quick phrases or one or two key words for each point. The more you've practiced your speech, the more useful the speaking outline will be as a reminder while you're delivering your speech.

Because you'll refer to this outline as needed while giving your presentation, make it easy on the eyes. If you use a word processor to create the outline, double-space, and select a large font size. If you handwrite your outline on note cards, write neatly, and leave space between each line.

IF YOU NEED TO CHECK YOUR NOTES DURING YOUR SPEECH...   ...WHICH OUTLINE WOULD YOU PREFER TO READ?

Base your speaking outline on your working outline. Create a similar structure by using roman numerals, capital letters, and arabic numerals and by indenting subordinate points. Number each note card or page of your speaking outline. This will help you reassemble the outline quickly if you drop your cards or pages while walking up to the front of the room or delivering your speech.

Note that your instructor may have specific requirements about the form and length of your speaking outline. Check to ensure that your outline meets these requirements.

Elements of Your Speaking Outline

Your speaking outline should be a condensed version of your long working outline that retains all of the points, subpoints, and source quotations of the longer version. Indicate main points and subpoints in no more than a sentence each, and trust yourself to develop these ideas

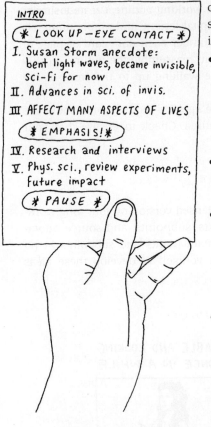

INTRO
(✳ LOOK UP – EYE CONTACT ✳)
I. Susan Storm anecdote:
   bent light waves, became invisible,
   Sci-Fi for now
II. Advances in sci. of invis.
III. AFFECT MANY ASPECTS OF LIVES
   (✳ EMPHASIS! ✳)
IV. Research and interviews
V. Phys. sci., review experiments,
   future impact
   (✳ PAUSE ✳)

conversationally while delivering your speech. Include the following elements in your extemporaneous outline:

- *Main points.* Write each main point as a brief phrase or as a single sentence. Stating your main points using similar words or parallel structure will signal to your listeners that these points are important.

- *Subpoints and sub-subpoints.* Write just enough to remind yourself of the key idea.

- *Abbreviations.* To condense your outline, use abbreviations whenever possible. However, as you have probably realized when going back to study notes you took in class, the abbreviations need to be easily recognized.

- *Evidence.* When providing evidence for your claims in your speaking outline, include necessary citation information and also word-for-word quotations or accurate paraphrases of evidence from the original source.

- *Difficult words.* If you'll be using words that are difficult to pronounce or remember, include them in your speaking outline.

- *Transitions.* Include a brief reminder of each transition in your speech. These reminders don't need to be word-for-word, but make them detailed enough to indicate to your audience that you're done with one idea *and* you're moving on to the next. Consider using brackets to set your transitions apart from your points.

- *Delivery notes.* Consider jotting down a **delivery reminder** to handle any speaking challenges effectively. For example, write "SLOW DOWN!" in places where you tend to rush, or "LOOK UP!" if you often read from your notes rather than making eye contact while presenting. Consider writing "KEY POINT" or "EMPHASIS!" to remind yourself to use inflections or gestures to highlight an important idea. Try writing "COVER WHEN DONE!" as a reminder for what to do after you've finished using a visual aid. To make reminders stand out, circle them, write them in capital letters, use a different colored ink, or highlight them.

> Ⓒ **To consider how delivery reminders could help a speaker's presentation, try Video Activity 11.3, "Rate: Too Fast (Needs Improvement)."**

A SAMPLE SPEAKING OUTLINE

INTRO

Look up—eye contact •
- I. Susan Storm anecdote: bent light waves, became invisible, sci-fi for now
- II. Advances in sci. of invis.
- III. Affect many aspects of lives

Emphasis!
- IV. Research and interviews
- V. Phys. sci., review experiments, future impact •

Pause
[TRANSITION   Begin with what it takes to make object invis.] •

BODY

- I. Must trans. light around object
  - A. Fiction—magic •
    1. Hades's invis. helmet
    2. HG Wells's magic elixir
    3. Harry Potter's invis. cloak
  - B. Researchers focus sci. principles
    1. Visibility depends on light. Interview with Prof. Rutan, Feb. 10, 2007: Must transport light around object. To be visible, light must travel toward blackboard. Block that light, board invisible. •
    2. Effect like mirage. Duke physicists David Smith and Dave Schurig, *Discover*, Nov. 2006, **"when light rays from the sky hit the hot, thin air just above the surface of the asphalt, they bend. . . . Rays once headed from the sky to the ground are redirected to your eye, making the road shimmer like water. In effect, the mirage is cloaking the (now invisible) road behind an image of the blue sky."**

Margin notes:

• Include all five parts of intro, limited to key words.

• Abbreviate *science* as *sci.*

• Remember to include transitions.

• Note anecdotes; trust yourself to explain in your own words.

• Include citations for all evidence sources.

Slowly

[TRANSITION   Now know what is required, look at sci. efforts.]

II. Invis. research progressing well
   A. Began w/ microwaves
      1. Josie Glausiusz, sr. ed., *Discover*, Nov. 2006, Duke physicists used microwaves because **"substantially longer wavelength, which makes the cloaking effect considerably easier to achieve."** •

• All word-for-word quotations go in quotation marks.

      2. Same source: used spec. created metamaterials, **"possess an ability, not found in nature, to bend light at extreme angles."** Placed rings of metamat. around cylinder to **"bend microwaves to flow around the cylinder like water flowing around a pebble in a stream."**

• Reminder to display presentation aid

Show Video •

   B. More recent trials cloak from visible light
      1. Lynn Yarris, Berkeley Lab Communications Dept., "Making 3D Objects Disappear," Sept. 17, 2015: Berk. research team headed by Prof. Zhang created ultrathin cloak about 80 nanometers wide (3 millionths of inch). Cloak placed around 3D object, **"the light reflected off the skin cloak was identical to light reflected off a flat mirror, making the object underneath it invisible."**

• Reminder to display presentation aid

Show Video •

      2. Professor Ni and colleagues, *Science*, Sept. 18, 2015, **"the cloak can also conceal objects with sharp features like abrupt edges and peaks."** If cloak is **"designed correctly, both the container and the objects inside the container will become invisible."**
   C. How long until cloak can shield large objects? Ulf Leonhardt, visiting prof., Natl. U. of Singapore, *National Geographic News*, Nov. 20, 2008, **"it's a question of the will and the money put into this field."**

SPEECH CHOICES

A CASE STUDY: *MIA*

Let's check Mia's plan for outlining her speech.

Countdown: There were two weeks to go before Mia's speech. With all her preparation work done, she was ready to move on to the detailed working outline. Mia checked out her class notes on outlining and the sample outline her class had been given. She didn't want to waste her time working on an outline in the wrong format.

Mia started with her main points, subpoints, and sub-subpoints, using the required alphanumeric format and indentation. Where Mia was using evidence, she provided a full citation for the source and idea. Mia was careful to use quotation marks each time she directly quoted an author because she didn't want to risk plagiarizing. She ended up combining a point and a subpoint together after she realized that they were very similar. Mia typed her introduction and conclusion, indicating each with a roman numeral. She inserted transitions, making sure that they made it clear when she was moving from one main point to the next. She included several signposts such as "One important use of smartphones" and "Another helpful app" to help the audience follow her development of main ideas.

Mia finished by creating her works cited section. She included only references that she actually used in her outline. Because she saved the citations during her research phase, it was easy to copy and paste them and then reformat them as needed. Whew! Now that her working outline was finished, Mia had two weeks to practice her delivery and consolidate her notes into a short speaking outline after she became familiar with the material. She was still nervous about actually giving the speech, but at least she'd be prepared.

YOUR TURN:
How will you make sure you know the format that you need for your speech outlines?

For more questions and activities for this case study, and to see a ◉ video clip from Mia's speech on using a speaking outline, please go to LaunchPad at macmillanhighered.com/speakup4e.

[TRANSITION   Have seen how research proceeding, next how affects lives]

III. Many practical apps. •

    A.   Improve visual environ. Ian Sample, sci. corresp., *Guardian*, Mar. 18, 2010: **"some scientists believe**

• Abbreviate terms you know well.

SPEECH CHOICES

A CASE STUDY: JACOB

Let's consider how Jacob got his outline together.

Jacob was due to give his speech the next day. During the previous class, the instructor had collected an outline from each student who spoke, so Jacob figured he needed one for the big day. Unfortunately, the notes on outlining that he had taken in class were sketchy, and he'd lost the sample outline that his instructor had passed out.

Jacob figured that he knew what an outline was and would be able to come up with one on his own. He liked to use bullet points on writing assignments, so he inserted these in a couple of places where he was presenting a series of examples. He decided not to write down each main point or structure them in a certain way (he distantly remembered roman numerals). Rather than be hyperstructured and boring, he'd go for something more free-flowing and spontaneous. (Hadn't his teacher mentioned she liked jazz?) Jacob remembered something about transitions, so he wrote the word *transition* in a couple key places where he would move on to a new point.

Jacob noted some of his research sources in the introduction, and he put down his sources in a bibliography. He hadn't kept track of all the full source citations, but he was able to remember most of the information. He cut and pasted some quotes for his speech so that he'd be able to read them at the right times. Done. True, there wasn't a lot of time to practice. But now Jacob felt even more confident—because he had a speech to read.

YOUR TURN:
How will you make sure you know the format that you need for your speech outlines?

For more questions and activities for this case study, please go to LaunchPad at macmillanhighered.com/speakup4e.

cloaking materials could be used to hide unsightly buildings or high-security facilities."

B. Save NRG. Helmholtz Assn. of German Research Centers, "Invisible Cloak Might Enhance Efficiency of Solar Cells," Oct. 1, 2015: "**Modules that are presently mounted on roofs convert just one-fifth of the light into electricity.**" Karlsruhe Tech scientists working on "**optical invisibility cloaks**" to "**guide sunlight around objects that cast a shadow on the solar panel."

C. Satellite connections. Jim Kerstetter, sr. ed., *CNET News*, Aug. 21, 2012: Intellectual Ventures (investors incl. Gates) patented metamat. tech. that elim. heavy and expensive equipment on planes. Tech. is laptop sized, could create **"personal satellite hot spot."**

D. Protect us from other waves. Adam Piore, contrib. ed., *Discover*, July–Aug. 2012: Cloak sound, seismic, and ocean waves.

[TRANSITION   Ventured into unseen world of invis.]

CONCLUSION

Look up! •

I. Sci. of invis., current research, future effects

II. Soon see benefits to defense, energy , satellites, safety. Susan Storm as Invis. Woman no longer fiction.

• Briefly note main points to summarize.

CHAPTER REVIEW

"A good outline strengthens organization and preparation."

In this chapter, we explained the importance of outlining. We showed you how to develop and use working and speaking outlines to organize your ideas, practice your presentation, and ultimately deliver an effective speech. A detailed working outline shows the structure of your speech and the hierarchy of your ideas, as well as full quotations for all evidence you'll provide in your speech. This long outline also includes notes for transitions and visual aids. Use your working outline to practice your speech until you're thoroughly familiar with it.

Your speaking outline is briefer and condenses your ideas, using phrases, key words, and abbreviations. It still should retain word-for-word quotations from your evidence sources. Speaking outlines usually are prepared on numbered note cards or on pieces of 8½ in. × 11 in. paper; the writing on these outlines must be clear and easy to read. You may want to develop your speaking outline only after you've practiced your speech extensively with your working outline. The speaking outline helps you present your speech conversationally—by conveying your ideas in your own words, maintaining eye contact with the audience, and not reading a word-for-word script or reciting your presentation from memory. The speaking outline also serves as a handy reminder if you lose your place while delivering your speech, if you need to quote evidence during your talk, or if you want to remember certain delivery tips (such as emphasizing a particular point while presenting your speech).

 LaunchPad
macmillan learning

LaunchPad for *Speak Up* offers videos and encourages self-assessment through adaptive quizzing. Go to **macmillanhighered.com/speakup4e** to get access to:

✓ **LearningCurve Adaptive Quizzes**

▶ **Video clips that help you understand public speaking concepts**

Key Terms

outlining *306*
working outline *308*
 speaking outline *309*
 extemporaneous delivery *309*
body *310*
subordination *311*

evidence *313*
 transition *314*
 introduction *314*
 conclusion *315*
list of works cited *315*
delivery reminder *326*

Review Questions

1. Explain the differences between a working outline and a speaking outline.

2. How does creating an outline help ensure that your ideas are well supported?

3. Describe the most important guidelines for creating a working outline for a speech's body, introduction, and conclusion.

4. What are the benefits of delivering your speech from a relatively brief speaking outline?

5. Describe the most important guidelines for creating an effective speaking outline.

Critical Thinking Questions

1. If you were to give a speech on the nature of working outlines, what would your main points be? How would they compare to the main points of a speech about the nature of speaking outlines?

2. How can the process of developing a working outline help you be more confident when delivering your final speech?

3. Can you think of a situation in everyday life in which you use subordination? How might you use subordination in a conversation with a friend? In a writing assignment? What does this lead you to believe about the importance of subordination in communication?

Activities

1. Select any of the sample speeches in this textbook. Working individually or in groups, condense the speech into a speaking outline.

2. Take a look at both the working outline (pp. 316–23) and the speaking outline (pp. 327–31) for Josh Betancur's speech, "Invisibility: Science Fiction No More!" Could you deliver the speech yourself using his working outline? Why would it be difficult to deliver the speech yourself, right now, using only his speaking outline? What type of preparation could help you deliver his speech from his speaking outline?

3. ⓒ **Video Activity 11.4, "DuBoise, Central Texas Coalition against Human Trafficking,"** Watch the clip from a persuasive speech against human trafficking. Prepare a brief speaking outline of the speaker's conclusion, and use that outline to deliver the excerpt from her speech. Then watch the video clip again. How closely did your speech match the presentation?

4. Open one of your textbooks from another course, and outline a chapter based on the headings, subheadings, and key terms that appear in boldfaced or colored text. Do these elements show a clear hierarchy of ideas? How clear is the picture of the chapter that the outline creates? Could you summarize the chapter using only the outline?

12

LANGUAGE AND STYLE

"Choose your words carefully."

Marvin was eager to present his speech about a law-enforcement intervention program called Operation Ceasefire to his classmates.[1] He explained that the program—led by police, clergy, teachers, neighbors, and community leaders—promotes outreach and prevention with repeat offenders in a community. In discussing the program, Marvin used technical terms such as "reentry felons" (former felons who are paroled and return from prison to their communities) and "recidivism" (a relapse into committing crimes again). He also used police slang, such as "deal with perps" and "guys on the job." At one point, he contrasted Operation Ceasefire with how police traditionally handle "certain neighborhoods" and provide "protection" from violent crime. When Marvin sat down after concluding his speech, he felt confident that he had conveyed his credibility and met his objective—informing the audience about his topic.

Marvin's classmates, however, had mixed reactions to his talk. Many found him credible because of his wide vocabulary of police slang and legal jargon, but others found his language impenetrable. Several audience members resented his use of phrases such as "guys on the job" for "police officers." Some listeners felt that the phrase "certain neighborhoods" was a veiled reference to socioeconomics, and others felt that it suggested racial profiling and reminded them that some police officers were too quick to use violence against African American males—perhaps because of racial profiling. Audience members also reacted differently to the word "protection," with some reminded of police officers' heroic efforts and sacrifices, and others thinking of their use of excessive force and corruption.

Clearly, Marvin failed to convey his message to many in his audience—in large part because of his word choice. **Word choice**, or **diction**, requires you to consider your audience, the occasion, and the nature of your message when choosing language for a speech. If Marvin had used the same language when talking to an audience of police officers, he might well have had more success, but his classmates consisted of diverse students who interpreted his words in their own ways and who had their own perspectives on law enforcement. Marvin failed because he didn't adapt his word choice to his listeners' expectations. When giving speeches, word choice can matter far more than you originally might think.

Similarly, word choice factored heavily in Martin Luther King Jr.'s "I Have a Dream" speech, which we discuss in Chapter 2. When King presented this address on August 28, 1963, at the March on Washington, he didn't give it an official title. Only later did people start calling it the "I Have a Dream" speech. Why has this phrase endured in people's memories? It was an exceptionally powerful expression that encapsulated King's vision of a time and place that would be free from prejudice and discrimination. Nearly fifty years after his death, people still experience profound emotions when they recall this expression. If King had calmly used the words "I hope" instead of "I have a dream," he would have had much less effect on his listeners.

An average speech may contain hundreds or even thousands of words, and every one of them matters. Selected carefully, your words can help you connect with your audience and get your message across clearly. Used thoughtlessly, they may confuse, offend, bore, or annoy your listeners, preventing them from absorbing your message. In this chapter, we examine the importance of choosing the right words for your speeches and the differences between oral and written language. Then we explain how to use language to present your message clearly, express your ideas effectively, and demonstrate respect for your audience.

THE IMPORTANCE OF LANGUAGE AND WORD CHOICE

You make thousands of word choices every day when you talk with friends and family, take notes in class, write emails, make phone calls, and send text messages. Most of us try to choose our words carefully in each of these situations. After all, our words have a lot of power: they can inform, inspire, and uplift others. But they also can confuse

people (for example, if you've used jargon or slang that others might not understand), and they can hurt others (for instance, if you've used biased language).

Your word choice defines you as a speaker. Recall that a speaker's *ethos*, or personal credibility, can influence an audience's perception of the presenter's message. Your words and phrases convey your ethos to your listeners because they say something about you as a person.

How do you use words in ways that clarify your message and enhance your credibility? Along with using appropriate and considerate language, you can explain technical terms and use helpful presentation aids (for clarity), thus effectively incorporating such terms into your speech (to enhance credibility).

A student speaker named Gillian applied these practices while delivering an informative presentation about armor plating used during the Ottoman empire. Gillian showed photographs depicting the armor worn by soldiers and their horses. She also used technical terms in a way the audience would understand. For instance, at one point she discussed a "gilded copper *chanfrein*," which she immediately explained was "forehead armor for the horse—like the helmet a soldier might wear." By using the correct technical terminology, Gillian showed authority and gained credibility in the eyes of her audience. And by explaining these terms through devices such as analogy ("like the helmet a soldier might wear"), she made her message accessible without coming across as condescending to her listeners.

EXPLAIN TECHNICAL TERMS

DIFFERENCES BETWEEN ORAL AND WRITTEN LANGUAGE

You may have noticed that words and sentences that are spoken aloud can come across quite differently from words that you read to yourself. In a public speaking context, the difference between spoken and written language can be even more pronounced. To help you craft better language for your speeches, consider these three key differences between oral and written language:

- *Oral language is more adaptive.* Writers seldom know exactly who will read their words or in what context. The best they can do is to take educated guesses and make language choices accordingly. When you speak before a live audience, however, you can get immediate feedback, which is virtually impossible for a writer. Thus, you can observe your audience members during your presentation, interact with them, and *respond* to the way they are receiving your message. Because a speech is a live, physical interaction that generates instantaneous audience feedback, you can adapt to the situation, such as by extending or simplifying an explanation if listeners seem confused or by choosing clearer or simpler language.

- *Oral language tends to be less formal.* Because writers have the luxury of getting their words down on paper (or on screen) and then going back to make changes, they typically use precise word choice and follow the formal rules of syntax and grammar. This careful use of language aligns well with most readers' expectations. In most speech situations, however, language choice tends toward a somewhat less formal style. Because listeners lack the chance to go back and reread your words, you will want to use shorter and less complicated sentences. (Of course, certain speech situations—such as political settings—require elevated sentence structure and word choice.) In addition, effective oral language is often simpler and less technically precise than written language is. Thus, consider incorporating appropriate colloquialisms, a conversational tone, and even sentence fragments into your speeches.

ORAL vs. WRITTEN LANGUAGE

- *Oral language incorporates repetition.* Most writing teachers and coaches advise their students to avoid repeating themselves or being *redundant* by covering the same ground more than once. But in speaking situations, repetition can be an especially effective tool because your listeners can't go back and revisit your points: your words are there and then suddenly are gone. Because most audience members don't take notes (especially outside a classroom setting), there is nothing for listeners to rely on except their own memory of your words. You can help your listeners remember your message by intentionally repeating key words and phrases throughout your presentation. If they hear certain words often enough, they will remember them.

DENOTATIVE AND CONNOTATIVE MEANING

In addition to using words to express your message clearly and to enhance your credibility, you need to be aware that words can have two very different kinds of meanings. By understanding these differences, you can select your language more strategically to create the effect you want. In the sections that follow, we look at this notion of two meanings—*denotative meaning* and *connotative meaning*.

Denotative Meaning

The **denotative meaning** of a word is its exact, literal dictionary definition. When you use a word that has one dictionary definition (and is not overly technical), you usually can expect that your audience will understand what you mean. But many words have several dictionary definitions. In these cases, you may need to take steps to avoid confusion.

Consider the word *run*. According to *Merriam-Webster's Collegiate Dictionary*, *run* has numerous definitions. It can be a verb meaning "to go faster than a walk" ("He runs every morning") or "to dissolve or spread when wet" ("The rain made the ink on the note run"). It can be a noun meaning "an unbroken course of performance" ("The company had a good run of profits this year"), and an adjective meaning "being in a melted state" (for instance, "runs like butter"). Suppose you wanted to use the word *run* in a speech to refer to a successful series of victories by your school's track team. If you said, "We've had a great run this season," your listeners may wonder if you're referring to a specific race or to a string of victories scored by the team against opponents during the season. In this case, you may want to avoid the risk of confusing your audience by saying instead, "We've consistently trounced the competition during this season."

Connotative Meaning

Many words also have at least one **connotative meaning**—an association that comes to mind when people hear or read the word. A word's connotative meanings may bear little or no resemblance to its denotative meanings. For example, when used as a noun in a statement about stocks, the word *dog* may connote a poor investment opportunity—yet the literal meaning of the noun *dog* is a canine animal.

By using words in your speeches deliberately for their connotative meanings, you can make a powerful impression on your audience. For example, a student named Betty made the following statement in her presentation on the history of hairstyles in the twentieth century: "In the roaring twenties, the short 'bob' or 'flapper' haircut exploded onto the scene through the rise of silent film star Louise Brooks." When Betty used the verb *exploded*, she triggered the strong, fiery association that most people have with the word. This savvy use of the connotations of *exploded* helped Betty make her point far more forcefully than if she had merely said that the bob "became very popular."

On the other hand, carelessly using a word that has very different denotative and connotative meanings can backfire and confuse your audience. Consider Albert, a student who made the following statement in an impromptu speech about a school district's refusal to lower the student-to-teacher ratio for class size in elementary schools:

"That kind of decision really demonstrates some bigotry by the school board." The word *bigotry* literally means the state of mind of a person who is intolerantly devoted to her or his personal opinions or prejudices—the meaning that Albert intended in his comment. Unfortunately, many people have come to associate the word *bigotry*

with racial prejudice. Albert did not intend a racial connotation. He just wanted to say that he thought the school district was unreasonably committed to its decision about class size. Because many students in Albert's class had experienced the pain of racial prejudice firsthand, they inferred from Albert's use of *bigotry* that issues of race underlay the school board's decision, which wasn't true. If Albert had analyzed his audience more carefully, he might have known to avoid using the word due to its potentially misleading connotative meaning. Instead, he could have said that the school board stubbornly refused to change its view about reducing class sizes.

PRESENTING YOUR MESSAGE CLEARLY

You can't get your message across to your audience unless you present it clearly. To make your message as clear as possible, use language that's *understandable, concrete, proper,* and *concise.*

Understandable Language

Understandable language consists of words your listeners find *recognizable.* In most situations, the best way to ensure that you're using understandable language is to choose words that reflect your audience's language skills, avoiding technical terms beyond their comprehension.

For example, if a cell biologist gave a talk to a roomful of English majors, she would quickly confuse her listeners with terms such as *ribosomal DNA* and *anaerobic cellular metabolism*. Yet those terms could be appropriate in a speech delivered to a group of experts or insiders—for example, when presenting a paper to scientists at a biology conference.

Thus, you need to analyze your audience to determine what language your listeners will recognize. Audience members' educational background can suggest their general vocabulary level. Meanwhile, demographic information and stories about listeners' life experiences can help you predict what language the audience will understand.

Also take care in using **jargon**—specialized or technical words or phrases that are familiar only to people in a specific field or group. Jargon includes technical terms as well as abbreviations, acronyms, slang, and other esoteric expressions. For example, people in the field of tele-communications use jargon extensively—including expressions such as *7G* (seventh-generation telecom networks), *CapEx* (capital expenditures), *first-tier ops* (telecom operators with the largest market share), and *the cloud* (servers available over the Internet). The jargon can be even trickier

to use if its definition is still in a state of evolution. The word *cloud* is one such case.[2]

Here are two simple guidelines for deciding whether to include a particular instance of jargon in a speech:

- *If you can say something in plain language, do so.* Unless you see a pressing reason to use jargon—such as to clarify an important point or to bolster your credibility—use widely accessible words.
- *If you do use jargon, explain it.* By clarifying your use of jargon, you can gain whatever advantages it offers and still ensure that your audience understands you.

For example, a student named Patrick was making a presentation about safe horseback-riding practices in his public speaking class. Most of his fellow students had grown up in the city and had little experience with horses. In explaining the steps required to prepare a horse for a trail ride, Patrick said, "Be very careful about how you tack up your horse— that is, how you put the bridle and saddle on." He guessed (correctly) that many of his listeners wouldn't understand the phrase *tack up*. By using the term—which is common among people who ride horses—he gained credibility as someone familiar with his topic, and by explaining it, he helped his audience understand the information.

Concrete Words

Whenever possible, strive to use concrete words instead of abstract ones. What's the difference? A **concrete word** is specific and suggests exactly what you mean. An **abstract word**, on the other hand, is general and can be confusing and ambiguous for your audience. Consider the following four sentences, which range from abstract to concrete:

- This past week, Jane arrived in a vehicle. *(abstract)*
- Four days ago, Jane arrived in a car. *(less abstract)*
- Last Tuesday at noon, Jane arrived in a blue Toyota. *(more concrete)*
- Last Tuesday at noon, Jane arrived in a blue 2008 Toyota Corolla. *(most concrete)*

Only the third and fourth sentences convey in specific terms how and when Jane arrived. If this information is relevant to the presentation,

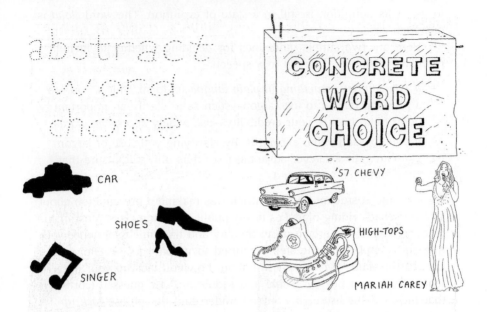

either of these sentences would help the speaker convey more information than the first and second sentences.

This does not mean that you should never use general language. In fact, some situations call for a general language style. In the language of speechwriters, this is the difference between speaking from "five thousand feet, as opposed to fifty feet." When you want to describe a concept or theory from a broad perspective and give the audience the *big picture* or the *grand vision*, you invariably will use general language. Sometimes speakers want to begin with general concepts (five thousand feet) and then move toward specific details (fifty feet). For example, in his 2015 State of the City address, New York mayor Bill de Blasio used both lofty language and grounded examples to describe his goals and accomplishments. He began with general language:

> If we do not act—and act boldly—New York risks taking on the qualities of a gated community. . . . A place defined by exclusivity, rather than opportunity. And we cannot let that happen. Over the past two years, I've spoken about the need to take dead aim at the Tale of Two Cities, and about our vision for creating One New York, rising together . . . a city where everyone has a shot at the middle class.

LANGUAGE FLYING AT 5,000 FEET

LANGUAGE FLYING AT 50 FEET

Mayor de Blasio then followed up with concrete examples:

> And while we have so much more work to do, 2014 was a year of great progress in our effort to address inequality and lift up our families. Some examples:
>
> We achieved full-day pre-K for more than 50,000 of our kids.
>
> We nearly doubled enrollment in after-school programs for middle school kids in all five boroughs.
>
> By executive order, we expanded living wage coverage to 18,000 workers.
>
> With the help of the City Council—and the strong leadership of my partner in government, Speaker Melissa Mark-Viverito—we secured paid sick leave for 500,000 more New Yorkers.[3]

Proper Use of Words

The audience's understanding of your message will improve if you use words that correctly express the point you want to make. Incorrect word choice can confuse listeners or undermine your credibility. For example, if you used the words *recession* and *depression* interchangeably in a speech

USE PROPER WORDS

on the economy, you probably would lose credibility with any audience members who know the difference between these two economic terms. At the same time, you might confuse or mislead audience members who do not understand the distinction. You also should watch out for words that commonly are misused (such as *literally* and *effect*) and for words that frequently are mispronounced (such as *probably*, *library*, and *nuclear*).

It's also easy to fall into the trap of mixing up words that sound alike. For example, one student delivering a speech on the Seattle music scene of the 1990s accused the late Kurt Cobain of "immortal behavior." The audience laughed, knowing that musicians clearly don't live forever and that the speaker probably meant "immoral behavior." Although this speaker's listeners were amused, the joke was on him: many of his audience members lost some respect for him.

Concise Language

Because audience members cannot reread or rehear portions of your speech, they have only one chance to grasp your ideas. For this reason, make sure that each of your sentences expresses just one thought. Although long sentences linking different ideas may be understandable in print, they're hard to follow in a speech.

As a rule of thumb, aim to be *concise*—that is, use the fewest words necessary to express an idea. If you are one of the millions of users of Twitter, the online social networking service, you already may be used to being succinct because tweets are limited to 140 characters; this restriction forces you to think and express yourself concisely. Giving a speech needn't be as restrictive as writing a tweet, but a similar philosophy can be used. When you outline your speech, focus on making your points in the fewest words possible. You occasionally may want to add words or phrases to incorporate color, eloquence, wit, or humor into your talk; just make sure you have a good reason to insert those extra words.

The term for unnecessary words in a presentation is **verbal clutter**—extraneous words that make it hard for the audience to follow your message. Here are three examples:

- "The death penalty cannot deter crime *for the reason that* murderers do not consider the consequences of their actions."

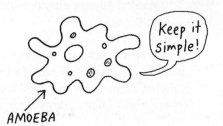

- "*Regardless of the fact that* you disagree with the government's position, you cannot dispute the FCC's ruling."

- "If we are to *make contact* with our bargaining opponents, we have to find a mutually acceptable schedule."

You could easily revise those sentences to eliminate verbal clutter:

- "The death penalty cannot deter crime *because* murderers do not consider the consequences of their actions."

- "*Although* you disagree with the government's position, you cannot dispute the FCC's ruling."

- "If we are to *meet* with our bargaining opponents, we have to find a mutually acceptable schedule."

EXPRESSING YOUR IDEAS EFFECTIVELY

Words have great power to move an audience, especially when used vividly. Empower your own language through the use of *repetition, hypothetical examples, personal anecdotes, vivid language,* and *figurative language.*

Repetition

Repetition—saying a specific word, phrase, or statement more than once—helps you grab your audience's attention and leave listeners with enduring memories of your speech:

> At the end of the battle, every soldier was killed. Every soldier.

This use of repetition draws listeners' attention to the fact that all the soldiers *on both sides of the conflict* died at the end of the battle, driving home a sobering point that the speaker wants to make.

To get the most from repetition, use it sparingly. If you repeat too many statements in your speech, your listeners won't be able to discern the truly important points in your presentation.

You also can use repetition by returning to a point later in a speech to provide a gentle reminder to your audience. In the following example, a student named Allyson employs this technique in a speech about trekking across Russia:

> When most people think about mountains in Russia, they think about the Urals. These are old mountains, stretching some twelve hundred miles from north to south. The mountains themselves are covered with taigas—large forests that blanket the area. . . .

As I mentioned a few minutes back, these twelve hundred miles of Ural Mountains are an impressive sight, with all sorts of wildlife, including wolves, bears, and many different game birds.

Later in her speech, Allyson again repeats the north-to-south distance ("twelve hundred miles") to emphasize the challenges of backpacking through the vast Ural mountain range.

Finally, you may want to repeat a point through *rewording* it—making the point again but in different words. When your original point might be confusing, rewording gives your audience another option for grasping what you mean. Rewording is similar to the technique you use to explain jargon. Here's one example:

According to the engineering report, the shuttle booster rockets had systems failure with the cooling system, not to mention serious problems with the outer hatch doors and the manually operated crane. Put another way, there were at least three mechanical problems we know of with this last shuttle mission.

Rewording works particularly well in those parts of your speech where you enumerate a list or make a technical statement that might be difficult for your audience to follow.

Hypothetical Examples

Consider using hypothetical examples with technical information, complicated messages, policy statements, and points in a speech where you want to focus your audience's attention. A **hypothetical example** is an imagined example or scenario you invite your listeners to consider to help them follow a complicated point presented immediately afterward.

For instance, a student named Blake wanted to inform his audience about the legal test for defamation of

As a speaker, you can help your listeners remember your message by intentionally repeating key words and phrases. As a speaker, you can help your listeners remember your message by intentionally repeating key words and phrases. As a speaker, you can help your listeners remember your message by intentionally repeating key words and phrases. As a speaker...

character. He introduced his presentation with the following hypothetical example:

> Suppose that a television news crew is shadowing a paramedic team to record its average day, and the paramedics are called out to a highway accident. Now suppose that the camera crew tapes the whole rescue, and the reporter talks to a badly injured victim who is sedated with painkillers. Under the influence of the painkillers, the victim says many foolish things, including some unkind words about her employer. Would the news station be justified in broadcasting the whole story—including everything the victim said to the reporter? What are the victim's rights here, if any? This scenario suggests the difficulty of determining whether defamation of character has taken place.

Personal Anecdotes

Illustrating a concept with *personal anecdotes* (brief stories) can help you further build credibility and reassure your listeners that you're not judging them. Peter, a senior in a speech class, used the following personal anecdote in a speech about phobias:

> Phobias come in many different forms—and most, if not all, can be cured with therapy, medication, or a combination of the two. I know this because I've lived with one of these myself. Although you would not know it to look at me today, I once had a horrible fear of swimming in the ocean. Just the thought of stepping into the open, boundless ocean—water that might have sharks swimming in it—used to give me the shakes, sweaty palms, the works. It was a real problem. But after lots of therapy, I took a doctor's advice and joined a bay swimming club. With the help of my new friends in the club, I forced myself to swim in the bay—including a swim under the Golden Gate Bridge at dawn and

during slack tide. Being out there with people I really trusted cured me of the fear.

Peter illustrates one type of phobia in a way that gives him credibility (he speaks from experience). His personal anecdote also demonstrates that he took his subject seriously. Finally, it enables him to avoid offending audience members who may have struggled with similar fears.

You can achieve similar effects with anecdotes about events your listeners may have experienced personally. In a speech on credit card debt, a freshman student named Jackson sought common ground with his audience through the following anecdote:

> You really have to be careful about credit cards. You usually get on somebody's mailing list right out of high school. Suddenly your mailbox is filled with offers for free credit cards. And they don't have a service charge for the first three months. You can get credit up to five thousand dollars and pay just a minimum payment each month. Hasn't that happened to most of you in this room? It happened to me, too. And we all know how fast that credit card debt can pile up!

Vivid Language

Vivid language grabs the attention of your audience with words and phrases that appeal to all the senses—sight, smell, touch, hearing, and taste. The following examples from an autobiographical presentation illustrate the differences between ordinary and vivid word choices. In the first example, Jamie describes his childhood years with his family in relatively uninspiring language:

> I remember those mornings at home only too well. Mom would call us if we overslept. She was downstairs making breakfast every morning at eight o'clock sharp. My brothers and I would fight to be the first into the bathroom.

Now consider this more vivid version of Jamie's story:

> Mornings were memorable in my house. It was always cold in the room I shared with my brothers. With no curtains on our windows, light streamed in, poking us in the eyes before Mom called us down for breakfast. The smell of bacon wafting upstairs did the rest. Routinely, we shoved one another, forming a line outside the bathroom, knowing Mom would demand to know if we had washed up before coming to the table.

The second version conveys the same basic information as the first. However, it paints a more graphic picture of the scene, with stronger **imagery**—mental pictures or impressions—for the audience. We can *see* the bright light. We can also smell the bacon and hear Mom's voice.

To use vivid language, select descriptive words that evoke pictures, smells, textures, sounds, and flavors in your listeners' minds. But use such language sparingly. If you overuse it, it may lose its effect.

> ▶ **To see an example of a speech introduction that could use more vivid language, try Video Activity 12.1, "Roth, Emergency in the Emergency Room."**

Figurative Language

Figurative language, or *figures of speech*, refers to the techniques that speakers employ to word specific types of claims or ideas. Although there are literally hundreds of kinds of figures of speech,[4] we focus on four of the most commonly used—*anaphora, antithesis, simile*, and *metaphor*.

Anaphora—the repetition of a word or phrase at the beginning of successive phrases, clauses, or sentences—is used to achieve emphasis and clarity, as well as a rhetorical sense of style. For example, in a special occasion speech known as a *eulogy*, a surviving relative of the deceased said the following:

> *He is watching over us* now, listening to me give a speech I wish I never had to give. And so it will go for everyone. *He is watching over us* as we drive his youngest daughter to school every morning. *He is watching over us* as we face the uncertainty of continuing to run the business he built.

Here the repetition of "He is watching over us" allows the speaker to imply that the deceased is not really gone and that those who grieve for his loss can be consoled by the suggestion of his continued presence.

Speakers may occasionally wish to compare or contrast topics in a speech, even if they know in advance how they would like their audience to resolve the points in conflict. When speakers do this, they employ **antithesis**—clauses set in opposition to one another, usually to distinguish between choices, concepts, and ideas.[5]

For example, a student named Stephen employed antithesis to persuade people to invest in solar power:

> Do we want to go forward or backward? Live in the future or be stuck in the past? Continue to be dependent on oil from other countries or invest in safe, free sunshine right here to meet many of our electricity and power needs?

Here Stephen contrasts "forward" and "future" with "backward" and "stuck in the past." He wants his audience to choose "safe, free sunshine" over being "dependent on oil from other countries."

Similes and metaphors suggest similarities between objects that are not alike. A **simile** makes explicit comparisons and contains the word *like* or *as*. Examples include "His mind works *like an adding machine*" and "The baby's crying was *as sweet as music* to his ears."

A **metaphor** makes implicit comparisons of unlike objects by identifying one object with the other. The comparisons, however, are not meant to be taken literally.[6] For example, the phrase "innovation is the engine that drives our economy" doesn't mean that innovation is an actual engine.

> ▶ To see a speaker using a simile, try Video Activity 12.2, "Gender-Based Responses in Sports Chatrooms."

> ▶ To view a speaker using a metaphor, try Video Activity 12.3, "Gender-Based Responses in Sports Chatrooms."

Similes and metaphors can add color, vividness, and imagery to your speech. When you use these devices, be sure to use clear and consistent terms so that the images make sense. Mixed metaphors—such as "it's not rocket surgery" or "he nailed that one out of the park"—can conjure images that either don't make sense or are unintentionally funny. Further, overly complicated metaphors can become tiresome in a speech.

Likewise, avoid mixing comparisons—that is, using more than one simile or metaphor at a time. Otherwise, you might produce some unintentionally funny statements. Here's an example of a mixed metaphor:

> Outlawing the possession of marijuana paraphernalia was exactly the *bullet* the House of Representatives needed to *cook* the new drug bill and *drive* it over to the Senate.

When used properly, a simile or metaphor can help your audience understand one idea through its reference to another. A metaphor also can help listeners experience a new idea "in terms that resonate with their past experience."[7]

CHOOSING RESPECTFUL AND UNBIASED LANGUAGE

When you use respectful language in your speeches—words, phrases, and expressions that are courteous and don't reflect bias against other cultures or individuals—you deliver far more effective presentations. Why? Your audience members remain open to your ideas and view you as trustworthy and fair. In this way, you gain immense personal credibility.

By contrast, using **biased language**—word choices that suggest prejudice or preconceptions about other people—erodes your credibility and distracts your audience from listening to your message. For these reasons, avoid language that suggests you're making judgments about your listeners' or someone else's race, ethnicity, gender, sexuality, religion, or mental or physical ability. In the rest of this section, we present ideas for keeping biased language out of your speech.

Avoid Stereotypes

A **stereotype** is a generalization based on the false assumption that characteristics displayed by some members of a group are shared by all members of that group. Stereotypes are often based on ethnicity, race, gender, religious beliefs, or sexual orientation. But stereotypes can also be based on people's economic backgrounds, the schools they attended, the regions they come from—even their appearance or musical taste. Stereotypes, especially negative ones, are a form of biased language that put a speaker's credibility at risk.

Stereotyping can come into play when speakers make claims beyond the facts that their evidence proves—by generalizing about their topic. Suppose a presenter offers a few examples of people who received jobs through affirmative action policies but who didn't have the skills or experience required for those jobs. The speaker argues that those few examples prove that everyone who benefits from affirmative action is unqualified. The speaker would be making a claim without proof and thus perpetuating a stereotype.

Take special care to use arguments that avoid stereotypes when discussing topics that are loaded with potential for controversy. For example, if you wanted to argue against affirmative action, you could claim that race or gender should play no role in any hiring decisions. Or you could advocate for other remedies for reducing discrimination in society, thereby acknowledging that discrimination does exist.

Use Gender-Neutral References

Experts in grammar recommended using the generic *he* as early as 1553,[8] and by 1850, this preference was legally supported (*he* was said to stand for *he* and *she*).[9] By the 1970s, however, modern linguists began questioning whether the generic use of masculine pronouns was reinforcing gender-based stereotypes.

Using gender-neutral references can be challenging at times. For instance, suppose you were giving a speech about jobs that can be held by both men and women—such as chief executive officer (CEO), nurse, and high school principal. Occasional use of *he or she* is fine, but frequent use gets tedious for listeners. How would *you* react if you heard a speaker say, "A good president keeps his or her meetings organized, listens to his or her employees, and puts his or her company's needs first"? Happily, there are ways to work around any awkwardness with pronouns. Using plurals where appropriate can help: "Good *presidents* keep *their* meetings organized, listen to *their* employees, and put *their* company's needs first." Or if a singular pronoun is more appropriate for your speech, alternate the use of *she* and *he* from paragraph to paragraph or from example to example.

Also avoid using gender-specific nouns or noun phrases, such as *poetess*, *chairman*, *congressman*, *cleaning lady*, and *fireman*. Instead, use a **gender-neutral term**—a word that does not suggest a particular gender—such as *poet*, *chair*, *representative*, *cleaner*, and *firefighter*.

Make Appropriate References to Ethnic Groups

To show respect for your audience, use the noun or phrase that a particular ethnic group prefers when you refer to that group. For example, *African American* is commonly preferred to *black*. Sometimes people from a group may use more than one name to refer to themselves—for example, *Latino/Latina* and *Chicano/Chicana* or a name derived from their country of origin. If you are uncertain about which term to use in such a case, ask friends or classmates who are members of that group which name they prefer.

When ethnicity is relevant to your audience, be sure to refer to ethnic groups correctly. Not all people from Laos are Hmong, a visiting professor from Nigeria is not African American, and people from Puerto Rico or Spain are not Mexican Americans. Moreover, when a word comes from a language that uses different masculine and feminine forms, pay attention to those forms. For example, author Ana Castillo is a Chicana, not a Chicano. Attentiveness to such distinctions during a speech will pay big dividends in the form of appreciation from your listeners.

Steer Clear of Unnecessary References to Ethnicity, Religion, Gender, or Sexuality

When a person's ethnicity, religion, gender, or sexuality is not relevant to a point you are making, there's no need to mention it in your speech. Including it can hurt your credibility. For instance, if you say "the *Chinese American* judge," "the *Jewish* player in Major League Baseball," "the *male* first-grade teacher," or "the *lesbian* CEO," listeners may believe that you find it odd for a judge to be Chinese American, a baseball player to be Jewish, a man to be a first-grade teacher, or a lesbian to run a company. On the other hand, in an informative speech about baseball great Jackie Robinson, you probably would want to refer to his African American heritage. Why? Robinson was subjected to many forms of racism and broke the "color barrier" in Major League Baseball when he joined the Brooklyn Dodgers in 1947. His enduring legacy stems just as much from his experiences as an African American as it does from his talent as a

SPEECH CHOICES

A CASE STUDY: *MIA*

Let's see what choices Mia is making about language and style.

Mia was not a huge fan of how her voice sounded when she was recorded. (Is anyone?) Still, Mia made sure this was part of her plan as she refined, edited, and practiced her speech. She also worked on *how* she wanted to tell the stories of refugees who had used cell phones during their journeys. She was already planning to use specific examples to compare journeys, show that many challenges were similar, and identify ways that smartphones had helped. For these examples, Mia wanted to use as many details as possible to engage her listeners.

She also planned to use as much vivid language as possible to bring the stories to life. To prepare for this, she rewrote passages of each story, using specific words and phrases that engaged the senses. Her description of a boat that began to sink as it moved across the sea toward Greece noted the substandard, overcrowded vessel, which became full of water after the engine died. As the boat sank, four emigrants had to jump into the sea without life jackets, relying on only two children's rubber rings to keep them afloat. They swam for seven hours in cold water, battling strong waves. In these ways, Mia hoped to paint a strong and moving image of the emigrants' harrowing journey.

YOUR TURN:
How might you use vivid language in your speeches?

For more questions and activities for this case study, please go to LaunchPad at macmillanhighered.com/speakup4e.

ballplayer. Thus, it would be appropriate and even necessary to acknowledge his race during that speech.

A Note on Appropriate Language and Political Correctness

The notions of *appropriate language* and *political correctness* have made it difficult for people to know how to avoid bias in their speeches. What do these terms mean exactly? The idea behind appropriate language is that words have tremendous power to influence the ways people think of, feel about, and treat each other. Thus, it is important to avoid—as

SPEECH CHOICES

A CASE STUDY: *JACOB*

Let's check in with Jacob to see his plans to utilize language and style for his speech.

Jacob considered himself to be a pretty confident person. For this reason, he didn't think he needed to practice much before the speech. In fact, he thought that practicing might prevent him from acting natural and casual. He'd seen a couple of his classmates act nervous, and he didn't understand it. All you needed was to act like you knew what you were doing. He allowed himself a few fantasies of how he'd look up there. He would make strong eye contact and end the speech with everyone applauding, fully convinced of his thesis. It was going to be pretty great, actually.

Jacob knew that he was going to pull in the audience by using examples of athletes. He was going to focus on two athlete profiles—one for a running back on the football team and the other for a starting guard/all league player on the men's basketball team. He knew one declaration he would make: "These guys are really being treated unfairly. They sacrifice everything for the game, and they get little to nothing in return." That would have to convince his audience, if they weren't already convinced.

YOUR TURN:
Do you feel confident giving speeches? If not, how could you increase your confidence?

For more questions and activities for this case study, please go to LaunchPad at macmillanhighered.com/speakup4e.

often as possible—words that could cause harm or pain to others, especially in terms of a person's or a group's identity.

Some people, on the other hand, argue that efforts to encourage the use of appropriate language often go too far. Rather than protecting certain vulnerable people from hurtful language, critics say that these guidelines limit people's precious right to freedom of expression by establishing strict rules of political correctness—written or unwritten codes of conduct requiring language that reflects a politically and socially liberal view.

The best way to avoid the debate over appropriate language and political correctness is to support your position on an issue—no matter what it is—with credible evidence and logical reasoning. Otherwise, your listeners probably will perceive you as prejudiced. Saying something like, "We all know that the Americans with Disabilities Act puts an unfair

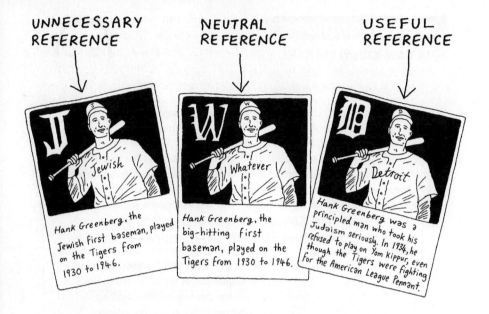

UNNECESSARY REFERENCE

NEUTRAL REFERENCE

USEFUL REFERENCE

Hank Greenberg, the Jewish first baseman, played on the Tigers from 1930 to 1946.

Hank Greenberg, the big-hitting first baseman, played on the Tigers from 1930 to 1946.

Hank Greenberg was a principled man who took his Judaism seriously. In 1934, he refused to play on Yom Kippur, even though the Tigers were fighting for the American League Pennant.

burden on employers" would instantly reveal bias and a lack of thought about your topic. On the other hand, you could build a much stronger case on the difficulties some businesses might encounter in complying with the Americans with Disabilities Act by making careful word choices and offering solid and unbiased evidence, such as compelling examples, credible statistics, and solid expert testimony.

CHAPTER REVIEW

"Choose your words carefully."

As Marvin's story revealed, word choice can make or break the effectiveness of your speech. In this chapter, we explained how to use language to clarify your message, captivate your audience, and enhance your credibility. Key practices include understanding the denotative and connotative meanings of words and evoking those meanings strategically. We also offered ideas for presenting your message clearly—including using understandable language and concrete words, employing words properly, and adopting concise language. And we suggested that to infuse your speech with color and evocative imagery, you can use devices such as repetition, hypothetical examples, personal anecdotes, vivid language, and various forms of figurative language. Finally, we addressed the importance of using unbiased language to show respect for your listeners. Suggestions on this front include avoiding stereotypes; using gender-neutral references; referring to ethnic groups appropriately; and avoiding references to ethnicity, religion, gender, or sexuality that are irrelevant to a point you're making.

 LaunchPad
macmillan learning

LaunchPad for *Speak Up* offers videos and encourages self-assessment through adaptive quizzing. Go to **macmillanhighered.com/speakup4e** to get access to:

✓ **LearningCurve**
Adaptive Quizzes

▶ **Video clips that help you understand**
public speaking concepts

Key Terms

word choice (diction) *336*
denotative meaning *341*
connotative meaning *342*
jargon *344*
concrete word *345*
abstract word *345*
verbal clutter *349*
hypothetical example *351*
 vivid language *353*

imagery *354*
 figurative language *355*
anaphora *355*
▶ antithesis *355*
▶ simile *356*
▶ metaphor *356*
biased language *357*
stereotype *357*
gender-neutral term *359*

Review Questions

1. How does a speaker's choice of words affect his or her credibility?
2. Describe three ways in which oral language differs from written language.
3. Define *denotative meaning* and *connotative meaning*, and describe the differences between the two.
4. What four qualities ensure clear language?

5. Describe five tools you can use to express your ideas more effectively.

6. Explain four steps you can take to ensure that the language you use is unbiased and respectful.

Critical Thinking Questions

1. Think of a topic you might describe at fifty feet. How might you describe or explain the same topic at five thousand feet?

2. Is the dictionary your only tool for checking that you understand a word's meaning and have used (and pronounced) it properly? How else can you assess connotative meanings that might be associated with a particular word?

3. When is it appropriate to use a rhetorical figure of speech known as antithesis? What advantages does it offer a speaker? How would you use antithesis?

4. What does the term *politically correct* mean to you? Are words like *fireman* and *cleaning lady* merely offensive to some people, or are they inaccurate? Are there any words that would offend you if they came up in a speech? Are there any politically correct terms that bother you? Why or why not?

Activities

1. Consider three examples of jargon that you use with your friends. Then try explaining them in ways that make them understandable to other people.

2. Open a dictionary at random, and look at one particularly long entry. How many different meanings are listed for the word you found? How do the meanings vary? Can you think of any connotative meanings not listed in the dictionary?

3. Find a news article that references a relatively complicated study, a piece of legislation, or a reputable survey. Compare the news article with the original item (which you can usually find through a Web link or search). How different is the language presented in each? What choices has the news writer made in deciphering the study, legislation, or survey for a more general audience?

4. Think about a funny and engaging story that you enjoy telling about yourself or your family. How might you use such a story or anecdote to illustrate a point in a speech? What kinds of topics might your story or anecdote lend itself to?

Study Plan

_____

_____

_____

_____

_____

_____

_____

_____

_____

_____

_____

_____

_____

_____

_____

_____

13

DELIVERING YOUR SPEECH

“How you say something is often as important as what you say.”

Lesli, a student in a political science class, just finished delivering an oral presentation of her essay in favor of more fiscal conservatism in the federal government. In just eight minutes, she commented on a wide range of issues—including federal income taxes, entitlement programs, and the national debt. An experienced writer, she structured her speech clearly and concisely. She carefully outlined her speech and delivered it using a small stack of note cards. She also used several helpful visual aids, such as charts showing government spending on various social programs.

Although Lesli worked hard to develop a well-organized speech, she received only a B– from her instructor. When she asked why she didn't receive a higher grade, her professor explained that the content of the speech was excellent but that her **delivery**—the combination of verbal and nonverbal communication skills used to present the speech—was less than ideal. The instructor explained that Lesli had spoken too fast, used a monotone voice, and fussed too much with her note cards. In addition, she had turned her back on her audience while pointing to and discussing her visual aids.

Lesli's experience reveals a major lesson for all public speakers: how you say something can be as important as what you say. Why is effective delivery crucial in public speaking? It helps make your speech compelling and memorable. In an age when audience members may be easily distracted by their many responsibilities, even the most carefully researched and clearly organized talk may not be enough to hold their attention. Speakers today need every advantage they can get to capture—and keep—their listeners' interest. Skillful delivery can give you that edge. Think about it: in your lifetime, you may have listened to dozens or even hundreds of speeches. Of these, how many did you find truly memorable? And what made them outstanding? If you're like most people, you'll realize that the best speech you've ever heard not only contained valuable ideas but also was delivered in a way that held your attention and had you remembering the speech long after it was over.

In fact, delivery is what comes to mind for most people when they think about speechmaking. Although audience analysis, research, preparation, and practice play vital roles in public speaking, it's how you deliver your speech that determines whether you'll be effective with your audience members. In this chapter, we discuss speech delivery—focusing on the various ways you can present a speech as well as the verbal and nonverbal skills you need to deliver a powerful, evocative, and exciting presentation.

SELECTING THE RIGHT MODE OF DELIVERY

Imagine yourself standing before an audience, preparing to make an address. How will you actually deliver your speech? Will you read from a manuscript? Recite from text you've memorized? Speak extemporaneously from an outline?

In most classroom settings (as well as many settings outside of class), speaking extemporaneously from an outline will allow you to achieve the best possible results. This delivery mode enables you to adopt a natural, conversational style that audiences appreciate. Yet there are certain situations in which you may want to read from a manuscript or recite your speech word-for-word from memory. We examine each of these three delivery modes in turn, starting with reading from a manuscript.

Reading from a Manuscript

In this delivery mode, you give your speech by reading directly from a **script**—a typed or handwritten document containing the entire text of your speech. As you read, you typically do not deviate from your script or improvise.

Although most people using this delivery mode read from a printed script, it has become increasingly popular for speakers to use teleprompter devices when addressing large audiences. From the audience's perspective, teleprompters are clear, appearing as small glass screens around the speaker; from the speaker's perspective, however, they display lines of text, which advance in time with the speech. Having more than one teleprompter allows the speaker to appear to shift his or her gaze toward different parts of the audience while continuing to read the text from the prompter. Although teleprompters might seem ubiquitous—they are used by television news anchors, politicians, presenters at award ceremonies, and so on—the technology is not available in most public speaking situations. Thus, for the purposes of our discussion, reading from a script means reading from a printed or handwritten manuscript that the speaker holds in his or her hands.

Delivery from a script is appropriate in circumstances in which speakers (or speechwriters) need to choose their words very carefully.

READING FROM A MANUSCRIPT   MEMORIZING FROM A MANUSCRIPT   SPEAKING FROM AN OUTLINE

ONLY SPECIFIC, FORMAL SITUATIONS CALL FOR MANUSCRIPT DELIVERY

Dear valued customers,
As a father of two, I know nothing is more important than the safety of children.
Quality and safety have always taken highest priority at ACME PLASTIC ANIMALS INCORPORATED. It is therefore with great regret that I must announce the total recall of our GREAT WHITE SHARK, model number 884A. During the manufacturing process an error was made...

CEO

#884A

LACERATION HAZARD

The word-for-word manuscript delivery ensures that listeners hear *exactly* what you want them to hear. For example, public speakers often use this mode of delivery in press conferences. Imagine a lawyer approaching the microphone to "make a statement" to the press about his client, a professional athlete accused of wrongdoing. The lawyer reads directly from a carefully prepared manuscript to ensure that his exact words are heard and reported in the news, with no deviations and no surprises. By closely controlling his message, he stands a better chance of controlling what journalists say about him or his client and therefore influencing public perception.

Still, reading from a script has its disadvantages. To begin with, the script itself becomes a prop—something you can hide behind as you read. And like other props, it can limit your eye contact with the audience.

In addition, when you read from a script, you tend to speak in a monotone rather than a conversational tone. Some listeners will find this mode dull and impersonal, while others may even consider it condescending. Consider the words of one student about a fellow classmate: "To tell you the truth, I almost found it insulting. If all [the speaker] wanted to do was read to us, he could have just given us the notes and let us read them ourselves."

Memorizing from a Manuscript

To recite a speech memorized from a script, you learn your script word-for-word and deliver it without looking at any text, notes, or outline. You behave like an actor on the stage who memorizes dialogue and recites

MEMORIZED DELIVERY CAN COME ACROSS AS SLICK... AND NOT IN A GOOD WAY

the words as part of a *performance*. When would you want to deliver a speech by memorizing from a script? Memorization is advisable only when you are called on to deliver a precise message and are already trained to memorize a great deal of text and deliver it flawlessly.

This delivery mode does offer some advantages over reading from a script. There's no barrier between you and your audience, so you can maintain eye contact with listeners throughout your speech. This allows you to be more natural when using gestures and visual aids. And like reading from a manuscript, you can control your word choice by repeating precisely what you've memorized. Memorization was a key feature of classical rhetorical training, but it is no longer considered the best form of speech preparation and delivery in most situations.

This mode of delivery has several disadvantages. For one thing, memorized presentations often come across as slick and prepackaged, or "canned." Listeners may view the speech as a stale performance delivered the same way every time, regardless of the audience. As a result, they may take offense or lose interest.

Memorizing is also very challenging, especially with a long speech. And people who speak from memory are typically wedded to their text; the presentation can grind to a halt if the speaker forgets even a single word or sentence.

ANOTHER DOWNSIDE
OF MEMORIZATION

Because this delivery mode's disadvantages outweigh its advantages, we recommend avoiding it unless you have a specific background in memorizing large bodies of text (as a trained actor, for example) *and* your speech situation requires it.

Speaking from an Outline

In this mode of delivery—which is the preferred mode in most speech situations—you deliver your speech by referring to a brief outline you prepared in advance. Typically, you will want to prepare and practice first with a full-sentence working outline. Next, you'll want to condense the working outline into a briefer speaking outline (complete with delivery cues), recorded on sheets of paper or note cards (for more information on outlines, see Chapter 11).

You should be able to glance at this brief outline and instantly remember what you want to say. If you've made the note cards easy to read (for example, by using large print and spaces between lines), you can maintain eye contact with your audience. Using this brief outline to deliver your speech will allow you to speak *extemporaneously*, meaning you will write the outline ahead of time, learn the material in the outline, and then speak spontaneously in the presentation with only the outline available for reference.

SPEAKING FROM AN OUTLINE

GOOD EYE CONTACT ⟶ 👁 - - - - 👁

COMFORTABLE GESTURES

GOOD MOVEMENT

FRESH, NOT CANNED, LANGUAGE

ORGANIC

SUPPORT AND GUIDANCE

POCKET MAP

STOPS YOU FROM GETTING LOST

Speaking from an outline offers the best aspects of reading from a script and memorizing your speech while avoiding their disadvantages. You can glance at the outline just long enough to spur your memory, so there's no barrier between you and your audience, and your eye contact does not suffer. Also, you don't have to worry about forgetting your place because the outline is at hand to remind you.

Equally important, when you speak from an outline, your delivery becomes more *conversational*. You sound as if you are talking with your listeners instead of reading a speech to and *at* them. Finally, with this delivery mode, you choose your words flexibly, so you can adapt your message as needed to the audience at hand. For instance, if you notice that a listener looks confused, you can provide further explanation for the point you're discussing.

Of course, speakers need to practice delivering from their outlines to give the best possible presentation. This practice is also beneficial in another way: research indicates that practice and preparation can lessen the anxiety that speakers feel when it is time to present.[1]

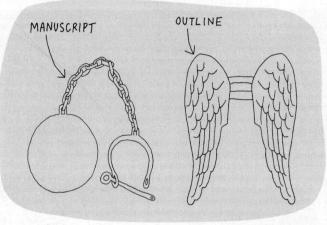

Impromptu Speaking

In some situations, you may be called on to speak unexpectedly. **Impromptu delivery** means that you are generating your speech content in the moment, without time to prepare in advance. These kinds of speeches are both quite common and very challenging for inexperienced speakers. They occur regularly in a variety of situations: you might be called on to speak at a meeting at the last minute, to comment in a class, or to offer a spur-of-the-moment toast at a wedding or party. You also use impromptu delivery while fielding unexpected questions after a presentation.

Although such situations can seem terrifying for new speakers, it is possible to handle them effectively if you follow a few simple guidelines for impromptu delivery. The key is to remember that even in a spontaneous speaking situation, you can still present from a mental outline that you draft quickly and keep in your mind, just as you would with a physical outline in an extemporaneous situation. (Or if you have a few moments to collect yourself, you might try to jot down your main points.) You can pull together a mental outline by quickly asking yourself the following questions:

- *What is the question or topic?* Begin by thinking carefully about the precise nature of the question or topic you have been asked to address. In speech parlance, this is sometimes referred to as

IMPROMPTU SPEAKING

thinking about the call of the question/topic. Ask yourself, "What is the specific topic to speak about? What is the specific question to answer?" Be precise here.

- *What is my answer or view?* As you are developing a mental outline, consider what you think about the topic or what you think the answer to the question is.

- *How do I support my position?* Consider the reasons that support your view or your answer.

Your answers to these questions should quickly yield a precise thesis or topic statement that also serves as a preview of the organization and body of the speech. This entire process can occur in a matter of seconds.

Because this is an impromptu speech, people will not expect a carefully prepared introduction; thus, a direct one will suffice (for example, "I'm delighted to tell you what our division has been developing this year"). Your conclusion need only summarize your points and restate your position (for example, "So that's what we've been working on this year. I hope you're all as excited about these new products as we are").

USING VERBAL DELIVERY SKILLS

To deliver a successful speech, you need to think about more than just your mode of delivery; you need to draw on a variety of speaking skills, both verbal and nonverbal. In this section, we examine the importance of **verbal delivery skills**—that is, the effective use of your voice when delivering a speech. Developing verbal delivery skills involves careful consideration of the use of *volume, tone, rate of delivery, projection, articulation, pronunciation,* and *pausing.*

Volume

Volume refers to how loud or soft your voice is as you deliver a speech. Some speakers are not audible enough, and others are too audible. A guiding rule for volume is to be loud enough so that everyone in your audience can hear you but not so loud as to drive away the listeners positioned closest to you.

The biggest challenge for many presenters is speaking loudly enough to be heard. Because audience members don't have the option of "turning up the volume," you will need to provide that volume yourself when no microphone is available. If you speak too softly and don't project enough, your listeners may have trouble hearing you. They may even see you as timid or uncertain—which could damage your credibility.

Yet speaking too loudly presents a different set of problems. A student named Jason once gave an informative presentation in one of our classes. During his speech, many listeners in the front row began leaning back in their chairs. He was speaking so loudly that his listeners were trying to put some distance between themselves and him.

When you begin preparing your delivery, think about your volume level. How loud is your natural speaking voice? If you aren't certain, ask some friends or relatives to give you an assessment. Then consider your

audience for the speech presentation, as well as your speaking forum. How will the size of the audience or the room affect you? Finally, focus on visual cues from your audience while delivering your speech to help you determine whether your volume level is appropriate, and adjust your volume as needed.

Tone

The **tone** of your speaking voice derives from *pitch*—the highs and lows in your voice. If you can mix high and low tones and achieve some tonal

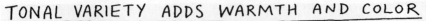

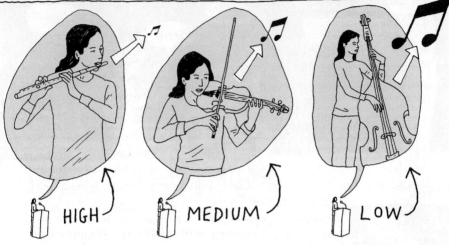

variety, you'll add warmth and color to your verbal delivery. By contrast, if your tone never varies (speaking in a **monotone**), listeners may perceive your presentation as bland, boring, or even annoying (in the case of a relentlessly high-pitched voice).

How much tonal variety should you aim for to make your voice interesting and enticing? Follow this guiding rule: use enough tonal variety to add warmth, intensity, and enthusiasm to your voice but not so much variety that you sound like an adolescent whose voice is cracking. As you practice your speech, try dropping your pitch in some places and raising it in others. If you're not sure whether you're achieving enough tonal variety, practice in front of a trusted friend, family member, classmate, or colleague, and solicit her or his feedback.

Additionally, consider using *inflection*—raising or lowering your pitch—to emphasize certain words or expressions. For instance, try a lower pitch to convey the seriousness of an idea, or end on a higher pitch if you are posing a question. Like italics on a printed page, inflection draws attention to the words or expressions you want your audience to notice and remember.

Rate of Delivery

Your **rate of delivery** refers to how quickly or slowly you speak during a presentation. As with other verbal delivery skills, going to one extreme or another (in this case, speaking too quickly or too slowly) can hurt your delivery.

Consider the example of Louis, a student at Harvard University who had a very slow rate of delivery. While giving a talk during a semi-nar on music theory, he noticed that many students (as well as the teacher) seemed inattentive. He also became aware that those listeners who *were* paying attention began interrupting him—not with questions about the content of his speech but with queries about his next point. Clearly, they were trying to move him along, which probably meant they were irritated and distracted.

Do you fall into the "slow speaker" category? Do people tend to finish your sentences for you—during conversations or while you're delivering a public address? Although people who try to finish your statements may seem rude, their behavior sends an important signal that you need to increase your rate of delivery. Fail to catch that signal, and you risk losing your audience's interest and appreciation.

Swinging to the other extreme—talking too fast—presents the opposite problem. Overly fast talkers tend to run their words together, particu-larly at the ends of sen-tences, preventing their audiences from track-ing what they're say-ing. Listeners often have a difficult time in this situation—not because they are disinterested or impatient but simply because they

cannot comprehend what is being said. In the worst-case scenario, potentially interested audience members may transform into defeated listeners because of a fast talker's verbal onslaught (see Chapter 4, Listening Skills).

> ⊙ **To view an example of someone speaking at too fast of a rate, try Video Activity 13.1, "Rate Too Fast (Needs Improvement)."**

The guiding rule for achieving an appropriate rate of delivery is this: speak fast enough to keep your presentation lively and interesting but not so fast that you become inarticulate. You also can ask a friend or relative to listen to you and give you feedback about your rate of delivery. Finally, resist any temptation to speed up your delivery to fit an overly long speech into the allocated time. Instead, shorten the content of the presentation.

Projection

Have you ever observed someone singing without a microphone and wondered how the person's voice managed to reach people near *and* far? What about actors on a stage who speak their lines quietly yet can still

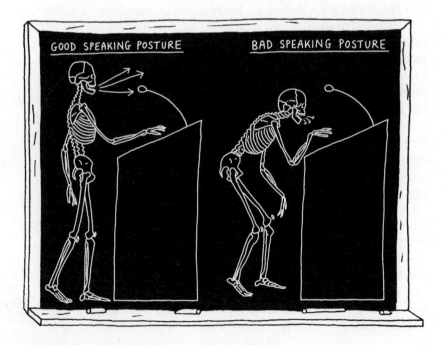

be heard by everyone in the theater? These individuals use **projection**—"booming" their voices across a forum to reach all audience members.

To project, use the air you exhale from your lungs to carry the sound of your voice across the room or auditorium. Projection is all about the mechanics of breathing. To send your voice clearly across a large space, first maintain good posture: sit or stand up straight, with your shoulders back and your head at a neutral position (not too far forward or back). Also, exhale from your diaphragm—that sheet of muscle just below your rib cage—to push your breath away from you.

Articulation

Articulation refers to the crispness or clarity of your spoken words. When you articulate, your vowels and consonants sound clear and distinct, and your listeners can distinguish your separate words as well as the syllables in your words. The result? Your audience can easily understand what you're saying.

Articulation problems are most common when nervousness increases a speaker's rate of delivery or when a speaker is being inattentive. Whatever the cause of your articulation issues, focus on this rule to get better results: when you deliver a speech, clearly and distinctly express all parts of the words in your presentation, and make sure not to round off the ends of words or lower your voice at the ends of sentences.

Pronunciation

Pronunciation refers to correctness in the way you say words. Are you saying them in a way that has been commonly agreed to? If you pronounce terms incorrectly, your listeners may have difficulty understanding you. Equally troublesome, they may question your credibility.

Elizabeth, a banking professional, related the following story about the problems that can arise when a speaker mispronounces words:

> In my job, I was required to work with lawyers because they drew up the trust documents for their clients. I worked with lawyers, but I was no lawyer myself. Sometimes they can be a little arrogant about their position, thinking that if you didn't go to law school, you shouldn't be working in a law-related field. I worked hard to earn their respect. But I noticed that when I used some legal terms in front of them, they occasionally looked at one another and smiled, as though they were sharing a private joke. One such word was *testator*. That's the person who creates a testament like a trust or a will. Whenever I used that word, I always said "TES-tah-tore," so that it sounded like it would rhyme with

USE CARE PRONOUNCING UNFAMILIAR WORDS OR TECHNICAL TERMS

matador. And the lawyers would smirk—but nobody ever corrected me. Eventually, I was embarrassed to learn that the word is pronounced "tes-TAY-ter."

How can you ensure that your pronunciation is accurate? The guideline here is simple: if you're not certain how to pronounce a word or a name you want to use in your speech, find out how to say it *before* you deliver your presentation. For names of public figures, search for radio or television interviews with the subject to find out the preferred pronunciation. For other words, you can ask for guidance from your instructors, classmates, coworkers, or friends who might be familiar with the term. Better still, refer to a reputable dictionary, which will provide phonetic spellings for each word as well as a general guide to pronunciation. Many online dictionaries and other resources provide useful audio clips that demonstrate proper pronunciation.[2]

Pausing

Used skillfully, **pausing**—leaving gaps between words or sentences in a speech—provides you with some significant advantages. Besides enabling you to collect your thoughts, it reinforces the seriousness of your subject because it shows that you're choosing your words carefully. Pausing can help you create a sense of importance as well. If you make a statement and then pause for the audience to weigh your words, your listeners may conclude that you've just said something especially important.

To get the most from pausing, use it judiciously, pausing every so often rather than after every sentence. Otherwise, your listeners may wonder if you're having repeated difficulty collecting your thoughts, or they may think you're being melodramatic. In either case, your audience will begin to take you less seriously.

When pausing during a speech, it's best to fill those pauses with silence rather than with verbal fillers or verbal tics. A **verbal filler** is a word or phrase, such as *like* or *you know*, that speakers use to fill uncomfortable silences. Here's an example of what verbal fillers do to a speaker's delivery:

> *And so*, the library was closed . . . *you know*. But I had to study somewhere. *But* . . . I didn't get to study there, *and* . . . *but* . . . I had to go somewhere . . . *but* . . . *and* . . . I tried the dorm reading room. *And, like* . . . it was so quiet there, *you know*?

USING A SPACE TO MAKE A POINT (and a bad pun)

FILLING SPACE POINTLESSLY

A **verbal tic** is a sound, such as *um* or *ah*, that speakers use when searching for a correct word or when they have lost their train of thought:

> *Um* . . . the purpose of my speech is . . . *ah*, to . . . *um* . . . make you see how . . . *um* . . . dangerous this action . . . *ah* . . . really is.

Everyone uses verbal fillers or tics at some point while giving speeches: it's hard *not* to. But using them too often can distract your listeners or make them wonder if you're tentative or ill-prepared. The best way to avoid overusing fillers and tics is by learning to be more aware of when you use them. How? Try speaking in front of a friend who is holding a clicker or other low-level noisemaker; have your friend use the noisemaker every time you use a filler or tic. At first you may be surprised by how often you do so, but with some practice, you will develop better awareness and better habits.

USING NONVERBAL DELIVERY SKILLS

In addition to verbal delivery, you will need to consider your nonverbal behavior as part of the delivery of your speech. **Nonverbal delivery skills** involve the use of physical behaviors to deliver a speech. In this section, we discuss how specific elements of nonverbal delivery—*eye contact, gestures, physical movement, proxemics,* and *personal appearance*—can help you connect with your audience and leave a lasting impression.

Eye Contact

To understand what **eye contact** is, you may find it helpful to think first about what it is not. Eye contact is not you looking at your audience members while they look at something else. Nor is it audience members looking directly at you while you stare at your notes or nervously gaze at the ceiling for some divine guidance on what to say next. Rather, with true eye contact, you look directly into the eyes of your audience members, and they look directly into yours.

Eye contact enables you to gauge the audience's interest in your speech. By looking into your listeners' eyes, you can discern how they're feeling about the speech (fascinated? confused? upset?). Armed with these impressions, you can adapt your delivery if needed. For example, you could provide more details about a particular point if your listeners look fascinated and hungry for more or reexplain a key point if your listeners look confused or overwhelmed.

Eye contact also helps you interact with your audience. By glancing at a particular listener, for instance, and noticing that he or she seems eager to ask a question, you might be prompted to stop and take queries from the audience.

Finally, eye contact helps you compel your audience's attention. Father Paul, a wise Episcopalian priest, once shared a secret of his effective sermonizing technique: "When I speak, I look right at my congregation. And when I do that, I make them look at me, too. And it is harder not to listen to me when I do that . . . precisely because of that!"[3]

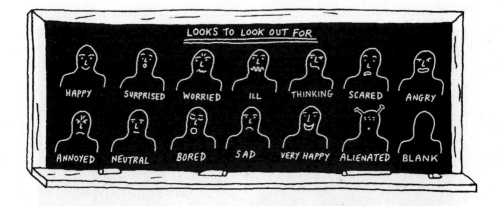

When you and your audience establish eye contact, it becomes difficult for listeners to look away or mentally drift as you're talking.

From the audience's perspective, eye contact is critical for another reason entirely. In Western cultures, many people consider a willingness to make eye contact evidence of a speaker's credibility—especially truthfulness. An old saying holds that "the eyes are the windows of the soul," meaning that our eyes can betray who we really are or what we really think or believe. Of course, just because someone makes eye contact doesn't necessarily mean that he or she is telling the truth. Likewise, a speaker's failure to look directly at the audience may stem from causes other than dishonesty, such as nervousness or shyness. Still, as long as people *believe* that the eyes reveal the soul, they will associate a lack of eye contact with deception. To communicate honesty, expertise, and confidence, maintain frequent eye contact with your audience.

PAN————————————————————————→NING

How you use eye contact depends on the size of your audience. With small audiences, try to establish and sustain direct eye contact with each listener at various points in your speech. With large audiences, this isn't practical. Therefore, you'll need to use a technique called **panning**. To pan your audience, think of your body as a tripod and your head as a movie camera that sits atop the tripod. Imagine yourself "filming" everyone in the group by moving your "camera" slowly from one side of your audience to the other. With this technique, you gradually survey all audience members—pausing and establishing extended eye contact with an individual listener for a few moments before moving on to do the same with another listener.

Panning with extended eye contact gives your audience the sense that you're looking at each listener, even if you aren't. And it still enables you to gauge your audience members' interest, hold their attention, and interact with individual listeners if needed.

Gestures

A **gesture** is a hand, head, or face movement that emphasizes, pantomimes, demonstrates, or calls attention to something.[4] Gestures can add flair to your speech delivery, especially when they seem natural rather than overly practiced.[5] Research also indicates that gestures can benefit a listener's

WORLD LEADERS USING GESTURES THEY PROBABLY SHOULDN'T

THE PUTIN CHOP

THE CLINTON TWO-GUN POINT

THE KERRY STEEPLE

THE TRUMP CONDUCTOR HAND

THE MERKEL PALM DOWN

ability to understand a speech's message.[6] The effectiveness of a gesture depends on how it links with the speech topic—so gestures depicting physical actions communicate more than those depicting abstract topics. Hand gestures that link with speech content are called co-speech gestures (CSGs). CSGs communicate thoughts and ideas in two different ways—linguistically (through words that are heard) and visually (through the gesture that is seen). Neuroimaging of the brain shows that when CSGs are used with speech, there is more activity in the parts of the brain involved with language processing—meaning that listeners understand and retain more.[7]

But gestures can backfire. For one thing, not all your listeners will interpret the same gesture—a clenched fist, an open palm, a raised forefinger—in the same way.[8] For example, some people see a fist as a symbol of violence, and others consider it a show of forcefulness or determination. If an audience member interprets a particular gesture differently from what you intended, you may inadvertently send the wrong message to that person.

You also should be aware that gestures may communicate a message that is inconsistent with your verbal message. For example, some people have criticized President Obama when he points an index finger straight up and wags it back and forth when speaking. This gesture can work if the intention is to criticize or dismiss an individual or a group, but it risks making the speaker seem arrogant, overly pious, or condescending. Gestures like this also can reinforce negative perceptions that a particular audience may already have. For example, many of the president's critics in Congress felt that he was book smart but not experienced in the political realities of Washington, DC, because he had served in the U.S. Senate for only four years before being elected president.

For them, the president's wagging finger may have reinforced the image of a professor lecturing them as if they were his students and not his political peers.

> ▶ To see an example of artificial-looking gestures, try Video Activity 13.2, "Gestures: Overly Scripted (Needs Improvement)."

In addition to ensuring that your gestures reinforce your spoken message, avoid using distracting gestures born of nervousness—such as stuffing your hands in your pockets; jingling keys or change in your pockets; or fiddling with a watch, ring, or pen. These behaviors can distract audience members to the point that they'll start focusing more on your gestures than on your speech.

To get the most from gestures, follow these guidelines:

- Use gestures deliberately to emphasize or illustrate points in your speech.
- Remain aware that not all audience members may interpret your gestures in the same way.
- Make sure your gestures reinforce your spoken message.
- Avoid nervous, distracting gestures.

Physical Movement

Physical movement describes how much or how little you move around while delivering a speech. Not surprisingly, standing still (sometimes referred to as the "tree trunk" approach) and shifting or walking restlessly from side to side or back and forth ("pacing") in front of your audience are not effective. A motionless speaker comes across as boring or odd, and a restless one is distracting and annoying.

Instead of going to either of these extremes, strive to incorporate a reasonable amount and variety of physical movement as you give your presentation. Skillful use of physical movement injects energy into your delivery *and* signals transitions between parts of your speech. For example, when making an important point in your presentation, you can take a few steps to the left in front of your audience and casually walk back to your original spot when you shift to the next major idea. One useful tip is to combine moderate movement with the panning approach to eye contact, discussed earlier in this section.

How much physical movement, if any, is right for you? Move as much as necessary to invigorate your speech (even if you must come out from behind a lectern or podium) but not so much that you confuse or distract your audience.

Finally, speaking from a lectern or podium might make you feel somewhat more comfortable because it usually acts as a barrier between you and your listeners. Unless you must be at the lectern because of a microphone, we recommend that you come out from behind it at least part of the time so that you can interact more fully with your audience. When you are at the lectern, be sure to avoid gripping the sides or top tightly with your hands; such a grip adds tension to your body and will be clearly visible to audience members.

MOVEMENT EMPHASIZES TRANSITIONS AND ENGAGES LISTENERS

X-------
STAND
HERE
TO DELIVER
THE FIRST
POINT

X
STAND
HERE
TO GIVE
THE SECOND
POINT

X
MAKE
CONCLUSION
HERE

AVOID STAYING ROOTED TO ONE SPOT

Proxemics

Proxemics—the use of space and distance between yourself and your audience—is related to physical movement. Through proxemics, you control how close you stand to your audience while delivering your speech.

The size and setup of the speech setting can help you determine how best to use proxemics. For example, in a large forum, you may want to come out from behind the podium and move closer to your audience so that listeners can see and hear you more easily. Moving toward your audience also can help you communicate intimacy;[9] it suggests you're about to convey something personal, which many audience members will find compelling. Research has shown that audiences perceive a strong association not only between closeness and intimacy but also between closeness and attraction[10] and that they see closeness as an indication of the immediacy/nonimmediacy of the speech message.[11]

Of course, people have different feelings about physical proximity. Whereas some welcome a speaker's nearness, others consider it a violation of their personal space or even a threat. Culture can influence a

THE POETICS OF SPACE (AKA PROXEMICS)

person's response to a speaker's proximity. In some cultures, physical closeness is considered offensive or invasive.[12] In others, it is considered essential to positive relationships.

To determine how much space to put between you and your listeners, consider your audience's background, the size and setup of your forum, and your ability to move around the forum. When speaking, move close enough to your listeners to interact with them and allow them to see and hear you but not so close that you violate anyone's sense of private space.

Personal Appearance

By **personal appearance**, we refer to the impression you make on your audience through your clothing, jewelry, hairstyle, and grooming, and other elements influencing how you look.[13] Personal appearance in a public speech matters for two reasons. First, many people in your

SPEECH CHOICES

A CASE STUDY: *MIA*

Let's check back with Mia and see what adjustments she made for her delivery.

Mia knew that she had a bad speaking habit: her tone of voice often rose at the end of a sentence as though she was asking a question instead of making a declarative statement. This made Mia sound as if she was constantly asking the audience if she was right instead of telling them what she really thought or believed. When she mentioned this to her teacher, her instructor advised her to "be confident in her own voice" by being more assertive and ending her sentences by lowering her tone. Mia also knew that anxiety made her lower her voice, which in turn made it difficult for people to hear her.

To work on her tone, Mia asked a friend to be her audience. At this point, Mia had already practiced the speech using her speaking outline, knew the material and the structure very well, and only occasionally had to glance at the outline for reference. When giving the speech to her friend, Mia focused on using an extemporaneous delivery style. Because she knew the speech, she also could engage with her audience with sweeping (panning) eye contact (even though for this practice run, she had only one audience member). Afterward, her friend congratulated her on her interesting speech and warm, natural delivery, boosting her confidence.

YOUR TURN:

Are there any friends or family members you could practice your speech with?

For more questions and activities for this case study, please go to LaunchPad at macmillanhighered.com/speakup4e.

---

audience will form their initial impression of you *before* you say anything—just by looking at you. Be sure your appearance communicates the right message. Second, studies show that this initial impression can be long lasting and very significant.[14] If you make a negative first impression because of a sloppy or an otherwise unappealing appearance, you'll need to expend a lot of time and effort to win back your audience's trust and rebuild your credibility.

The rule for personal appearance is to do what is appropriate for the audience you are addressing, given the occasion and the forum. If you're addressing a somber and formally dressed audience while eulogizing the life of a fallen friend, don't show up in brightly colored casual

SPEECH CHOICES

A CASE STUDY: *JACOB*

Let's see what decisions Jacob made for delivering his speech.

Two days before he was to deliver his speech, Jacob felt a twinge of fear. Was he as fully prepared as he thought he was? At that moment, Jacob decided that the best way for him to give this speech would be to read the text to the audience. That way, he could be sure that nothing was left out. The notion of reading his speech text calmed him down greatly.

The next morning, he stopped in an empty classroom to practice his speech. He picked up his five-page speech text and held it directly before his face. As Jacob read, he realized he was blocking his face from his (imaginary) audience. Even though he lowered the paper, he wasn't able to make eye contact because he had to focus on the words on his papers. He also felt stuck in one place. Maybe he should move, but that would require walking and reading at the same time!

Jacob noticed something else: his voice was coming out at a flat volume and tone. He'd imagined himself chatting conversationally with the class as he gave his speech, but this was not going as he'd planned. After his practice run, Jacob decided that perhaps he should practice his speech a little more so that he could give it without staring at his notes. After all, he was passionate about his topic, and he wanted to be able to convince his classmates of his topic—that student athletes should be paid.

YOUR TURN:

How would your delivery change if you were reading from a full speech text versus reading from a working outline?

For more questions and activities for this case study, please go to LaunchPad at macmillanhighered.com/speakup4e.

garb and loud jewelry. Likewise, if you're delivering a presentation to a potential client in an industry known for its relaxed and playful corporate culture, consider dressing down for the occasion rather than donning a blue pin-striped suit and power tie.

But in any speaking situation, you should always strive to look presentable through good grooming (neat hair, clean nails, and moderate makeup) and an overall tidy appearance (no clothes that are shabby or inappropriately revealing). That way, you show respect for the audience, the situation, and yourself.

IT'S NOT JUST WHAT YOU WEAR, IT'S WHERE YOU WEAR IT

IT'S NOT JUST WHAT YOU WEAR, IT'S HOW YOU WEAR IT

CHAPTER REVIEW

> How you say something is often as important as what you say.

As Lesli's story shows, how you deliver your speech and the verbal and nonverbal skills you use while making your presentation can spell the difference between success and failure. In this chapter, we shared the pros and cons of three modes of prepared delivery—reading from a manuscript, reciting from a memorized text, and speaking extemporaneously from an outline—and noted that extemporaneous delivery is preferred in most contemporary settings. For unprepared delivery, or impromptu speaking, we offered guidelines for coming up with a presentation on the spot. We also discussed the many different elements of verbal delivery—volume, tone, rate of delivery, projection, articulation, pronunciation, and pausing—and the ways that you can use them to create more effective speeches. Employing elements of nonverbal delivery—such as eye contact, gestures, physical movement, proxemics, and personal appearance—can further captivate and engage your audience. By applying the right delivery mode and the right blend of verbal and nonverbal skills, you can get your message across to your listeners—and leave them wanting more.

 LaunchPad
macmillan learning

LaunchPad for *Speak Up* offers videos and encourages self-assessment through adaptive quizzing. Go to **macmillanhighered.com/speakup4e** to get access to:

✓ **LearningCurve**
Adaptive Quizzes

▶ **Video clips that help you understand public speaking concepts**

Key Terms

 delivery *367*
script *369*
◎ impromptu delivery *374*
verbal delivery skills *376*
◎ volume *376*
tone *377*
monotone *378*
◎ rate of delivery *378*
projection *381*
articulation *381*
◎ pronunciation *382*

pausing *383*
 verbal filler *383*
verbal tic *384*
nonverbal delivery skills *385*
◎ eye contact *385*
panning *388*
◎ gesture *388*
◎ physical movement *391*
proxemics *392*
◎ personal appearance *393*

Review Questions

1. Describe four methods of speech delivery.
2. What are verbal delivery skills? Describe seven elements of verbal delivery discussed in the chapter.
3. Explain what is meant by nonverbal delivery. Describe five elements of nonverbal delivery discussed in the chapter.

Critical Thinking Questions

1. What is the advantage of memorized delivery over other forms of delivery? What is its chief disadvantage? In what public speaking situations might memorization be appropriate for you?

2. What kinds of audience considerations should you take into account when making decisions about your nonverbal delivery? How might gender, culture, age, and other factors affect the way particular gestures are perceived?

3. What hand gestures would you use in an informative speech that describes kitchen knives and techniques for chopping vegetables or making thin slices of tender meat? How would you use the visual imagery of co-speech gestures (CSGs) to enhance the literal meaning of your speech words?

Activities

1. Think back to the example of Obama's finger wagging in the section on gestures in this chapter. Come up with two speech topics for which this gesture would be appropriate. Now think of two speech topics for which this gesture would not be appropriate.

2. Without practicing, make a brief recording of yourself explaining a simple and familiar task—for example, providing directions for traveling from your home to campus. Then make another recording of yourself describing a less concrete concept, such as the musical qualities of a favorite song. Take note of how often you use verbal fillers and verbal tics in each case. Do you think you would have used them as often if you had prepared an outline and rehearsed? Try it, and compare your results.

3. Check out a few stand-up comedy performances on YouTube or DVD. Take note of how the comics use nonverbal delivery skills—such as eye contact, panning techniques, and movement—to engage with their audience. Which comics are most effective at using nonverbal delivery skills? Why?

Study Plan

_____

_____

_____

_____

_____

_____

_____

_____

_____

_____

_____

_____

_____

_____

_____

_____

_____

_____

_____

_____

_____

USING PRESENTATION AIDS

14

> "Listening can lead to understanding; seeing can lead to believing."

Phil couldn't wait to deliver his speech about Harley-Davidson motorcycles to his class. The purpose of the speech was to inform his audience of the differences in quality between American motorcycles and those made in Japan and Germany. A longtime Harley owner, Phil felt that if audience members could *see* a Harley up close and *hear* the distinctive rumble of its engine, they would understand his point in a visceral way. But how could he provide this experience without driving his Harley into the classroom?

Phil considered other possibilities, such as playing a recording of a Harley engine being revved, showing enlarged photos of different Harley models, or playing some video footage from a recent motorcycle convention he'd attended. He knew that any of these presentation aids would help him convey the unique character and quality of Harley-Davidson bikes. But for him, they still weren't as potent as showing his listeners an actual motorcycle.

That night, Phil shared his concerns with his wife, Claire. She came up with a solution: she would park the family Harley outside the classroom's windows during Phil's talk. When the day of the speech arrived, Phil opened the window shades and invited his classmates to stand near him as he extolled the virtues of Harley motorcycles. Outside, Claire pointed to various parts of the bike as he mentioned them. Phil's audience immediately grasped his passion for Harleys (not to mention his wife's love for him!). Through creative use of presentation aids—in this case, an actual bike and an assistant who focused his listeners' attention on various aspects of the machine—Phil was able to deliver an exceptionally engaging and interesting speech.

In this chapter, we take a close look at presentation aids, examining their advantages, the many different forms they can take, and strategies for using them effectively.

WHY USE PRESENTATION AIDS?

Speech communication experts have long believed that listeners are much more likely to grasp spoken facts and concepts if presenters also provide visual and other nonverbal cues.[1] As early as the 1950s, studies showed that the use of audio and visual aids in a speech could increase learning by as much as 55 percent,[2] and today teachers recognize that aids helped students learn the course material.[3] Recent studies show that aids enhance learning for both inexperienced audience members and those who are experienced and knowledgeable about the subject matter.[4] A **presentation aid** is anything beyond your spoken words that you employ to help your audience members understand and remember your message. Also known as *audiovisual aids*, presentation aids include any materials you might use to support and convey the points and subpoints in your speech.

Consider your own learning experiences over the years. For example, how did you come to understand difficult math concepts? Did your teacher expect you to know how to solve complex problems after merely lecturing to you about algebra or geometry? Or did she *illustrate* the problems and concepts on the chalkboard—with plenty of examples? Most likely, you found the illustrations helpful and even essential for grasping the concepts. Likewise, if you studied a language not native to you, did your teacher merely lecture to you about the language in your native tongue? Or did he model the language for you, demonstrating correct pronunciation and perhaps playing recordings of native speakers using the language? Again, you probably found the demonstrations and recordings crucial for mastering the basics of the new language.

Savvy use of presentation aids can help you gain several important advantages as you deliver a speech.

Presentation Aids Can Make Your Speech More Interesting

A colorful and attractive presentation aid can help you spice up any presentation, especially one on a slightly dry topic. For instance, a financial-services salesperson giving a talk on retirement savings might display a photo of an older couple looking relaxed, happy, and healthy. The salesperson also could provide graphs that show the makeup of sensible investments.

ADDING INTEREST WITH A VISUAL AID

Presentation Aids Can Simplify a Complex Topic

If you are giving a speech on a technical or complicated topic, a presentation aid can help you simplify your message so that your listeners can better understand you. For example, a student giving a presentation on how to skydive could show a drawing of a simplified parachute, with labels highlighting each part of the equipment.

Presentation Aids Can Help Your Audience Remember Your Speech

Many individuals find visual information much easier to recall than spoken information.[5] Thus, the right presentation aids can help ensure that you leave a lasting impression on your listeners. For example, a speaker sharing a long list of reasons for changing the entrance requirements at a community college might hammer home his message by displaying a bulleted list of his main points at the end of his speech.

HELPING YOUR AUDIENCE REMEMBER YOUR SPEECH

TYPES OF PRESENTATION AIDS

A presentation aid may provide only audio assistance (such as a recording of a Harley-Davidson motorcycle engine), only visual assistance (such as a photograph of a person on a surfboard), or both audio and visual assistance simultaneously (as in a digital video recording of an exotic bird singing). Traditional aids include *the speaker*, *assistants*, *objects*, *visual images* (maps, photographs and drawings, diagrams), *graphs* (line, bar, pie), *text-based visuals*, and *audio and video*. Here, we take a closer look at each type of presentation aid.

The Speaker

You yourself can be an effective visual aid, particularly if your topic calls for an explanation of an action. Consider Zoya, a student who loved rock

YOU CAN BE YOUR OWN PRESENTATION AID

climbing and gave a presentation on the sport's basics. During her speech, she covered some common climbing moves and provided tips for taking lessons and finding the best beginner climbing spots. To illustrate her points, Zoya wore the clothes, special shoes, and equipment (harness, belay device, carabiners) that she used while climbing. Through her attire, she served as a visual aid.

In addition to wearing clothing or other apparel or equipment related to your topic, you can be a visual aid by demonstrating or acting out an aspect of your speech topic. Shenille, a college sophomore in a speech class, prepared an informative presentation about three styles of African dance. She described them and then demonstrated each one by dancing briefly before the audience.

Assistants

If serving as a presentation aid yourself would complicate things too much or prevent you from interacting with your audience, consider asking someone to help you reinforce points from your speech or to

demonstrate something. For example, in speeches about lifesaving techniques and the use of cardiopulmonary resuscitation (CPR), lifeguards teaching new recruits often ask an assistant to play the role of a victim of a drowning accident, concussion, heart attack, or stroke. The lifeguard then demonstrates techniques and procedures on the assistant while the class watches. As we saw earlier in the chapter, using an assistant can also help you surmount unique challenges in using presentation aids— such as how to show a motorcycle to a classroom of students.

Objects

Any object can be a visual aid. For example, in a speech about James Bond movies, one student presented a collection of posters depicting all the actors who ever played 007, from Sean Connery to Daniel Craig. By contrast, in a 2014 TED (Technology, Entertainment, and Design) talk, Hugh Herr introduced a new generation of bionic limbs. Herr, a professor at the Massachusetts Institute of Technology and director of the biomechatronics research group at the MIT Media Lab, had lost both legs in a climbing accident three decades earlier. In this speech, he described the science behind the new bionic limbs, including mechanical interface (how bionic limbs attach to the physical body), dynamic interface (how bionic limbs move like flesh and bone), and electrical interface (how bionic limbs connect to the central nervous system). As he described each point, he also wore and modeled the bionic limbs—effectively becoming the object he was describing. He also ran in place, showing how this equipment was the first that allowed for running in place after only a neural command from the brain.

Herr also brought onstage Adrianne Haslet-Davis. a former dancer and marathoner who lost a leg after finishing the 2013 Boston Marathon during the terrorist bombing attack. Serenaded by music, Haslet-Davis and her partner performed a ballroom dance routine that brought audience members to their feet for a standing ovation. They knew they were witnessing a new technology that had the potential to improve the lives of millions of people.[6]

Herr spoke to a large audience, and for this reason he used a large projection screen behind him to make the components of a bionic limb accessible to all. If you are using a small object as a presentation aid in a speech to your classmates, consider walking closer to them and holding up the object for them to see.

What if you have the opposite challenge: your object is too large or unwieldy to present in its entirety to your audience? This situation calls for equally creative problem solving. Consider Alan, a student who gave a speech about the "physics of bowling." He explained everything about bowling—including the science behind the holes drilled into the balls, the effect of the rotation and angle of the bowler's arm on the ball's momentum, and the ball's effect on the pins. Alan couldn't bring an entire bowling alley into the classroom, so he came up with an ingenious alternative. He showed his audience three bowling balls—all with different kinds of holes. Then he rolled each ball down a slanted table and into the hands of an assistant. As he rolled the balls, he pointed out to

his audience how each ball's speed and path differed based on its design and his technique.

Visual Images

As the old saying goes, a picture can be worth a thousand words. When giving a speech, you sometimes can save time and improve clarity by presenting a simple visual representation rather than describing something. If you are explaining the layout of a room, for example, showing audience members a scale drawing will provide them with a clearer image than verbally describing the room's dimensions. Several types of visual aids can give your audience a clearer image of what you are talking about, including *maps*, *photographs and drawings*, and *diagrams*.

Maps. A map is a visual representation of geography and can contain as much or as little information as you wish. In addition to the map itself, you can add highlighting or labels to make the map more useful to your audience. For example, if you're giving a talk on the architecture of a particular city, you could show a map with labels for the city's most important buildings. In a presentation about competing in the Ironman triathlon in Hawaii, a speaker could use a map to show the route traveled for the race.

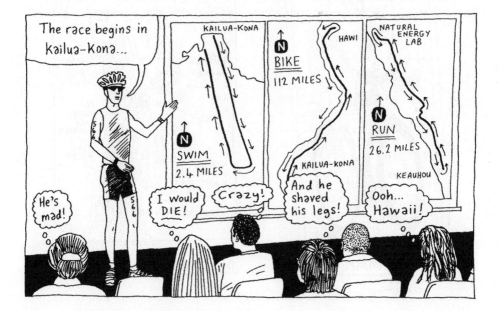

Photographs and Drawings. Photographs can help you provide an exact depiction. For example, if you're giving a speech about the *Mona Lisa*, you could display a photograph of the painting and point out certain aspects of Leonardo da Vinci's technique. Drawings enable you to emphasize certain details about your topic. For instance, in a speech about how mosquitoes spread malaria, you could display a drawing of the insect that shows how its proboscis is the tool for spreading disease. As with maps, you can add labels or other types of highlighting to a photograph or drawing to focus your audience's attention on specific details.

Diagrams. If you are explaining how something works or describing its parts, a diagram can be helpful. A **diagram** is a drawing that details an object or action and the relationships among its parts. Diagrams can be drawn by hand or rendered on computers, and they typically include visual images, labels, and other important information. Coaches routinely diagram plays to convey strategy to their players. You also might use an

PHOTO OF COMPETITOR

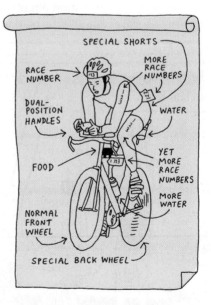

DIAGRAM OF COMPETITOR

annotated diagram to provide instructions or point out the elements of something, such as bicycle equipment.

Graphs

A **graph** is a visual representation of the relationship among different numbers, measurements, or quantities. Graphs are especially useful when presenting a great deal of statistical evidence. Some common types of graphs are *line graphs*, *bar graphs*, and *pie charts*.

Line Graphs. A **line graph** uses lines plotted on vertical and horizontal axes to show relationships between two elements. For example, you could use a line graph to show the various elevations of the Ironman race or the profits that a company made over a ten-year period.

Bar Graphs. A **bar graph** consists of parallel bars of varying height or length that compare several pieces of information. For instance, you could use a bar graph to compare the weight loss of three categories of tri-athletes in a series of races.

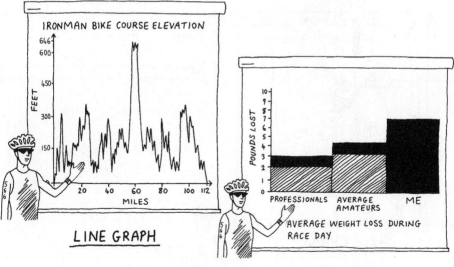

Pie Charts. A **pie chart** (also known as a **circle graph**) is used to show how percentages and proportions relate to one another and add up to a whole. A pie chart resembles a pie that has been divided up into slices, with each slice representing a percentage of the total sum. You could use a pie chart to show the percentages of different types of foods in a recommended diet for triathletes or the money that your town spent in a given year on various services, such as education or road repair.

Text-Based Visuals

In some cases, presenting text graphically can help your audience organize and understand information. For example, to highlight key ideas or important "takeaways" from your speech, you could use a **verbal chart**, which arranges words in a certain format, such as bullet points or columns. You might use a verbal chart to list tips for last-minute Ironman triathlon race preparation, show the parts of a motorcycle engine, or compare the pros and cons of a particular issue.

Text and graphics can be combined to convey both information and action. A **flowchart** is a text-based visual that demonstrates the direction of information, processes, and ideas. You might use a flowchart to show

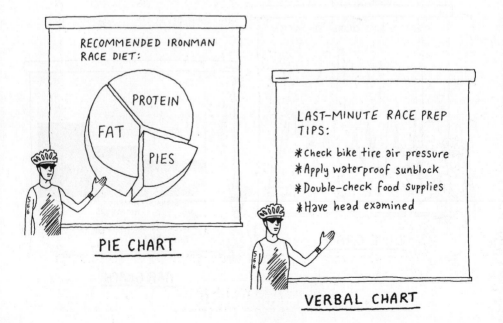

RECOMMENDED IRONMAN RACE DIET:

PROTEIN

FAT

PIES

PIE CHART

LAST–MINUTE RACE PREP TIPS:

* Check bike tire air pressure
* Apply waterproof sunblock
* Double-check food supplies
* Have head examined

VERBAL CHART

FLOWCHART

the steps that someone takes to prepare for the Ironman competition or the process that a bank uses to decide whether to lend money to a mortgage applicant. It is important to use text-based visuals sparingly; you do not want to present your entire speech outline as a visual aid.

Audio and Video

In many speech situations, it can be useful to demonstrate an action that cannot easily be described in words or presented in a still image. In such cases, you may incorporate audio selections or video clips into your presentation to explain, demonstrate, or illustrate a key point. We discuss several means of sharing audio and video, as well as practical considerations for doing so, in the section on technology. But first, let's consider the circumstances in which this type of content is most useful.

Audio. Presenting sound recordings or effects can greatly enhance a presentation if used well. In a speech about a particular musician or composer, for example, it makes sense to play a recording of his or her work for the audience. Audio also can make abstract concepts easier to understand. For example, Monica prepared a speech about the effects of loud music on hearing. Because *loud* is a relative term, Monica decided to play audio recordings of different sounds (the engine of a compact car, a radio turned up all the way, a jet engine during takeoff) at different volumes. Although Monica couldn't subject her audience to a roar as loud as a real jet engine, she arranged the *relative* loudness of the sounds to demonstrate noise levels by decibel and to help her audience understand the nature of sound and the ways it is measured.

Video. A video is useful to your presentation whenever showing the subject in action or motion would enhance the audience's understanding more than showing a still photo or describing the subject verbally would. For example, a photograph depicting alpine ski racer and Olympic gold medalist Lindsey Vonn would identify her as a world-class athlete and celebrity, but a video showing her skill during a race would be more useful if the speech focused on racing techniques.

In the same vein, video may be a better choice for your presentation aid if a moving image can better capture the scene or setting. For example, a photograph of a redwood tree on fire might be useful in a

speech about forest fires, but a digital video of a burning tree could better demonstrate how quickly a fire can spread.

Not all video clips are useful. Video works best when it is clear, compelling, and easy to see. For example, Meg is a bird-watcher, and she wants to give a speech about a type of seabird that nests near her home. Showing a grainy video clip of the fast-moving bird in flight probably would not add much to her presentation because it would not provide a clear image of the bird or a real sense of how it moves. However, a color illustration or photo of the bird, along with an audio clip of its call, would greatly enhance her presentation.

USING TECHNOLOGY WISELY

You've prepared your speech, and you've collected visual and audio aids that will support your points in an interesting way. Now you need to decide how to present them. Should you download all of your audio and video onto a laptop and create a digital slide show, complete with video clips and audio? Or will a simple flip chart and CD player do the job more effectively? In this section, we look at various means of incorporating both low- and high-tech presentation aids and examine the pros and cons of each.

Using Presentation Software

Presentation software (sometimes referred to as *slideware*) enables users to create, edit, and present information, usually in a slide-show format. You can use presentation software to create tables, charts, graphs, and illustrations. Digital cameras, cell phones, and MP3 players have further transformed the world of presentation aids by enabling you to capture, download, and share photos, audio, and video cheaply and easily. If you have access to a computer as well as a digital projector and audio speakers, this software makes it relatively easy to incorporate all of your aids into a digital slide show and present it to your audience. Such digital presentations have become widespread in business settings, in communities across the world, and on college campuses; indeed, some instructors may require a digital presentation for a public speaking course.

The most commonly used presentation software is Microsoft Power-Point,[7] but other software products are also available, including Adobe Flash, Apple Keynote, Articulate Presenter, Camtasia, Camstudio, ClearSlide (SlideRocket), CustomShow, Emaze, GoAnimate, Google Docs Presentations, Haiku Deck, Knowledge Vision, MediaShout, OpenOffice Impress, Projeqt, Powtoon, Prezi, Reallusion, Slide Bureau, SlideDog, Slideshare, Slideshark, Snagit, Wink, and Zoho Show.[8] The instructions for using these programs vary and change with each new version (refer to your program's user guide for technical guidance). Along with the general guidelines for any presentation aid, there are certain things you should keep in mind when developing a digital slide-show presentation.

Use it to unify a mixed-media presentation. If you have many different types of aids (pictures, data graphs, lists, video, and audio), presenting them in a unified way helps keep the audience focused on your message. Digital slide shows allow you to incorporate a variety of presentation aids and present them in one consistent frame. They also make it easy to print out parts of your slide show for audience members to take home. Such handouts are especially useful in informational presentations.

Remember, content is king. Don't let your speech be eclipsed by technological bells and whistles. As with any presentation aid, you should use presentation software to share material that supports your points. A slick digital presentation that lacks substance might look good, but it is unlikely to impress your audience (or your instructor). Your speech should be solid enough to deliver without any aids at all.

Don't let the software steal the show. Presentation software should be used to assist you in delivering your speech: it shouldn't deliver your speech for you. Remember that *you* need to be the center of attention, not your slides. Help your listeners focus on you and your message: avoid reading from your slides, move around as you speak, maintain eye contact with listeners, and limit the amount of text in your slides. Use your slides to show material; use your speech to talk about the material you show.

Using Other Technology

Although presentation software may seem ubiquitous, it is far from the only option you have for sharing your aids. Your choice of technology—analog or digital—may be dictated by the limitations of your forum or budget as much as by content or personal choice. Furthermore, in many cases, traditional presentation aids are more appropriate and make for more dynamic presentations than do their digital counterparts. A speaker can interact with printed photographs, marker boards, and flip charts, keeping the audience focused on the speaker rather than just on the aid. If you want to share a basic visual as part of your speech, these simple options are often the best choice.

You have similar options when it comes to audio and video. Although in recent years it has become possible to integrate audio and video into presentations using computer software and a digital projector, it often is more convenient or downright necessary to present audio and video using more traditional means—a laptop and a DVD.

When you incorporate audio and visual aids into a presentation, some speeches benefit from a mixed approach. A student named Justine did this when she gave an informative speech to her classmates on the history of jazz. During her presentation, she showed actual instruments—a tenor saxophone and an electronic keyboard—and demonstrated a few riffs on each. She later used a record player to play a vintage long-play (LP) recording of a rare Charlie Parker selection. Finally, she shared a digital recording of saxophonist Sadao Watanabe from an MP3 player with speakers attached.

GUIDELINES FOR DEVELOPING PRESENTATION AIDS

Effectively developing your presentation aids—that is, figuring out exactly what aids to use and how they should appear and be organized—can make your speech more interesting, simplify your topic, and help your audience remember your speech. Even if you have a general idea of what you want your aids to achieve—for example, show audience members some paintings from Pablo Picasso's Blue Period or help them remember the most important aspects of the job-interview process—you still have many factors to consider to achieve maximum impact. As you develop your presentation aids, *consider the forum, consider your audience, make sure your aids support your points, keep your aids simple and clear,* and *make sure to rehearse with your presentation aids.* Let's address each of these important factors in turn.

Consider the Forum

As we discuss in Chapter 5, consider the location, or **forum**, as you're mulling over which presentation aids to use. Where will the audience

hear your speech? Is the forum equipped to handle presentation aids? For example, is a large screen available? Are outlets available for a laptop computer, computer projector, slide projector, television monitor, or DVD player? If you want to visit a Web site during your presentation and show it to your audience, is wireless access available? If you plan to use printed visual aids, do you have access to poster boards, flip charts, marker boards, or chalkboards?

Consider Your Audience

Because presentation aids become part of the message you are sharing with listeners, your analysis of your audience should drive your aid selection. When choosing appropriate aids, be sure to consider audience demographics and listeners' prior exposure. Ask yourself, "Of all the possible aids for this speech, which one or which combination would work best with this audience?"

Demographics. Think about the *demographics* of your audience. Demographics—such as listeners' age, gender, and place of birth—can easily predetermine how audience members respond to a particular audio or visual aid.

For example, a student named Anna is giving a presentation on costume design in film. The main point of her speech is that clothing plays an important role in defining film characters. As she speaks, she clicks through images from films to show that costume designers have carefully chosen contemporary clothing that can offer insights into characters' personalities and experiences. In presenting this speech to a class of traditional-aged college students, Anna might include images of Ben Stiller and Naomi Watts in the 2015 film *While We're Young*. But if Anna is presenting her speech to people in their forties and fifties, she might make the same points, present the same evidence, but choose images of characters from earlier films, such as *Annie Hall* (1977) or *Do the Right Thing* (1989).

Prior Exposure. As noted in Chapter 5, **prior exposure** to certain elements of your speech may positively or negatively influence how your audience responds to those elements. This can be true of presentation aids as well. Consider Crystal, a student who gave a persuasive speech opposing abortion. She knew from interviews that many of her listeners identified themselves as pro-choice. Therefore, she avoided using graphic photos or images of abortion procedures, which these audience

members had probably seen many times before and would likely find offensive. Instead, Crystal chose visual aids to make her argument that all life has value, including pictures of healthy infants and the children and young adults they grew up to be. Although she may not have persuaded all her listeners to change their viewpoints on abortion, her speech was thought provoking and held her audience's attention.

How can you determine whether your audience has had prior exposure to the presentation aids you're considering—and what that exposure implies? Ask the same kinds of questions we introduced in Chapter 5:

1. *Has my audience seen or heard this aid before?* If so, proceed to the next question.

2. *What was the result of this prior exposure?* Were listeners persuaded to take the action the speaker advocated? If not, proceed to the next question.

3. *Why was the prior exposure ineffective?* Ask yourself how you can avoid repeating the mistakes made by the previous presenter, who failed to persuade his or her audience through those particular aids.

Make Sure Your Aids Support Your Points

Can your points be enhanced by specific images or sounds? For example, if you're giving a speech on a particular city's architecture, a map would strongly support your message. A recording of a song about that same city would be less relevant to your speech.

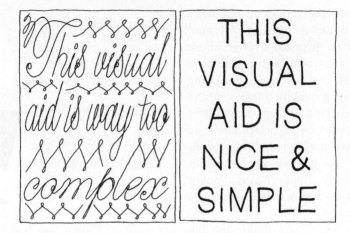

Keep Your Aids Simple and Clear

Consider the following suggestions for making your presentation aids simple and clear:

- *Keep your aids simple.* A presentation aid works best when audience members can simply glance at it or hear it once and quickly grasp what you're trying to communicate. If they have to stare at it, see it more than once, or listen to it several times, the aid is too complex and detailed.

- *Test the size of visual aids.* Make sure each visual aid is large enough to be seen by everyone in your audience. The bigger your audience is, and the farther they are from you and your visual aid, the larger the aid should be.

TIPS FOR HOW A CANDIDATE CAN SPIN A POLITICAL CRISIS
- Deny, deny, deny.
- Accuse your opponent of the same thing.
- Do the "mea culpa."

WRONG   RIGHT

- *Create contrast.* On visual aids, contrast increases readability. To create contrast, place dark colors against a light background or light colors against a dark background. On a poster, for example, place dark text against a lighter background.

- *Test the legibility of visual aids.* Be sure to check whether all the numbers, letters, words, sentences, and graphics in your visual aids are legible—that is, easily distinguished at a distance. For instance, ask a classmate, friend, or roommate to view a poster or projected slide from a distance and tell you whether she or he can see everything on it. If not, continue refining your aid—for example, by increasing font size and adding white space between elements.

- *Test the volume and clarity of audio aids.* Be certain that your audio aids will be loud enough *and* clear enough (that is, free of static or other "noise") for all your listeners to hear.

Rehearse with Your Presentation Aids

We strongly advise that you create your aids while developing your speech—and then practice using them as you rehearse your presentation. Don't put yourself in the risky position of needing to create aids on the fly while delivering your speech. At the same time, we suggest that you prepare for the unexpected—including power failures and technology glitches (frozen programs, system crashes, or a failed Internet

TEST LEGIBILITY

connection). As many public speakers have discovered, technology can fail just when you need it most. Imagine how you'd feel if, at a key point in your speech, you turned on your computer to project an important photo and the device didn't work. To avoid this scenario, always prepare a hard copy of any presentation aids you plan to present through computers or other technology or equipment. You can always pass the copy around the room as a last resort. To further cover yourself, make sure you practice giving your speech without using the aids.

When delivering PowerPoint or other sorts of digital presentations, make sure to practice a number of times with your slides, just as you would with speech outlines. To guard against any surprises, check that your media will work with the computers in the speech setting before it's time to speak, and bring hard copies of your aids with you on the day of the presentation. When incorporating a computer or DVD player into a presentation, keep in mind basic principles of using aids: practice with the aids (ideally, in the room where you will be presenting and on the same equipment), consider taping power cables to the floor (to avoid

BE PREPARED TO SPEAK WITHOUT AIDS

tripping over them during your speech), and make sure you have the video cued to the right scene before beginning your speech.

> ▶ To see an example of a speaker making a mistake with a presentation aid, try Video Activity 14.1, "Presentation Software: Checking Beforehand (Needs Improvement)."

USING PRESENTATION AIDS DURING YOUR SPEECH

Skillful development of your presentation aids isn't enough to ensure a successful speech. You also need to use the aids correctly during your presentation. Otherwise, you risk making all-too-common mistakes, such as distracting your audience by keeping aids displayed after you're finished with them or losing eye contact with your listeners while discussing an aid. The following strategies can help you use your presentation aids successfully.

SPEECH CHOICES

A CASE STUDY: *MIA*

Let's look in on Mia to learn which presentation aids she decided to include.

Mia knew that her topic would allow her to use a variety of multimedia visual aids in her speech. She decided to make a PowerPoint presentation of simple but impactful photos, along with some visual aids that she would create herself.

She researched the types of images she wanted to use from online, making sure that they were from trustworthy sources. These included: a photograph of smartphones, a photograph of emigrants charging their phones, a photograph of an emigrant taking a picture of a map with his phone, and, finally, a photograph of an overcrowded raft at sea. All of these photos would provide impact for different points in her speech.

As for the visual aids that Mia decided to make, she first created a slide asking students how many Macedonian Denars were worth $1,000. The second slide showed that $1,000 equaled $56,000 Macedonian Denars. If emigrants were not aware of the exchange rate, they might be conned into giving someone too much money. For the second set of slides that Mia made, she showed two "text messages"—one with location coordinates, and the other saying, "The Coast Guard said they can see you." She would use these slides when sharing her closing story, in which an emigrant was on a boat that lost its engine in the Mediterranean Sea. He was able to look up his coordinates and send them to his cousin in Hawaii. His cousin contacted the Coast Guard, and they were able to transport those on the boat back to land.

YOUR TURN:

What presentation aids would you create for your speech? Would you use any aids besides visual ones (audio, etc.)?

For more questions and activities for this case study, and to see a ◉ video clip from Mia's speech on visual aids, please go to LaunchPad at **macmillanhighered.com/speakup4e.**

Make Sure Everyone Can See and Hear Your Aids

Position stereo speakers so that all listeners can hear the audio recordings you're playing. In the same vein, position a computer screen so that everyone can see it. Place a printed graph, chart, or picture prominently on the wall or flip chart so that your entire audience can view it.

SPEECH CHOICES

A CASE STUDY: *JACOB*

Let's check in on Jacob and see what choices he made for presentation aids.

Jacob believed that he might be more credible with his audience if he could mention that he was a former high school athlete. To introduce the idea to his audience, he planned to hold a baseball and wear his catcher's mitt when starting his speech. Unfortunately, on the day of the speech, Jacob left these at home. He didn't mind too much—his speech was strong enough on its own.

Jacob also developed a PowerPoint presentation for his arguments. His best slide showed the amount of money made by the National Collegiate Athletic Association (NCAA) and individual schools. These amounts were depicted as bullet points on the slide. He used blue text on a green background, thinking that the audience would like to see the school colors for the college's football team—the fighting Broncos.

YOUR TURN:

If you were to want to prove your credibility during a speech, what aids might you bring to help?

After the speech, he found out that his color choices had rendered the words nearly illegible. A classmate named Will even told Jacob that he had raised his hand during the speech to ask Jacob to read the words on the slide out loud. Jacob hadn't noticed Will's raised hand.

For more questions and activities for this case study, please go to LaunchPad at macmillanhighered.com/speakup4e.

Control Audience Interaction with Your Aids

To avoid distracting your audience unnecessarily, do not show or play an aid until you are ready for listeners to see or hear it. When you're finished presenting the aid, put it away or shut it off. This strategy keeps your audience's attention focused on you instead of your aids— and helps ensure that listeners don't miss important parts of your speech.

You can control audience interaction with your aids in several ways. For example, if you are using an audio recording, cue up the desired track ahead of time so that you can play it promptly when you're ready. Avoid playing background music (from an MP3 player or a cell phone) during your speech. If you plan to tape or pin a chart to the wall, do so in advance, but fold half of the display over the other half and tape or pin it down. That way, you'll block the audience's view until you are ready to refer to the chart in your speech, at which point you'll undo the tape or pin.

Use the same technique when displaying a series of images on successive sheets of a flip chart. Insert blank sheets between each sheet

containing an image. When you finish with one image, flip the page so that your audience sees a blank page. This technique also works well with overhead transparencies, slide shows, and computer images in a PowerPoint presentation. Remove each image after you've discussed it, leaving a blank screen, or turn off the equipment and refocus the audience on you.

What about handouts? To ensure that they're informative rather than distracting, issue clear instructions about how to use them. For example, pass out handouts facedown, and tell the audience not to look at them until you say so. Explain that you don't want listeners to get ahead of you. Of course, there always will be someone who ignores this instruction and takes a peek. To keep audience members focused on your speech, watch them during your presentation. Look for listeners who are paging through the handouts. Then adjust your delivery by increasing your volume or moving closer to those audience members to draw their attention back to you.

Maintain Eye Contact

Many inexperienced speakers look at their visual aids during their presentation instead of maintaining eye contact with their audience. Of course, you need to glance at visual aids as you present them—especially if you're referring to something specific on an aid. But this should be *only* a glance—not a gaze.

> ⊚ To view an example of a speaker making a common mistake with her presentation aid, try Video Activity 14.2, "Presentation Software (Needs Improvement)."

Remember the Purpose of Your Aids

As we've mentioned, you should treat your presentation aids as tools that supplement your speech—not as the main vehicle for delivering your speech. Your presentation contains your message, and you are the messenger. If you forget this, your audience might focus on your aids instead of you. For instance, many inexperienced salespeople rely too heavily on brochures and handouts during a presentation. They assume—mistakenly—that good marketing materials are all they need to sell a product or a service. But a brochure can't answer listeners' questions or interact spontaneously with them. Only a human being can connect with audiences in these crucial ways. The best speakers understand that presentation aids support a speech—not the other way around.

CHAPTER REVIEW

> Listening can lead to understanding; seeing can lead to believing.

In this chapter, we examined how the right selection and strategic use of presentation aids enhance your audience's interest in, comprehension of, and retention of your speech. Aids can take many forms, including the speaker him- or herself, assistants, objects, visual images (such as maps, photographs and drawings, and diagrams), graphs, text-based visuals, audio recordings, and video. You can display presentation aids in a variety of ways—such as in printed form or through presentation software and other technology. To get the most impact from your aids, you need to develop them with the following points in mind: consider your forum, consider your audience, make sure your aids support your points, keep your aids simple and clear, and rehearse with your presentation aids. Then use your aids judiciously during your presentation to support your points—not to deliver your message for you. A key point to remember is that presentation aids supplement your message, but they can never replace you. *You* are the messenger!

LaunchPad
macmillan learning

LaunchPad for *Speak Up* offers videos and encourages self-assessment through adaptive quizzing. Go to **macmillanhighered.com/speakup4e** to get access to:

 LearningCurve
   Adaptive Quizzes

 Video clips that help you understand public speaking concepts

Key Terms

presentation aid *402*
diagram *410*
graph *411*
line graph *411*
bar graph *411*
pie chart (circle graph) *412*

verbal chart *412*
flowchart *412*
⊙ presentation software *416*
forum *418*
prior exposure *420*

Review Questions

1. What are three key reasons for using presentation aids in a speech?
2. Describe at least seven types of presentation aids you might use in a speech.
3. According to the chapter, when is presentation software most useful?
4. What factors should you consider while developing your presentation aids?
5. What four things does a speaker need to keep in mind when delivering a speech with presentation aids?

Critical Thinking Questions

1. Are all presentation aids visual aids? What other senses might a good presentation aid engage?
2. What advantages does presentation software offer over more traditional ways of presenting visual and audio aids?
3. Do some types of speeches work better with presentation aids, and if so, which types of aids work best with which types of speeches?

Activities

1. ▰ Take a look at the illustration on page 422, which shows a speaker using a visual aid that's the wrong size. If you were to redraw this illustration to correct the speaker's mistake, what would that illustration look like?

2. Television commercials are persuasive appeals created from video and audio elements. With this in mind, consider a few television commercials you have found especially memorable. How do they use presentation aids (such as music and images) to grab your attention? How do these aids relate to the commercials' main points? How could you apply lessons from these effective commercials to your own presentations?

3. Think of ways that you, as the speaker, are a visual aid. How can you tailor your nonverbal delivery—things like your posture or your appearance—to reinforce your main point?

Study Plan

_____

_____

_____

_____

_____

_____

_____

_____

_____

_____

_____

Jaws was the turning point for Steven Spielberg. It grossed $470 million at the box office worldwide. His next movie, Close Encounters of the Third Kind...
This movie I'm making of my speech is not going to gross $470 million, but it's a lot more fun than I thought it would be.
THE MOVIES OF STEVEN SPIELBERG
JAW$: The Invention of the Blockbuster

MEDIATED PUBLIC SPEAKING

"Effective mediated public speaking offers a new world of challenges and opportunities."

Marshawn signed up to take his required public speaking course in an online format. His work schedule was unpredictable, and he appreciated the flexible hours that an online class would provide. Because the class would never meet face-to-face, he figured he would not be required to deliver any speeches. Besides quelling his nerves, he thought that this would make the course a bit easier to manage.

However, when Marshawn logged on to the course Web site for the first time, he received a surprise. Four speeches were required for the course, and although they would not be presented live in a classroom, students were responsible for making video recordings of their presentations and submitting them to the instructor electronically. This was not good news. Not only would Marshawn have to do all the work required to prepare and present his speeches, but he also would need to worry about recording them. "Who does my instructor think I am?" he wondered. "Steven Spielberg?"

After the first week of classes, Marshawn began to reconsider. He had been involved in making videos for most of his life. He had recorded special events with friends and family members on his cell phone and posted them on YouTube. His church choir had made a DVD of its best work, which featured Marshawn singing a solo. And whenever he brought a new romantic interest home to meet his parents, Marshawn's mom could not resist showing a video of his campaign speech for sixth-grade class president. Maybe he had more video experience than he'd originally thought.

Marshawn's experience is not unique. Twenty-first-century technology has increased the ways that we can communicate with one another. Today, speeches can be presented in real time to audiences in different locations, and they can be saved for future playback. Messages transmitted through either a mechanical or an electronic medium are examples of **mediated communication**. You may be called on to use mediated channels for presentations on campus, in your career, or as part of your community involvement. Therefore, you will benefit from gaining skills and experience with such methods of communicating.

Fortunately, much as you follow a set of manageable steps to prepare and deliver successful speeches in a face-to-face (F2F) environment, you can use a similar approach when called on to deliver a mediated presentation. This chapter will help you learn how to adapt when you speak to a remote audience and also how to become comfortable when speaking to a camera instead of live listeners. We begin by discussing the rise of mediated communication and the advantages and challenges of real-time and prerecorded presentations. Then we move on to strategies for optimizing delivery of effective messages in a mediated environment. Finally, we discuss the procedures for recording a classroom presentation and some special considerations for real-time presentations.

THE RISE OF MEDIATED COMMUNICATION

Since the 1990s, rapidly evolving communication technology has changed many of the ways we live and interact with one another. Before then, people wrote letters and used their landline telephones to stay in touch with friends and family members. Now you are far more likely to use text messages, emails, and social media instead. Back then, people had no choice but to visit the library to begin a research project, but now most students can access quality library resources online. Rather than commuting to your job every day, you may end up telecommuting from remote locations, using mobile devices such as laptops or smartphones to stay connected with colleagues and clients.

How do these trends relate to public speaking? These technological changes have created more options for public speakers to reach an audience. But face-to-face presentations are not on the way out; on the contrary, they remain the gold standard of public speaking formats. Technology cannot replicate the naturalness of F2F communication and the bond that can be created when speaker and audience share the same space. If you are taking an online public speaking class, you may be asked to come to campus to deliver your speeches in person. (This is often the case in "hybrid" speaking courses.)

Many remote classes—and perhaps some in-person courses—will ask that you record your speeches. You also may face situations in school and life in which a mediated format is your best available option. Mediated presentations offer some specific benefits, such as cost savings and the ability to reach a wide audience. Let's consider how mediated options are expanding and look at two basic formats for mediated speeches.

The Expansion of Mediated Public Speaking

There are many situations in which you may deliver a mediated presentation at school, on the job, or in your community. Consider the following examples:

- Recording a presentation for a class and uploading it on the course Web site
- Participating in a job or scholarship interview on Skype
- Creating a video for a favorite charity and posting it on YouTube
- Podcasting a program you produced for your campus radio station
- Delivering a sales presentation by videoconference to clients in several different states

Research confirms that the use of mediated presentations is expanding. A recent survey of college presidents found that over three-fourths of institutions teach online classes.[1] This has meant that teachers may be teaching substantially more students—particularly in massive open online courses (MOOCs), which are free and open to all.[2] Worldwide, spending on videoconferencing technology grew from $2 billion in 2011[3] to $7 billion by 2014.[4] The expectation going forward is that the market for video conferencing will grow by almost 10 percent per year until 2019.[5] Detroit's City Council is one of an expanding number of governmental organizations that allow people to use technology such as Skype to make comments during public meetings.[6] In fact, many of the this country's cities use Skype, and many more have embraced multiple

MEDIATED PRESENTATIONS CAN BE FUN...

It's 6:00 a.m., and it's time for BRAIN YOGA!

ZZz

...IF YOU LOVE YOUR SPOT ON CAMPUS RADIO BUT HATE GETTING UP EARLY.

Just look at this chart! Great!

...IF YOU NEED TO DO A SALES PITCH BUT COULD ALSO DO WITH A BREAK.

What are your salary expectations? Well, anywhere between... LIVE

...IF YOU CAN'T FIND YOUR SUIT PANTS AND YOU HAVE A JOB INTERVIEW.*

*Actually, just find your pants.

forms of social media.[7] Social media such as Skype can allow people to address a city council or a board of supervisors, even if they can't be at the meeting in person. This kind of technology has the potential to increase civic engagement in a meaningful way.

Prerecorded and Real-Time Presentations

The options for mediated delivery can be divided into two categories— prerecorded and real-time. A **prerecorded** (also known as **asynchronous**) mediated presentation is recorded by the speaker for later viewing by one or more audiences. For example, a speaker might create a podcast or a YouTube video of a presentation. If you are taking an online public speaking class in which you will be recording your speech assignments and submitting them to your instructor, you will be delivering a prerecorded speech.

A **real-time** (also known as **synchronous**) mediated presentation is delivered directly to the audience as the speaker presents the message from a remote location. For example, a speaker might make a presentation during a videoconference or a speech presented to a group via Skype. These speeches are similar to face-to-face presentations but with one crucial difference: the audience and speaker are not together.

Mediated presentations pose both opportunities and challenges, and these can vary depending on whether they are in a prerecorded or real-time format.

ADVANTAGES OF MEDIATED PRESENTATIONS

Why—and when—might a mediated presentation be a good choice? Let's consider the main benefits to presenting a mediated speech to a remote audience and the types of situations in which you may want to deliver a mediated speech.

General Advantages

This first group of advantages applies to both prerecorded and real-time presentations.

Flexibility. One advantage of mediated presentations is increased flexibility. Unlike face-to-face presentations, where you need to be at a specific place at a specific time, real-time technologies (such as videoconferencing) allow audience members to be at multiple (and presumably more convenient) locations. Prerecorded speeches also can be viewed at different locations *and* at different times. You may choose to sign up for an online public speaking class because of the flexibility it offers for your schedule.

Savings. Both forms of mediated presentations can save time and money. It can be expensive for an organization to bring everyone who should hear a message to a common location. The travel involved also places demands on participants' time. Rather than having the audience come to the speech, mediated technology can more efficiently bring the speech to the audience.

Audience Size. Attendance at a face-to-face presentation is limited to the number of people who can be accommodated in the available space and who can be there at the designated time. Because mediated presentations can be viewed by audiences in different locations and even at different times (for prerecorded speeches), they give you an opportunity to address a greater number of people.

Advantages of Prerecorded Speeches

Prerecorded presentations come with several specific advantages—*do-overs, pause and rewind buttons,* and the *option to save.*

Do-Overs. One benefit of prerecorded messages is the opportunity to do another "take" if your speech does not go well the first time. In a real-time speech, if you make a mistake (or perhaps your technology fails), there is no do-over. You need to adapt to the problem as best you can and continue the presentation. When you prerecord your speech, you have the chance to start over as many times as you like until you are pleased with the outcome. If you are adept with your equipment, you might also be tempted to edit your presentation. But be careful: your instructor may not allow editing in classroom speeches. If this is the case, it would be an ethical violation to do any editing, so be sure to check with your instructor first.

Pause and Rewind Buttons. Prerecorded speeches can provide audience members with additional opportunities to process and reflect on your message. A viewer can go back and review a section of the

presentation or watch the entire speech again. Audience members may also pause the video and discuss a part of the speech before moving on to the next main idea.

Option to Save. A final advantage is that prerecording creates a permanent record of your speech so that future audiences can view it. Suppose that you make a clear and concise training video for new employees at your job or you create an outstanding presentation about how to set up a food distribution program for a nonprofit organization where you volunteer. The company or the nonprofit organization could use your video to provide future audiences with the benefits of your good work. In addition, having recordings of your classroom speeches allows you to provide prospective employers with a sample of your public speaking skills, much as you might provide them with a writing sample.

Advantages of Real-Time Technologies

Video-based technologies such as videoconferencing, Webinars, and Skype allow speakers to communicate with audience members in diverse locations and in real time. The decision to use a real-time mediated format may depend on the purpose of the presentation. If the message is straightforward and not complex, this format is more likely to be appropriate.[8] Videoconferencing is also more likely to be successful when participants have already met and built a relationship with one another.[9] When participants are not acquainted, it may be more difficult for them to develop a sense of togetherness or cohesion in mediated formats.[10]

In any real-time mediated presentation, the technologies cannot create the sense of presence that comes when a speaker and an audience share the same physical space. However, they do allow for some of the benefits of a face-to-face speech, including *audience feedback* and *audience interaction*, and they offer the *option to save*.

Audience Feedback. Depending on the type of technology available, you might be able to experience audience feedback and adapt your speech in the moment. If you have the advantage of top-flight technology and large screens, you will be able to observe more of your audience's nonverbal responses.[11]

Audience Interaction. Real-time technology allows audience members to interact with the speaker during or immediately after the speech. For

example, there can be a question-and-answer session. Or if the speaker encourages it, audience members may ask questions during the presentation.

Option to Save. An additional benefit to real-time presentations is that they often can be saved. Depending on what technology you use, audience members may have the ability to go back to any part of your speech if they didn't understand something or want to reinforce the information shared. If you are able to record your real-time speech, you have the opportunity to share it with an even wider audience.

Now that we have considered some of the potential advantages to mediated presentations, let's turn our attention to the main challenges.

> ▶ For an example of a prerecorded (aka asynchronous) mediated speech recorded by the speaker for later viewing by one or more audience members, see Video Activity 15.1, "McAlister, Arsenic in Our Water Supply."

CHALLENGES OF MEDIATED PRESENTATIONS

Think of a political rally, a commencement speech, or a technology conference. Even with a large crowd, the speaker is able to connect personally to his or her audience. The main concern with mediated communication is that the in-person connection is missing. This section explores specific challenges that are created by mediated presentations, including loss of naturalness, loss of immediacy, decreased nonverbal communication, diminished feedback, difficulty managing distractions, and technological difficulties that are not found in face-to-face communication. After discussing these challenges, we explain how to overcome them in the next section of this chapter.

Loss of Naturalness

Our brains are hardwired for face-to-face interaction. Since the Stone Age, humans have used facial expressions and sound as primary means of communication. Over time, evolution has resulted in biological adaptations that enhance the effectiveness of F2F interactions. For example, the location of the larynx, the development of the vocal tract, and accompanying changes in the brain now allow human beings to create the many sounds needed to speak modern languages. Similarly, adaptations of muscles in the human face enable a diverse range of facial expressions used to communicate.[12]

The **naturalness** of a communication medium is determined by the extent to which it matches the features of face-to-face interaction.[13] Key factors that contribute to feelings of naturalness include sharing the same space, sending and receiving messages quickly, and being able to send and receive both verbal and nonverbal expressions.[14]

The human brain enables us to send and receive messages in our natural face-to-face mode with a minimum of effort. However, when we use a less natural medium, we face greater barriers to effective communication. In this way, videoconferencing can be seen as more natural than text-based media because it has the ability to convey vocal and visual cues (such as tone and body posture) synchronously, not unlike face-to-face communication. By contrast, emails provide mostly text-based cues and typically are asynchronous. Emoticons can be added to email messages, but they lack the richness and variety of cues found in F2F communicating.[15]

In the following section, we explore some of the specific challenges caused by mediated presentations in terms of the naturalness we often take for granted in F2F communication. Unless otherwise noted, these challenges apply to both prerecorded and real-time communication.

Loss of Immediacy

When you and your audience do not share the same space, the sense of connection is reduced. When you deliver a speech face-to-face—especially in a typical classroom setting—audience members are closer to you physically. They can observe your eye contact and sense your movement. Such actions create "interest and warmth between communicators."[16] Conversely, when you and your audience are in different locations, you will both feel less of a psychological link.[17] In a less natural environment, speakers face greater challenges establishing credibility and building common ground.[18] You may also feel less of a bond with your audience when presenting to a camera, which can feel like "presenting into the void."[19]

Decreased Nonverbal Communication

In Chapter 13, we noted the central role that nonverbal expressions play in communication. In a face-to-face speech, audience members can observe the full range of your nonverbal behaviors.[20] In a mediated presentation, however, this is less likely, especially when the camera is in a fixed position. For example, if you are being filmed from the waist up, the audience will see your facial expressions and most of your hand gestures, but the camera may not capture large arm gestures. Similarly, if you are using a fixed camera, your opportunities for moving around will be limited. Thus, you would not be able to move closer to the audience to emphasize a key point or move a few steps in either direction to signify a transition.

Mediated presentations also alter how listeners see and interpret your nonverbal messages. For example, the flat images of facial gestures that appear on a screen are not the same as the ones that would be perceived in a three-dimensional face-to-face environment.[21]

Diminished Feedback

A face-to-face environment provides your audience with the best opportunity to provide feedback while you are speaking. Even with real-time technology, it's difficult for listeners to provide that same quality of feedback.[22] When a speech is prerecorded, your audience has no chance to provide real-time feedback. (They may be able to leave real-time comments or tags on your recorded speech if you post it on specific sites that allow commenting.)

This decrease in audience response leads to several disadvantages. Normally, feedback lets you know if you are speaking clearly or presenting at the right pace. If it suggests that audience members do not understand an idea, you can expand on your explanation.[23] If you do not have a clear view of your entire audience, you cannot determine if they are losing interest and thus add some energy to your presentation.[24] It also prevents you from gathering positive reactions—such as attentive listening, a smile, or a nod of the head—to show that you are on the right track.

Difficulty Managing Distractions

When you are speaking from a remote location, audience members may be more likely to engage in **multitasking**. This practice, which refers to "juggling multiple tasks with and without technological devices," is increasingly common in the workplace, in meetings, and on campus.[25] For example, if you observe another student texting or checking Facebook during a classroom lecture, you are witnessing multitasking in action.

When you are delivering a speech face-to-face, common courtesy should discourage listeners from multitasking, but when audience members are watching you on a screen, it is easier for them to give in to distractions around them. This is particularly true for workplace presentations when audience members are watching in their offices or cubicles and can easily be interrupted by a coworker.[26] If you are not speaking on location, you also lose opportunities to use nonverbal strategies (such as moving closer to a person who is multitasking or changing the volume of your voice to gain attention).

From a remote location, you will have few opportunities to notice things that might be distracting your listeners. This is especially problematic during real-time presentations, when listeners can't immediately replay what they might have missed. You will not hear a lawn mower or an airplane passing overhead and temporarily drowning out your voice. If you are speaking to audience members in different locations, you may not be aware that one viewer's computer has crashed.

Technological Difficulties

In addition to challenges based on a lack of in-person interaction, mediated presentations are subject to unique technological difficulties.

Mediated speakers often fear that their technology (including upload-ing tools, computer recording devices, and Internet connections) will fail them.

Technological challenges do happen, but there are simple things you can do to try to prevent them. Practice beforehand with the technology you plan to use (we discuss this more in the following section). If you have trouble with your recording device, make sure that a backup is available. If the site you're using stops working, try opening it in a dif-ferent browser or disconnecting and reconnecting to the Internet. Con-tact the help team if you're using a submission site (like YouTube or a class Web site) that's not allowing you to upload. If you're having trouble with an online video service (Skype, Google Hangouts, ooVoo), consider switching to another.

Real-time presentations have more room for technological error, and we discuss these further in the last section of the chapter.

OPTIMIZING DELIVERY AND MESSAGES IN MEDIATED PRESENTATIONS

The key principles of speech delivery, content, and practice discussed in this book apply to both mediated and face-to-face speeches. However, there are a few unique considerations to keep in mind when your pre-sentation is mediated. In this section, we discuss *delivery considerations*, *message adaptations*, and *practicing delivery and recording*.

Delivery Considerations

First, let's discuss some considerations for delivery. These points apply to both prerecorded and real-time speeches unless otherwise noted.

Voice. To make sure your speaking voice is effective in a mediated presentation, a good general rule is to speak at about the same volume you would use to address people seated in a conference room. If you are prerecording, consider doing a quick "voice check": record yourself saying the beginning of your introduction, and play it back to ensure ap-propriate volume.

Maintaining an effective rate of delivery can be a challenge. There is a natural tendency to speed up your presentation if no audience is present, and the absence of an audience means you will not receive feedback if you speak too fast. To keep your rate under control, be sure to pause at natural stopping points in your speech.[27] For example, you might pause before you transition to the next main point, after you display a visual aid, or after you present evidence. Recall that speaking to a camera rather than a roomful of people can make it seem as though you are communicating with a vast empty space, which can cause you to lose energy. Imagine that you are speaking to a live audience, and consciously try to maintain an energetic delivery. Include some reminders on your extemporaneous notes, such as "Energy!" or "Enthusiasm!"

If your audience is watching you from different locations (say, for an online class), consider asking them to use high-quality earbuds. This will help them hear you clearly and will be more comfortable for them.

Eye Contact. Maintaining eye contact with your listeners is a challenge in mediated presentations because you can't look at them directly. (Even in real-time presentations, both the speaker and the audience are looking at each other on a screen.) Nevertheless, your audience will notice where your eyes are looking. To avoid looking as though you're gazing off into space, you should always look toward the camera (or a visual, like a small

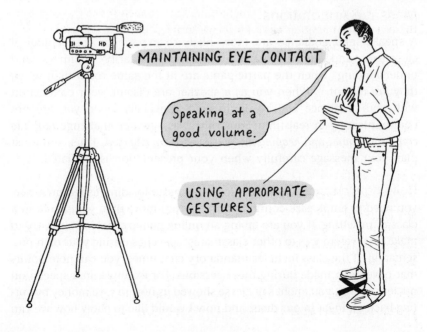

stuffed animal taped to the top) while presenting.[28] While speaking, imagine your audience in front of you. Make extended eye contact in several directions, just as you would with real people in a live audience.

Movement and Gestures. Elements of nonverbal delivery such as movement and gestures are also affected in a mediated presentation. On a screen, your gestures will appear more prominent because you are being displayed in a smaller area. Expansive gestures may also move out of the frame of your video. (Even if you have a skilled cameraperson, she or he can't anticipate your natural, conversational gestures.) It is important to gesture when you are recording a speech, but be careful not to gesture too expansively.[29]

Movement also needs to be controlled. Ensure that all movement remains within the range of the camera so that you do not move in and out of the screen. If your camera cannot move because you are recording your own speech or speaking at a fixed microphone, you may need to speak from a fixed location. If this is the case and you can't use nonverbal cues (such as pointing to an item on a visual aid or moving to indicate a transition), be sure to provide clear verbal cues to help audience members understand your point.

Message Adaptations

A speaker and audience are more likely to experience "psychological closeness" and feel a sense of "similarity, solidarity, openness, and understanding" when the participants are in the same room than when they are distant.[30] When you as a speaker are distant, your connection with your audience will be diminished, especially when you are not communicating in real time. You will have a greater challenge *building common ground* and *keeping audience members engaged*. Thus, you must plan your message carefully when your presentation is mediated.

Building Common Ground. To compensate for diminished presence, you need to emphasize common ground even more than you would in a classroom setting. If you are taking an online public speaking class, try to make brief references to other classmates' speeches during your own presentation. If the class includes mandatory chat times, you can note points that have been made during these sessions. For example, in a speech on nuclear energy, you might say, "Jesse showed us how to save money by cutting back on meat in our diets, and now I would like to show how we can

all save money on our utility bills."
You also might be able to relate common experiences of online students
to concepts in your speech. In an
informative speech on the use of
smoke signals, you might note
how this ancient system of
communication was used
to warn soldiers up and
down the Great Wall of
China when the enemy
was near.[31] Thus, students can
see how methods for communicating over great distances have evolved,
with technology now enabling them to interact with one another online.

You also want to emphasize common ground during mediated workplace or community presentations. If you have interacted with audience
members in the past, use relevant ideas from your previous discussions.
If you do not know your audience, you might emphasize goals or principles that are familiar to everyone in the group. For example, you might
refer to a company's logo or the mission of a nonprofit organization.

Keeping Audience Members Engaged. It is more difficult for
listeners to remain attentive when staring at a screen than when watching a live human being.[32] Remote listeners may feel more comfortable
multitasking, and you won't be able to see their nonverbal cues that may
indicate lack of interest. Thus, you will need to make it easier for them to
focus on what you are saying. There are several strategies you can use to
maintain audience interest when speaking in a mediated setting. Many of
these approaches are helpful in a face-to-face context, but they are especially important when your speech is being recorded.

- *Ask rhetorical questions.* One strategy is to make greater use of
  rhetorical questions and other strategies that encourage active participation. In a speech on the need to get more sleep, a speaker
  might ask, "How many hours do you think the average college
  student sleeps?" Even if you are not physically present, this type
  of question invites the audience to think about the answer and
  wait with anticipation for you to explain the correct response.
- *Increase the variety of supporting materials.* Another way to maintain interest is to increase the variety of materials you present. A

remote audience is more likely to lose interest if a speaker seems to be talking on and on. Conversely, a switch to another mode of presentation can recapture audience interest. For instance, a speaker who participates in rodeos might discuss rodeo equipment, focusing on the proper saddle in one of her main points. Her first subpoint might be an explanation of why a proper saddle is needed—and what went wrong the time she brought the wrong saddle to a barrel-racing event. Next, the speaker could display an actual saddle as a visual aid. Finally, the speaker might show a video clip of a rider in action while explaining how this rider used the saddle effectively.

- *Keep it simple and relevant.* A third strategy for maintaining engagement is to reduce complexity when explaining a main point or subpoint. Instead of discussing five ways for college students to decrease stress, pick the three that will be most relevant to the audience. If two credible research sources make the same basic point, choose the shorter quotation. Rather than presenting a long list of statistics, choose the most important one or two, and invest more time in helping the audience understand and remember them. If you must go into more detail on a particular main point, use signposts along with an internal preview or summary to help the audience keep track of your train of thought (see Chapter 9).

- *Highlight takeaways.* Finally, emphasize key takeaways for your audience to remember. A **takeaway** is a memorable phrase or sentence that captures the essence of your speech and can be repeated at key points in the speech. For example, in her speech on cardiovascular disease, Aubrey focused on three risk factors in her main points—stress, poor nutrition, and lack of exercise. Her subpoints explained the importance of minimizing these risks and the many feasible steps students could take. At the end of each main point, Aubrey used repetition, noting, "If you focus on this preventive measure now, your heart will thank you later." She also closed with this key sentence in her clincher.

Practicing Delivery and Recording

Now that you've considered strategies to combat the challenges of mediated presentations, it's time to move to the next stage—practice. Whether

you are giving a prerecorded or a real-time speech, you should allocate time to practice your presentation, just as you would if you were addressing your audience face-to-face. If you'll be using a camera operator, have this person record your practice so that he or she can become familiar with both the equipment and your speech. If there are points in your speech where the operator should zoom in on a visual aid, take a closer shot of you, or pan a live audience (if you have one), this can be practiced to ensure that it is handled smoothly.

After you record yourself practicing, play back the recording to see how your speech will appear to your audience. As you watch, note areas for possible change by considering the following questions:

- Are your rate and volume appropriate?
- Do you appear to be looking at the audience?
- Are all of your movements and gestures within view?
- Can your presentation aids be clearly seen? Does the audience have sufficient time to process the content of each one?
- Does the setting of your speech look professional?
- Do the lighting and background work to make a clear picture of you?

Practicing should minimize problems when you do a "final take" for a prerecorded presentation. However, allow sufficient time for a do-over if you experience any issues during filming. As with your practice takes, watch to make sure you have a quality recording before you submit your speech. Also, remember to save your final speech in more than one place (such as the cloud, a USB drive, or an external hard drive) as you would any important school materials.

RECORDING YOUR CLASSROOM SPEECH

After preparation and lots of practice, it's time to turn to the nitty-gritty of recording. In this section, we discuss how to set up and record your speech effectively. These suggestions will help you record both in-class and out-of-class presentations, such as a video for a scholarship application or a sales presentation your employer might require. Although this section focuses on prerecorded speeches, many of the tips about the *camera, setting and background, attire,* and *camera positioning* can be applied to real-time presentations.

Camera

There is no need to buy an expensive, top-of-the-line camcorder. You can make a very good recording with an iPad or a smartphone camera[33] (small tripods for these can cost under $10). If you have a smartphone, go to your camera features. For iPhones, slide the toggle at the bottom from Photo to Video, and press the red button to start recording. If you

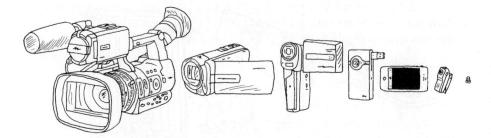

decide to use a smartphone to shoot video, remember these tips: (1) use a tripod to steady your shot; (2) shoot your video horizontally (wide screen) instead of vertically (narrow screen) because it will help you catch more in the shot; and (3) shoot a ten-second sample video, and replay it to make sure the lighting and sound quality are acceptable. For best results, do any editing on your computer, where a larger screen will allow you to see everything in more detail.

Check to see if your college has video cameras available for students to borrow. If you want to buy a camcorder, look at online reviews to find one that meets your need. You also might consider buying a camcorder with other classmates and then selling it and splitting the proceeds once the term has ended. Whichever option you choose, be sure to use a device that is familiar and easy to use.

Setting and Background

The background for your recorded presentation should look professional. Consider finding a conference room you can use at your college or in a neighborhood library. If you need to record the speech at your home, be sure the setting is neat and clean. Look through the viewer to see what your audience will see. Make sure your inflatable gorilla, the pile of unwashed clothes, and half-eaten bags of chips are out of sight. Even an attractive item may create a distraction. For example, be sure that the plant or lamp you're standing in front of doesn't appear to be growing out of your head.[34]

Avoid background noises that might compete with your speech in the video. The last thing you need is to have an episode of *Project Runway* blaring in the background or a boisterous friend barging into your room with concert tickets. Select a time when your roommates will not be home, or be sure you can count on them not to disrupt your speech.

The primary light source should be behind the camera operator and directed toward you. Avoid standing in front of a sunny window or a bright light; otherwise, you will be in shadow. It is generally better to have more light than less, so be sure to select a well-lit room. You can also bring in additional light if the room seems too dark.[35] However, if you're blond, beware of standing directly beneath a bright light (it might make your head appear to glow).

> ▶ To see an example of how lighting and clothing choices can affect a speech, try Video Activity 15.2, "Attention-Getter (Needs Improvement)."

Attire

In addition to selecting clothing that is appropriate for public speaking (see Chapter 13), you need to choose clothing that will make a good impression on camera. Single, neutral colors are generally better than plaids or stripes.[36] If you wear striped clothing, it can result in a "strobing effect" that will distract the audience.[37] Checked clothing may blur, and the brightness of pure white may make it difficult to see your face clearly.[38] When you practice your speech, you will be able to see how you and your speech setting will appear to the audience, so be sure to wear the clothes you will wear for the actual speech. A special note to those who wear jewelry: avoid bangles or anything that can make noise because it will be an audible distraction during your presentation.

Camera Positioning

You or your carefully chosen camera operator should check that the camera is trained on the correct shot. Your instructor may have specific visual requirements (such as having the video show you only from the waist up as you deliver your speech). If you are required to speak to an audience, your instructor may ask you to record the comments of listeners both before and after your speech.

When recording your speech, be sure the view is wide enough to capture your movements and gestures. If no specific shot is required, avoid using "talking head" shots, in which the audience can see only your head and upper body. These tend to be perceived as boring by the audience, and they limit much of your nonverbal communication. Also, if someone is taping you with a cell phone or other handheld device, be sure to have her or him place the device on a flat surface to avoid camera shakiness.

> ▶ To see an example of a speech with camera operator problems, try Video Activity 15.3, "Fallacy: Red Herring (Needs Improvement)."

Be sure the camera is positioned at the level of your eyes. This will make you appear to be having conversational eye contact with audience members rather than looking down on them.[39] Changing the camera shot while recording presents challenges, but it can help enliven your speech.[40] If you have a skilled camera operator and are confident he or she can make these kinds of moves look seamless (or if your professor suggests you incorporate different moves), consider having your operator

DO NOT ASK ANY OF THESE PEOPLE TO BE YOUR CAMERA OPERATOR

Mr. Sleepy   Ms. Clumsy   Ms. Distracted

take close-up shots when you emphasize key points, zoom in on visual aids, or shoot you from different angles. These moves need to be coordinated between you and your camera operator so that they are done at the correct points in your speech. If the microphone is in the camera, it should remain about the same distance from you for the entire speech. If that distance becomes greater, you will sound farther away: a microphone can't zoom in or out the way a lens can.[41]

SPECIAL CONSIDERATIONS FOR REAL-TIME PRESENTATIONS

Many students have experience with real-time communication, whether through joining Google Hangouts with friends or using Skype during an internship interview. Real-time communication is also highly important in today's workforce, and employers may expect you to know how to give an effective mediated speech.

Although many of the previous suggestions about delivery mechanics apply here as well, some additional tips and suggestions are unique to real-time technology, including *practicing with your equipment to make sure it works, selecting a robust Internet connection, using group chat/video and screen sharing, creating opportunities for audience interaction*, and *soliciting feedback through an alternative medium*.

Practicing with Your Equipment to Make Sure It Works

As mentioned previously, we strongly advocate practicing mediated speeches before the actual presentation date. For real-time presentations, it's vital to practice with the technology you plan to use. For example, if you are using Skype, practice in the room or location where you will be presenting at least one day before your speech. Go through a dry run, using and sharing any slides or video you plan to use in the speech. Ideally, you should ask a friend or colleague to view your speech remotely and make sure everything works smoothly.

Selecting a Robust Internet Connection

Be sure that your Internet connection is strong enough to handle all parts of your presentation. Your room may have a weak wireless signal or a signal strength that varies within the room. In these cases, you

should find either a better room or a spot with the strongest signal. Sometimes you will have a choice of using an Ethernet connection or wifi. In our experience with technologies like Skype, if you have a choice, indicate a preference for Ethernet. In nearly every situation, it will provide a stronger, more reliable, more consistent connection. Wifi works, but other devices in the immediate vicinity drain its signal strength, which can freeze or crash your program.

Using Group Chat/ Video and Screen Sharing

In a presentation via technology such as Skype or Google Hangouts, you can establish your audience and manage what audience members see with group chat/video and screen sharing. Group chat

can be used on the day of your presentation to add audience participants from a contact list. You can then change the name of the chat to reflect the purpose of the meeting (your presentation), type in a welcome message, and send out files (such as an agenda or slides) before the speech. Group video will allow you to see all participants individually. If available, you can also use screen sharing to allow your audience members to view your presentation aids on their computers.

Creating Opportunities for Audience Interaction

As we mentioned earlier, mediated presentations can never take the place of face-to-face interaction. However, with technology such as Skype, you can take some easy actions to decrease the barrier between you and your audience as much as possible.

For starters, make sure you position yourself directly in front of your computer so that you look at audience members as they watch you on their screens. Create the appearance that you are really in their presence. Encourage them to ask questions at deliberate points in your speech, or ask them for comments and feedback. As you watch them, study their reactions as you would in a live audience situation. Do they appear engaged? Distracted? Are they checking emails or texting on their

phones? The more you can do to focus their attention, the more likely they will be to interact with you.

Soliciting Feedback through an Alternative Medium

Finally, you may decide to ask someone who is at the audience's location to send you the reactions of other listeners, especially if you are

giving a long presentation with time for questions and comments. A simple way to do this is to have this individual (usually a session moderator) send you simple text messages regarding the audience's level of engagement, comprehension, skepticism, interest, enthusiasm, or even boredom. Be sure to check your phone discreetly so that your audience doesn't think that *you* are distracted. (If you're using a group chat function, your observer may be able to use it to send you private real-time feedback.) Ask this individual to keep the feedback simple so that you can check it and adjust your delivery as needed. In this instance, the backchannel feedback source becomes a second pair of eyes for you.

CHAPTER REVIEW

> Effective mediated public speaking offers a new world of challenges and opportunities.

In this chapter, we examined mediated public speaking, in which a message is transmitted through an electronic or a mechanical medium. We contrasted mediated communication with face-to-face (F2F) communication. Although mediated communications do not have the immediacy of F2F communications, they offer several advantages and are used increasingly in schools and the workplace. They fall into one of two categories—prerecorded presentations and real-time presentations.

Some of the advantages of all mediated presentations are flexibility, savings, and audience size. Prerecorded advantages include do-overs, pause and rewind buttons, and the ability to save. Real-time advantages include audience feedback, audience interaction, and the option to save. Due to the loss of naturalness in mediated presentations, there are also some challenges to meet, including loss of immediacy, decreased nonverbal communication, diminished feedback, and difficulty managing distractions. Still, there are ways to combat these challenges—by optimizing delivery methods (voice, eye contact, movement, and gestures) and adapting your message appropriately (focusing on building common ground and keeping audience members engaged). It's also important to practice a mediated speech beforehand.

When recording a presentation, you should consider choice of camera, setting/background, attire, and camera positioning. For real-time presentations, keep in mind the following suggestions: practice with your equipment to make sure it works, select a robust Internet connection, use group chat/video and screen sharing, create opportunities for audience interaction, and solicit feedback through an alternative medium.

 LaunchPad
macmillan learning

LaunchPad for *Speak Up* offers videos and encourages self-assessment through adaptive quizzing. Go to **macmillanhighered.com/speakup4e** to get access to:

 LearningCurve
Adaptive Quizzes

 Video clips that help you understand
public speaking concepts

Key Terms

mediated communication *436*
prerecorded (asynchronous)
  presentation *439*
real-time (synchronous)
  presentation *439*

naturalness *444*
multitasking *447*
takeaway *452*

Review Questions

1. Define *mediated public speaking*, and provide three examples of situations in which a mediated presentation might be used.
2. Name and define the two major categories of mediated presentations.
3. Identify three advantages of mediated presentations.
4. Define *naturalness*, and explain the challenges speakers face when not presenting in a face-to-face situation.
5. Identify three things to keep in mind for effective delivery of mediated presentations.
6. Name four ways of keeping your audience engaged during a mediated presentation.
7. Name three tips for practicing the delivery and recording of a prerecorded speech.

8. Explain how the background for a prerecorded speech should look.

9. Explain the advantages of group chat/video or screen sharing in a real-time mediated presentation.

Critical Thinking Questions

1. Will mediated public speaking ever replace face-to-face speeches as the preferred format for presentations? Explain your answer.

2. Some colleges have created courses in which all lectures are presented online. Does this format improve the quality of education? Why or why not?

3. You have been assigned to videotape a presentation for your class, and you have three choices for locations—the campus study lounge, your apartment, or the campus bar. The campus study lounge may be occupied by students who are prepping for final exams, your apartment has stains on the carpet and the sofa, and the campus bar (where you work) will be moderately empty when it opens a little before lunchtime. Which location would you choose, and why?

Activities

1. Working individually or in groups, prepare a plan to prerecord a speech. Include the type of camera, setting and background, speaker's attire, and camera positioning.

2. ▟ Look at the illustration on page 458. How would you redraw this picture to correct the three camera operators? What should each person do differently?

3. ◉ Video Activity 15.4: "Gentz, My Hero, Marilyn Hamilton." Watch Lillian Gentz's speech. How does the limited view of the speaker make it difficult to observe all of her nonverbal communication? Her presentation aids? If you were the camera operator, what changes would you make in recording Gentz's presentation?

Study Plan

16

INFORMATIVE SPEAKING

"Effective informative speakers share accessible, understandable information in a compelling way."

Suppose you have a work-study job at the campus health center. To help promote campus health, the center will offer free influenza inoculations to students in the coming weeks. The center's director has asked you to deliver a brief presentation at the student union to inform students about the program.

An informative presentation teaches the audience something and increases listeners' understanding, awareness, or sensitivity to your topic. Your speech might include information about the way the flu spreads, its symptoms, and the dangers it poses, particularly for college students. It would be helpful to talk about simple measures students can take to prevent the spread of the flu, especially students who live in dense campus housing and commuters who share homes with young children or pregnant women. You could present information about the three methods for inoculating people from the flu—including a standard flu shot; the flu mist, which is a simple spray that goes into the nose; or an Intradermal, which is a new injection that is administered by a needle so small that subjects barely feel it.[1] Finally, you'd need to describe the logistics of your school's program—where and when the shots will be given, how to get an appointment, and what information students will need to give to the professionals who are administering the shots.

Your goal should be to provide all the information students need to decide whether they want to get a shot and how to get one if they decide to do so. Although the presentation is primarily informative, it also may contain a bit of persuasion. After all, you are speaking about something that you and your school believe is an important health concern and hope that students who are armed with good information will take advantage of the program.

In this chapter, we take a close look at informative speaking. First, we examine specific techniques for informing. Next, we consider the common types of informative speaking. Finally, we address how to develop an informative speech, including strategies for analyzing your audience and simplifying complex information in your presentation.

TECHNIQUES FOR INFORMING

Most informative speeches rely on one of the following techniques for conveying information—*definition, explanation, description, demonstration,* or *narrative*. Although some topics may lend themselves to one or another of these techniques, you usually will use a blend of techniques in your informative presentation.

Definition

Through **definition**, you break down something by its parts and explain how they add up to identify the topic. In short, you explain the essence, meaning, purpose, or identity of something. That "something" could be any of the following:

- An object—for example, "What is a bicycle derailleur?"
- A person or group—for instance, "What are hipsters?"
- An event—such as, "What was 'the Play' in college football?"
- A process—for instance, "What is reverse engineering?"
- An idea or concept—for example, "What is obscenity?"

As we discuss in Chapter 8, there are four types of definitions. An example of each is shown in the table on page 469, which demonstrates how you might use each of the four types to define the word *obscenity*.

TYPES OF DEFINITIONS

Type	Explanation	Example
Dictionary	The meaning of a term as it appears in a dictionary	*Merriam-Webster's Collegiate Dictionary*, Eleventh Edition, defines *obscenity* as "something that is obscene"—that is, "disgusting to the senses."
Expert	The meaning of a term that comes from a person or an organization that is a credible source of information on your speech's topic	According to Chief Justice Warren Burger of the U.S. Supreme Court in the 1973 case *Miller v. California*, obscenity is expression that appeals to a "prurient" (sick or unhealthy) interest in sex or sexual matters; depicts sexual conduct in a "patently offensive way"; and, when taken as a whole, "lacks serious literary, artistic, political, or scientific value."
Etymological	The understanding of a word or concept that is obtained by tracing its roots in the same or other languages	The word *obscenity* may derive from the Latin word *obscaenus*, combining the prefix *ob* (meaning "to") and the word *caenum* (meaning "dirt," "filth," "mire," and "excrement").
Functional	The meaning of a term that comes from examining how it is applied or how it functions	In practice, American law recognizes obscenity as hard-core pornography (and not as violence, disease, or other social ills).

*JUSTICE POTTER STEWART, CONCURRING OPINION ON *JACOBELLIS V. OHIO* (1964)

Explanation

Through **explanation**, you analyze something clearly and specifically by tracing a line of reasoning or a series of causal connections between events. In this process of interpretation, you also may offer examples to illustrate the information you're sharing. Explanation works well when you're giving a speech about a process, tracing the end of an important event, or describing how an interesting object works. For instance, you could use explanation to help your audience understand any one of the following:

- The most common causes of running injuries
- The events and decisions that led to the end of World War II
- How the engine in a hybrid car works
- The stages that a person usually goes through when grieving
- How cell mitosis works
- How Skype technology can be used for civic engagement at a city council meeting

Let's assume you are giving a speech to explain how Skype technology can be used by private citizens for civic engagement with local government (a topic mentioned in Chapter 15). Your speech might begin by explaining how residents used to have to travel to city council meetings and wait for a chance to make short presentations on matters that were of concern to them. You might talk about how this effort showed a commitment to democracy—but wasn't feasible for people who had family and work-related obligations. You also could explain how Skype allows a speaker to be present at the city council meetings without having to be there in person.

Description

When you use **description**, you use words to paint a mental picture for your listeners so that they can close their eyes and imagine what you are saying. If you provide sufficient information and detail, your audience may be able to experience vividly what you describe—and through multiple senses. For example, you might decide to use description to help your audience understand one of the following:

- What the aurora borealis looks like
- What it's like to work on a presidential campaign

- What the people you see (every day) on public transportation look like
- How you felt when you drove a car alone for the first time
- What the call of a blackbird sounds like
- How your city would look if people stopped littering
- What it's like to attend the Burning Man festival in Nevada
- What it looks like when humpback whales breach
- What a freshly applied tattoo feels like

Your descriptions can have maximum effect when you use vivid language, presentation aids, and details that evoke the senses of sight, sound, smell, touch, and taste. This can be especially effective if you use a description as a subpoint to engage listeners' imaginations and place it in the middle of what you're defining, explaining, demonstrating, or telling a story about. (See Chapter 12 for more on effective description.)

Demonstration

You might choose to provide a **demonstration** of a topic if your goal is to teach your audience how a process or a set of guidelines works. Demonstrations often call for both physical modeling and verbal elements as you lead the audience through the parts or steps of whatever

you are demonstrating. Your audience learns by watching your modeling and listening to your words. Because physical modeling often requires the use of props and visual aids, be sure to practice with the aids before giving your speech. And because you'll be teaching your audience, you need to be confident that you know your topic thoroughly.

Demonstrations could be helpful for a wide range of informative speeches. For example, you might use a demonstration to show your listeners how to do one of the following:

- Fix a flat tire on a bicycle
- Care for an orchid
- Create a Zen garden sandbox
- Sell something on Craigslist
- Milk a goat
- Perform a praise dance
- Practice self-defense
- Properly display and store an American flag

🅒 **To see an example of a speaker demonstrating what to look for when buying a guitar, try Video Activity 16.1, "Garza, How to Buy a Guitar."**

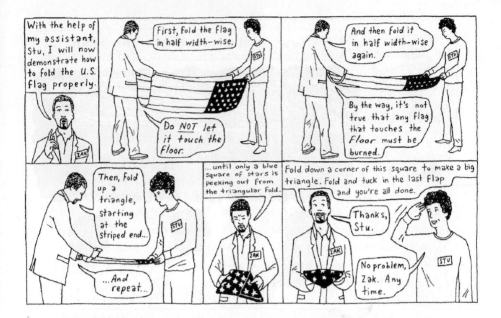

For some of these demonstrations, you could take the needed props to your speech forum. For instance, to demonstrate how to fold an American flag, you could easily bring in a large flag and—with an assistant—show the proper way to fold it for storage according to military custom.[2] You also could improvise by asking members of your audience about the flags that they've seen in advertising, used as decoration in dorm rooms, or printed on T-shirts and other clothing—before noting that such seemingly patriotic displays are actually violations of the U.S. Flag Code.[3]

Demonstration coupled with repetition of the speech message has proven especially effective as a learning and memory-enhancement tool. A good example of this can be seen in the practices of an organization called Per Scholas, which provides job training to low-income individuals. This program has been spectacularly effective with helping to train computer-repair technicians who have little or no previous formal education. The practice of demonstrating the repair process and repeating the message has been key to the program's success.[4]

Narrative

A **narrative** is a story. When you use a narrative in an informative speech, the story enables you to share information and capture the audience's attention. The story itself can take the form of a personal remembrance, a humorous anecdote, or a serious account of an event that happened in someone else's life—all told in a way that informs the audience about your topic. Used skillfully, narratives can help "humanize" a speaker for listeners and thus enhance the speaker's credibility, or ethos.

Using narrative in an informative speech is a good way to get your point across in an engaging, memorable way. For example, you could use narrative to do one of the following:

- *Open a speech on the risks and dangers associated with playing tackle football.* A poignant introductory story—perhaps about Chris Borland, the star rookie player for the San Francisco 49ers who retired after only one season because he was concerned that repetitive head trauma could cause him permanent brain damage— could help win your listeners' attention and stir up their emotions right from the start.

- *Emphasize the importance of communication in sustaining intimate relationships.* An entertaining narrative about a misunderstanding that you and your romantic partner ultimately cleared up through skillful communication could help you make your point in a light-hearted but meaningful way.

- *Help your listeners appreciate the need for careful preparation before a job interview.* A story about a friend who failed to research the dress code of a company she was interviewing with and felt embarrassed when she showed up wearing overly casual attire could leave a lasting impression on your listeners.

- *Reveal the difficulty of getting a job after serving time in prison.* A story about the hardships that released inmates face when trying to find jobs and rebuild their lives could raise audience awareness.

> ▶ **To watch an example of a speaker using a narrative, try Video Activity 16.2, "Conveying Information: Narrative (Needs Improvement)."**

Using narrative effectively takes careful thought and preparation. You need to choose a story that supports your message and not throw in a narrative simply to entertain or captivate your audience. The stories that you select—and the details that go into them—should be

based on audience analysis. If you are giving a speech about the risks and dangers of playing tackle football to an audience made up of people who know little about football, you might need to explain who Chris Borland is and why he was important to the San Francisco 49ers team and fans. You might also need to explain how he became aware of a study that found degenerative brain disease in posthumous examinations of seventy-six out of seventy-nine former National Football League players.[5] You probably would want to describe how Borland believed that he should walk away from the game before the head injuries seriously damaged him. Even if you know the elements of the narrative well, you may want to research background information and specific details of the story and weave the information you find into the speech.

Finally, remember that it's a bit of an art to tell a compelling story in a way that also informs and educates your audience. You want to come across as casual and natural (rather than over-rehearsed) but also authoritative, which requires extensive preparation and practice. It's as if you need to practice acting unrehearsed. In truth, using narrative in a speech can be risky, but if you do it well, it offers you and your audience real rewards. (For more on narrative, see Chapter 8.)

TYPES OF INFORMATIVE SPEECHES

Informative speeches seek to share information, explanations, or even ideas with an audience. Unlike persuasive speeches, which seek to make an argument and therefore confirm or alter an audience's beliefs or actions, informative speeches are meant to give audience members knowledge they might not have possessed before the speech. Informative speeches can be about a wide range of topics—*objects, individuals or groups, events, processes,* and *ideas.* In this section, we take a closer look at each of these types of informative speeches.

Objects

If you're giving an informative speech about an object, you have a virtually unlimited range of possibilities to choose from. The one thing all objects have in common, though, is that they're not human. The table below shows a small sampling of the much larger universe of possible objects your speech could address.

TYPES OF OBJECTS SUITABLE FOR AN INFORMATIVE SPEECH

Type	Examples
Mechanical or technological	motorcycle blender cell phone weapons system
Natural	flowering plant river elephant planet
Cultural	painting building book gourmet dish
Personal	jacket credit card ice skates necklace

In giving an informative speech about a particular object, you could use a number of techniques. For example, suppose you're preparing a presentation about the benefits of chocolate—which is a food and therefore an object. In this case, you could easily use description to inform your audience. You might describe the smooth, creamy texture and sumptuous flavor of a high-quality chocolate truffle and the feeling of well-being that can come from eating it.

Depending on the purpose of your speech, you also could use one or more of the other techniques. For example, you might use

- *definition* to clarify what chocolate is and how it differs from other consumable products derived from cacao beans,
- *explanation* to trace the process by which chocolate bars are made,
- *demonstration* to show how you might bake a chocolate cake, or
- *narrative* to convey chocolate's popularity as a romantic gift.

Finally, note that an informative speech about an object may also contain elements of process—especially if that object has moving parts. For instance, to deliver a presentation on how a motorcycle operates, you might explain how the bike's fuel and transmission systems work together to create the process of acceleration.

Individuals or Groups

Giving an informative speech about an individual or a group offers an equally wide range of possibilities. People are fascinated by others, as can be seen from the popularity of celebrity-focused magazines, reality-based television shows, and personal memoirs. Human subjects with extraordinary physical or emotional characteristics or compelling life stories can provide engaging and informative material for speeches. Groups, likewise, are collections of people with whom your audience can identify; these can include famous politicians in the same party or musical performers who capture tremendous amounts of attention. To illustrate, you could focus your talk on one of the following:

- *A famous politician, entertainer, sports star, explorer, or artist.* For example, you might give a speech about Shirley Chisholm, the first African American woman elected to the U.S. Congress (in 1968) and a candidate for president in the 1972 Democratic primary, nearly four decades before Barack Obama or Hillary Clinton.

A FAMOUS POLITICIAN

- *An unsung hero* (a person or group that did something great but never won recognition for the accomplishment). For instance, you could tell your audience about members of a small tribe in the forests of Burma who survived persecution by the ruling junta.

AN UNSUNG HERO

- *A tragic figure whose life provides a cautionary tale.* For example, you might discuss Philip Seymour Hoffman's untimely death from mixed drug

A TRAGIC FIGURE

intoxication after starring in many critically acclaimed films.

- *An influential political party, artistic movement, sports team, or musical group.* For instance, you might discuss the rise of women in comedy—both those writing and starring in their own television shows, such as Lena Dunham, Amy Schumer, Ilana Glazer, and Abbi Jacobson, as well as those who have helped to diversify existing shows, such as Leslie Jones of *Saturday Night Live.*

As with objects, you could easily use description to deliver your informative speech about an individual or a group. For example, if your speech focused on aviator Amelia Earhart, you could describe her youth and personal qualities along with her famed accomplishments. You also might use narrative to tell a story about the defining experience that led her to become a pilot (namely, attending a stunt-flying exhibition in her late teens). Or you could use explanation to trace the events that led her to attempt her biggest challenge—flying around the world.

Remember that although you will not be able to describe all of a person's life experiences in a single speech, you can use life events to make a larger point about a person's character—what kind of person he or she is. You could support such claims by using narratives supplied by the person's family, friends, associates, and even critics or enemies.

A presentation on a person or group might effectively incorporate information about an object or a process as well. Consider a talk on renowned inventor Thomas Edison. To convey Edison's innovative spirit, you could discuss the life experiences that led to his great achievements and also several of his most famous inventions—objects such as the lightbulb and the phonograph. Or you could describe the process by which he developed one of his best-known inventions, including how he resolved problems that arose while designing it.

Events

An event is a notable or exceptional occurrence, either from the present time or from some point in the past. Here are just a few examples of events on which you could focus an informative speech:

- The signing into law of the Twenty-Sixth Amendment, which lowered the voting age to eighteen
- The discovery of a new planet or species
- The outcome of a high-profile murder trial
- The publication of an important new book
- An underdog's surprising victory over the front-runner in a sporting event
- The emergence in the business world of a new and different kind of company
- The unearthing of new evidence suggesting the origins of humankind
- A wedding, funeral, or religious ritual in your family
- The Republican or Democratic National Convention
- The Billabong Pipeline Masters at Banzai Pipeline
- A commemoration at the Tomb of the Unknowns
- Your town's extraordinary Fourth of July celebration
- Fashion Week in New York City

BLENDING NARRATIVE AND DESCRIPTION

How do you decide what event would make a good topic for an informative speech? Look for events that your audience will consider exciting, newsworthy, historically important, or interesting because they are unfamiliar or surprising.

In delivering an informative speech about an event, you could easily use narrative to tell the story of how the event unfolded. You also could use description to explain how the event affected a group of people. Or you could employ a blend of both narrative and description. For instance, suppose you were presenting a speech about the day you became an American citizen. You might begin with a narrative about your experiences as an immigrant, including anecdotes about your travels from your home country and your family's struggle to establish itself in America. You might then detail the process of applying for citizenship. Finally, you might describe what happened at your naturalization ceremony and how it felt for you to take the citizenship pledge.

Processes

Imagine that you're filing a tax return, changing a tire, planting a vegetable garden, or giving a haircut to a friend. Or maybe you're thinking about how two countries resolve a border dispute, how Major League Baseball owners and the players' union negotiate the baseball salary cap for each team, or how marriages are arranged in a particular culture.

Each of these is a process—a series of steps or stages that lead to a particular outcome. You can detect processes at the level of something localized and simple (such as how to change a tire) and at a much broader level (such as how changes in labor and immigration laws and trade policies affect the cost of automobiles, including tires, in different countries and markets). Thus, we sometimes suggest that processes can be seen at both the micro level (the view of a process from fifty feet) and the macro level (the view from five thousand feet). Many of the informative presentations in a speech class will involve the micro level (which is easier to explain and grasp), but that shouldn't discourage you from trying a macro-level topic (such as the ways in which global warming occurs). When presented as a process, even large topics can be digestible for most audiences.

Remember that some topics (such as how changes in the tax code will affect the alternative minimum tax) do not lend themselves well to a discussion of process because they are highly technical. Does this mean you should avoid a technical topic? No, but it does mean that if you select a topic because it is process oriented, you should focus on

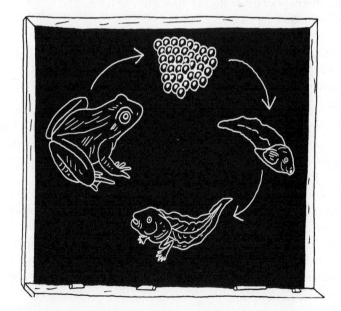

subject matter that is within your audience's level of understanding, break down the topic into smaller parts, and only then show how those parts work together as part of a larger process.

When you deliver an informative speech about a process, you probably will want to walk your listeners through the steps that make up that process, explaining how each is carried out and in what order.

> ▶ To see a speaker describing a complex process, try **Video Activity 16.3,** **"Conveying Information: Description."**

Depending on your goal, use a variety of techniques to inform your audience about a particular process. For example, if you want listeners to understand how a specific object is made or how it works, you might use explanation to clarify what each step is and how it leads to the creation of the object.

By contrast, if your goal is to teach audience members how to perform the process themselves, combine both explanation and *demonstration*— that is, verbally and physically model the steps of the process.

To illustrate, suppose you're giving a presentation on cake decorating. You'd probably want to explain what tools are needed and what kinds of icings are appropriate for particular styles of decoration. You also might demonstrate by showing the actual techniques used to produce a certain decoration—for example, a basket-weave design—through enlarged photographs or a video. If you are in a relatively intimate environment, you might even decorate an actual cake as part of your presentation.

In deciding which process to focus on in an informative speech, take care to avoid overused topics (such as how to make the perfect peanut butter and jelly sandwich) and topics related to alcohol (such as how to make Jell-O shots or brew beer at home). Instead, think about processes that would be interesting and fresh for your listeners. Also, consider how you might discuss the effects of an important process. For instance, suppose you're informing your audience about how the baseball farm system works. In this case, you could add interest to the topic by using a narrative to convey how the process changes young players' lives by giving them a shot at the big leagues.

Ideas

An idea is a theory, principle, belief, or value. Ideas are relatively abstract compared to other informative speech topics, such as an object, a person, or a process. For example, it's easier to explain what the aurora borealis looks like or how a motorcycle engine works than it is to describe the notion of freedom of speech. The idea of freedom of speech is more difficult to explain for two reasons: first, it's an idea and not a physical object or process, and second, there are limits to freedom of speech. Indeed, this concept has several subtleties that restrict its application in many situations (for example, it is illegal to incite certain kinds of violence or to threaten to kill another person).[6]

Some ideas are emotionally loaded because people have difficulty agreeing on their meaning. Consider the notion of terrorism. Its meaning seems obvious to many after the September 11, 2001, attacks in New York, Washington, DC, and Pennsylvania and their repercussions. But are all violent acts against civilians or noncombatants terrorism? Are nation-states guilty of terrorism when their troops accidentally kill civilians? Why do people say things like "One man's terrorist is another man's freedom fighter?" Like freedom of expression, terrorism is a more complex and abstract notion than it may initially appear.

Here are some additional ideas that could be topics for an informative speech about an idea:

- Family values
- Income inequality
- The economic effects of globalization
- Generational theft
- The disadvantages of technology
- "It's better to give than to receive."
- The separation of church and state
- The advantages of working for employers who contribute to social or ethical causes

Because ideas are abstract, it's important to select an idea carefully as you consider topics for an informative speech. Otherwise, you may fail to connect with your audience during your presentation. Be sure to consider your audience's interests and level of education when you weigh potential ideas to discuss in your speech. For example, if you want to inform your listeners about the economic effects of globalization, think about how much your audience already knows about the topic. If audience members' knowledge is scanty, you'll need to provide more background on globalization during your speech, or you may decide to select another topic with which your listeners are more familiar.

Also ask yourself whether audience members have had prior exposure to the idea you want to discuss in your presentation. If they have—and did not find the idea compelling—you may want to consider selecting a different topic.

Finally, consider how you might make particularly abstract ideas more understandable to your listeners during your presentation. In a talk on the effects of globalization, for example, you could draw the following analogy: "Globalization is like agriculture. In agriculture, the more evenly you spread seeds across a large field, the more certain you can be that crops will grow in every corner of the field. Likewise, the more you allow commercial activity to flourish across many countries, the more you'll encourage economic well-being among the world's populations."

Most informative speeches about ideas require the use of definition or explanation, both of which enable you to clarify the meaning of the idea you're discussing and to examine its various ramifications. For instance, although the meaning of the word *terrorism* is hotly debated in academic and political circles, most people define it as a form of calculated violence (or the threat thereof) against civilians or noncombatants for the purpose of creating mass anxiety and panic while publicizing a political or social agenda.[7] An informative speech on terrorism might begin with that definition, but to further clarify the idea of terrorism, you could separate each part of the definition and explain it individually. For instance, to clarify what "publicizing a political or social agenda" means, you could offer several examples of groups that have committed violent acts and used the resulting publicity to advance their cause.

DEVELOPING YOUR INFORMATIVE SPEECH

To develop an informative speech, you use the same strategies described in earlier chapters—such as analyzing your audience's background and needs, deciding which supporting materials to include, and determining how to organize your content. In this section, we examine *analyzing your audience, selecting a technique* for organizing your speech, and *focusing on your goal to inform.* Appropriate audience analysis and organization help ensure that you prepare a solid foundation and structure for your speech.

Analyzing Your Audience

As with any type of public presentation, audience analysis is essential for developing a successful informative speech. Yet analyzing your audience for an informative presentation raises unique challenges. You'll want to focus on where and how your audience is situated for the presentation, what your audience's specific demographics are, and what the common ground you share with your audience is.

To analyze your audience, start by considering the characteristics of your speaking situation. If you are presenting an informative speech in class, note any requirements for the topic, format, and content of the presentation. If you're planning to deliver your speech outside of class, consider the occasion for your speech. Also note the forum (the setting where you will be speaking), the time of day intended for your presentation, the size of your audience, and the expected length of your speech.

Next, remember to examine audience **demographics**—particularly those most likely to influence your listeners' interest in and disposition toward your topic. These include political affiliation, group membership, occupation or academic major, race, ethnicity, gender, sexual orientation, socioeconomic background, age, religious affiliation, and family status.

Also look for common ground you might have with your audience— such as shared values, interests, and experiences. By noting common ground while developing an informative speech, you can incorporate strategies to strengthen your credibility, or ethos. (For more on audience analysis, see Chapter 5.)

Selecting a Technique

Your audience analysis also informs your choice of technique—or organizational pattern—for delivering the informative speech. Which technique would *most* help you inform your audience about your topic— definition, explanation, description, demonstration, narrative, or a combination of these? Your choice of technique is crucial because it helps you decide how you'll develop and organize the main points and supporting materials in your presentation.

For example, suppose you were considering using demonstration to present your informative speech. In this case, you would want to ask yourself the following questions:

- *Forum:* "Where will the audience be situated—and will there be ample space for me to move around as I give my demonstration?"
- *Audience size:* "How many people will be in my audience—and will they all be able to see and hear my demonstration?"

You also should consider audience size and details of the speaking forum when planning presentation aids for your informative speech. If you anticipate a small audience and cramped space, a PowerPoint presentation may be unnecessary. Showing objects or offering simple handouts might create an intimate setting. In a big forum with a large audience, you may be best served by projecting PowerPoint slides onto a large screen (or even several large screens) and adequately amplifying your voice. When speaking in such situations, make sure you plan carefully where you will stand. You may want to stand in the center of the room, directly before the screen or screens, and control the audience's interaction with the presentation aids by making the screen go blank after each point is made.

SELECTING A TECHNIQUE TO INFORM

Conversely, let's say you were considering using explanation or description to deliver your speech. In this case, you would focus more on demographics to analyze your audience. Look for anything in your listeners' backgrounds and characteristics that may make it difficult for them to understand the explanation or description you're planning to offer in your speech. For instance, if you're planning to describe a Hmong wedding ceremony and your listeners have no knowledge of Hmong culture, you'll need to provide more details in your description. Or if you're planning to explain the events leading up to the assassination of U.S. president John F. Kennedy and your listeners are too young to have lived through the event, you'll want to provide a fuller explanation than you would for an older audience. Of course, cultural background and age are not the only examples of demographics. You'll also need to consider other characteristics to develop an effective informative speech.

What if you're thinking about using narrative to present your speech? Common ground becomes particularly important in this case. To tell a story that will interest and move your listeners, it helps if you have had some of the same life experiences or share some of the same values. When you and your audience have common ground,

listeners will find it easier to believe you and identify with the narrative you're presenting.

Focusing on Your Goal to Inform

When developing an informative speech, it's particularly important to remain focused on your rhetorical purpose—to inform—at every phase (see the table on p. 492). If you know your subject well enough not to have to do research, be sure to establish your own credentials— noting, for example, "As someone who's played in poolrooms all over this state for more than two decades, I am fairly well schooled in the rules of the game." You also should remember that it's your responsibility to remain objective. If you find yourself choosing evidence that supports a particular point of view, you are going beyond informing. Remember that it's easy to remain objective on some subjects (such as knitting or explaining how an engine works), but other topics (such as defining *terrorism* or *freedom of speech*) invariably wander into more persuasive territory. We discuss persuasion further in Chapters 17 and 18.

ORGANIZING YOUR INFORMATIVE SPEECH

Organizational Pattern	Pattern Description	Example
Spatial	Describes or explains elements or events as they occur in space	A speech to explain the trajectory of a meteor that may come dangerously close to Earth
Chronological (temporal)	Moves from the beginning to the end by referencing points in time	A speech that describes a negotiation process, breaking down each bargaining step as it occurs
Causal	Explains the roots of a phenomenon or process	A presentation that explains how plate tectonics causes earthquakes and tsunamis
Comparison	Presents major similarities and differences between two items	A speech that compares the global reach and power of twenty-first-century United States with that of ancient Rome
Categorical (topical)	Main points constitute separate topics, each of which supports the thesis	A presentation to explain running a marathon, breaking it down into separate categories for training, nutrition, technique and style, and mental preparation

CLARIFYING AND SIMPLIFYING YOUR MESSAGE

As you prepare your informative speech, focus on clarifying and simplifying your message as much as possible. It will help your audience understand and thus retain your message.

Clarity is something you'll want to strive for in every informative speech, no matter what your topic is or who your listeners are. If you present a message that's confusing or use words that have vague meanings, it will be hard to connect with your audience.

In addition to clarifying your message, your audience analysis will help you decide how much to simplify your informative speech. For example, if listeners have little knowledge of your topic and the topic is complex, simplicity will be vital. A student named Jean once gave an informative presentation on a complex experimental genetic treatment that doctors and research scientists could use to fight cancer. Her audience was made up of students in her speech class—few of whom had sufficient background to follow the technical details in her speech. Jean wisely simplified things by first narrowing the broad topic of "treatment" to the more specific term "gene therapy." She then simplified her topic further by describing a simple three-step process for introducing genes into cells to prevent disease.

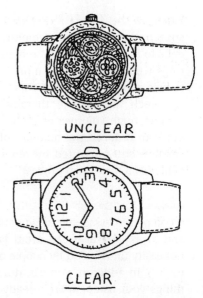

UNCLEAR

CLEAR

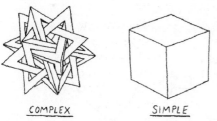

COMPLEX   SIMPLE

To clarify or simplify complex messages, consider the following techniques:

Move from General to Specific. Ask yourself, "At a minimum, what do I want my audience to take away from my speech? What basic message should the audience carry away?" Your answer can help you narrow a general or broad topic to a specific, simpler one—as in Jean's speech on gene therapy.

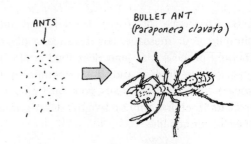

ANTS

BULLET ANT
(Paraponera clavata)

Reduce the Quantity of Information You Present. An informative speech may contain a tremendous amount of information for the audience to hear, process, and remember. An old adage still rings true here: "Less is more." Look for ways to reduce the number of details you present. A speech about gene therapy could contain huge volumes of information, but Jean reduced the quantity of information she presented by reducing the details to a three-step process.

Make Complex Information Seem Familiar. You can further clarify a complex message by using definition to explain difficult-to-follow terms and ideas. You also can avoid **jargon**—technical or insider terminology not easily understood by people outside a certain group or field (see Chapter 12). In addition, you can draw analogies between complex ideas and things your listeners are already familiar with.[8] For example, Jean could have made an analogy between gene therapy (a new concept for her audience) and a vaccine against polio (something that probably is familiar to her audience).

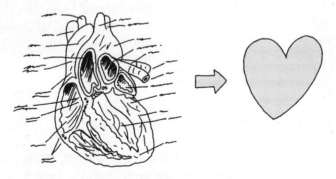

Use Presentation Aids. Presentation aids can help you clarify and simplify your message. For instance, a diagram of the three-step gene-therapy process that Jean described could have helped her listeners to envision the process and thus remember it. Likewise, if you are giving a speech on various bird calls, you could play a recording of a particular call instead of relying only on lengthy descriptions or demonstrations of what the call sounds like.

Reiterate Your Message. Through *reiteration*, you clarify a complex message by referring to it several times, using different words each time. For example, in an informative presentation about training for a triathlon, a speaker referred three times to the importance of using a heart-rate monitor. The first time he made the point, he said, "It's vital to use a heart-rate monitor to track your progress while you're training." The second time, he said, "Using a heart-rate monitor can really help you track your progress." The third time, he said, "The more you use the monitor, the more information you'll have on how you're progressing." By reiterating key points, you help your audience remember your message.

Repeat Your Message. Conveying a key point several times using the same words can also help ensure that your audience understands your message. For example, while introducing the gene-therapy process, Jean could have said something like, "This three-step process offers the best hope for treating cancer in the future." Then, in the conclusion of her speech, she could have said, "Let me repeat: this three-step process offers the best hope for treating cancer in the future."

SAMPLE INFORMATIVE SPEECH

SPIDER SILK: A MIRACLE MATERIAL DERIVED FROM . . . GOATS?

Rachel Parish
Southeastern Illinois College

Student Rachel Parish gave this informative speech in the 2007 finals of an annual national tournament hosted by Phi Rho Pi, a group that fosters public speaking and debate for junior and community college students throughout the United States. In this speech about an object, Rachel explains the astonishing strength and versatility of a material that may surprise her listeners—spider silk. Rachel's speech is organized categorically, or by topic, with the main points describing spider silk's properties, the means of producing it, and a number of its applications.

In the classic book *Charlotte's Web*, we find the story of a loving spider saving pitiful Wilbur from becoming bacon through messages spun in her webs. However, this is not the first time that such power has come from such a seemingly delicate medium.

In ancient Greece, spider webs were used to stop bleeding in open wounds. Aborigines use spider silk in small fishing lines. And how could we not mention Peter Parker's amazing ability to swing from buildings and catch the bad guys, all through the power of the web?

Now, that last example may be fictional, but Spider-Man's formidable weapon, the web, is no less amazing in real life. Spider silk is one of the strongest fibers known. It is incredibly fine and tough, and as the November 9, 2006, *London Daily Mail* tells us, "When woven into a fiber, it is weight-for-weight five times stronger than steel." •

So we know that the spider web, or spider silk, is tough, and over the past decade we found it to have both practical and medicinal benefits for us. However, to date we've never actually seen any of the benefits. Why? Well, gathering large quantities of spider silk has been relatively impossible until now. You see, while we may not have a real-life Spider-Man, we do have Spider*goat*. This is a transgenic goat that's

• Rachel's attention-getter includes stories and compelling facts.

producing spider silk on a much larger scale than Charlotte ever could. •

Today we'll learn about the value of spider silk and how these scientifically altered goats are allowing its once unavailable advantages to become a reality. First, we'll look at the background of spider silk; second, the goat's role in its production; and finally, its current and future uses. •

Let's first learn about the value of spider silk and how these goats are allowing its once unobtainable potential to be a reality. According to BBCNews.com, July 12, 2006, "Spider silk has been admired by scientists for decades due to its unique combination of strength, toughness, flexibility, and light weight; its thickness is less than one-tenth the size of a human hair, but it has 400,000 pounds per square inch of strength." To put this in perspective, if you built a massive spider web in which each strand was the width of a pencil, you could catch a 747 jumbo jet in full flight.

So if spider silk is indeed the strongest fiber on earth, why haven't we taken advantage of this miracle material before? The June 16, 2006, *Science and Technology* tells us that "spiders are incredibly hard to farm so silk can be harvested, mainly due to a spider's nature." • Basically, if you put two spiders together in a confined space, due to their cannibalistic nature, you'll suddenly find yourself with only one spider.

In addition, even when they are contained properly, you can milk only so much silk from a spider. A study this past November by Randy Lewis of the University of Wyoming showed that even when dealing with large spiders, on a good day you can gather only 1.5 mg of silk. Thus, even if you could get the cannibals to get along, a spider farm capable of raising enough useful silk would simply be impossible. •

However, all that has now changed. Last year, Nexia Biotechnologies—a Canadian research firm—began looking at normal farm goats as the key to bringing spider silk to the masses. According to Christopher Helman in Forbes.com, February 19, 2001, Jeffrey Turner, a geneticist at Nexia, discovered that the silk gland of spiders and the milk gland of goats were almost identical, but the goat's is obviously much bigger. At the turn of the millennium, Nexia began implanting spider genes into goats in order to breed "spider goats" capable of producing spider silk in large enough quantities

---

• "What's in it for them?": Here she provides a startling fact about goats and spider silk.

• Rachel quickly gives her thesis and previews her three main points, organized topically.

• Rachel establishes her source's credibility here by citing publication title and date. She could add more credibility by consistently including the author's name and credentials.

• Here and throughout, Rachel offers a variety of supporting materials— mainly examples, expert testimony, and statistics.

for commercial use. The end result was Webster and Pete, the first two goats born with the spider-web gene.

So now that we've looked past the roadblocks to cultivating spider silk by showing the creation of a feasible silk resource thanks to Webster and Pete here, let's examine the process by which the spider gene was passed on to the goats. • According to the January 15, 2006, issue of the journal *Nature*, "Spider silk starts out as a substance called scleroprotein, which shoots out from the spider's web spinnerets. . . . [I]t dries into a thread, and when this thread hardens we end up with something that looks a little more familiar to us."

• An effective transition signals the end of a previous point and introduces the next one.

When Nexia discovered that the silk glands of spiders were similar to goats' mammary glands, Nexia applied this discovery to dairy goats. Taking a goat embryo, Nexia injected the spider gene controlling the creation of silk into the goat's mammary cells. These cells then took effect and activated the female goats when they started lactating, or creating milk for their young. When the lactation period in the goat is over, these cells stop functioning and stop producing silk until the goat starts lactating again. According to *Materials Today*, December 2002, Jeffrey Turner reports that each transgenic goat is "capable of making 'literally miles' of this spider silk–based material." Fifteen thousand goats could produce enough silk to meet projected medical and industrial demands. Plus, because they're not cannibalistic, we're able to farm goats on a large scale. •

• Rachel offers this explanation of a process within her larger topical organization.

However, the spiders do have one advantage: the goats can't spin the silk they produce, so then there's a weaving process. As explained in the October 10, 2006, airing of *Modern Marvels* on the History Channel, "The goats are milked as they normally would be, then the milk is put into a centrifuge that spins rapidly. This causes the silk fibers to separate from the milk so they can be extracted. Salts are then added to the silk fibers to help them harden. Once this step is completed, you have what researchers have dubbed 'bio-steel.'" According to the June 3, 2006, *Journal of Biological Chemistry*, this new silk made from spider-enhanced goats is the same strength and composition as normal spider silk. The method is environmentally safe, and the goats are not harmed in any way during the milking process. •

• Rachel shows solid audience analysis by anticipating listener concerns: the process is environmentally safe and doesn't harm the goats.

So we've examined the background of spider silk, its genetic switch to goats, and how it has evolved into bio-steel. But what benefits can we anticipate from this evolution? Will the use of goat silk bring us from the research lab to the battlefield and the operating room? •

Biotech Week, December 13, 2006, reports that bio-steel is now being used to construct bulletproof clothing for soldiers and police. Dr. Randolph Lewis, a biologist at the University of Wyoming, stated in the same issue of *Biotech Week* that Kevlar, the most popular fiber used in bulletproof vests, is very difficult to make and requires a chemical processing that is highly damaging to the environment. Unlike Kevlar, spider silk bio-steel is made in water-based conditions, and it's completely biodegradable. • In addition, in tests performed in early 2006 at the University of Wyoming, it was proven that when woven into a bulletproof vest, spider silk was stronger and more durable than the now-outdated Kevlar.

Yet bio-steel's most promising benefits are medicinal rather than military. According to the Royal College of Surgeons of England, in "Secrets of the Spider Web," March 9, 2007, "the demand for spider silk in the medical profession is high with a myriad of potential uses such as scaffolds, bone grafts, or ligament repair." The real strength of bio-steel as an internal support is its great wall strength and its ability to naturally dissolve over time without the need of additional surgeries. In addition, the spider silk bio-steel can be used as wonderful, durable, and biodegradable stitches that can be used in the most delicate of areas due to the material's thinness and strength. What's more, as *Science*, June 23, 2006, reports, spider silk bio-steel provokes a very low immune response when introduced into the body. What does that mean for us? Well, heavy immune responses cause rejection of artificial medical implants, thus making bio-steel a much more successful option than any previous materials. •

The main challenge for researchers is breeding enough goats to meet the demand for bio-steel. However, according to the October 31, 2006, *CBC News*, "If breeding continues as is, then the University of Wyoming's herd of goats alone will be bountiful enough to meet commercial demands by the end of 2008." In 2006 they produced over 5,200 pounds of spider silk, and just this past August the UW researchers

• Questions act as a transition and keep listeners involved.

• Rachel returns to the theme of environmental safety.

• By outlining bio-steel's medical uses, Rachel again shows what's in it for listeners.

SPEECH CHOICES

A CASE STUDY: *MIA*

Let's look at how Mia decided what techniques to use in her informative speech.

Mia kept two choices in mind as she finalized her informative speech. First, she needed to decide what informative techniques to use. Did she want to provide technical information about how the cell phones were used, focus on the journeys made possible by cell phones, or share narrative stories? In the end, Mia settled on all three: she would explain the technical aspects of how emigrants used smartphones for their journeys, use vivid language and word choice to paint a verbal picture of emigrants' smartphone use, and occasionally tell the stories of specific emigrants.

The other choice Mia had to make was to decide whether her speech would be about an object (cell phones) or a process (using cell phones to navigate a journey). After thinking it over, Mia decided that she wanted her speech to be about the process of using smartphones, so she organized her speech using a series of steps in chronological order that demonstrated all the ways that a smartphone could assist in the journey. Mia occasionally used analogies to help her audience understand the steps of this process.

YOUR TURN:
What types of techniques will you use in your informative speech? How will your choices affect the type of speech you'll give?

Even though she had personal connections to this topic, Mia also made sure to document her main points so that no one would raise concerns about where she had gotten her information or whether she was representing other people's work as her own. She knew that this kind of honesty would make it easier for the audience to believe her claims.

For more questions and activities for this case study, and to see a ⊙ video clip from Mia's speech on informative techniques, please go to LaunchPad at macmillanhighered.com/speakup4e.

received a quarter-million-dollar grant from the Department of Defense to expand their output, so the future of goat bio-steel looks very promising.

• The conclusion brings the speech full circle with a reference to Spider-Man.

Today we looked at the background of spider silk, the goat's role in its production, and finally its current and future applications. We can see the value of goat bio-steel for both military and medicinal uses, and in time perhaps we could imagine America's favorite web slinger changing from Peter Parker to Pete and Webster. •

CHAPTER REVIEW

> "Effective informative speakers share accessible, understandable information in a compelling way."

As the chapter's opening example about the speech on influenza vaccines suggests, informative speaking is about teaching your listeners something and increasing their awareness of your topic. You probably use informative speaking many times during a typical day—whenever you're defining, explaining, describing, demonstrating, or telling a story about something. Whether you're speaking informatively in everyday situations or delivering a formal presentation to a class or another type of audience, you can greatly enhance your effectiveness by applying the key practices presented in this chapter.

First, know how and when to use the five techniques for informative speaking—definition, explanation, description, demonstration, and narrative. Second, decide on the type of informative speech you want to give—whether it will be about an object, an individual or a group, an event, a process, or an idea. Third, use audience analysis to decide which technique you should use to organize your speech and how much to simplify your message. And fourth, stay focused on informing and maintaining an objective viewpoint.

When you apply these practices, you improve the odds of achieving your purpose in giving an informative speech. You enable your audience members to learn something new and important, and you hone their understanding, awareness, or sensitivity to your topic.

 **LaunchPad**
macmillan learning

LaunchPad for *Speak Up* offers videos and encourages self-assessment through adaptive quizzing. Go to **macmillanhighered.com/speakup4e** to get access to:

 LearningCurve
Adaptive Quizzes

 Video clips that help you understand
public speaking concepts

Key Terms

definition *468*

explanation *471*

description *471*

demonstration *472*

narrative *474*

demographics *488*

jargon *494*

Review Questions

1. Name and explain five techniques for informing.

2. What five types of topics for informative speeches are offered in the chapter?

3. What basic steps must be considered as you develop your informative speech?

4. Name the six basic techniques you can use to clarify and simplify your informative message.

Critical Thinking Questions

1. What subjects could you give an informative speech about without doing any research at all? How would you establish your credibility absent outside evidence?

2. Have you ever felt that someone who claimed to be informing you was in fact trying to persuade you? What was it about the speaker's presentation that tipped you off? Did this feeling make you more or less receptive to the information he or she was presenting?

3. Is it possible to define and describe a controversial idea, such as assisted suicide for terminally ill patients, without becoming emotional? Can an informative speech be emotional without becoming persuasive?

4. If you had to give a speech that explains that your fellow college students are at risk by not getting flu shots and provides some options for them, what would you choose to say? Also, how would your audience analysis of your listeners (especially with respect to their age and generation) inform your choices?

Activities

1. Take a look at any persuasive speech (you can find one at the end of Chapter 18 or search at the library or online for any political campaign speech). Edit it so that the focus of the speech is only on informing. How much of the speech is left?

2. Do you know a topic well enough to prepare a fifteen-minute informative presentation on it? Create a quick outline showing how you would do it.

3. Look up a "how-to" topic (such as how to make compost, play blackjack, or file your taxes) at the library or online. What kinds of sources do you find? Which ones do you find most helpful—and credible—and why?

Study Plan

_____

_____

_____

_____

_____

_____

_____

_____

_____

_____

_____

_____

We should TOTALLY volunteer to help Community TV with their membership drive. It'll be AH-MAZING! I LOVE so many of their programs. We could all work the phones next Sunday. I'm going to pass out a sign-up sheet. What do you think?
ACTION
Hey, why are they so UNENTHUSIASTIC?
Er...
COMMUNITY TV SIGN UP
Doesn't that channel show nothing but boring British costume dramas?
What's in it for ME?
ACTION
I don't even have a TV.
Telemarketing, yuck, no way!
ACTION
I have a big exam the day after. I can't do it.
I am thinking about something else...

17

PERSUASIVE SPEAKING

66Good persuaders make
strategic choices in
an ethical manner.99 Kaliya was excited about a community
service opportunity she discovered. The
local public television station was going
to hold a membership drive, and the station manager was looking for
groups that could spend four hours on the phones helping callers set
up their pledges. She couldn't wait for the next meeting of ACTION, her
service club on campus, so that she could ask the members to volunteer
at the station, which broadcasted several of her favorite programs.

At the next club meeting, Kaliya stood up and presented her idea.
She listed the programs that were scheduled that day on the station and
talked about the mission of public television. Then she suggested that
the club volunteer as a group to work on the phones at the membership
drive on Sunday from 3 to 7 p.m. Finally, she passed out a sign-up sheet.
Much to her disappointment, the other club members had little enthusiasm for her idea, and only two people volunteered.

Kaliya had made a common error that frustrates the best intentions
of those attempting to persuade others to adopt their ideas. Although
she loved her local public television station, she had not considered how

other club members might respond to her plan. For one thing, she failed to explain how volunteering would benefit the participants—an important consideration in any persuasive speech. Furthermore, she lost her audience's attention when she began listing the programs, so by the time she suggested that club members should work on the phones, many were only half listening. Some club members thought that they would have to make cold calls to ask for money, and they were uncomfortable with telemarketing. In addition, she had not considered the fact that final exams were starting the next day, and many students were stressed out and studying. No wonder she was unsuccessful.

Kaliya should have done more to tailor her message to the audience. She might have drawn club members into her speech by asking about popular public television shows that they probably watched as children. Because she knew many club members well, she might have focused on programs she knew they would like rather than listing every show on the schedule. She might have told listeners that this service opportunity would be helpful when they went job searching because many local businesses supported this station. If she had interested her listeners, then they would have been more attentive when she explained that they would be taking calls from people who wanted to donate—not cold calling. And she could have selected a better time to participate rather than the afternoon before finals started.

As Kaliya discovered firsthand, knowing how to speak persuasively is a vital skill in all areas of life. Consider your own situation: Do you want to get a new policy adopted on campus? Advance in your career? Influence members of your community to support an important cause? Convince your roommate to listen to the music you want to hear? Win a major contract for your company from a new customer? Get an extension on the deadline of a paper? In these and many other cases, you'll need to master the art of persuasive speaking if you hope to generate the outcomes you want.

In this chapter, we introduce the topic of persuasive speaking. We start by explaining the nature of a persuasive speech, followed by the process of persuasion. Then we show you how to select your thesis, main points, and supporting materials based on your audience analysis. We also consider the ethical obligations of a persuasive speaker and present several strategies for organizing your persuasive message. In the following chapter, we go into more detail about specific methods of persuasion.

THE NATURE OF A PERSUASIVE SPEECH

In a **persuasive speech**, your goal is to *influence audience members' beliefs, attitudes, or actions* and to *advocate fact, value, or policy claims*. Let's take a closer look at these characteristics.

Persuasive Speeches Attempt to Influence Audience Members

Depending on your goal, influencing audience members might mean trying to *strengthen audience commitment, weaken audience commitment,* or *promote audience action*.

Strengthen Audience Commitment.

If audience members already agree with your perspective, you may try to strengthen their commitment. For instance, your classmates may already believe that there are not enough healthy food and drink options in campus vending machines. In this case, you could seek to convince them to take immediate action to address the problem.

Weaken Audience Commitment.

If many audience members disagree with your perspective on an issue, you may attempt to weaken their commitment to their viewpoint. For example, suppose that you support the removal of all fast-food outlets on campus but your audience survey reveals that most of your classmates like to eat at those establishments. Your speech is unlikely to succeed if you advocate a ban on campus fast food. Instead, you could try to weaken your listeners' commitment to fast food; for example, you might attempt to persuade them that eating fast food less frequently has many benefits.

Promote Audience Action.

You also may seek to persuade audience members to take a specific action. Asking students to drink less caffeine, serve on the college's Library Improvement Committee, or vote for an activity-fee increase would be examples of this type of speech. You also might advocate taking action in the community, such as volunteering to help assemble bags of food for a local food bank.

THREE GOALS OF PERSUASION

Persuasive Speeches Advocate Fact, Value, or Policy Claims

In any persuasive speech, you will make one of three types of claims—a *fact claim*, a *value claim*, or a *policy claim*.

Fact Claim. A **fact claim** asserts that something is true or false. Fact claims that are debatable make for especially strong persuasive speech topics. For example, do energy drinks cause more health problems than coffee does? Have charter schools improved student achievement in your state? Do first-person-shooter video games cause players to commit violent crimes? Because each of these questions is debatable, you could come up with an argument supporting either a yes or a no answer.

Value Claim. A **value claim** attaches a judgment (such as good, bad, moral, or immoral) to a subject. Examples of persuasive speech topics making these claims include "physician-assisted suicide is immoral," "full-body scanners are a justified intrusion on airline-passenger privacy," and "it is better to cut funding for prisons than for higher education."

Many people can reach agreement on fact claims when presented with enough evidence, but value claims often provide greater challenges. Audience members' ideas of right and wrong may be deeply held and may stem from religious or philosophical beliefs—and thus be difficult to change. If you decide to make a value claim in a persuasive speech, select one that your audience is at least open to considering.

Policy Claim. A **policy claim** advocates that action should be taken by organizations, institutions, or members of your audience. Examples include advocating that the federal government should provide student loans with a zero percent interest rate, that the Food and Drug Administration should regulate e-cigarettes, or that listeners should adopt a "grandfriend" and regularly visit or help a senior citizen in need.

> ▣ Video Activity 17.1: To see examples of different types of claims, try Video Activity 17.1: "Claims: Policy" and "Claims: Fact."

Now that you know typical objectives of persuasive speeches, let's turn our attention to how persuasion works.

THE NATURE OF PERSUASION

Two Paths to Persuasion

How do audience members make a decision to accept or reject a speaker's persuasive message? Richard Petty and John Cacioppo's **elaboration likelihood model**[1] provides a well-respected explanation.[2] This model shows two ways that audience members may evaluate a persuasive speaker's message—the central and peripheral routes. The **central route** denotes a high level of elaboration—a mental process that involves actively processing a speaker's argument. Audience members reflect on the message and consider it in light of their preexisting ideas about the issue.[3] Central route listeners are more likely to develop a positive attitude when the speaker's arguments are strong. After considering your points, they may view your arguments favorably: in other words, if you've argued well enough, they are more likely to agree with you.[4] We provide a detailed discussion of how to develop strong arguments in Chapter 18.

Audience members who follow the **peripheral route** do not actively process your message (low elaboration). Instead, they're more easily influenced by cues that are tangential, or peripheral, to the message's content.[5] Such cues may include the likeability or attractiveness of the speaker, flashy presentation aids that add little to the message, or aspects of the speaker's delivery. These peripheral factors allow receivers to take an easier path to agreement or disagreement without carefully considering the speaker's arguments.

The Importance of Central Route Processing

The positive effects of central route processing continue even after your speech. When audience members seriously evaluate the content of a

TWO PATHS TO PERSUASION

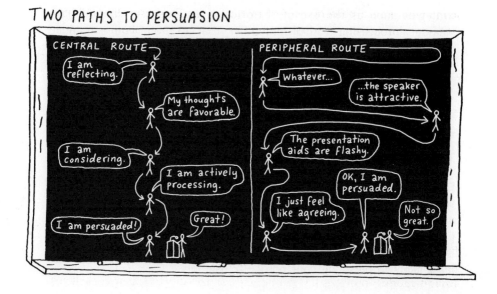

persuasive message, they form attitudes that are longer lasting and less likely to change in response to future counterarguments. They are also more likely to take action based on those attitudes.[6]

Conversely, the effects of the peripheral route are more likely to fade quickly. Furthermore, trying to convince an audience with peripheral factors can raise major ethical concerns. You can probably think of commercials that use celebrities or trendy music to sell their product, rather than offering factual evidence to prove a product's benefits. These marketing schemes may be successful, but they often miss the ethical mark by relying on fallacious instead of rational appeals. Similarly, if a speaker manages to persuade audience members by playing a catchy song during transitions or by quoting a pop-culture celebrity (who has no expertise on your topic), he or she has not persuaded ethically. This is because the speaker failed to help audience members make a rational decision. (See Chapter 3 for more on ethical standards.)

Which Route Will Audience Members Follow?

Audience members will most likely take the central route when your topic is relevant or important to them and they are able to follow your argument.[7] Strategies for adapting to your audience are discussed in the following section as well as in Chapter 5. Audience-involving strategies such as the use of rhetorical questions also can increase message processing.[8] Also remember that to help your audience understand your presentation, you need to present a well-organized message (see Chapter 9) and make effective use of language (see Chapter 12).

TAILORING YOUR PERSUASIVE MESSAGE TO THE AUDIENCE

Effective persuasive speakers use **strategic discourse**—the process of selecting supporting arguments that will best persuade the audience in an ethical manner. There are many supporting ideas that you could present, typically far more than can fit into the available time. Your job is to make strategic choices by selecting the ethical arguments that are *most* likely to persuade your particular listeners.

Adapting to Audience Disposition

Your listeners' disposition—their attitude toward your topic—should affect your approach to persuading them. As we discuss in Chapter 5, your audience may be hostile, sympathetic, or neutral toward the topic of your speech, and you should adjust your thesis depending on which audience type you are addressing.

The starting point is to determine where your audience stands on the issue. For example, suppose your goal is to change your college's mascot from the one that was selected by the school's founders a century ago to an animal that lives in the wild near your school. You might have the chance to advocate for your idea before several different audiences:

- Student groups that believe that the current mascot is disrespectful of their heritage and are looking for a new one
- Organizations on campus that support the traditional mascot or are concerned about the cost of making a change
- A group of students who are not interested in college sports and are worried about other issues in their lives

Although you want to advocate in favor of changing the mascot with each of these audiences, you wouldn't use the same supporting arguments

AUDIENCE DISPOSITION

SYMPATHETIC	HOSTILE	NEUTRAL
Yes, please change the mascot. We are not cartoon people with feathers on our heads!	No, keep the old mascot. It's part of college tradition.	It's only a sports logo. We don't care what it is; we're too busy studying.

with each. Groups on campus that oppose the current mascot would be sympathetic toward your proposal. Organizations that back the current mascot (or do not believe the cost would be affordable) would be hostile to your plan. Finally, busy students who have little interest in college sports may not care about getting involved in your campaign.

After you know where your audience stands, you can tailor your thesis appropriately. **Social judgment theory** explains that audience members make a decision about your thesis by comparing it with their own perspectives on the issue. Listeners have a **latitude of acceptance**, which is the range of positions on a given issue that are acceptable to them. Likewise, they also have a range of positions that are unacceptable, constituting their **latitude of rejection**.[9] Listeners who are very concerned about your issue tend to have a narrower latitude of acceptance. If the issue is not important to them, they will be open to a broader range of positions.[10]

Therefore, you're most likely to persuade your listeners to change their minds if the position you take on your topic falls within their latitude of acceptance. Conversely, you probably won't persuade audience members if your position falls within their latitude of rejection—especially if they have very strong viewpoints that differ from yours. Under these conditions, your speech may even produce a **boomerang effect**—the act of pushing your listeners to oppose your idea even more vigorously than they did before hearing your speech.[11]

How does all of this work in practice? Let's return to the example of your effort to change the school's mascot. If you are addressing student groups that support the change, their latitude of acceptance may

THE LAND OF AUDIENCE DISPOSITION

include support for your idea and a desire to take an active role. Such audience members might be willing to attend meetings with college officials, pass out pamphlets on campus, or help make a YouTube video featuring the proposed new mascot.

If you are addressing a group that supports the current mascot (a hostile audience), however, a speech calling for a new mascot is likely to be counterproductive because it falls within their latitude of rejection. Your audience analysis might reveal that these listeners would be open to talking to groups on campus that object to the current mascot and learning about their concerns or to making the change slowly over a few years so it would be more affordable. If so, you could advocate one of these options.

Finally, you would take still another approach for the students who are not interested in sports (a neutral audience). Asking them to sign a petition or vote in an election to change the mascot could fall within their latitude of acceptance. However, if you ask them to take a greater role in your campaign, this greater demand on their time might fall within their latitude of rejection.

SAYING THE WRONG THING CAN PUSH YOUR AUDIENCE AWAY

Appealing to Your Audience's Needs

Audience members have **needs**—objects they desire and feelings that must be satisfied. Human needs powerfully affect how we behave and how we respond to one another's ideas. As we note in Chapter 5, your message is more likely to succeed when it is relevant to the audience— that is, when it answers their question, "What's in it for me?"[12] Experts from previous eras, such as psychologist Abraham Maslow[13] and social critic Vance Packard,[14] have identified specific sets of needs, which continue to be emphasized in many persuasive appeals.

According to Maslow's **hierarchy of needs**, people's most basic needs must be met before they will focus on less essential ones. The most basic human needs are physiological: we require food, drink, health, and shelter to survive. After these needs are met, we attend to safety needs, which include economic security and protection from danger. If our physiological and safety needs are fulfilled, we seek to satisfy social needs, including love and friendship. From there, we strive for self-esteem, the feeling that comes from being respected and valued as a contributing member of society. Finally, to satisfy what Maslow called self-actualization needs, we seek opportunities for creativity, personal growth, and self-fulfillment.

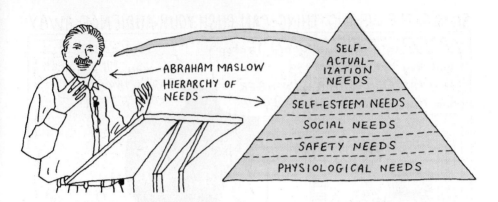

You should consider this hierarchy when analyzing your audience. If most audience members are struggling to pay their rent, it will be difficult to persuade them to donate to a political campaign, eat organic food, or sign up for an elective class in pottery. These activities may be worthy, but they will not help students who are dealing with late fees or the threat of eviction. Ideas that cost money are likely to fall outside these audience members' latitude of acceptance, potentially resulting in a boomerang effect.

By focusing on needs that are of concern to audience members, your speech will be more likely to persuade. For example, let's say you want to give a speech convincing your classmates to exercise more often. Exercise fulfills a number of different needs: it can improve people's health, help them perform better at work and in school, increase their self-esteem, mitigate the dangers that come with obesity, and (if done in a social setting) provide opportunities to forge friendships and meet romantic partners. You should determine which of these needs are most important to your audience and then emphasize them in your main points and subpoints.

Connecting to Your Listeners' Values

Values are "core conceptions" of what is desirable for our own life and for society.[15] They guide people's judgments and actions.[16] Each of us has values that guide how we live—for example, being helpful, honest, logical, imaginative, or responsible. We also have ideas about what kind of society we want to live in, such as one that offers equality, freedom, happiness, peace, or security.[17] All of these are values. Because values play a central role in guiding our lives, adapting an argument to audience values is one of the most important considerations for ensuring that your argument will be persuasive.[18]

VALUES GUIDE AUDIENCE JUDGMENTS —AND SOMETIMES VALUES ARE IN CONFLICT

A speech about airline safety provides one example of how a message can be tailored to audience values. Suppose you support installing more extensive security screening at airports. If national security is an important value for your listeners and you document how extended screening would reduce the risk of terrorist hijackings, you would have a persuasive argument. On the other hand, suppose efficiency and liberty are fundamental values to your audience. To persuade these listeners, you would need to explain how the screening you're advocating would not slow down airport lines and could be done with minimal intrusion on travelers. If you could prove a high risk of terrorist hijacking, you also could argue that even though efficiency and liberty are generally important values, *in this case*, the value of national security is paramount.[19]

Accounting for Audience Beliefs

Audience **beliefs** (the facts about your topic that they consider to be true) will have a significant effect on their **attitude** (their favorable or

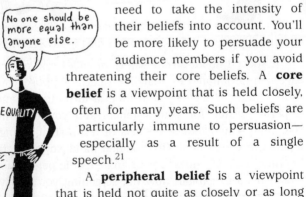

unfavorable feeling) toward your thesis. For example, think back to the opener for Chapter 16 regarding flu prevention. Suppose you want to convince the students in your speech class to get a flu shot. Audience members might believe that the flu affects mostly senior citizens and that the effects of the flu are not serious for younger people. If listeners do not believe that their risk from the flu is serious, their attitude toward your proposal is likely to be negative. To persuade audience members that they need to act, you could present credible evidence to show that the risk from the flu is significant for college students and that the flu can seriously affect their ability to study and work.[20]

Focusing on Peripheral Beliefs

In addition to considering what audience members' beliefs are, you need to take the intensity of their beliefs into account. You'll be more likely to persuade your audience members if you avoid threatening their core beliefs. A **core belief** is a viewpoint that is held closely, often for many years. Such beliefs are particularly immune to persuasion—especially as a result of a single speech.[21]

A **peripheral belief** is a viewpoint that is held not quite as closely or as long as a core belief. People may form peripheral beliefs by hearing a news report, reading a book or magazine, or listening to a statement made by a political or religious leader. These beliefs are more open than core beliefs are to change by a persuasive message. Thus, you can boost your chances of success if you focus your appeal on your listeners' peripheral beliefs.

A study of 12,000 college students found that vaccinated students were less likely to have flu-like illness and missed less class and work.*

*Kristin Nichol et al., *Archives of Pediatrics and Adolescent Medicine,* December 1, 2008, p. 1113.

For example, suppose you want to persuade various groups of people at your college to spend one Saturday morning working on a campus beautification project. You first address the Parkour Club, whose members usually practice their sport on Saturday mornings. (Parkour is a physical activity that involves getting past obstacles efficiently using skills like running, climbing, and jumping rather than walking around them.) If you argue that parkour is a pointless activity, you probably won't gain volunteers because you'd be attacking a core belief. On the other hand, the tradition of practicing on Saturday morning is more peripheral. You would have a better chance of winning these listeners' support if you said that devoting one Saturday morning to doing something to benefit the campus community would be a worthy cause—and that club members could practice afterward.

Demonstrating How Your Audience Benefits

Audience members weigh the costs and benefits whenever they are deciding whether to take action in response to a persuasive appeal.[22] They are most likely to support your proposal when you show how they will benefit from doing so and when they feel that the costs involved are minimal— or at least worth the benefits.

To increase your persuasive power, help your listeners visualize themselves experiencing the benefit they'll gain if they take the action you're advocating. Here is how one speaker showed audience members how they could benefit by volunteering to spend time with young children:

> Imagine yourself volunteering to help young kids in our community. You do not even need to go downtown to help. Students can volunteer to read to children at the day-care center in our library at story hour each day. The next time you are using the library in the afternoon, walk past the center, and see what a good time the kids and your classmates are having. Share a story from your culture or a book you loved as a child. If you enjoy volunteering, you can even sign up for a community service course and earn academic credit.

In addition to demonstrating how your listeners will benefit from taking the actions you're advocating, you may want to show them that the costs of these actions are low. This can be particularly important when your listeners are seriously considering taking action. If this is the case, they probably already recognize the benefits of doing so, and showing them that taking action has limited disadvantages could be the final step in gaining their support.[23]

Acknowledging Listeners' Reservations

In analyzing your audience, you may discover the reasons that your listeners are opposed to your thesis or at least uncommitted or neutral

toward it. To address these reservations, consider using a two-sided argument. This does not mean that you simply present two different perspectives to audience members and leave it for them to decide. Rather, in a **two-sided argument**, you briefly note an argument *against* your thesis and then use evidence and reasoning to refute that argument.

For example, suppose you are advocating that all students should pass a comprehensive exam in their major subject before graduation. You anticipate that many classmates will find this option stressful, fearing that a low score would keep them from graduating. In a two-sided argument, you would first acknowledge that a comprehensive exam could be stressful, but then you might cite statistics showing that at a similar college, most students pass such an exam. You also could show how study guides and review sessions successfully prepare students.

A well-presented two-sided argument can help you change audience members' attitudes in favor of your thesis and strengthen your credibility.[24] This is because people are more likely to support an idea if they know that its proponent is sensitive to their concerns and understands their views.

MAKING A TWO-SIDED ARGUMENT

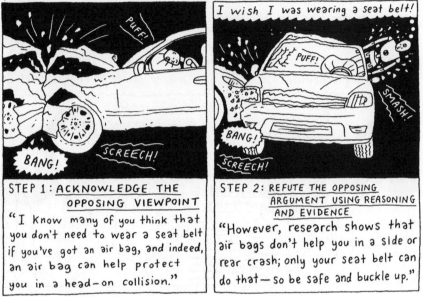

STEP 1: ACKNOWLEDGE THE OPPOSING VIEWPOINT

"I know many of you think that you don't need to wear a seat belt if you've got an air bag, and indeed, an air bag can help protect you in a head-on collision."

STEP 2: REFUTE THE OPPOSING ARGUMENT USING REASONING AND EVIDENCE

"However, research shows that air bags don't help you in a side or rear crash; only your seat belt can do that—so be safe and buckle up."

ETHICAL PERSUASION

As we note in Chapter 3, a public speaker must be ethical as well as effective. You want your audience members to accept your thesis, but you should earn their support with honest—not deceptive—persuasion. In this section, we highlight important ethical considerations for persuasive speakers.

Help Your Audience Make an Informed Decision

Ethical speakers help their listeners reach well-informed decisions rather than manipulating them into agreement. Unfortunately, some persuaders use unethical tactics. For example, one study found that a detailed description of a single individual who had been on welfare for sixteen years exerted a greater influence on an audience's perception of welfare recipients than statewide statistics showing that 90 percent of welfare recipients go off the rolls within four years.[25] Using vivid evidence that depicts an atypical situation is an unethical half-truth unless the speaker informs the audience that the situation described is not the norm.

To persuade ethically, present solid, truthful claims that support your thesis. Scrupulously avoid arguments based on faulty reasoning, and include all the key facts you know that would help your audience carefully weigh what you're proposing. Remember, you can address counterarguments to your position by using a two-sided argument.

Research Your Facts

As a public speaker, you have an ethical duty to research your topic so that you can be sure the facts you present to your audience are accurate. If your research reveals that a fact is supported by a consensus of credible sources, you can confidently use that fact in your speech. Conversely, if you find that the jury is still out on a claim you wish to make, don't present that point as an established fact. Instead, acknowledge that the point is being debated. Then use a two-sided argument to show why you believe the support for your side outweighs the support for the other side. If you find that few credible sources support your claim and that most sources disagree, do not include the point in your speech. Research other arguments for your position instead.

FIND THE DIFFERENCE

Note Any Biases

Some communicators stand to benefit personally if they succeed in persuading their audience. For example, a former homeland security official who advocated full-body scanners at airports was a consultant for a company that made these devices, and a health economist who discussed government health care policies had a contract with the government.[26] Audience members will understandably feel cheated if such potential conflicts of interest are not disclosed because such facts are relevant to their decision of whether to believe a speaker. Therefore, you should practice **full disclosure** to your audience. This means that you acknowledge any vested interest you may have in your topic. For example, if you'd receive extra credit for persuading students to participate in a professor's study, your audience members deserve to know that information. They also will be more likely to respect you if you're honest enough to reveal such biases.

Attribute Your Research Properly

Include citations *every* time you present ideas that you found from other sources. Make sure that quotations and paraphrases are accurate and that they represent the original author's point of view. For more information on presenting evidence ethically and accurately, see Chapter 7.

ORGANIZING YOUR PERSUASIVE SPEECH

Audience members must be able to follow your message in order to process it carefully. Thus, you need to choose an organizational pattern that clearly conveys your message *and* maximizes your persuasive impact. There are different patterns to consider, depending on whether your thesis advances a fact, value, or policy claim.

Organizing Fact Claims

If you're planning to make a fact claim, you will be seeking to prove that something is true or false. In this type of persuasive speech, consider using a *causal* or *categorical pattern*, depending on the main points you'll be presenting.

Causal Pattern. Many fact claims argue that one thing causes another. If this describes your fact claim, a **causal pattern** is ideal. To illustrate, here is how a presenter might organize a speech claiming that fast food causes health problems:

> THESIS   Fast-food restaurants are a significant cause of health problems in the United States.

MAIN POINTS

   I. Low prices encourage frequent fast-food consumption.

  II. Fast-food meals are high in fat and calories.

 III. High-fat, high-calorie foods cause obesity, diabetes, and heart disease.

Categorical Pattern. Sometimes each main point in your speech will reflect a different reason that you believe your fact claim to be true. In this case, you can use a **categorical pattern** to organize your presentation. Consider the following example from a speech intended to convince listeners that climate change is actually happening:

> THESIS   The earth is experiencing climate change.

MAIN POINTS

   I. Droughts are lasting longer, and their effects are more critical.

  II. Extreme weather is on the rise.

 III. Greenland's ice sheet and glaciers are melting at an accelerating rate.

 IV. Coral reefs are disintegrating.

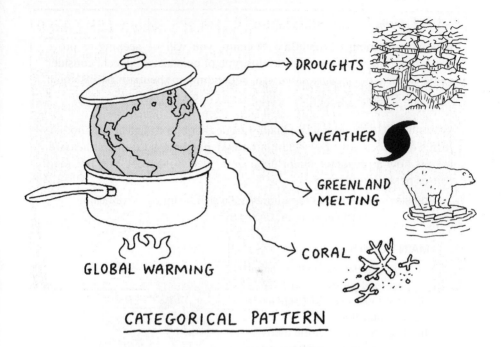

CATEGORICAL PATTERN

Organizing Value Claims

In making a value claim in a persuasive speech, you attach a judgment to your subject and then try to get the audience to agree with your evaluation. Three organizing patterns—*criteria-application*, *comparison*, and *categorical*—can help you.

Criteria-Application Pattern. A **criteria-application pattern** has two main points. One establishes standards for the value judgment you are making; the other applies those standards to the subject of your thesis. Here is how you could use this pattern in a persuasive speech on the value of community service in college:

THESIS   Community service is a valuable part of the college experience.

MAIN POINTS

  I. A college education should provide students with several benefits.
  A. New knowledge and skills
  B. Preparation for the workforce

CRITERIA–APPLICATION PATTERN

    C. Participation in new experiences
    D. Clarification of students' values and their place in the world
 II. Community service provides college students with the opportunity to gain all these benefits.
    A. It leads to higher grade-point averages and stronger communication skills.
    B. It provides valuable work experience and a chance to discover career interests.
    C. It offers an opportunity to experience new situations and work with people from diverse backgrounds.
    D. It encourages students to consider their values and see how they can help society.

Comparison Pattern. When you want to claim that two situations are similar or different, a **comparison pattern** can help you support that claim. Here is an example of how this pattern could be used in a speech about the benefits of nuclear fusion (producing energy by colliding atomic nuclei together) compared to current sources of energy.[27]

THESIS   Nuclear fusion is a more beneficial power source than present energy sources.

COMPARISON PATTERN

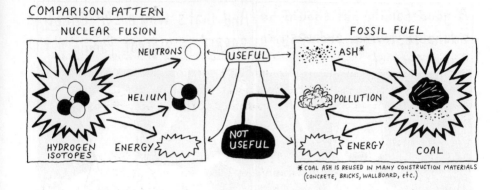

MAIN POINTS

I. Fusion relies on abundant resources, unlike fossil fuels, which are scarce.

II. Fusion produces no pollution, unlike fossil fuels, which harm the environment.

III. Fusion reactors do not risk meltdowns, unlike nuclear fission plants.

Categorical Pattern. In some persuasive speeches, you may decide that it isn't necessary to explain how each main point supports the value judgment you are making because your audience already understands each point's relevance. In this case, you can use a categorical pattern.

To illustrate, suppose you want to convince your audience that advanced driver-training courses are beneficial. Your listeners probably know that they could judge the value of a driver-training course by considering such factors as reduced accident risk and lower insurance premiums. Therefore, you could organize your main points in a categorical pattern, such as the following:

THESIS   Advanced driver-training courses are beneficial.

MAIN POINTS

I. They reduce the risk of accidents.

II. They lower drivers' insurance premiums.

III. They lower drivers' maintenance and gas costs.

IV. The savings gained from the course exceed the cost of the course.

Organizing Policy Claims

When you advance a policy claim, you call for action. You might want audience members to do something in particular, or you might want to convince them that an organization or institution (such as a state or local government) should take a particular action. For this type of persuasive speech, you can use a *motivated sequence* or *problem-cause-solution pattern*.

Monroe's Motivated Sequence. Developed by Alan Monroe nearly eighty years ago, this organizational pattern remains popular.[28] Monroe's motivated sequence follows the stages of thinking that people often go through while solving a problem or considering new ideas.[29] A **motivated sequence** aims to establish five main points, as shown in the following example from a persuasive speech encouraging students to study abroad:

MAIN POINTS

   I. *Attention* (creating a willingness to listen to your message). Few members of our class are looking forward to final exams next month. Do you think it would be more exciting if your finals were happening in Rome, Beijing, Sydney, or Buenos Aires?

  II. *Need* (identifying a need relevant to your audience). Every member of this class plans to get a job after graduation. The job market is highly competitive.

 III. *Satisfaction* (showing how your proposal will fulfill the need you identified). Participating in our college's Study Abroad Program will strengthen your credentials in the job market. Employers report that they are more likely to hire a candidate with international experience.

 IV. *Visualization* (helping listeners form a mental picture of the benefits of your proposal). Imagine that you have returned to the United States after an amazing semester in Spain or Japan. At an interview for a job you really want, the interviewer asks if you have experience with other cultures. You answer yes, and you see the interviewer's interest perk up. The next day, the company makes you an offer.

  V. *Action* (clarifying what you want listeners to do). Attend an informational session on next year's Study Abroad Program in the Student Union next Wednesday. You can learn more about the exciting options open to you, hear from past participants, and ask questions.

After that, I hope you will decide to make Montreal, Mumbai, or Madrid your home for next fall.

> ▶ To see an example of a presentation using Monroe's motivated sequence, try Video Activity 17.2: "Patterns of Arrangement, Monroe's Motivated Sequence," which is used in a persuasive speech about radio frequency identification (RFID) technology.

Problem-Cause-Solution Pattern. With a **problem-cause-solution pattern**, the first main point describes a problem that needs to be addressed, the second explains the cause of the problem, and the third presents a solution that can minimize the problem. This pattern can be especially helpful if you are asking the audience to support a policy change by an organization or institution. Because your ultimate goal is

SPEECH CHOICES

A CASE STUDY: *JACOB*

Let's see whether Jacob used audience-centered persuasive strategies.

Jacob selected a policy thesis for his persuasive speech: college athletes in revenue-producing sports should be paid a salary. However, he forgot that persuasive speeches use strategic discourse and need to include arguments that best persuade a particular audience. Instead of thinking about his audience, he wrote down ideas that he himself believed. And because he waited until the last minute to prepare his speech, he didn't have any time left to think about how his speech might be made more audience-centered.

Jacob prepared a speech that connected with his own beliefs and values rather than those of the audience. He didn't provide any evidence that classmates who did not follow or participate in sports would benefit from his plan. Most of his examples focused on other colleges, so he did not even relate his speech to classmates who did follow his college's sports teams. In addition, he did not consider the audience's possible objections to his proposal. For example, some students might be concerned about how his plan would affect women's sports, and others might be worried that their student fees might be increased to pay athletes. Jacob didn't think about addressing these concerns with a two-sided argument.

There also were problems with the logic of Jacob's speech. He had proposed an annual salary of $35,000 plus free tuition. But he did not investigate whether the revenue earned by these teams could cover the players' salaries and tuition costs. Jacob had no idea how his plan would affect the college's finances, which already had been hit by three years of budget cuts.

Finally, Jacob did not follow the ethical obligations of a persuasive speaker. He did not research his topic carefully so that he could be sure that the facts he presented were accurate. Because he was unaware that his college recently agreed to provide a stipend of almost $3,000 per year to student athletes, he didn't investigate how this stipend affected athletes' standard of living and the college's financial situation. He also made minimal effort to attribute the ideas he borrowed from research sources to those sources in his presentation.

YOUR TURN:
At what point in the speechmaking process should Jacob have taken a closer look at these issues? If you were Jacob and became aware of the issues raised here, what would you do to address them?

For more questions and activities for this case study, please go to LaunchPad at macmillandhighered.com/speakup4e.

new behavior on the part of the organization or institution, the problem-cause-solution pattern builds to the action you are advocating.

Here is an example of how a speaker might use this pattern in a persuasive speech advocating the installation of public bike racks near bus stops and train stations:

THESIS   The local government should install secure bike racks near heavily used bus stops and train stations.

MAIN POINTS

I. *Problem*. Parking is scarce, and traffic is congested near commuter bus stops and train stations in our county.

II. *Cause*. Many suburban commuters who would take mass transit live more than a mile from the closest bus stop or train station.

III. *Solution*. Providing secure bike racks will encourage alternative means of transportation to and from stops and stations, opening up parking spaces and alleviating traffic.

CHAPTER REVIEW

> "Good persuaders make strategic choices in an ethical manner."

In this chapter, we explored how persuasive speakers strengthen or weaken their audience's commitment to a particular topic or motivate their listeners to take a particular action. In doing so, persuasive speakers make one of three types of claims—fact, value, or policy. In evaluating a message, audience members may take the central route and carefully process the message or take the peripheral route and be influenced by cues that have little to do with speech content. If they are interested in the topic, they will most likely follow the central route, resulting in more effective and longer-lasting attitude change.

We also shared strategies for relating a persuasive message to your audience, including choosing a thesis based on your listeners' disposition, linking your message to your audience's needs and values, demonstrating how the costs of your proposal are worth the benefits, addressing audience reservations about your thesis, and focusing on your listeners' peripheral beliefs.

Additionally, you can develop your message in an ethical manner by helping your listeners make an informed decision, researching your facts thoroughly, disclosing any biases, and properly attributing your research sources. Finally, we offered strategies for organizing your message, depending on whether you are making a fact, value, or policy claim.

LaunchPad
macmillan learning

LaunchPad for *Speak Up* offers videos and encourages self-assessment through adaptive quizzing. Go to **macmillanhighered.com/speakup4e** to get access to:

✓ **LearningCurve**
Adaptive Quizzes

▶ **Video clips that help you understand public speaking concepts**

Key Terms

persuasive speech *507*

fact claim *508*

value claim *508*

policy claim *509*

533

Review Questions

1. Describe three goals of persuasive speeches.

2. What are the three types of claims used in a persuasive speech?

3. Describe the elaboration likelihood model. What are the differences between central route processing and peripheral route processing of a message?

4. Describe six ways in which a speaker may adapt his or her message for an audience.

5. What four steps can you take to ensure that your persuasive speech is ethical?

6. Describe two ways to organize a persuasive speech for each of the following—a fact claim, a value claim, and a policy claim.

Critical Thinking Questions

1. Why do you think that persuasion that is created when audience members follow central route processing is more effective than persuasion created through peripheral route processing?

2. How does using strategic discourse to craft a persuasive speech differ from preparing a speech in which you explain how you feel about a particular issue?

3. How would understanding Maslow's hierarchy of needs help you deliver more effective persuasive speeches? How could it hurt your effectiveness if you do not consider it?

4. Consider the way that talking heads and audiences for twenty-four-hour news channels tend to break along ideological and party lines. What does this tell you about latitudes of acceptance and rejection? How would you characterize the latitudes of acceptance and rejection for people who do not like to listen to commentators on either end of the political spectrum?

Activities

1. Working individually or in groups, select a persuasive speech topic. Identify three possible audiences for that speech—sympathetic, hostile, and neutral. Select a thesis and at least three main points for each audience. Discuss how your thesis and main points should differ for each audience type.

2. Select any thesis for a persuasive speech that advocates action by the audience. How could you use each of the strategies for adapting your argument to the audience in a speech on the topic you have chosen?

3. ⓒ Video Activity 17.3: "Martinez, Extra Credit You Can Live Without." Watch Anna Martinez's speech. How does Martinez tailor her thesis to fall within audience members' latitude of acceptance? Identify other strategies she uses to adjust her speech to the audience.

4. Review the editorial page in several newspapers, and consider their attempts to persuade you. How many editorials make fact claims? Value claims? Policy claims? Can you tell what organizational pattern the writers are using?

5. Visit factcheck.org, the Web site of a nonpartisan group that investigates claims made by politicians, news organizations, and interest groups to determine how truthful they are. Are you surprised by any of the information presented there? What examples of unethical speech did you come across?

Study Plan

LaunchPad
macmillan learning

Look for the ✓ and ▶ throughout the chapter for adaptive quizzing and online video activities at **macmillanhighered.com/speakup4e**.

METHODS OF PERSUASION

18

"Persuasive speakers
are credible, logical,
and emotionally
affecting."

For an upcoming persuasive speech, Maya
picked a unique topic that hit particularly
close to home. Three years earlier, her
uncle was released from a twenty-two-year
imprisonment after DNA tests revealed that
he hadn't committed the murder for which he was jailed. During her
presentation, she planned to ask the audience to lobby for states to
provide compensation to innocent prisoners who are exonerated by new
DNA evidence.

Maya knew she would face a challenge in persuading her listeners.
After all, not many people are wrongly imprisoned, so why should her
audience members take time out of their busy lives to lobby state governments for a new policy? In short, why should they care?

To build the most persuasive case possible, Maya decided to use
three powerful tools—ethos (demonstrating her credibility), logos (presenting sound reasoning for her claims), and pathos (evoking intense
emotion in her audience). She established her credibility by citing trusted
researchers' findings on the accuracy of DNA testing and the inaccuracy

of eyewitness accounts (which typically lead to wrongful convictions). She demonstrated solid reasoning for her proposal by presenting statistics about the difficulties that exonerated prisoners face in finding paid work after their innocence is proven. And she evoked her listeners' compassion and empathy for exonerees by describing the harsh realities that her uncle had endured since his release from prison—including long stretches of unemployment.

Maya's presentation proved a resounding success. By skillfully blending ethos, logos, and pathos, she not only captured her listeners' attention but also convinced them that exonerees deserve to be compensated for the ordeals they suffer as a result of errors made in the justice system. By the time Maya wrapped up her speech, some students were jotting down the tips she shared for lobbying state governments to introduce an exoneree compensation law. Her audience embraced her proposal, and some listeners intended to take the actions she recommended—solid evidence that she had given an effective persuasive speech.

You can use these strategies as successfully as Maya did. In this chapter, we discuss the use of ethos, logos, and pathos to create an effective speech.

ETHOS: YOUR CREDIBILITY AS A SPEAKER

Since ancient times, people have recognized that a speaker with **ethos (credibility)** has far more persuasive power than one without. A credible speaker is seen as knowledgeable, honest, and genuinely interested in doing the right thing for his or her audience. Ethos can help you win audience members' trust and persuade them to embrace your viewpoint. But what is credibility, exactly? By taking a closer look at what it consists of, we can get a deeper understanding of this crucial persuasive tool.

Understanding the Elements of Credibility

The ancient Greek philosopher Aristotle believed that practical wisdom and virtue are major components of ethos. Modern communication scholars use the term **competence** to refer to practical wisdom and the word **trustworthiness** instead of *virtue*. When audience members perceive a speaker to be both competent (knowledgeable and experienced) about a subject and trustworthy (honest and fair), they find it easier to believe that speaker's claims.[1]

Aristotle also urged public speakers to exhibit **goodwill** toward their audiences—by wanting what is best for their listeners rather than what would most benefit themselves.[2] According to contemporary researchers, speakers who demonstrate goodwill do the following:

- Understand their listeners' needs and feelings,
- Empathize with their audiences' views (even if they don't share them), and
- Respond quickly to others' communication.[3]

Building Your Credibility

When you're just starting out as a public speaker, your audience members may not immediately recognize your credibility. You'll need to build your ethos through what you say during your speech—and how you say it. Here are some helpful strategies:

- *Share your qualifications to speak on the topic.* If you have some expertise in the subject, outline your credentials for your audience. In some cases, this might involve listing your educational qualifications and work experience ("I have a degree in finance and have worked in banking for six years"). In others, it might mean telling the audience about your personal stake in the subject, just as Maya did when she spoke about her uncle's having been exonerated of murder by DNA evidence. If your knowledge is based mostly on your research, that should be indicated, too.

THE SPEAKER HAS CREDIBILITY AND SHOWS EMPATHY

- *Present strong evidence from reputable sources.* When you provide evidence for your claims, you indicate that you have carefully researched your topic, which communicates your competence. Citing a number of well-balanced and credible sources shows the audience the extent of your research and helps establish your credibility in the process.

- *Highlight common ground with the audience.* Reminding the audience of your shared experiences can make your message—and you—more credible. A teacher speaking to parents of preschoolers, for example, might mention the anxiety he felt the first time he dropped his own young son at preschool before attempting to persuade them that their nervous child will have fun when school activities start.

- *Choose your words carefully.* The words you select for your speech also can demonstrate your understanding of your listeners and thus your goodwill toward them. Be careful to use any technical terminology appropriately to show that you understand the subject matter, and make sure to avoid language that your audience might find insensitive or offensive.

- *Show respect for conflicting opinions.* Throughout your speech, use respectful language to refer to people who disagree with you. For example, "Some of you may not share my thinking on this, and that's OK. There are lots of ways to look at this issue."

- *Practice your speech until your delivery is fluent.* When you demonstrate effective delivery skills during your presentation—for example, by interacting comfortably with the audience—you are more likely to come across as trustworthy.

Avoiding Loss of Your Credibility

You have many strategies available for enhancing your credibility during a speech. But there are just as many ways to make a misstep and erode your ethos while giving a talk. Anytime you say something that shows a lack of competence, trustworthiness, or goodwill, you damage your credibility.

Such errors are common during political campaigns, and you can probably think of examples of gaffes that dimmed the chances of a candidate for office. But we also have seen such errors hurt the credibility of student speakers. In your speeches, careful preparation can help you avoid credibility-draining mistakes. Here are some common sources of this type of error:

- *Getting your facts wrong.* Your competence and preparation will be questioned if you present factual information that is just plain inaccurate. Mushers and dog-show enthusiasts would immediately recognize the error of calling the Alaskan husky a purebred dog because these sled dogs are crossbred from diverse bloodlines. Likewise, a speaker who mixed up the Brontë sisters would alienate fans of Victorian literature, and Internet radio fans would be skeptical of a presenter who referred to the music streaming service Pandora as Pandora's Box. One benefit of selecting a topic you know well is that you are less likely to present factual errors on a familiar subject.

- *Pronouncing words incorrectly.* Your experience in a topic area will be questioned if you mispronounce the names of key persons or concepts related to the topic. For example, a student who referred to hip-hop pioneer Afrika Bambaataa (*Bam-BAH-Tah*) as Afrika *BOM-bait-a* would not be credible to audience members who know that genre of music well, and a charitable organization seeking volunteers in the southern Bay Area of California would quickly lose credibility by referring to the region as SIL-i-cone Valley, rather than SIL-i-con.

- *Failing to acknowledge potential conflicts of interest.* In Chapter 17, we note the importance of disclosing your biases. If you fail to acknowledge any personal interest in your topic, it will hurt your credibility when it is revealed. For example, suppose a classmate advocated that all students who serve in student government

KNOW YOUR FACTS OR RISK LOSING CREDIBILITY

should receive a thousand-dollar scholarship and asked the class to sign a petition supporting this policy. When you read an article in the campus newspaper that says that the speaker serves in the student senate, you think, "No wonder he wanted that scholarship policy!" You would view that student more suspiciously the next time he presented a speech and might be less inclined to vote for him in the next election.

- *Stretching to find a connection with the audience.* Have you ever seen speakers attempt to speak a language they do not know well, try to use local or professional slang, or act interested in the audience members' favorite sports team? They often end up mangling words or using terms incorrectly, getting distracted from their message, and worrying about possible mistakes. These errors end up highlighting how disconnected a speaker is. Local dialect also can be a challenge. For example, when speakers address a Missouri audience, they must decide whether to refer to the state as *Missouree* or *Missouruh*.[4] You should always show respect to your audience, but the best choice is to be your authentic self. If a change in your typical pronunciation seems forced rather than sincere, you will lose credibility.

After a speaker's credibility has come into question, it's very difficult to repair the damage. Thus, before giving a speech, examine the language you intend to use, and make sure that it communicates competence, trustworthiness, and goodwill. However, even bulletproof ethos isn't enough to deliver an effective speech. You also need to deliver a solid set of facts to prove the claims you're making.

LOGOS: THE EVIDENCE AND REASONING BEHIND YOUR MESSAGE

Reliable facts can further strengthen your credibility and help your audience members make well-informed decisions—key effects of ethical public speaking. Sound reasoning that supports your claims is also essential if you hope to persuade audience members to change their beliefs or behaviors. When you present trustworthy facts to back your claims and clearly show how those facts have led you to those claims, you use **logos** effectively.

For example, suppose you want to deliver a persuasive speech arguing that diet soft drinks do not help people lose weight, a claim that might seem counterintuitive to many of your listeners. To convince them that you know what you're talking about, you'll need to supply proof, or **evidence**, of your claim. To further strengthen your logos, you'll need to show that the conclusions you've drawn from the evidence make sense. Is your train of thought logical? Or are you using **fallacious (faulty) reasoning** to twist or distort the facts in your favor?

In the following sections, we discuss how *using evidence*, *using reasoning*, and *avoiding logical fallacies* can help you to build a persuasive message.

Using Evidence

When your audience analysis suggests that listeners may not accept a claim you want to make, you'll need to supply proof. One of the best ways to do so is to research evidence from credible sources (see Chapter 7) and then present that evidence in your speech. To use evidence effectively, apply the following principles.

Identify your sources and their qualifications. Indicate who your source is for each piece of evidence you present, along with her or his qualifications, before providing the evidence during your speech. Concrete documentation strengthens your credibility.[5] To ensure your sources' credibility, use facts provided by unbiased experts.[6]

A BUNCH OF LOGICAL PEOPLE

If you gain, you gain all; if you lose, you lose nothing. Wager, then, without hesitating, that He exists.

BLAISE PASCAL

This isn't magic—it's logic—a puzzle. A lot of the greatest wizards haven't got an ounce of logic; they'd be stuck here forever.

HERMIONE GRANGER

The length of life takes the leading place among inquiries about events following birth.

PTOLEMY

So many women, learned in every kind of knowledge, have flourished in almost every age.

MARIA AGNESIS

I am an omnivorous reader with a strangely retentive memory for trifles.

SHERLOCK HOLMES

That is a most illogical attitude.

Mr. SPOCK

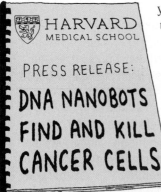

THIS JUST IN...

HARVARD
MEDICAL SCHOOL

PRESS RELEASE:

DNA NANOBOTS FIND AND KILL CANCER CELLS

Give listeners new evidence. Use audience analysis to determine what evidence is likely to be new to your listeners. Facts that they're not yet familiar with are more likely to increase their perception of your credibility.[7]

Provide precise evidence. Precise evidence consists of specific dates, places, numbers, and other facts. Here's an example of this kind of precision:

A study by Sharon Fowler and her colleagues at the University of Texas Health Science Center found that the risk of becoming obese or overweight

for regular soft drink drinkers consuming one to two cans daily is 32.8 percent. For those who consume a comparable amount of diet soft drinks, the risk is 54.5 percent.[8]

This citation provides a specific percentage as well as the lead researcher's name and affiliation.

Look for compelling evidence. Audiences are more likely to be persuaded by compelling evidence that includes concrete or detailed examples. Such evidence engages listeners' senses, helps them visualize the point you're presenting, and increases the likelihood that they will remember the information.[9] For example, in your speech about diet sodas, you could include a compelling anecdote about a student who gained weight after switching from sugared to diet soft drinks.

*EXTRACURRICULAR ACTIVITIES REPORT 2013,
published by Elm Park Board of Education

Credible evidence documenting the significance of a problem to the audience also can be compelling. A study of public health messages found that evidence documenting the severity of a health condition to which audience members are susceptible made the message more persuasive.[10]

Characterize your evidence accurately. Carefully word your claim so that it accurately reflects what your evidence proves. For example, if all the facts you've gathered strongly support the idea that diet drinks don't help people lose weight, then use those very words to state your claim about the drinks, rather than saying something like "Diet soft drinks aren't as healthy as people think."

Using Reasoning

Reasoning is the line of thought that connects the facts you present and the conclusions you draw from those facts. Persuasive speakers typically use **inductive reasoning**—generalizing from facts, instances, or examples and then making a claim based on that generalization. The table on page 547 shows several examples of inductive reasoning from everyday life.

EXAMPLES OF INDUCTIVE REASONING

Fact	Claim
At three different locations at this university, food service was slow.	All food-service outlets at this school are probably slow.
Lonyae is good at football.	It's plausible that Lonyae would be good at soccer.
Two students in the back row just fell asleep.	This is a boring class.
Sarah does not save enough time to study or write papers.	Sarah is likely to receive a low grade.

There are four types of inductive reasoning—*example, comparison, sign,* and *causal reasoning.* Let's explore each type in detail and consider how to use them effectively.

Example Reasoning. When you use **example reasoning**, you present specific instances to support a general claim. Your goal is to persuade the audience that your examples supply sufficient proof of your claim.

For instance, here's how you could use example reasoning to argue that endangered species are making a comeback:

The Fortymile caribou herd reached a low of 5,000 members in Alaska and the Yukon in 1976. Now, the herd exceeds 46,000 and

INDUCTIVE REASONING

I know Jana is a good *TRUMPET* player.

Jana would probably be a good *TROMBONE* player, too.

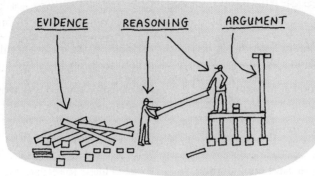

is growing in range.[11] In California, the peregrine falcon has been taken off the endangered species list, and Yosemite National Park has been a key site for recovery.[12] And there are now more than 9,700 breeding pairs of bald eagles in the lower 48 states, far more than the 487 pairs in 1963.[13]

REPRESENTATIVE EXAMPLES

To use example reasoning skillfully, be sure to provide enough instances to persuade your audience that your general claim is reasonable. The more examples you can find, the more confident you can be that your claim is correct.

Of course, in a short speech, you may have time to present only three or four examples to back up your argument. In this situation, you'll need to choose the most representative examples. A **representative example** is an instance typical of the class it represents. For example, if you wanted to present an even more compelling case that endangered species are making a comeback, you might want to provide examples of species that live in a variety of regions in North America.

If you're planning to use example reasoning in a speech you're researching, think about counterexamples your audience may consider. For instance, some listeners may argue that whereas certain species are recovering their populations, others are still endangered. Thus, they may view your claim that "endangered species are making a comeback" as inaccurate. If such counterexamples have merit, you may need to revise your claim to "*some* endangered species are making a comeback."

Comparison Reasoning. When you use **comparison reasoning**, you argue that two instances are similar and that what you know is true for one instance is likely to be true for the other. For example, if you argue that the prohibition of marijuana can't succeed because prohibition of alcohol failed, you would be using this type of reasoning.

For comparison reasoning to work, your audience must agree (or be persuaded) that the two instances are in fact comparable. To illustrate, suppose you can show that marijuana use is similar to alcohol use and that current marijuana laws resemble earlier alcohol-prohibition laws. By emphasizing these similarities, you can make a more convincing argument that marijuana prohibition probably will be just as ineffective as alcohol prohibition was.

To further strengthen your comparison reasoning, make sure your audience accepts the "known facts" as true. For example, perhaps your listeners would argue that alcohol prohibition in the United States wasn't actually a failure if it reduced alcohol consumption significantly. In this case, you might have to note other ways in which such prohibition could be considered a failure. For example, it led to the rise of organized crime when entities such as the Mafia took over bootlegging operations to counter government raids on speakeasies.

Sign Reasoning. When you use **sign reasoning**, you claim that a fact is true because indirect indicators (signs) are consistent with that fact. For example, you might claim that college students are facing serious financial challenges, as evidenced by students working longer hours.

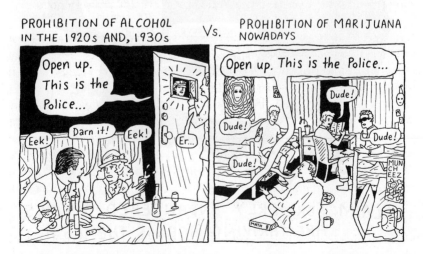

PROHIBITION OF ALCOHOL IN THE 1920s AND, 1930s Vs. PROHIBITION OF MARIJUANA NOWADAYS

SIGNS OF RISING TUITION

This type of reasoning is most effective if you can cite multiple consistent signs of the fact you are claiming. For instance, you could strengthen your claim that students' financial challenges are rising by also noting an increase in student loans and a higher rate of students dropping out of school. However, as you're researching your speech, be sure to look for signs that are *inconsistent* with your argument. If you discover that students are spending more money on entertainment and clothes, you may find it difficult to convince your audience that the signs prove that financial struggles are on the rise.

You might use sign reasoning to decide whether you should take a particular class. For example, you might note that on the first day of the semester, the classroom is so full that students are sitting on the floor. Furthermore, there is a long waiting list for the class, and the book for the course is sold out at the bookstore. Each of these facts would be an indirect indicator that the course and the instructor are very good.

Causal Reasoning. When you use **causal reasoning**, you argue that one event has caused another. For instance, you would be using causal reasoning if you claimed that playing violent video games leads children to get involved in destructive and illegal activities.

You can strengthen your causal reasoning in several ways. One way is to explain the link between cause and effect. For example, you might contend that when children play violent games, some may empathize with the violent character they control in the games. Thus, they are more likely to emulate that character in their everyday lives. Another way to use causal reasoning effectively is to support the cause-and-effect link with evidence from credible sources. For instance, you could use quotations from the American Academy of Pediatrics or a Senate Judiciary Committee Report to bolster your argument about the effects of violent

SUPPORTING CAUSAL REASONING

1. EXPLAIN THE LINK BETWEEN CAUSE AND EFFECT

2. PROVIDE CREDIBLE EVIDENCE

3. DEMONSTRATE A CORRELATION

* M. DE LISI ET AL., "VIOLENT VIDEO GAMES, DELINQUENCY, AND YOUTH VIOLENCE: NEW EVIDENCE," YOUTH VIOLENCE AND JUVENILE JUSTICE 11.2 (2013): 132–42, 138.

video games on children's behavior. Finally, you could show a correlation between cause and effect—for example, by presenting a study indicating that "playing violent video games is correlated with delinquency and violence," even after controlling for other factors associated with juvenile delinquency.[14]

Causal reasoning can be tricky because it is easy to misinterpret the evidence or come to the wrong conclusion. We take a look at errors in causal reasoning and other common reasoning errors in the following section.

> ▶ To see an example of a speaker using inductive reasoning, try Video Activity 18.1, "Reasoning: Inductive."

Avoiding Logical Fallacies

Reasoning is fallacious (faulty) when the link between your claim and supporting material is weak. We briefly mention several fallacies in Chapter 3 in the context of unethical persuasion—*hasty generalization*, post hoc *fallacy*, ad hominem *(personal attack) fallacy*, and ad populum *(bandwagon) fallacy*. Here, we explain the logical error in these four fallacies and highlight five other common fallacies—*causal reasoning errors* (including *reversed causality*), *straw person fallacy*, *slippery slope fallacy*, *false dilemma fallacy*, and *appeal to tradition fallacy*—that you'll want to avoid in your speeches.

Hasty Generalization. When using example reasoning, be sure to avoid **hasty generalization**. This fallacy occurs when a speaker bases a conclusion on limited or unrepresentative examples. For example, it would be fallacious to reason that jobs could be created in any city whose leaders put their minds to it based on the example of Austin, Texas. Austin has a number of unique job-creation advantages that other cities may not be able to match: it is the home of a first-rate university, a highly educated population, the state capitol, and a robust venture capital scene.[15]

Causal Reasoning Errors. One common error in causal reasoning is the ***post hoc* fallacy**. The fallacy lies in the assumption that just because one event followed another, the first event caused the second. But this sequence of events, in itself, does not prove causality. For example, suppose a college expands the size of its library, and students' grades subsequently increase. It might be tempting to conclude that the expansion of the

HASTY GENERALIZATION

library caused the improvement in grades. However, other factors could have led to the higher grades—rising admission standards, increased student motivation to achieve, or grade inflation. Before you can confidently claim that library expansion was the cause of the higher grades, other likely factors would need to be ruled out.

POST HOC FALLACY

It's also important to watch out for **reversed causality**, in which speakers miss the fact that the effect is actually the cause. For example, an improvement in students' academic quality may have led the college to expand the library to accommodate the study habits of these highly motivated students.

Ad Populum (Bandwagon) Fallacy.

You've committed the ***ad populum* (bandwagon) fallacy** if you assume that a statement (for example, "The police are adequately trained to avoid excessive force," "Millennials and members of Generation X will receive no social security benefits when they retire," or "Sending U.S. troops to the Middle East to attack ISIS would reduce the risk of terrorism") is true or false simply because a large number of people say it is. (*Ad populum* is Latin for "to the people.")

The problem with basing the truth of a statement on the number of people who believe it is that most people have neither the expertise nor the time to conduct the research needed to arrive at an informed opinion about the big questions of the day. For this reason, it's best to avoid using public-opinion polls to prove facts.

Ad Hominem (Personal Attack) Fallacy.

Some speakers try to compensate for weak arguments by making personal attacks against an opponent rather than addressing the issue in question. These speakers have committed the ***ad hominem* (personal attack) fallacy.** (*Ad hominem* is Latin for "to the person.") For example, in a campaign speech for student body president, one candidate referred to her opponent as a "tree-hugging environmental whack job." Her goal was to stir up listeners' biases against outspoken environmentalists on campus and persuade

them to reject her opponent as an extremist. This tactic was unethical because she supplied no evidence to support her claims, and those claims were not relevant to her opponent's qualifications for the position.

Straw Person Fallacy.

You commit the **straw person fallacy** if you replace your opponent's real claim with a weaker claim that you can more easily rebut. This weaker claim may sound relevant to the issue, but it is not; you're presenting it just because it's easy to knock down, like a person made of straw.

During the 1999 impeachment trial of former U.S. president Bill Clinton, some of his defenders committed this fallacy when they argued that an extramarital affair is part of a person's private life and not a sufficient justification for impeaching a president. However, Clinton's

political opponents maintained that whether the president had an affair was irrelevant: he had lied under oath, an action that in their minds justified impeachment.

Slippery Slope Fallacy. You've fallen victim to the **slippery slope fallacy** if you argue against a policy because you assume (without proof) that it will lead to a second policy that is undesirable. Like the straw person fallacy, this type of argument distracts the audience from the real issue at hand. Here's one example of a slippery slope argument during a televised community forum on gun control:

> We cannot expand background checks on gun purchases. That would lead us down the road to allowing the federal government to confiscate the guns of law-abiding citizens.

In this example, the speaker had no evidence or reasoning to explain how the first policy (background checks on gun purchases) would lead to the second (confiscation of guns from persons who have a legal right to own them).

False Dilemma Fallacy. You fall prey to the **false dilemma fallacy** if you claim that there are only two possible choices to address a problem, that one of those choices is wrong or infeasible, and that therefore your listeners must embrace the other choice. For example:

Either you must get an advanced degree immediately after you graduate, or you'll never find a job in this difficult market.

The weakness in a false dilemma argument is that most problems have more than just two possible solutions. To illustrate, in the previous example, the two options expressed (either pursue a graduate degree or remain jobless) are certainly not the only possibilities. Many people with bachelor's degrees are able to get jobs, and graduate programs often prefer that their candidates have a few years of real-world experience.

Appeal to Tradition Fallacy. You've committed the **appeal to tradition fallacy** if you argue that an idea or a policy is good simply because people have accepted or followed it for a long time. For example:

We must continue to require general education courses at this college. For the past fifty-three years, the students at State U have taken general education classes.

FALSE DILEMMA FALLACY

This argument is weak because it offers no explanation for why the tradition of general education courses is a good thing in the first place. The fallacy lies in presenting history and tradition as proof that a policy is good. A speaker defending something historic or traditional must show why it is worth preserving. In the previous example, a speaker might support the point by noting the benefits that students gain from taking general education courses (versus taking more classes of their choice or in their major) or the increased career options that students with broad general education backgrounds have after college.

> ⏵ To watch a speaker using a fallacy in his speech, try Video Activity 18.2, "Fallacy: Either-Or (False Dilemma): Diplomacy vs. WWIII (Needs Improvement)."

APPEAL TO TRADITION

PATHOS: EVOKING YOUR LISTENERS' EMOTIONS

When used with ethos and logos, emotional appeals—known as **pathos**—help you put a human face on a problem you're addressing. When you stir your listeners' feelings, you enhance your persuasive power. Indeed, some experts have referred to human emotions as "the primary motivating system of all activity."[16] Thus, by providing a heartwarming example of a person who benefited from an action you're recommending in your speech, you could complement statistical evidence that indicates all who could benefit. An emotional appeal can be an effective, ethical component of a strong persuasive speech; however, this kind of appeal can also be abused, so they need to be used responsibly.

Using Emotional Appeals

Humans have the capacity to experience a wide range of emotions—including empathy, anger, shame, fear, and pity—and each of these feelings can be used to enhance pathos when you prepare a persuasive speech. For example, in a presentation in which a speaker advocated greater freedom in doctor selection for health maintenance organization (HMO) patients, she used the following emotional appeal:

> Trey McPherson was born with half of his heart shrunken and nearly useless, a condition that causes most children to die in infancy. Fortunately, Trey was not one of these victims because he was treated by a leading pediatric heart surgeon. After two surgeries, Trey's parents were able to experience the joy of seeing their ten-month-old son climb out of his crib at the hospital. Except for a bandage on his tiny chest, it was difficult to tell that Trey had recently experienced open-heart surgery.
>
> Sadly, many babies are not as lucky as Trey. Although this skillful surgeon's patients have far-above-average survival rates, many pediatric cardiologists in the New York area find that their "favorite surgeon is frequently off limits because of price if a child belongs to an HMO."[17]

This example evokes a variety of emotions. It stimulates listeners' *anger* and *pity* at the thought that small children are being denied the best available care. It prompts them to *empathize* by imagining how they would feel if a loved one with a serious disease were forced to accept low-quality medical care. It also causes *joy* at the thought of how Trey's parents must have felt when their child recovered from surgery.

Notice that this emotional appeal is accompanied by sound reasoning. The speaker provides evidence that Trey's access to excellent care is atypical, which justifies the anger she evokes.

> ▶ To see a speaker using logos and pathos, try Video Activity 18.3, "Claims: Fact (Appeals to Emotion and Credibility)."

A **fear appeal**—an argument that arouses fear in the minds of audience members—can be a particularly powerful form of pathos.[18] However, to be effective, a fear appeal must demonstrate a serious threat to listeners' well-being.[19] To be ethical, it must be based on accurate information and not exaggerated to make your argument sound more persuasive.

A fear appeal is also more likely to succeed if your audience members believe that they have the power to remedy the problem you're describing.[20] Consider messages by National Park Service rangers advocating safe storage of food in national parks. The rangers provide statistics showing how often bears have broken into cars or tents when people have left food out. They augment these statistics with videos that show bears smashing car windows and climbing inside the vehicles to get food. These images usually strike fear into viewers' hearts. The rangers then show how easy it is to store food safely in lockers or bear-proof canisters. Because audience members realize they *can* readily adopt these practices, they *do* adopt them.

Effective *word choice* (see Chapter 12) also can strengthen the power of an emotional appeal. When a speaker's language connects with the values and passions of audience members, the persuasive effectiveness of a message is enhanced. Political consultants on both the right and the left carefully consider the exact words that are used to express an idea to voters. Emory University psychology and psychiatry professor Drew Westen notes that "every word we utter activates what neuroscientists call networks of association—interconnected sets of thoughts and emotions."[21] The selection of metaphors, for instance, has a significant influence in framing how audience members perceive an issue. For example, labeling participants in armed conflict as "freedom fighters" primes the listener to have a favorable view of the cause for which they

HOW A FEAR APPEAL SUCCEEDS

are fighting.[22] Political consultant Frank Luntz has had a successful career assessing the instant responses of focus-group members who are exposed to different words used to communicate the same basic message and then recommending optimal word choice for his clients.

How does this work in practice? Take the question of whether the government should take an active role in solving the problem of income inequality in the United States. When working with state governors who opposed government involvement in solving this problem, Luntz offered the following advice about word choice: use the terms *economic freedom* and *free market* instead of *capitalism*, and refer to "government taking money from hardworking Americans" instead of the phrase "raising taxes on the rich."[23]

Although you are unlikely to hire a high-priced consultant to help you choose the words that will be most compelling to your classmates, you can use your audience analysis to inform the language you select. If you express the key points of your message with words that relate to the values, needs, and aspirations of your audience members, your ideas are more likely to resonate. For example, in a classroom speech that took a stance on a campus issue, Taja advocated moving the campus's print newspaper to an online-only format. Her audience analysis revealed that many students read news and blogs online and that they were concerned that losing the printed newspaper would break a long tradition and result in less reliable reporting. Taja argued that "the online format we all rely on today could not be a better match for the campus newspaper's long tradition of excellent reporting." Thus, she depicted the change as a move from one medium to an even better one rather than a complete overhaul of the paper's tradition of excellence. As was true for Taja, the words you choose to express your message can strengthen your persuasive appeal. However, they must also be used in an accurate and ethical manner.

Ensuring Ethical Use of Pathos

As we've discussed, emotional appeals, when combined with ethos and logos, can be very effective. But emotional appeals can have a dark side, too. You may be able to persuade some of your audience members even if you don't establish a sound connection between your point and the emotion you are invoking, but your appeal will not be logical and certainly will not be ethical. This is unacceptable. History is replete with persuaders (including Adolf Hitler) who used pathos to achieve unethical and even horrific ends. Recall the old adage "With great power comes great responsibility," and don't use emotional appeals to manipulate your audience.

Let's take the HMO example previously discussed. The key to that appeal to pathos was that the speaker used sound reasoning to connect a relatively rare health emergency (a baby born with a damaged heart) with a broader challenge facing many potential patients (access to a wide selection of qualified physicians). If the speaker had failed to make the logical connection between the points, however, she would have been acting unethically. How might that happen? Suppose she could not provide evidence that access to a wide range of doctors would actually help families in Trey's situation and other health crises as well. In that case, her speech would merely be an emotional ploy to manipulate the audience into accepting her argument.

Numerous examples of fear appeals are premised on "facts" that are blatantly untrue. One instance involves politicians who offer "misbeliefs about the alleged risks of autism and other injuries from childhood vaccines" despite detailed analyses of vaccine safety that "disprove completely claims of vaccine-linked autism."[24] Certain climate scientists lost credibility after inaccurately stating that the Himalayan glaciers, which feed many rivers in Asia, could melt by 2035.[25] Fear appeals that exaggerate the health consequences of drug use (such as claims that using marijuana is similar to playing Russian roulette) have rarely succeeded.[26] Indeed, poorly substantiated claims can have a boomerang effect.[27] To present a convincing fear appeal and preserve your own

UNETHICAL USE OF AN EMOTIONAL APPEAL

ethos, you must use credible evidence to substantiate the harmful consequences that you predict.

Ethical speakers also must ensure that they select language that accurately describes the ideas they are discussing. Although compelling *word choice* can be used as an ethical persuasive tool, it can cross the line into manipulation, exaggeration, or untruth. The **loaded language fallacy** is committed when emotionally charged words convey a meaning that cannot be supported by the facts presented by the speaker. For example, a speaker arguing against a proposal to tax sugar-sweetened beverages referred to the plan as a "healthy choice tax" and implied that the plan would require consumers to pay a sales tax on orange, apple, and grape juices, which were included in the U.S. Department of Agriculture's recommendations for healthy eating.[28] The charge evoked anger in many audience members who agreed with the speaker that taxing such healthy choices would be absurd. The ethical problem was that the proposal applied only to sugar-sweetened fruit drinks, not to the 100 percent fruit juices recommended by the USDA.[29] Audience members were persuaded by the *loaded language* that described the proposal inaccurately, not by a credible argument against the true plan.

SAMPLE PERSUASIVE SPEECH

▶ EXTRA CREDIT YOU CAN LIVE WITHOUT

Anna Martinez

California State University–Fresno

Anna Martinez selected student credit card debt as the topic of her persuasive speech. Based on her survey of the audience, she determined that it would not be feasible to argue that students should not use credit cards. She selected a different thesis that was within their latitude of acceptance—encouraging students to be more careful credit card consumers.

Anna's speech is targeted to an audience of college students, and she refers to information gleaned from her survey to support her points. Anna consistently uses evidence to support her claims, and she has organized her speech in the problem-cause-solution format.

There is a dangerous product on our campus. It is marketed on tables outside the student union and advertised on the bulletin board in this classroom. Based on my audience survey, it is likely that most of you have this product in your possession right now. By the end of my speech, this product may be costing you more than it is right now. This dangerous product is credit cards. •

• Suspense-building attention-getter

Today I would like to discuss the problems created by college students' credit cards and hopefully persuade you to be a careful credit card consumer. If your credit card situation is anything like mine—and over two-thirds of this class indicated that they are currently carrying a balance on one or more cards—take note: you can save money.

My husband and I paid for our own wedding. More accurately, we used our credit cards to charge many of our wedding expenses. And thanks to Visa, we are still paying for our wedding every month! We have saved money with some of the suggestions I will present today, and you can do the same.

To that end, let's cover some of the problems created by students' credit card debt, then analyze causes of the problem, and finally consider steps you can take to be a careful credit card consumer. •

• Anna includes her thesis, connects with the audience, establishes credibility, and previews her main points.

We'll start with a look at the problems created by these "hazardous products."

Credit card debt on campus is a significant and growing problem. Many students have credit card debt. According to Matthew Scott, in *Black Collegian*, April 2007, "College financial aid provider Nellie Mae reported that 76 percent of undergraduate students had credit cards in 2005, with an average balance of $2,169. An alarming 25 percent of undergraduates had credit card balances totaling $3,000 or more." In *Business Week*, September 5, 2007, Jessica Silver-Greenberg notes that "the freshman 15, a fleshy souvenir of beer and late-night pizza, is now taking on a new meaning, with some freshmen racking up more than $15,000 in credit card debt before they can legally drink." If you are not sure how your own balances compare, you are not alone. The previously mentioned Nellie Mae study found that the average balance reported by students was 47 percent lower than the average balance computed from data provided by credit bureaus. •

- Anna consistently uses research sources to support her points.

High credit card use can change our lives for the worse. According to the April 2007 *Black Collegian* article, Rhonda Reynolds of Bernard Baruch College built up $8,000 worth of debt and was unable to make even the minimum payment. Her account went into collections. *Business Week*, March 15, 1999, provided another example: Jason Britton, a senior at Georgetown University, accumulated $21,000 in debt over four years on sixteen cards! Jason reports, "When I first started, my attitude was 'I'll get a job after college to pay off all my debt.'" Then he realized that he was in a hole because he could not meet his minimum monthly payments. He had to obtain financial assistance from his parents and now works three part-time jobs. •

- Supporting material: examples

You probably do not owe $20,000 on your credit cards, but even smaller balances take their toll. Robert Frick, associate editor for *Kiplinger's Personal Finance* magazine, March 1997, states that if you make the minimum payments on a $500 balance at an 18 percent interest rate, it will take over seven years to pay off the loan and cost $365 in interest.

High credit card debt can also haunt your finances after you graduate. Matthew Scott, previously cited, notes that credit bureaus assign you a credit score, which is "your economic report card to the rest of the world." That score will "determine the interest rates you pay for many forms of credit and insurance." He also notes that prospective employers will check your credit score and use that number to decide whether or not you are responsible.

Many people in this class are carrying student loans, which will need to be paid back upon graduation. When you add credit card debt to student loan payments, rent, utilities, food, the payment on the new car you want to buy, family expenses, and so on, the toll can be heavy. Alan Blair, director of credit management for the New England Educational Loan Marketing Corporation, in a 1998 report on the corporation's Web site, notes serious consequences for students who cannot balance monthly expenses and debts, including "poor credit ratings, inability to apply for car loans or a mortgage, collection activity, and at worst, a bankruptcy filing." •

- Relating the problem to a college audience

Don't let this happen to you. After all that hard work earning a degree and finally landing a job where you don't have to wear a plastic name tag and induce people to get "fries with that order," the last thing any of us needs is to be spending our hard-earned money paying off debt, being turned down for loans, or, worse yet, being harassed by collection agencies.

Credit card debt is hazardous to students' financial health, so why are these debts piling up? Let's move on to the causes of this problem. •

The reality is that credit card issuers want and aggressively seek the business of students like ourselves. As Jessica Silver-Greenberg writes in her previously cited September 2007 article, "Over the next month, as 17 million college students flood the nation's campuses, they will be greeted by swarms of credit-card marketers. Frisbees, T-shirts, and even iPods will be used as enticements to sign up, and marketing on the Web will reinforce the message."

Card issuers actually troll for customers on campus because student business is profitable. Daniel Eisenberg, writer of the Your Money column for *Time* magazine, September 28, 1998, notes that "college students are suckers for free stuff, and many are collecting extra credit cards and heavier debts as a result." Eisenberg refers to a U.S. Public Interest Research Group survey, which found that students who sign up for cards at campus tables in return for "gifts" typically carry higher unpaid balances than do other students. Jessica Silver-Greenberg, in an October 15, 2007, *Business Week* article, writes that "college kids are a potential gold mine— one of the few growing customer segments in the saturated credit-card market. And they're loyal, eventually taking three additional loans, on average, with the bank that gives them their first card." •

Companies use "sucker rates" to induce students to apply for credit. *Business Week*, March 15, 1999, writes that "credit card marketers may advertise a low annual percentage rate, but it often jumps substantially after three to nine months. First USA's student Visa has a 9.9% introductory rate that soars to 17.99% after five months. Teaser rates aren't unique to student cards, but a 1998 study by the Washington-based U.S. Public Interest Research Group found that 26% of college students found them misleading."

* Transition to main point II

* Supporting material: explanation of why card issuers market to students

So it appears that credit card companies will not stop demanding student business any time soon. What can we do about it?

My proposed solution is to be a careful credit card consumer.

Why not get rid of your credit cards before it's too late? All right, maybe you won't go for that solution. My survey indicated that most of you enjoy the flexibility in spending that credit cards provide. •

• Anna notes that her listeners are likely to reject her strongest suggestion. She then advocates a solution within her audience's latitude of acceptance.

So here are some other ways you should be credit card smart. One practice is to shop carefully for the best credit card deals. The companies that are not spending their money giving away pizzas and iPods on campus may be able to offer you a better deal. In her September 7, 2007, *Business Week* article, Silver-Greenberg recommends that you beware of offers from South Dakota or Delaware corporations. Those states are "considered 'safe harbors' for credit card companies because they have no cap on interest rates or late payment [fees]."

A second solution is to read the fine print on credit card applications to learn what your actual interest rate will be. Alison Barros, a staff writer for the Lane Community College *Torch*, October 29, 1998, quotes Jonathan Woolworth, consumer protection director for the Oregon Public Interest Research Group, who wrote that "students need to read the fine print and find out how long those low interest rates last. Rates that are as low as 3% can jump to 18% within three months, and the credit card company doesn't want the student to know that."

Here is an example of the fine print on an ad that begins at 1.9 percent and soon rises. If you read the fine print, you note that the rate can rise to more than 20 percent. •

• Anna shows a visual aid here.

• *Second* and *third* are examples of signposts.

Third, even if you can only make the minimum payment on your cards, pay your bills on time. • Silver-Greenberg's September 5 article indicates that students' "credit scores can plunge particularly quickly, with one or two missed payments, because their track records are so short." She further cautions students to be aware of "universal default" provisions in their credit agreements. These provide that if you miss a payment on one card, other credit card companies can also raise your interest rate (even if you have paid those cards on time), perhaps to 30 percent. *Business Week*,

March 15, 1999, cautions that "because students move often and may not get their mail forwarded quickly, bills can get lost. Then the students fall prey to late fees." •

Finally, you can keep money in your pocket and out of the credit card company's by paying attention to your credit report. If any agencies are "talking trash" about you with inaccurate information, be sure to have it corrected.

To sum up these solutions, even if you do not want to stop using credit cards, there are many ways to be a careful credit card consumer. Shop for a good rate, and be careful to read the fine print so you know what the rate really is. Know what you owe, and take the responsibility to make payments on time. •

This morning, we have learned about a hazardous product on campus—credit cards. We have noted the problem of high student credit card debt, analyzed some of the causes of this problem, and considered several methods for being a careful credit card consumer. •

If your instructor offers you a chance for extra credit in his or her class, take advantage of the opportunity. But when a credit card issuer offers you a free T-shirt or phone card if you will sign up for their extra credit, just say no. When you pay off a credit card with a 19.9 percent interest rate, that "free" T-shirt could turn out to be the most expensive clothing you will ever buy. •

• Adapting the solution to a college audience

• Internal summary of main point III

• Summary of main points

• The clincher sums up Anna's speech with irony.

CHAPTER REVIEW

Persuasive speakers are credible, logical, and emotionally affecting.

After you have selected a topic for your persuasive speech, analyzed your audience, and chosen an effective thesis, you need to develop a message that compels listeners to accept your thesis—and your ultimate goal of changing or strengthening their beliefs, attitudes, or actions. You can do this by combining ethos, logos, and pathos.

Through ethos, you establish your credibility as a speaker. The audience must perceive that you are competent and trustworthy and have their best interests at heart. You can avoid losing credibility by avoiding statements that raise doubts about your knowledge, honesty, or goodwill.

Through logos, you use credible evidence to support your claims. You also present sound reasoning to establish these claims by using examples, comparisons, signs, and cause-effect relationships. When reasoning, it is essential to avoid logical fallacies.

Through pathos, you further strengthen your persuasive power by evoking your audience members' emotions—not to manipulate your listeners but to move them in an ethical and responsible manner to take the action you're proposing or adopt the belief you're advocating.

Together, ethos, logos, and pathos can help you win your listeners' heads (their reason), hearts (their emotions), and hands (their commitment to action). Master these three tools, and you'll greatly enhance your prowess as a persuasive speaker.

 LaunchPad
macmillan learning

LaunchPad for *Speak Up* offers videos and encourages self-assessment through adaptive quizzing. Go to **macmillanhighered.com/speakup4e** to get access to:

✓ **LearningCurve**
Adaptive Quizzes

▶ **Video clips that help you understand public speaking concepts**

Key Terms

ethos (credibility) *538*
competence *538*
trustworthiness *538*
goodwill *539*
 logos *543*
evidence *543*
fallacious (faulty) reasoning *543*
precise evidence *544*
 inductive reasoning *547*
example reasoning *547*
representative example *549*

comparison reasoning *550*
sign reasoning *550*
causal reasoning *551*
▶ hasty generalization *553*
post hoc fallacy *553*
reversed causality *555*
▶ *ad populum* (bandwagon)
fallacy *555*
▶ *ad hominem* (personal attack)
fallacy *555*
straw person fallacy *556*

◎ slippery slope fallacy *557*　　◎ pathos *560*
◎ false dilemma fallacy *557*　　　fear appeal *561*
　appeal to tradition fallacy *558*　　loaded language fallacy *565*

Review Questions

1. Explain the three primary elements of credibility.
2. Indicate six steps you can take to enhance your own credibility.
3. What are four mistakes you can make that may harm your credibility?
4. What are three fundamental components of a logical message?
5. Identify and explain eight logical fallacies.
6. What factors come into play when making an emotional appeal?
7. What kinds of practices can harm an emotional appeal?

Critical Thinking Questions

1. What role does audience analysis play in establishing your credibility? Is the speaker's responsibility to back up claims with solid evidence the same for a sympathetic audience as it is for a hostile or neutral audience?
2. As an audience member, how can you identify logical fallacies during a speech? How can you identify weak or misleading evidence? How do you react when a speaker's claims are based on unsound evidence or reasoning?
3. How should a speaker who favors a particular tradition develop a logical argument in favor of that tradition that avoids committing an appeal to tradition fallacy? For example, how might a speaker build a case for the general education requirement described in the text on page 558? In a broader sense, how can you build a strong and ethical argument for maintaining a tradition that you support?
4. What types of presentation aids can you use to build your credibility?
5. Reflect on your position on a controversial issue in society. What evidence could persuade you to change your mind or adopt a neutral position? Who or what would be a credible source that might induce you to rethink your position? How can the answers to these questions help you in your own efforts as a persuasive speaker?

Activities

1. Working in a group, select a thesis for a persuasive speech. Then prepare four supporting arguments for that thesis, using a different type of inductive reasoning (example, comparison, sign, and causal) for each supporting argument.

2. Select an issue that would be appropriate for a persuasive speech. Construct three different arguments for that issue using powerful language (see p. 562). Break into groups, and share your arguments. After each person shares, have the others rate the effectiveness of the argument on a scale of 1 (not convincing) to 10 (highly convincing). After providing ratings, group members should explain why they found some words and phrases more powerful than others.

3. Create a credibility checklist based on the bulleted list on pages 539 to 540. Review a persuasive speech in this text or one that you find on the Internet, and see how many of the criteria the speaker fulfills.

4. ⊙ **Video Activity 18.4: "Morales, Without Liberty and Justice for All."** Watch Enrique Morales's persuasive speech. Identify where he uses ethos, pathos, and logos in an effort to persuade his audience. Evaluate how well he uses evidence and reasoning to build his case. Are there any changes you would advise him to make?

5. ▧ Review the illustration "Supporting Causal Reasoning" on page 552. Working individually or in groups, select a claim based on causal reasoning that you could make in a persuasive speech. Then think of one argument in support of that claim that explains the link between cause and effect, explain the type of credentials that would make an author credible on this claim, and identify a correlation that would help show a link between cause and effect.

6. Watch a few episodes of a program such as *The Daily Show*. For one episode, assess each comedic bit or segment, and identify those that focus on pundits' and politicians' use of loaded language *and* fear appeals. Characterize a few of the fallacies being exposed.

Study Plan

_____

_____

_____

_____

_____

_____

_____

_____

_____

_____

_____

_____

_____

_____

_____

_____

_____

_____

_____

_____

_____

_____

_____

SPECIAL-OCCASION SPEAKING

19

> "Whether to mark a celebration, a milestone, or a passing, we all participate in special-occasion speaking as speakers or listeners."

Speeches that praise, celebrate, memorialize, or otherwise commemorate special occasions have a long history. A Sumerian tablet dating back to about 2000 BCE records the funeral utterances of Ludingirra, a teacher and poet, as he laments the loss of his father and his wife by eulogizing (or memorializing) their achievements and personal qualities. Indeed, **epideictic** rhetoric—speaking that praises or blames—was one of the three genres of oratory identified by the fourth-century BCE Greek philosopher Aristotle.[1] Speakers typically used this form of address to celebrate timeless virtues during occasions such as funerals or holidays.[2] And ever since Aristotle's lifetime, people around the world have continued to use public speaking to help themselves and others celebrate joyous occasions, mourn the passing of loved ones, honor friends' or colleagues' achievements, and observe other milestones in their communities.

Think about the times you've been moved by a speech marking a special occasion. Perhaps on a Labor Day, you heard a speaker praising workers who helped build some of the great bridges and highways in your area. Or maybe you've attended a gathering to observe the passing of another September 11 on the calendar, and the speaker's words helped you reflect once again on the magnitude of the terrorist attacks in 2001. You also might have attended a wedding, clapping and cheering along with the other guests as friends and relatives of the bride and groom offered toasts to the new couple. And if you've excelled at your job, perhaps you've been presented with an award, along with words of praise from your boss, during a department meeting or party. If you've attended a formal dinner for your company or a community organization, you may have listened to an after-dinner speech—a traditional presentation designed to entertain an audience after a meal. Certainly, you'll have the opportunity to listen to many speeches of congratulation and advice if you take part in graduation ceremonies after completing your college degree.

Special-occasion speeches mark some of the most important events in our lives—those that bring us together with others in our community and those that unite us in our humanity. As you go through life, you'll hear many such speeches and probably will be called on to give one or more yourself. Even if you never have to deliver a formal presentation in an official capacity (such as at work or in a civic setting), you almost certainly will be invited to "say a few words" at various points in your life. For example, your grandmother might ask you to say good-bye to your deceased grandfather during an intimate graveside service. Or you might host a large gathering of family at your home for Thanksgiving, and your guests will expect you to start things off by sharing some inspiring words about the meaning of the holiday. Or perhaps you've

arranged for your friend's band to play for the first time at a local pub, and he asks you to introduce the performers to the crowd.

Whatever your special speaking occasion, you'll have to face that ever-daunting question: "What am I going to say?" This chapter will help you answer that question. We start by introducing six types of special-occasion speeches and discussing the purposes each type serves. Next, we offer some general guidelines for speaking at a special occasion. After that, we go into detail about each of the six types of special-occasion speeches, providing tips tailored to each type. Finally, we revisit a few preparation and delivery strategies discussed earlier in the book.

TYPES OF SPECIAL-OCCASION SPEECHES

Although there are various types of special-occasion speeches, the six most common are as follows:

- *Speech of introduction.* Sometimes referred to as "the speech before the speech," this is a brief presentation designed to prepare an audience for the "main event"—a speaker, a performance, or an activity that will follow. A speech of introduction provides context and gives credentials for the main speaker or performer.

- *Speech of presentation.* Awards, honors, and special designations often require speeches before they are conferred. A presentation speech explains the background and significance of the award and the reasons that the recipient is deserving of it.

- *Speech of acceptance.* Recipients of honors, awards, or designations are often expected to give a short presentation of their own—something beyond a simple thank-you. Recipients typically express gratitude for the award, extol the award's significance to them and others, and acknowledge others' support and contributions.

SPEECH OF INTRODUCTION

SPEECH OF PRESENTATION

SPEECH OF ACCEPTANCE

- *Speech to memorialize or eulogize.* A **eulogy** comments on the passing of an individual, celebrates his or her life, and often shares personal reflections and stories about the deceased. It offers an appropriate method for recovering from grief, helps people feel consolation, and pays tribute to their sense of loss.[3] A speech to memorialize uses the same approach but is expanded to honor the sacrifice and heroism of a group of individuals— often on a significant anniversary, such as Veterans Day or September 11.

- *Speech to celebrate.* Events that represent rites of passage—such as christenings and circumcisions, bar and bat mitzvahs, graduations, weddings, reunions, and retirements—often demand celebration speeches. These may take the form of a toast or special observance that focuses the audience's attention on the milestone achieved and recognizes the joy and pride the participants feel.

- *After-dinner speech.* At times, a speaker needs to use humor and good storytelling to lighten the mood of an occasion or soften up an audience. Although these presentations are called "after-dinner speeches" (in the tradition of Mark Twain), they can follow or precede a meal. Light in tone, they can help a speaker entertain her

SPEECH TO MEMORIALIZE

or his listeners or set the stage for an event that follows the meal, such as a fund-raising effort for a charitable cause.

At some events, you'll hear more than one type of special-occasion speech being delivered. Consider the Academy Awards (or Oscars) ceremony hosted in Los Angeles by the Academy of Motion Picture Arts and Sciences. This star-studded annual event begins with a *speech of introduction*. A master of ceremonies—perhaps Chris Rock, Neil Patrick Harris, or Ellen DeGeneres—prepares the audience for the main event, often acknowledging the honored tradition of the Oscars while also tell-ing jokes to loosen up the crowd. At some point during the evening, a well-known actor gives a *presentation speech* before announcing a lifetime achieve-ment award for a long-famous director or producer. Recipients of Oscars and lifetime achieve-ment awards deliver *acceptance speeches* thanking the academy, exclaiming how much the award means to them, and acknowledging (sometimes seemingly endlessly) the support they've received from their families and colleagues. Later in the evening, a pre-senter might *eulogize* a recently departed luminary from the motion-picture industry.

Each of the six types of special-occasion speeches serves a unique purpose and evokes a different mood, but they all have something in common: to deliver them effectively, you must apply certain common skills (such as evoking your listeners' emotions and being mindful of their expectations). We present the following guidelines to give you a basic foundation of knowledge and then explore strategies tailored to each of the six types of speeches.

GENERAL GUIDELINES FOR SPECIAL-OCCASION SPEECHES

A handful of general guidelines can boost your chances of delivering an effective special-occasion speech, no matter what type you'll be giving. These guidelines include *appealing to your audience's emotions*, *matching your delivery to the mood of the occasion*, *adapting to your audience's expectations*, *evoking shared values*, and *respecting time constraints*.

Appealing to Your Audience's Emotions

Successful special-occasion speeches often evoke emotional responses, such as laughter, tears, joy, and pride. Because many special occasions are intimately connected with important human events, your audience will likely be predisposed to experiencing a particular feeling during the occasion. Your job in giving the speech will be to signal when it's time for that emotion to come to the surface.

For example, suppose you're about to deliver a eulogy at a graveside service for your grandmother. Although generally designed to comment on a loved one's passing, a eulogy can be presented in several formats—to celebrate, to mourn, to commemorate, or to honor.[4] Let's imagine that in this case your grandmother was a loving family woman, an accomplished artist, and a dedicated supporter of important causes. Family members and friends are gathered around the headstone under a canopy of maple and oak trees. Everyone present is reflecting on your grandmother's life, and the sorrow of saying good-bye begins to settle around their hearts. The moment arrives for you to walk to the headstone and deliver the eulogy. You begin speaking. As you recall your grandmother's special qualities and achievements and talk about how much she meant to you, your eyes fill and your voice breaks at times. The combination of your words and the expression of your grief gives the others gathered around the gravesite permission to let their own feelings well up. By enabling your family and friends to begin experiencing and expressing their grief, you help them embark on the mourning process—something we all must do when we have lost a loved one.

> ▶ To see a speech that appeals to an audience's emotions, try Video Activity 19.1, "Gentz, My Hero, Marilyn Hamilton."

Matching Your Delivery to the Mood of the Occasion

Whether joyous or solemn, lighthearted or serious, your demeanor and words should match the overall mood of the special occasion for which you're giving a speech. As the saying goes, there's a time and a place for everything—a time to tell funny stories, a time to show respect, and a time to share your own sadness. By ensuring that what you say and how you say it are appropriate for the occasion, you will enhance your effectiveness.

THE ELEMENTS OF AN EFFECTIVE SPECIAL-OCCASION SPEECH

For example, a eulogy calls primarily for a somber, sad tone, although a lovingly humorous recollection about the deceased may also be appropriate and appreciated. At the graveside service for your grandmother, for instance, family members and friends might smile through their tears and nod their heads knowingly when you help them recall her famous midnight excursions into the kitchen for chocolate ice cream.

If you're the best man at your older brother's wedding and you're giving a toast at the reception, you'll evoke a different overall mood. You'll want to express your happiness that your brother has found a loving spouse as well as give voice to everyone's wish that the new couple will share a long and joyous life together. Depending on the traditions of your culture, you also might introduce a

bit of humor by hinting at the wild escapades your brother had in his younger years and expressing your satisfaction that he's finally settling down with a wonderful partner. You decidedly would not go on and on about any hard or painful times the couple experienced while dating. Nor would you be in any way critical of their relationship.

Adapting to Your Audience's Expectations

Listeners' cultural background, age, values, and other characteristics all affect how they perceive a special occasion and what they expect from a speech delivered during that occasion. For example, a community of Christian Arab immigrants living in Chicago would likely want to attend a church funeral service after one of their community members died. Moreover, they probably would expect a mostly religious service with only a brief discussion of the deceased, including comments focused on how he or she cared about the community and shared its traditions. At a community dinner in honor of the deceased later in the day, speakers may share more personal stories.

On the other hand, an audience of amateur comedians might expect a fun and lighthearted presentation at a roast for a fellow entertainer, with speakers revealing funny stories about the individual being roasted. At this kind of event, it would run against audience expectations to bring up painful events from the person's childhood and thus bring an overly serious turn to the proceedings.

The lesson? Before giving any special-occasion speech, be sure you're familiar with your audience's expectations regarding what should be said during the speech and how it should be said.

Evoking Shared Values

Many effective special-occasion speeches appeal to values shared by members of the audience and the speaker. For instance, suppose you're presenting a plaque to Olivia, a fellow member of PeopleAid, an organization that helps homeless members of your community. The award is for Olivia's steady dedication to PeopleAid's mission of helping the homeless. She has recruited an unusual number of volunteers to serve boxed lunches to the homeless at shelters throughout the community and led other valuable projects for the organization. Before handing the plaque to Olivia, you deliver a speech extolling her ability to embody PeopleAid's values, which include compassion for those in need and a strong work ethic. Your speech about Olivia reaffirms your listeners' own dedication to these values and inspires them to strive for the same high standards she has set.

> © To watch a video that evokes shared values, try Video Activity 19.2, "Language, Delivery, and Special-Occasion Speeches."

Other special-occasion speeches may touch on values such as patriotism, fairness, shared sacrifice, and religious belief. To illustrate, let's say you're giving a speech at a ceremony recognizing the first anniversary of the death of Frank, a close friend who lost his life while serving in the U.S. Army in Afghanistan. The ceremony is held at the town hall near where you and Frank grew up. Neighbors and family members have gathered to remember Frank and honor the one-year anniversary of his death. In your speech, you note that "Frank felt the same love for his country that everyone in this room feels. We have all made sacrifices for that love. Frank lost his life, and we lost him all too soon. We will never forget our lost friend, brother, son, and neighbor." Through these words, you tap into the patriotism in your listeners' hearts and their sense of shared sacrifice— reminding them that you are all connected in a close community.

Respecting Time Constraints

Most special occasions are carefully planned affairs. Recall a wedding or retirement dinner you've recently attended. The occasion likely had a program that listed specific times for certain events. The program for a retirement dinner, for example, might look something like this: "Cocktails at 4:00. Award ceremony at 5:00. Dinner at 6:00." The occasion also may feature several speeches. Whenever refreshments, meal service, and multiple speakers are involved, skillful management of the overall program schedule becomes important. If an event listed in the program starts late or if one speaker uses up more time than the program has allotted, then the entire event can quickly go off the rails. For this reason, if you're giving a speech at such an occasion, make sure you know beforehand when you're scheduled to speak and what your time allotment is. Then be certain to stick to these logistics while delivering your presentation. As a courtesy, be willing to modify the time for your own presentation if a previous speaker has gone overtime.

STRATEGIES FOR EACH TYPE OF SPECIAL-OCCASION SPEECH

Although the general guidelines described in the preceding section can help you deliver an effective special-occasion speech, you'll also want to master strategies tailored to each of the six types of speeches. By pairing these specific practices with the general suggestions, you'll increase the odds of delivering a top-notch speech—no matter what the occasion.

Strategies for Speeches of Introduction

When you're giving a speech to introduce another speaker, a performer, or an event, you have three goals:

- Shifting your listeners' focus from interacting with one another to paying attention to the upcoming event,
- Building anticipation and excitement for the upcoming topic and speaker or presentation, and
- Introducing the person, performance, or event that's coming next.

When making an introduction, remember that you are not the main entertainment. Your primary goal is to facilitate what's coming next, and there is nothing more disastrous than an introductory speaker who goes on too long or tries too hard. Thus, take care not to upstage the speaker or event you're introducing. In particular, resist any urge to talk at length about yourself. Also, be sure to express some of your own appreciation for and anticipation of the upcoming event. The following tips can help you keep your audience focused on the main event and effectively achieve your three-part goal in giving a speech of introduction.

Be Patient. When the time comes for you to start your introduction, many listeners may still be settling into their seats, finishing a meal, or simply chatting with one another. To help them gradually shift their attention to you, stand up and begin talking above the background noise and voices in the room. But be patient: it takes time for people to transition away from what they're doing at the moment.

Use Attention-Getters. To help focus your listeners on the upcoming speaker or event, use attention-getters to cut through any noise or conversation in the room, making sure that you remain appropriate for the setting. Consider the attention-getters mentioned in Chapter 10, particularly one of the following: incorporate a striking statement, use a little bit of humor, or take the opportunity to let listeners know that you're one of them.

Modulate Your Volume. Even if you are working with a microphone, you may need to speak loudly at first to overcome the prevailing noise in the room and grab listeners' attention. After your speech is under way, be sure to lower your voice as the room quiets down. If conversation

THE ART OF INTRODUCTION

stirs again later during your speech, you can always raise your voice once more to an appropriate level.

Be Focused and Brief. Remember that your job is to prepare the audience to pay attention to the speaker or performance that will follow you. To that end, keep your comments focused on that event. Also, make sure your introduction is concise. Otherwise, audience members may start seeing you as the main entertainment, or they may lose interest in the next part of the program.

Strategies for Speeches of Presentation

Like a speech of introduction, the presentation of an award or a commendation precedes and facilitates what comes next for the audience. But unlike a speech of introduction, a presentation speech usually

celebrates the person, organization, or cause being honored—whether it's a service commendation for a teacher at a local PTA meeting, an award for team members at a sports banquet, or even an Emmy Award for lifetime achievement in television.

Thus, in a presentation speech, your role will be more fundamental than in a speech of introduction; you must provide your listeners with background and context for the honor to follow. This might seem unnecessary because listeners probably already know what the honor is and why they are there to observe it. Yet your job is to highlight the significance of the award and to build excitement and even reverence for it. You can do this by describing in detail the importance of the award itself and the background and contributions of the recipient.

Handled skillfully, a presentation speech can inspire intense emotion in listeners and even move them to dedicate themselves to the award recipient's work. Strong and enthusiastic applause after you've presented the award or commendation is another sure sign that you've nailed the speech. The following tips can help you achieve this kind of effect.

Adopt the Persona of a Presenter. In this type of speech, you're not just announcing the conferring of an award or honor; you're also presenting it. To demonstrate your authority as a presenter, be sure to speak respectfully and knowledgeably about your subject.

Explain the Significance and Background of the Award or Honor. Most people in your audience will understand that they are there for the presentation of an award. But they may not know why the honor or award really matters. What is its significance? Does it have an interesting history you could share? In a nutshell, a major goal of your presentation speech is to make clear why your listeners should care about the award about to be bestowed.

Connect the Recipient's Background to the Award's Criteria. Every award has qualifications or criteria that a potential recipient must meet and perhaps exceed. But these may not be obvious to the audience. In your speech, be sure to explain the criteria—and then point out how and why the recipient has met or surpassed them. Consider using stories and examples of the recipient's achievements to show dramatically (and perhaps humorously) why she or he deserves this honor.

THE ART OF PRESENTING

Use Appropriate Presentation Aids. A video or a slide presentation, perhaps with a light music or audio accompaniment, can complement your speech. Consider using presentation aids to explain both the criteria for an award and the ways that the recipient fulfilled the criteria. For example, if you're presenting an award for a person who has helped teach literacy to children in need, you could provide a short slide show depicting the recipient performing this work and some audio snippets of children who benefited from the person's efforts.

Strategies for Speeches of Acceptance

Imagine this: you're the beneficiary of a prestigious award, and the presenter has just handed it to you. What do you say now?

A high-quality acceptance speech is less about what you're saying ("Thank-you. I couldn't have done this without the rest of the team.") and more about how you're behaving while accepting the honor. By being there, you transform the presentation into a kind of public spectacle. The audience will expect you to show both humility and responsibility. You can fulfill those expectations by giving a brief, gracious, and heartfelt speech that expresses your gratitude while also recognizing the efforts of others who contributed to your achievement. The following tips can help you attain this blend of important qualities.

Use Appropriate Volume and Articulation.
Accepting an award can stir intense emotions within you, causing your voice to drop or break—and if you are using a microphone, such lapses will be amplified. To overcome this challenge, anticipate the effects of strong feelings, and feel free to gather yourself for a moment or two before you start talking. Strive to speak with sufficient volume and clarity throughout, especially when thanking others during your acceptance.

Your Majesty, Your Royal Highnesses, Ladies and Gentlemen. The work I have done has, already, been greatly rewarded and recognized. Imagination reaches out, repeatedly trying to achieve some higher level of understanding, until suddenly I find myself momentarily alone before one corner of nature's pattern of beauty and true majesty revealed. That was my reward.

RICHARD FEYNMAN
1965 NOBEL PRIZE IN PHYSICS

Show Genuine Humility.
Listeners can easily spot the difference between someone who's genuinely modest and humbled by an honor and someone who's just acting humble. Think about it: you've probably seen people stand at a podium, gush about how this award has "caught me off guard" and "left me speechless," but then pull out a sheet of paper and give a canned speech. Irritating, isn't it? To avoid making this mistake, don't act surprised if you knew you would be receiving the award. But definitely express your genuine gratitude for the honor and for the people who helped you achieve it.

Remember That Less Is More. Going on too long while accepting an award can give the impression that you always talk about yourself and rarely exhibit interest in others. To avoid conveying this impression, aim for brevity in your acceptance speech. Say enough to demonstrate your humility (perhaps through a bit of self-deprecating humor) and to acknowledge your deep appreciation for the award or honor. Briefly thank those to whom you are indebted. And then sit down. Otherwise, the music may start playing, and your presenter may take you by the elbow and start ushering you offstage.

WESTMINSTER KENNEL CLUB
DOG SHOW 2015

Woof, woof wooooooof!*

BEST IN SHOW
Ch Tastins
Looking for Trouble
a.k.a. Miss P

*Thanks. I'm hungry. Is it dinnertime?

Strategies for Speeches to Memorialize or Eulogize

Because death is a part of life, at some point you inevitably will lose a beloved family member or friend. You may be asked to deliver a eulogy about the person at a memorial service after his or her passing. As noted earlier, your purpose during this type of speech is to review and celebrate the life of your loved one and to console your listeners while helping them grieve publicly. It may seem that the two goals (consoling and facilitating grief) are in conflict, but consolation actually supports grieving—primarily because you can express these strong emotions as you encourage your audience to feel the same. Witnessing a eulogist publicly expressing grief gives the audience license to do so as well.

Delivering an effective eulogy is about helping the living by showing your own emotion as well as extolling the departed loved one's virtues and achievements. The following tips can help you provide this assistance when giving this kind of speech.

Focus on Celebrating the Person's Life. Each person's life has both high and low points, good experiences and bad. Instead of focusing on negative memories in your eulogy, highlight the departed loved one's accomplishments, important relationships, and unique qualities, citing examples and stories familiar to your listeners. You'll establish common ground with your audience members and help them collectively celebrate the best of the person they've lost.

Use Humor Judiciously. At most memorial services, several people will stand up and say something about the deceased. If each person in a series of speakers focuses unrelentingly on the profound sorrow of the occasion, the collective heaviness may become too much for the audience to bear. For this reason, consider providing a humorous (but appropriate) anecdote about the deceased at some point during your remarks to relieve the tension. Listeners may feel profound relief when they can laugh through their tears.

Don't Be Afraid to Show Your Emotions. The best way to give the audience permission to grieve openly during a memorial service is to show your emotions. A display of feeling can set loose a flood of feelings in your listeners, which can provide a healthy emotional release.

Strategies for Speeches to Celebrate

Life is as much about joy and celebration as it is about tragedy and loss. The birth of a child, a couple's decision to spend their lives together, a

IT'S OK TO HELP LISTENERS LAUGH THROUGH THEIR TEARS

*Central Intelligence Agency **Culinary Institute of America

graduation, a rite of passage from youth to adulthood: these and other major milestones in our lives are all causes for happiness. And they're all marked by special occasions at which people deliver speeches to help celebrate the joyous event.

If you're delivering a speech of celebration at such an occasion, your role is to explain the significance of the occasion, acknowledge the joy everyone is feeling, and inspire the audience to take part in the celebration. The following tips can help you achieve this goal.

Aim for Brevity. Take enough time to remind your audience why the gathering is important and joyful—but not so much time that you tire, bore, or distract the audience from the subject of the celebration.

Use Humor Appropriately. Different cultures define "appropriate" humor in different ways. Use audience analysis to determine whether humor is OK for the particular celebration or whether listeners would find it distracting or offensive. Never use humor to hurt; instead, use it to highlight endearing qualities of the people being celebrated. Tell stories about the celebrant that he or she finds funny, and avoid making jokes about matters the person is embarrassed about or considers sensitive. Consider using humor in a self-deprecating way, so that the story you're sharing is funny rather than hurtful.

THE WRONG WAY TO GIVE A SPEECH OF CELEBRATION

Good luck, Robb and Sandra... Er... I mean, Cindy! Whatever, this marriage won't last long anyway. Robb's a player—not a henpecked hubby... Hic!

THE RIGHT WAY TO GIVE A SPEECH OF CELEBRATION

Good luck, Cindy and Robb—and for Cindy, a fond farewell to those times we spent puzzling over Robb's cryptic text messages. Turns out, his ironic use of emoticons actually worked!

Strategies for After-Dinner Speeches

After-dinner speeches have a long and storied tradition in the United States. They emerged in an age before television and other mass media were on the scene and when speaking was a major form of entertainment. This tradition produced such literary giants as Mark Twain, who gave several hundred of these kinds of addresses, always after a meal.[5] Like others who delivered these types of presentations, Twain usually salted his after-dinner speeches with entertaining stories, personal references, and a great deal of wit.

After-dinner speeches in the United States have developed their own unique flavor, but other cultures have their own after-dinner speaking traditions. Some scholars argue that the North American style of toasting arose from a long-standing tradition from Great Britain, centered in formal affairs and especially in traditional British men's clubs. And Russia has a tradition of sharing many toasts—studded with anecdotes and stories for each drink—at formal occasions and especially at group meals.

MARK TWAIN (1835 TO 1910)

It usually takes me more than three weeks to prepare a good impromptu speech.

To cease smoking is the easiest thing I ever did. I ought to know, I've done it a thousand times.

Always acknowledge a fault. This will throw those in authority off their guard and give you an opportunity to commit more.

It is my custom to keep on talking until I get the audience cowed.

Effective after-dinner speakers assume the role of entertainers and have a talent for amusing and delighting their audiences while occasionally making a more serious point. Indeed, many after-dinner speeches are given at gatherings designed to raise funds for a particular cause, such as a charitable organization or a politician's election campaign. These speeches are longer and more involved than simple toasts, and they require the ability to thrill and captivate an audience, often after listeners have consumed a full meal and perhaps a few glasses of wine. To overcome these challenges, apply the following strategies for delivering an effective after-dinner speech.

Focus on Humorous Anecdotes and Narrative Delivery, Not Jokes.

In after-dinner speeches, the tradition has always been to employ witty stories and anecdotes as opposed to a series of one-liners or jokes with punch lines. Remember that your after-dinner speech should be a combination of anecdotal references and storytelling wrapped around a larger theme, not a stand-up comedy routine.

Practice Your Storytelling and Narrative Delivery.

The success of your after-dinner speech depends on *how* you tell a story as much as it

THE WRONG WAY TO GIVE AN AFTER-DINNER SPEECH	THE RIGHT WAY TO GIVE AN AFTER-DINNER SPEECH
A priest, a rabbi, an imam, a German, a Russian, a Japanese guy, a Korean, a West Indian guy, and George Bush all walk into a bar, and the bartender says, "Oh, I get it, this is your idea of a joke, right?"	Ladies and Gentlemen, it gives me great joy to stand before you tonight. Let me start by saying that, as a rabbi, I've starred in many bad jokes...

does on what you say in the story itself. Sufficiently rehearse your narrative so that you will feel comfortable and relaxed sharing it during the actual speech. Think of your after-dinner speech as a kind of performance, and understand that—like all performances—this one will benefit from lots of practice and polish.

Link Your Speech to the Occasion's Theme. If the dinner gathering has a serious theme—for example, the importance of raising funds to support cancer research—consider linking a lighter narrative to that weightier theme. You'll help the audience adopt a relaxed and receptive frame of mind while still accepting the urgency of the topic.

Adapt Your Delivery to Your Audience and the Occasion. Be prepared to make spontaneous adjustments to your structure and content based on what's happening around you. Look for opportunities to focus your wit or good-natured satire on something that another speaker or a member of the audience has said. For example, by commenting on a point that a previous speaker made or a question that an audience member has asked, you show that you're delivering an original rather than a canned or prepackaged speech. You thus let your audience know that you consider them worthy of a fresh presentation tailored specifically to them.

ADAPT YOUR DELIVERY TO YOUR AUDIENCE AND THE OCCASION

SAMPLE SPECIAL-OCCASION SPEECH

SWEARING-IN CEREMONY FOR NEW U.S. CITIZENS

Joseph Tuman
San Francisco State University

In addition to being one of the authors of this book, Joseph S. Tuman has worked in broadcast news media as a political analyst for various news services, including ABC News and CBS News. In 2009, Tuman—who was born in Texas to parents who immigrated to the United States—was invited by the U.S. Immigration and Naturalization Service to give the keynote address at a swearing-in ceremony in San Francisco for people from around the world who were about to become new citizens of this country. What follows is the text of his speech to this large and diverse audience.

Good morning! I didn't quite hear you. Let's try that again: good morning! I still can't quite hear you. Don't be polite! This is a special day. This is *your* day! Come on, say it like you mean it. Scream it. One more time: good morning! •

That's better.

This *is* a special day. And I want to tell you how honored I am to be here to share it with you. I'm not going to say congratulations just yet because I have a few words I would like to share with you first. You may have noticed that I have someone sitting up here with me on the stage as I'm speaking. This is my mother. Her name is Turan. Turan Tuman! • When the people putting on the ceremony asked the folks I work with at CBS5 if I would be willing to speak today, I immediately thought about my mom and this particular year.

It's a significant year for her, because fifty years ago the woman you see sitting with me up on the stage was out in the audience with *you*. In that year she was being sworn in as a new citizen of the United States of America, just like all of you. And so I asked their permission for her to join me today as I speak. Mostly because I wanted her to be more proud of me—than my brothers. . . . But also because some of what I'm going to say for you also hopefully will have some meaning for her. So I'm looking at her now, and she's

• The call and response with the audience is an attention-getting device that focuses everyone and generates excitement for what is to come.

• Tuman is using his mother as a visual aid because she was sworn in as a citizen fifty years earlier. Her experience allows Tuman to share common ground with his audience.

blushing. Either that means I've embarrassed her, or she's annoyed with me. Well, we'll see. The person who is not up on the stage with me today, sadly, is my father. We lost him two years ago. But he's with me here today in spirit. •

My father's name was Vladimir. Vladimir S. Tuman. In this country, it was a hard name for people to pronounce, so his colleagues and friends just called him "Bill." As an accommodation, my mom called him "Villa." He was born, like some of you, on the other side of the world, in a country called Iran and in a place called Kermanshah. At a young age, because he was gifted at math and science, my father won a scholarship. The scholarship allowed him to travel to England, where he earned degrees in engineering and physics and geology. After many years, he returned to the place where he had grown up. And there he faced the dilemma that many people who become immigrants face.

He had developed a worldview outside of the Iran. A larger worldview. He was Westernized. He wore different clothes, and he spoke more and different languages. He had seen other parts of the world. And, sadly, he realized it would be difficult for him to fit in, back in the place he had once called home. He worked for a time in the petroleum industry as an engineer. At some point, his boss took him aside and said to him: "Tuman, you're a good man, and a good employee. But this is a Muslim country, and you are a Christian. You will never go further in this company than you already have." My father was somewhat devastated at this news. "What should I do?" he asked. The man said with a straight face: "You should go to America!"

"America?" my father asked. "Why?"

And the man responded: "Because in America they don't mind if you are a Christian!" •

Yes, my father thought that was funny later too. Little did he realize, how close to correct the man was.

When my father came to this country, he landed in Texas, and my mother and my older brother soon joined him. Texas is where I was born and where I entered the picture. My father eventually became a professor. We moved from Texas to Illinois and eventually to California. He was at Stanford University for a time, before moving our family to Turlock, a place that seemed very different from Palo Alto.

• Tuman invokes the memory of his father, who also was an immigrant to America, to find more common ground.

• This anecdote injects some humor into a serious subject. The audience laughed, which means they understood the joke even if English was not their first language.

I spent my younger years there, up through high school. My brothers—I have two of them—always wondered why my father moved us there. It wasn't until he died a few years ago and I went to speak at his funeral that it occurred to me why he moved us to Turlock. Turlock was a small agricultural town, with the anomaly of having a new liberal arts college in its midst. My father started the first physics department there. But he would've been just as happy to stay at Palo Alto at Stanford. For years we wondered: why had he left Palo Alto for Turlock? That day as I spoke at his funeral, it finally occurred to me.

As I stared out into the hundreds of people who had come to the tiny Assyrian church for his funeral, I realized that most of them also came from the town he grew up in, in Iran. You see, all his life, my father wanted to go back to the place he called home. But he realized when he went home, he no longer belonged there. America became his new home—but he never stopped missing the place of his birth. And so at a later stage in life, he decided he would bring home to him here. With my father's assistance, many of those people in the church that day had already become citizens like you . . . and like my father. •

• The description of his father's funeral and the many people from his father's hometown is dramatic and poignant. It also provides some ethos for the advice to come, which Tuman borrowed from his father.

As a new citizen of this country, my father immediately embraced the culture here, especially the politics of this place. He loved it. Most of all, he loved the fact that he could express himself openly without fear of retaliation or punishment. He adored this country. It is in his memory today that I offer you these three small pieces of advice that my father often shared with others who wanted to become citizens here.

First, he always said that everyone who came to this country should be educated. If they were uneducated when they came, he insisted that they become educated once they were here. And more important, he always insisted that they made sure that their children and their grandchildren would not only finish high school but go to college and graduate. In our family, all of my brothers and myself earned not only undergraduate degrees but graduate degrees as well. And all of us, incidentally, became professors and teachers. My mother, who sits up here with me, was in the PhD program at UC Berkeley as well and taught for many years in Turlock.

My father understood that education was not just an end unto itself, but really for all immigrants to this country it was the great equalizer. It is not a cliché to say that America is the land of opportunity. And what all of us get when we come here is a chance to *do better*. The thing that equalizes everything for everyone in the end is education. That's what makes the American dream possible. So to paraphrase my father, make sure you are educated. Make sure that your children go to college. And if you really want to follow his advice, make sure they go to graduate school after college, too! •

    • This message about education is bolstered by and reinforces Tuman's ethos as a professor.

The second thing my father would always say to people who wanted to become citizens of this country was this: once you are a citizen, make sure that you always exercise your right to vote. Our country graciously allows all citizens the right to vote, but sadly in America today, too many of the people who could vote, don't vote. I can't tell you how important it is that you not only register to vote but also become what is known as a *likely voter*—meaning that you establish a pattern and history of voting regularly in elections.

In this country, voters choose our leaders. Voters provide input about policy and decision making by exercising their choices in the ballot box. If you never vote, you shouldn't complain about things you don't like. Also, by not voting you are ignoring your responsibility as a citizen. Take this responsibility seriously. Make sure that you vote. Make sure that everyone in your family votes. And make sure that your children are ingrained with the same sense of responsibility. It is an awesome responsibility and *also one of the greatest gifts of this country*. •

    • The point about voting is bolstered by and reinforces Tuman's other ethos as a television political analyst.

I'm getting near the end of my speech now. And I want to share one last piece of wisdom with you. This was something I once heard my father say in slightly different words to a man who was very timid about becoming a citizen here. It wasn't that he didn't want to be a citizen but rather that he feared people would still see him as a foreigner. So let me say to you in my words the equivalent of what my father said that day. Now that you have been sworn in and you are citizens of this country, *don't ever let someone tell you that you aren't a real American*. Let me repeat that: *don't ever let someone tell you that because you came from somewhere else and you had to get sworn in as a citizen here, somehow that makes you less of an American. Or not a real American at all.* Nothing could be further from the truth.

Anyone can be born here. And when you're born here, it's not as if you had to exercise your choice to be born in America. That was a decision that your parents made for you. But when you are a person who has to fight to come to this country, who has to suffer, who has to work hard, who has to endure many hardships and challenges to get to this place—well, at that moment, the very moment you're at today, you know exactly what it is to not only be a citizen of this country but also to be a real American. *You weren't born here. You chose this country. You took affirmative steps to become a citizen here. And you are as much, if not more, an American as any other citizen here today. Never, ever let someone speak down to you or tell you otherwise.* •

• Tuman's advice is an inspirational call to action.

So now, say it with me: say it out loud! *I am an American!* Geez, this is as bad as when I said good morning. Come on, say it louder: *I am an American!* Again! *I am an American!* •

• Another call and response, which brings the audience vocally back into the speech.

And this last part is also for you, Mom. This year you celebrate fifty years of citizenship in this country. And for nearly fifty years, I have listened to you make jokes about how you will always be seen as a foreigner. Well, Mom, you're not a foreigner. You are a citizen of this country. And I guess I need to remind you that you've lived in this country longer than you lived anywhere else, by several times over. *Mom, you are an American, too.* And you are as much an American in this country as anyone. •

• Tuman gives another message to his mother, who has become an additional audience member. She now serves as an example of what people in the audience can become in time.

Oh, she's blushing again; I guess I am going to hear about this after the speech. So let me wrap this up by saying once again: my hearty congratulations to all of you. Welcome to your new country. Welcome, fellow Americans! Thank you and good day!

CHAPTER REVIEW

 Whether to mark a celebration, a milestone, or a passing, we all participate in special-occasion speaking as speakers or listeners.

At some point in your life, you almost certainly will be asked to deliver a special-occasion speech, whether it's to mark a joyous or sorrowful event, present or accept an award, introduce another speaker or performer, or give a witty but evocative talk after a formal dinner.

By applying the general guidelines described in this chapter as well as the strategies tailored specifically to each of the six types of special-occasion speeches, you can lay the groundwork for a successful presentation that will make your listeners remember the event for many years to come. If you are asked to deliver a speech on such an occasion, be aware of the type of speech your audience will expect, and follow specific strategies designed to tailor your special-occasion speech for both the occasion and the audience.

 LaunchPad
macmillan learning

LaunchPad for *Speak Up* offers videos and encourages self-assessment through adaptive quizzing. Go to **macmillanhighered.com/speakup4e** to get access to:

✓ **LearningCurve**
Adaptive Quizzes

▶ **Video clips that help you understand public speaking concepts**

Key Terms

epideictic *577*

eulogy *580*

Review Questions

1. Name and describe six types of special-occasion speeches identified in the chapter.
2. What five guidelines should be adhered to when delivering a special-occasion speech?

3. What four strategies for speeches of introduction are offered in the chapter?

4. Describe four strategies for speeches of presentation.

5. What three strategies should you use when delivering a speech of acceptance?

6. What three strategies should you use when speaking to memorialize or eulogize?

7. Describe two strategies that can help you deliver a celebratory speech.

8. Offer four strategies for effective after-dinner speeches.

Critical Thinking Questions

1. What characteristics do television hosts like Jimmy Fallon and Stephan Colbert share with famous speakers like Mark Twain? In what ways are after-dinner speeches and late-night monologues similar? Which one do you think would be more difficult to prepare and deliver, and why?

2. How does a eulogy differ from a celebratory speech? How are they the same?

3. Are there occasions when you might need to deliver a celebratory speech in front of a somewhat hostile audience? How might you change your speech in those circumstances?

Activities

1. Imagine that you have been tasked with delivering a speech of introduction for a controversial figure (such as Roman Polanski, Ann Coulter, Lance Armstrong, or Charlie Sheen). How would you handle introducing someone whom you dislike or do not respect or whom the audience might view negatively? Craft an attention-getter for this type of speech.

2. Suppose that a close friend or a brother or sister has asked you to give a toast at his or her wedding. What would you say? How would you use humor?

3. Imagine that you have to give a special-occasion speech honoring someone important to you. Prepare three outlines—for a speech of introduction for this person, for a speech of presentation of an

imaginary award, and for a speech that toasts the person for a life event (such as a wedding, graduation, or retirement). How do your three outlines differ?

Study Plan

_____

_____

_____

_____

_____

_____

_____

_____

_____

_____

_____

_____

_____

_____

_____

_____

_____

_____

GROUP COMMUNICATION

20

"Several heads are better than one." Jenny, Sam, Juan, Ashley, and Yolanda were taking a course called Community Service 101, which gave students credit for performing volunteer work. The instructor organized the students into five groups, and Jenny, Sam, Juan, Ashley, and Yolanda were placed together as a group. Each group had to choose one volunteer project, and each member of the group had to contribute at least thirty hours of service to the project. At the end of the term, each group would deliver a thirty-minute multimedia presentation informing the class about its project.

Throughout the term, Jenny, Sam, June, Ashley, and Yolanda experienced firsthand the challenges and benefits of working in a group. For example, they argued over what to call themselves and, after an intense and uncomfortable debate, eventually settled on HELP (Hands-on, Empowering, Loving People). In their first few meetings, Sam and Yolanda kept interrupting each other, and Ashley tried to dominate the discussion. Eventually, Juan reminded the others that to fulfill the requirements of the course, they needed to select a volunteer project and work out a plan for

609

implementing the project. Jenny realized that smoother cooperation would help them achieve this goal, so she suggested that group members agree on rules for communicating and making decisions. They settled on several rules, including these: no one can interrupt when someone else is speaking, everyone gets a chance to contribute ideas, and all decisions must be unanimous.

As the project unfolded, HELP's attention to effective leadership and productive participation enabled the group's members to select and carry out a worthy project—supporting an after-school program at a nearby elementary school. Through spirited but respectful discussions, each member was able to offer unique and valuable ideas for carrying out the project.

Despite the rocky start, the group's commitment to the mission and to one another paid big dividends. By the time HELP was scheduled to deliver its presentation on the project to the rest of the class, Jenny, Sam, Juan, Ashley, and Yolanda had mastered the challenges of managing group dynamics. Each member described a different aspect of how HELP carried out its project and what results the group achieved, and the speech was a success.

Through their project, these students discovered both the difficulties and the advantages of working in a **small group**—a limited number of people (three or more) gathered for a specific purpose. This classroom experience showed them that **group dynamics**—the ways in which members relate to one another and view their functions—can determine whether a group achieves its mission.

Learning how to master group dynamics, work well with others in pursuit of a common goal, and communicate your group's achievements to others are valuable life skills. Although group interactions can sometimes be frustrating, you will inevitably be asked or decide to participate in a group at some point in your educational and professional lives—whether in the classroom, in your community, or at work.[1]

Why is working effectively in a group important? Small groups offer important advantages over individual efforts. Often, people can achieve a better outcome by collaborating on a task rather than working alone. Each group member has unique experiences and perspectives to offer. By sharing ideas, each member has the chance to spot potential problems or improvements in a plan that a lone individual might miss.

And each person in a group has different strengths and interests. The group can divide up a project so that each member takes responsibility for the portions of the job he or she is best suited for.

But as we've seen with HELP's story, to gain the benefits of collaboration, group members must interact productively. This chapter provides suggestions for managing key elements of group dynamics—including how to lead a group, how to participate in one, how to make decisions as a group, and how to present your findings or decisions to an audience.

EFFECTIVE GROUP LEADERSHIP

When the coach of a gold medal–winning Olympic team, the leader of a Nobel Prize–winning medical research team, or the director of a successful play is interviewed, that person usually is being recognized as a successful leader. Successful groups depend on capable participation by each group member, but the leader's actions are critical.

This is true because it's difficult for any group to function without an effective leader. Somebody needs to organize group meetings, keep the group focused, encourage participation by all members, mediate conflict, and facilitate decision making. The leader need not have total control, but she or he must help group members reach a decision and achieve goals together. How do groups acquire leaders? They do so through several means, as we discuss in this section.

Selecting a Leader

Groups gain leaders in various ways. Sometimes an external authority selects a **designated leader** to help the group move quickly forward with its mission. For example, a mayor may appoint a blue-ribbon committee to investigate ways to improve mass transit, designating a leader to guide the inquiry. Or an army lieutenant who needs to send soldiers on a reconnaissance mission may designate a leader from the group of troops selected.

In other situations, there may be an **implied leader**, someone with preexisting authority or skills who is well suited to the task at hand although not formally assigned the role. For instance, a marketing manager may decide to form a task force to evaluate her company's advertising strategies. At the task force's first meeting, she's the implied leader because she formed the group.

In still other situations, a group may have an **emergent leader**, one who comes to be recognized as a leader by the group's members over time. Although not officially elected or even named as such, an emergent

DESIGNATED LEADER

IMPLIED LEADER

leader usually comes to assume the role because he or she has the most time to commit to the group, demonstrates exceptional competence and goodwill, or simply takes the initiative and starts leading. Juan and Jenny did this for HELP.

Leading Meetings

Effective group leaders conduct meetings in ways that enable members to work together productively, contribute their ideas, and make well-informed decisions. If you're the leader of a group, consider these tips for facilitating group meetings.

Address Procedural Needs. Where and when will meetings take place? Who will start meetings and record notes? And how will notes be circulated to members who cannot attend a particular meeting?

Model the Behavior You Expect. Avoid interrupting others or dismissing their questions or comments. Make group members feel they can interact comfortably with you. And resist any urge to dominate discussions or decisions.

Facilitate Discussion. Ensure that all members of your group have the opportunity to participate in each discussion. If some group members are not speaking during a meeting, strive to bring them into the discussion

MODEL THE BEHAVIOR YOU EXPECT

("Anil, what do you think?" or "That's a good point, Sarah. You've clearly researched this carefully. But let's also give Tyler a chance to share his ideas"). Although it's important to contribute when you have an idea that nobody else has raised, try to let other members speak first. If you make your position known early, members may hesitate to contradict you.

Keep Members on Task. If the discussion begins to stray from the item under consideration, keep members on task in a friendly manner. For example, "I agree with Harry that our department's holiday party is going to be a blast. But let's talk about how we're going to tackle reserving the space for the event."

Help Members Avoid Groupthink.

Groupthink is members' tendency to accept ideas and information uncritically because of strong feelings of loyalty or single-mindedness within the group.[2] Groupthink erodes the lively and open exchange of ideas necessary for informed decisions. Worse, it also suggests that being increasingly amiable with other members of a group can eliminate independent, critical thinking, and replace it with groupthink.[3] If one person advocates a course of action in your group and everybody else nods in agreement, try to broaden the discussion before moving the group toward making a final decision. For instance, ask a particularly insightful participant if she or he can think of any potential risks to the proposed course of action. If nobody is willing to offer any reservations, consider raising some concerns yourself: "I like Sangeeta's idea, but let me play devil's advocate for a minute. . . ." Be sure that the group has considered the pros *and* cons of the proposed options before selecting one.

Facilitate Decisions.

When it seems that members of your group have thoroughly discussed the issue at hand, help them come to a decision. As leader, you will participate in the final decision, but your leadership role does not entitle you to make the decision for the group. In other words, never use your power to manipulate the group. After the decision has been

made, ensure that it is recorded, and then move the group on to the next issue. Revisit decisions only when new circumstances make the original decision unfeasible.

Help Organize the Group's Presentation. Does your group need to present its conclusions? If so, who will serve as the speaker or speakers? How will the presentation be framed to best meet the audience's needs? As leader, you don't necessarily need to make all the decisions yourself, but you do need to coordinate the decisions on these topics.

Managing Conflict

Whatever the situation or setting, disagreements inevitably crop up as a group works together on a project. Some conflict is helpful. For example,

when members express honest disagreement about proposed plans of
action, they help minimize the risk
of groupthink. But interpersonal
conflicts that have nothing to do
with the group's mission can create distractions. Whenever conflict
arises in your group, strive to
minimize it or channel it in
a productive direction. The
following guidelines can help.

Refer to Ideas by Topic, Not by Person.
Focus on the content
of specific suggestions rather than attributing those suggestions to individual members. For example, suppose you're part of a group that's trying to get a candidate elected
as head of the town council.
Monique advocates sending a
mass email to build support
for the candidate, but Tim
thinks that leafleting would
be better. Refer to these ideas
as "the email plan" and "the
leafleting plan" rather than
"Monique's idea" and "Tim's
suggestion." When ideas get
associated with an individual,
that person may develop a feeling of personal investment in that option.
He or she may thus become defensive if the proposal is criticized—even if
it has real shortcomings.

Resolve Conflicts Quickly.
If a conflict between group members
becomes distracting, try to resolve it rather than allowing it to continue
or repressing it. Give the members who disagree an equal opportunity to
explain their perspective; let each person speak without interruption, and
then ask other members for their views. If both people's ideas have merit,
perhaps you can help the group find a solution that draws the best from
each perspective. As leader, you may ultimately need to offer your opinion or vote to break a deadlock on an issue, but try to give group members
an opportunity to speak before injecting your opinion.

Focus on Tasks, Not Disagreements. Help members concentrate on the task at hand rather than on interpersonal tensions that may be simmering. Rather than criticizing individuals (by saying things like, "Sally, your answers to Noah's questions are always sarcastic"), articulate desired changes in behavior (by saying things like, "Let's get back to discussing our project").

A personality clash may be best solved by discussing the problem in private with the members who disagree rather than airing the conflict in front of the entire group. If a member gets along well with the people experiencing the conflict, she or he may be able to help them find a way to manage their disagreement.

Manage Disruptive Emotions. Conflicts can spark intense and disruptive emotions within a group. Even after a conflict has been resolved, members may still feel angry, upset, or embarrassed and may withdraw from the discussion. If this happens, bring reluctant members back into the discussion by inviting their input on important issues.

Seek to Create a Diverse Group Atmosphere. Working with others allows us to draw on everyone's unique experiences and perspectives. Group members with different ideas can tackle complex problems by offering up, weighing, and trying out multiple solutions. Greater group **heterogeneity**, or member difference (as compared to **homogeneity**, or member similarity), is not without its challenges. In groups that are highly heterogeneous, members may have to provide more background information for their ideas and may be more likely to disagree with one another. But although homogeneous groups may run more smoothly, heterogeneous groups find ways to coordinate multiple perspectives more productively.[4] In other words, a group with

diverse perspectives that values all of those perspectives and is able to use them effectively has the best chance of reaching their goals.

EFFECTIVE GROUP MEMBERSHIP

Although strong leadership is essential to effective group communication, productive participation by members is equally vital. To contribute your best to a group as a member, start by understanding the types of roles you can take on to support your group's success.

Three Types of Member Roles

There are three types of roles that group members can fill.[5] Two of them—*task-oriented roles* and *maintenance-oriented roles*—are helpful. The third type—*self-oriented roles*—is not productive and should be avoided. People can take on different types of roles, even during the course of a single meeting, although most have the tendency to focus on one or two. If you're able to note which roles you often take on, you can consider if they are the most helpful for the situation you're in and adapt accordingly.

Task-Oriented Roles. Task-oriented roles contribute to a group's ability to accomplish its goals through enhancing members' participation and the free flow of information within the group. In a group in which members are fulfilling these roles, you'll likely see people asking helpful questions and making constructive comments. There are eight task-oriented roles:

I'm constructive!

- *Initiators* suggest the group's goals and offer new ideas or propose new solutions.

- *Information providers* offer facts relevant to the issue under discussion. These facts might include researched evidence or examples based on personal experience.

- *Information gatherers* ask other members to share facts they know, or they seek out needed information from other sources.

- *Elaborators* add supporting facts, examples, or ideas to a point that someone else has made during the discussion.

- *Clarifiers* attempt to make the meaning of another member's statement more precise.

- *Evaluators* offer their own judgments about the ideas put forward during a discussion.

- *Synthesizers* identify emerging agreements and disagreements among the group as a whole.

INITIATORS

INFORMATION PROVIDERS

INFORMATION GATHERERS

ELABORATORS

CLARIFIERS

EVALUATORS

SYNTHESIZERS

RECORDERS

- *Recorders* take notes during the meeting, tracking major decisions and plans made by the group. They may send memos or emails to group members summarizing previous meetings, providing agendas for future meetings, or reminding people of tasks they agreed to work on between meetings.

I'm encouraging!

Maintenance-Oriented Roles. Maintenance-oriented roles help sustain and strengthen efficient and effective interpersonal relations in a group. When members perform maintenance roles effectively, they are more likely to work together comfortably as a team, support one another, and present findings or recommendations that reflect group consensus. There are five maintenance-oriented roles:

- *Harmonizers* decrease tension in the group, perhaps by infusing humor at just the right time or by making positive and optimistic comments.
- *Compromisers* attempt to find common ground between adversaries within the group and offer solutions that may be palatable to people on both sides of the conflict.
- *Encouragers* inspire other group members by complimenting their ideas and work.
- *Gatekeepers* facilitate the exchange of information among group members.
- *Norm facilitators* reinforce healthy group norms and discourage unproductive ones.

HARMONIZERS   COMPROMISERS   ENCOURAGERS   GATEKEEPERS   NORM FACILITATORS

Self-Oriented Roles. Self-oriented roles accomplish little for a group and are motivated by the selfish ends of individual members. Groups with a heavy emphasis on these roles may experience incomplete findings, infighting, and dissension. There are four self-oriented roles:

- *Blockers* stop the group from moving toward its objective—by refusing to accept decisions the group has made or by arbitrarily rejecting other members' ideas or opinions.

- *Withdrawers* refuse to make any contribution or to participate in the discussion. They may feel out of their element in the group or may be having difficulty following other members' comments and ideas.

- *Dominators* monopolize group interactions by interrupting others, arguing for the sake of arguing, and insisting on having the last word. This behavior may stem from feelings of insecurity, an aggressive personality, or some other factor.

- *Distracters*—the opposite of *harmonizers*—send the group in irrelevant directions with off-topic comments or extraneous conversation, perhaps because they have trouble concentrating on a topic or focusing on the completion of a process.

When you're participating in a group, focus on how you can fulfill task-oriented and maintenance-oriented roles (or encourage others to do so). Also, avoid playing self-oriented roles, and discourage others from adopting them.

BLOCKERS   WITHDRAWERS   DOMINATORS   DISTRACTERS

Tips for Participating in a Small Group

In addition to fulfilling task- and maintenance-oriented roles, you can improve your effectiveness at group participation by applying the following practices.

Prepare for Group Meetings. If an agenda has been distributed for an upcoming meeting, think about the topics under consideration *before* you gather with other group members. Keep track of any commitments you made for the meeting (such as researching the answer to a question or bringing your laptop), and be sure to fulfill them. If you are planning to disseminate information to group members, be sure to iron out any wrinkles in your presentation beforehand.

Treat Other Members Courteously. Courtesy begins with arriving at a group meeting on time (or at least informing the group if you will be late). Turn off your cell phone unless you are expecting a call that will help the group conduct its business. During the discussion, treat other members with respect, even when you disagree with their views. If you do disagree with other members, be sure to focus on the issue at hand rather than on personalities. For example, if someone proposes an idea you find question-

able, don't say, "I'm not sure you have the patience to carry out this idea." Instead, try to learn more, perhaps by asking, "What's your experience in doing this sort of thing? Can you tell us more about the kinds of challenges we can expect?"

Listen Interactively. Inattention between members can cause tension in a group. Someone who doesn't feel heard may turn a deaf ear to another person's comments at later meetings. To avoid this problem, practice interactive listening (see Chapter 4). As other members of your

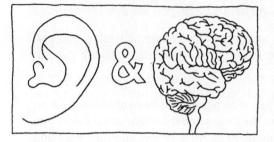

group share their ideas and comments, try to understand their viewpoints and show that you are listening. Ask for clarification if you need it, and make sure you understand a point before challenging it.

Participate, Don't Dominate.   To gain the benefit of diverse perspectives, a group needs contributions from each member. When you have a relevant point to make, share your idea. Your participation is particularly important when you have experience with a topic or a unique viewpoint that hasn't been expressed.

At the same time, avoid monopolizing the discussion. If you find yourself speaking a disproportionate amount of the time, take a break and let other members contribute. You may even ask another member to chime in if it seems that he or she has an idea but is reluctant to speak.

Participate Authentically.   A group functions at its best when members put diverse ideas and perspectives on the table. Therefore, be guided by honesty, not popularity, when considering problems and solutions. If you have an idea that you believe is important, don't be afraid to mention it, even if you're worried about how others might perceive it. If you have concerns about another member's suggestion, explain your reservations to the group.

Be sure to balance candor with tact when questioning or challenging a colleague's idea. Critique the idea, not the person, in a manner that makes your concerns clear. For example, "I'm not sure our group can afford to rent that facility for our project," not "Where in the world do you think we're going to get the money for that?"

In the same vein, if others disagree with an idea you have presented, avoid overreacting. Instead, let others explain their position. If you disagree with what you're hearing, explain your position calmly and rationally. If you listen to their criticism and find it to be valid, then be honest and acknowledge that you agree.

Fulfill Your Commitments. For a group to achieve its goals, it's vital that members accept responsibility for performing certain tasks—both the ones assigned to them individually and the ones required of all participating members. For example, you may promise to research the cost of an item that your group needs to purchase, or perhaps you've agreed to distribute notes from the last meeting to the group.

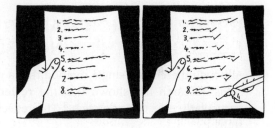

When group members make commitments, the rest of the group will rely on them to fulfill those commitments; if people drop the ball enough times, the group as a whole will find it more and more difficult to carry out its work. Moreover, in most situations, work assigned to another group member will depend on work you've been assigned, so failing to follow up on your commitments will hurt not just you but also the other member.

Use Technology to Your Advantage. Because you probably will need to use technology for group work, keep the following suggestions in mind. Figure out which type of technology is the most useful for your purposes. All forms have drawbacks, and it's important to be aware of both benefits and limitations. For example, instant messaging may be useful in meetings because it allows immediate feedback between participants; however, members can't always retrieve the content for future reference.[6] Use audio conferences for simpler information sharing. If your meeting requires thorough discussions of group issues, you may want to consider videoconferencing so that you can see and hear one another.[7] In a similar vein, because technological mishaps can happen, test all necessary equipment beforehand. Ensure that everyone can see and hear one another, and use names to clarify who is being addressed.

Although computer technology seems widespread, not everyone has access to it or is comfortable using it. Make sure that all group members have access to the technology you'd like to use. Finally, try to imitate or facilitate face-to-face immediacy whenever you can. Whether by sending an email containing personal references ("How was your trip?") or by using Skype or FaceTime for meetings to allow members to see one another and talk with one another, you can use technology to make group members feel as if they are all together.

GROUP DECISION MAKING AND THE REFLECTIVE-THINKING PROCESS

Although there is no single method that a group *must* use to make decisions, research has shown that the **reflective-thinking process** is a particularly effective approach.[8] The reflective-thinking process has five steps:

1. Define the problem.
2. Analyze the problem.
3. Establish criteria for solving the problem.
4. Generate possible solutions.
5. Select the best solution.

In this section, we take a closer look at each of these steps.

Define the Problem

Before your group can select a course of action, you must know exactly what problem (or objective) you will address. As a group, work to define the problem or goal as precisely as possible.

Analyze the Problem

After your group has defined the problem, analyze its nature. What are the primary aspects of the problem? Which of these are most important for the group to focus on?

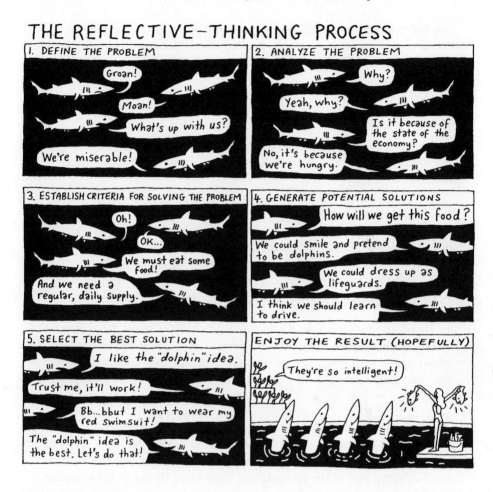

Establish Criteria for Solving the Problem

Decide which factors will be most important when weighing possible solutions to the problem your group will be addressing. Each proposed solution will have strengths and weaknesses, and establishing criteria will help you select the best overall solution.

Generate Possible Solutions

Create a list of potential solutions to the problem your group is addressing. Brainstorming (see Chapter 6) is an effective technique for building this list. Remember that during brainstorming, the goal is to generate as many ideas as possible without judging them. Research can also be a good way to find out how other individuals or groups may have handled similar problems.

Select the Best Solution

After your group has developed a number of potential solutions, evaluate the advantages and disadvantages of each based on the criteria you've defined.

After a group has reached a consensus, it often needs to communicate its findings to others. In the following section, we explain how to plan and deliver effective group presentations.

DELIVERING GROUP PRESENTATIONS

To share its ideas with an audience, a group may select from several common approaches, including a *symposium*, a *panel discussion*, or a presentation by a *single group representative*. In this section, we offer tips for using each of these three approaches.

Symposium

During a **symposium**, in which several or all group members speak to the audience in turn, each group member takes responsibility for delivering a different part of the presentation, depending on her or his expertise or interest or the needs of the group. For example, suppose that a product team at a computer company wants to propose a design for a new hand-held device to its research and development department. One member might describe the competing handheld designs the team used as reference points for its own design. Another member might then present the technical resources that will be required to manufacture the device. And a third member might conclude the presentation by sharing the group's thoughts about how to minimize the costs of producing the design.

If your group has decided to use this presentation format, plan your symposium carefully. Make sure everyone in the group agrees on the topic that each speaker will address and the time she or he will take. Check that all members know what will go into each presentation, so that no one unwittingly repeats points made by someone else (or forgets to mention important ideas).

When you participate in a symposium, avoid speaking longer than your allotted time. Otherwise, subsequent speakers may have insufficient time to deliver their parts of the presentation. Also, treat other speakers' ideas with respect. If you need to mention points on which group members disagree, present others' ideas in a professional manner, without judging the individuals who advocate those ideas.

As you close your part of the presentation, make sure to introduce the next speaker briefly and note any connections between topics in your transition. As a courtesy to both the next speaker and the audience, introduce the speaker by name.

Like a speech by an individual, an effective symposium has an introduction, a body, and a conclusion. In addition to presenting her or his ideas, the first speaker should begin with an introduction that gains the audience's attention, reveals the topic of the presentation, establishes credibility, connects with the audience, and previews the main idea that each subsequent speaker will develop. The final speaker should conclude by summarizing each presenter's main idea and leaving the audience with a memorable clincher.

Panel Discussion

In a **panel discussion**, members engage in discourse with one another, observed by the audience. Group members sit at a table and speak as if conversing among themselves, while the audience watches and listens. There may be time for audience questions after the discussion, but the panel members' primary role is to speak, and the audience's primary role is to listen. For example, a professor might ask a team of students to come back the next semester and conduct a panel discussion for a new class about a research project they successfully conducted.

A panel discussion usually requires a **moderator** who introduces each **panelist** (participant) and facilitates the discussion. The moderator's role is similar to that of a leader in a group discussion. He or she monitors the time, asks questions that keep the discussion moving, and ensures that each panel member has an opportunity to participate. A

moderator also may participate in the discussion, although he or she should not dominate the presentation.

Panel participants, too, should contribute to the discussion without monopolizing the presentation. It is important to participate if you have special experience or expertise with the point being made. If you have less information on a given issue or you have been speaking more than other members, give other panelists the opportunity to talk. Also, be tactful and professional when disagreeing with another member's point.

The atmosphere in a panel discussion is usually more casual than that in a symposium, and panelists may interact with the speaker, make comments, or ask questions. Talk about the panel discussion in advance with your group so that you all know which questions or topics you want to bring up. That way, the group will be well prepared and able to prioritize the most important issues to be covered.

Single Group Representative

Sometimes one person will be responsible for presenting on behalf of the entire group. If your group has selected this format, keep the following considerations in mind.

First, check that your group has discussed and decided on the best approach for the presentation. Which person is most qualified to present the group's opinions? Who would have the most effective delivery? Is this a topic that requires the ethos or authority of a group leader or a group member with particular expertise? Select the member who best meets these criteria.

Second, if you're the person chosen to give the presentation, be sure

your group has carefully thought through all aspects of the speech. There's an important difference between a speech that you prepare, research, and deliver yourself and one that emerges from a group: in the latter instance, the group contributes substantially to the invention process. Get input from all group members before you start preparing the presentation, and solicit their feedback after you outline your speech.

Third, as you are delivering the talk, take care to distinguish whether you are representing your own views, the views of some members of the group, or a consensus of all group members. Be fair and accurate when summarizing other members' viewpoints. Acknowledge other members' good ideas rather than presenting them as your own.

CHAPTER REVIEW

> **Several heads are better than one.**

An effective group discussion requires skillful leadership and constructive participation. The leader must manage key elements of group dynamics, including the flow of the discussion. She or he has to ensure that all perspectives receive consideration, encourage participation, keep the group on task, and minimize interpersonal conflict. In terms of group members, the most effective focus on task- and maintenance-oriented roles and avoid self-oriented ones. They actively share their ideas, consider one another's viewpoints, constructively participate, and help the group reach a sound decision—perhaps through the five-step reflective-thinking process.

Groups may present their findings in a symposium, during which each member presents part of the group's message. At other times, the group may use a panel discussion format, in which there is less formal structure and more give-and-take among members. In either case, thorough preparation will allow each member to know who will present which topics.

If you're called on to deliver a presentation for your entire group, preparation will again help ensure that you're accurately reflecting the group's decisions, opinions, or findings. Be sure to get input from other group members while preparing the presentation, and acknowledge other members' viewpoints as you're giving the speech.

 LaunchPad
macmillan learning

LaunchPad for *Speak Up* offers videos and encourages self-assessment through adaptive quizzing. Go to **macmillanhighered.com/speakup4e** to get access to:

✓ **LearningCurve**
   Adaptive Quizzes

 Video clips that help you understand public speaking concepts

---

Key Terms

small group *610*
group dynamics *610*
designated leader *612*
implied leader *612*
emergent leader *612*
groupthink *617*
heterogeneity *621*

homogeneity *621*
reflective-thinking process *628*
symposium *630*
panel discussion *631*
moderator *631*
panelist *631*

Review Questions

1. Name and describe three types of leaders and the ways they are selected.
2. What are the two main roles of the group leader?
3. What are the three main types of member roles in a group?

4. What six strategies should group members employ to participate in a small group effectively?

5. Explain the five steps of the reflective-thinking process.

6. Describe the three common approaches to group presentations identified in the chapter.

Critical Thinking Questions

1. In what ways do the public speaking skills you have developed in this course increase your ability to participate effectively in groups? Offer specific examples.

2. If you are participating in a group for this speech course, are you performing task-oriented roles, maintenance-oriented roles, or self-oriented roles? Do your roles change depending on the nature and circumstances of the group you are in?

3. How might the reflective-thinking process for groups help you make better decisions on an individual basis?

Activities

1. Watch a television reality competition that involves group projects (such as *Survivor* or *The Apprentice*). Write a brief report that provides five examples of how the individuals in these competitions conform to the group leader and member roles described in the chapter. Then provide one example of how the group dynamic affects their outcomes on a specific task.

2. Make a list of individuals with whom you share a group identity—for example, your classmates in a study group. Is there a leader among you? How did this person come to be the leader? In different circumstances (for example, if all of you volunteered to help with a grassroots political campaign), do you think the leader and group roles would be the same?

3. Have you ever been part of a group that came to a bad decision? Having read the chapter, explain how you would modify your behavior to produce a better outcome if given the chance to redo it.

APPENDIX A
Speech Choices Outlines and Full-Length Speeches

HOW EMIGRANTS USE SMARTPHONES: SPEECH OUTLINE

As you have progressed through the chapters in Speak Up, *you have followed the story of Mia's preparation for her informative speech. Here is a full-sentence outline of her presentation. Mia's hard work at each stage of the process has paid off. She has a well-organized outline that displays her audience adaptation, research, planning of main points, selection of supporting materials, and choice of presentation aids.*

HOW EMIGRANTS USE SMARTPHONES

SPECIFIC PURPOSE   To inform my audience about the crucial importance of smartphones for emigrants to Europe

INTRODUCTION

• Use of rhetorical question for attention-getter

I. Imagine that you are a refugee from a war-torn country, trying to migrate across Europe with what you can carry in your backpack. What would be the most important possession to bring with you? • Most of you have one with you right now. And although your water bottle and the California roll you brought for lunch would help, I'm not referring to these necessities. The answer, for many emigrants, is a smartphone.

[SHOW A VISUAL AID OF A SMARTPHONE SCREEN WITH USEFUL INFO FOR EMIGRANTS.]

II. Today, we'll take a look at how smartphones are central to the success of emigrants' journeys.

III. Many members of this class have their own stories of how their families came to the United States. And most of you are very familiar with a multitude of apps on your own smartphones. So let's put these two ideas together and see why smartphones are so useful for migrants.

IV. I have always been interested in my own family's story of emigration through Europe and on to North America and have been fascinated while researching the twenty-first-century version of this narrative.

V. We'll start by taking a look at the widespread use of smartphones by emigrants, then consider how smartphones are vital to emigrants' journeys, and finally see how smartphones are especially essential in dangerous situations. •

• Mia includes the five components of a good introduction— attention-getter, thesis, relevance to audience, credibility, and preview.

[TRANSITION   So let's begin by observing that smartphones are a prized possession for emigrants.] •

• A transition is noted in brackets.

BODY

I. Smartphones are essential for emigrants.

A. Smartphones are one of the most important possessions of many college students, and our class surveys indicated that many of you spend hours each day on yours. •

B. Smartphones are even more vital for immigrants.

• Subpoints and sub-subpoints are indented properly.

1. Hannah Kozlowska, staff reporter for *Quartz*, indicated on September 14, 2015, that "more than a billion people around the world rely on smartphones and their ubiquitous messaging and social media apps, but none more so than the hundreds of thousands of people who are fleeing war, hunger, and famine in the Middle East and Africa." •

• Mia uses a full citation for each research source and quotation marks for direct quotations.

2. In an October 9, 2015, *MTV News* article, Melita Šunjić, UN Relief and Works Agency senior public information officer, stated that at refugee camps, emigrants not only

ask about where to eat and sleep but also "where they can get WiFi" and "is it possible to help them charge their phones."

[SHOW A VISUAL AID OF MULTIPLE EMIGRANTS CHARGING PHONES.]

3. For example, a music teacher named Osama Aljasem, who had migrated from Syria to Belgrade, Serbia, told the *New York Times* on August 25, 2015, that "every time I go to a new country, I buy a SIM card and activate the Internet and download the map to locate myself." Mr. Aljasem acknowledges that "I get stressed out when the battery even starts to get low." •

• Mia uses a variety of supporting materials, such as lay testimony and a brief example.

4. The need for Internet access can spur creative solutions. When refugees experienced connectivity problems after crossing the border into Croatia, Louise Dewast, a digital news associate for *ABC News* described a unique fix on September 22, 2015. Otvorena Mreža (Project Open Network), a tech start-up, sent "volunteers carry[ing] backpacks with mobile Wi-Fi devices," creating human hotspots.

[SHOW A VISUAL AID OF HUMAN WI-FI HOTSPOTS.]

[TRANSITION   Now that you have seen that many emigrants rely on smartphones, let's take a look at how and why these phones are so helpful.]

II. Smartphones are essential for navigating, negotiating, and communicating in new environments.

A. Imagine that you have just arrived in a country for the first time and you need to cross it on your journey. You don't speak the language, could be all alone, have no local currency, and don't know where you can stay or how to safely travel. What apps on your phones might you use? Don't say "Order a pizza" because the closest Domino's is over one hundred miles away and they won't deliver. And what new

apps would you download before you left? Your
phone could be your lifeline. •

B. Communicating with family members is one
important use of smartphones.

  1. In *Time* magazine, October 19, 2015, news
     photographer Patrick Witty tells the story
     of Rami Shahhoud, who uses his phone to
     connect with his wife and family back in
     Damascus. Rami explains that "if it were
     five years ago, they'd maybe be thinking
     what's happening to me and I'd be wonder-
     ing what's happening to them. . . . But now,
     thank God for this technology."

  2. Emigrants who have become separated
     from family members can use the Red Cross
     Web site, Trace the Face: Migrants in Europe,
     to post their own picture or search for pic-
     tures of loved ones that have been posted.

  3. Another helpful app is a foreign currency
     conversion calculator. •

     a. Picture yourself newly arrived in Mace-
        donia with $1,000—your life savings. If
        a trader offers you 30,000 Macedonian
        denars for these dollars, the right deci-
        sion could determine whether you can
        afford to make it through Macedonia
        and on to your ultimate destination.
        That sounds like a lot of denars. Should
        you make this deal? •

[SHOW A VISUAL AID WITH THIS EQUATION AT THE TOP:
$1,000 = _____$ MACEDONIAN DENARS.]

     b. The answer is no!

[SHOW A VISUAL AID WITH THIS EQUATION AT THE TOP: $1,000 =$
54,855 MACEDONIAN DENARS (ON JUNE 16, 2016).]

     c. You would get only about half of what
        your money was worth. No emigrant
        could finance travel for long at this rate.
        Fortunately, as Rob Price, a technol-
        ogy reporter, writes in *Business Insider*,
        September 9, 2015, "foreign currency

Margin notes:

• Relate topic to audience

• Use of signposts in subpoints, such as "another"

• Use of example that engages audience

conversion calculators are [a] popular choice, helping people to avoid getting ripped off as they cross borders and currency areas."

4. After obtaining the right currency, another question is where to eat and stay.

a. Emigrants share this information with one another online. For instance, on September 15, 2015, *CNN* reported the experience of Kenan al Beni and six friends, who relied on Facebook pages from other migrants. These pages included advice about which tent to purchase and directions to a reasonably priced Athens hotel. They relied on social media sites for "everything we need," according to Kenan.

b. Nonprofit organizations' sites also can be accessed. The International Rescue Committee's Web site, Refugee Info, can be accessed for information about lodging, services, and food in a number of different European cities. In *Wired*, December 5, 2015, Rey Rodrigues, the organization's technology coordinator, states, "We're trying to reach as many people in as many spots as possible, to make sure it's not outdated information. . . . My team then goes in to map those services and validate it across peer groups in each city."

5. The next morning, it may be time to move on toward the ultimate destination, and again smartphones play a useful role.

a. Investigative journalist Matthew Brunwasser wrote in the *New York Times*, August 25, 2015, that emigrants "share photos and videos of their journeys taken on their smartphones" with Facebook groups such as How to Emigrate to Europe, which has over 39,000 members.

b. In *The Telegraph*, September 20, 2015, reporters Josie Ensor and Magdy Samaan describe a 120,000-member Facebook group, Karajat Al Mushunti-teen (Travelers Platform), as "an eBay or one-stop shop for migrants" from Africa and the Middle East. On this site, members provide maps with "the best routes and good stopping points on the way." When one route is closed off, this is noted, and new options are suggested. ●

                                     ● Analogy to eBay

[SHOW A VISUAL AID OF EMIGRANTS USING THEIR PHONES TO TAKE A PICTURE OF A MAP.]

[TRANSITION   We have seen how emigrants use smartphones to take care of daily needs. Next, let's look at uses of these phones in riskier situations.]

III. Smartphones help emigrants deal with danger.

   A. One problem is coping with traffickers.

      1. In his *Business Insider* article, Rob Price noted that thanks to apps such as Google Maps, "refugees are able to make their own way like never before, without having to rely on the high prices and often horrendous conditions offered by people-traffickers."

      2. In the previously cited *New York Times*, article, Mohammed Haj Ali of the Adventist Development and Relief Agency concurs that "the traffickers are losing business because people are going it alone, thanks to Facebook."

      3. Smartphones also provide vital information for emigrants who decide to rely on traffickers for all or part of their journey.

         a. Many members of our class have relied on reviews on sites such as Uber and Yelp to make decisions as consumers. ●

         b. And according to social media manager Alessandra Ram in *Wired*, December 5, 2015, social media allows migrants to

                                       ● Use of analogy that will be familiar to audience

review trafficking services and the opportunity to compare prices. Matthew Brunwasser, previously cited, provides an example of one trafficker who offered a half-price discount for young children and received thirty-nine Facebook "likes."

c. In a September 11, 2015, *CNBC* article, Kate Coyer, director of the Civil Society and Technology Project at Central European University, indicates that although online tools may not bring an end to trafficking, they can reduce the "costs and dangers of trafficking."

B. A second danger is crossing the high seas, often in substandard and overcrowded watercraft.

1. In the *World Post*, October 14, 2015, International Rescue Committee press manager Paul Donohoe reports that "the mobile phone has also become a 'fundamental' tool in surviving the harrowing water-crossing from Turkey to Greece, which has claimed almost 3,000 lives in 2015 alone, according to the U.N. Human Rights Council."

• Visual representation of unsafe watercraft

[SHOW A VISUAL AID OF AN OVERCROWDED RAFT AT SEA.] •

2. In *The Independent*, September 3, 2015, reporter Lizzie Dearden related the story of one twenty-year-old emigrant, Firas (the author kept his real name private), describing his experience on a boat that headed to Greece only to have the engine die after one half hour at sea:

> Quickly the boat became full of water and started to sink. . . . So I sent a Whatsapp message giving my GPS and asking them [the Greek coast guard] to help us. . . . Me and my three friends from Syria jumped into the sea. We didn't have any life jackets, just two children's rubber rings for the four of us. . . . The water was very cold,

and the waves were very strong. . . . But I
never lost my faith or my hope. . . . I was
picked up by the coast guard after seven
hours of swimming. . . . I've managed to
call my mother and tell her I made it. •

• A narrative shows the importance of smartphones.

3. Sometimes a smartphone can literally make
the difference between life and death.

[TRANSITION   Today, I hope you have learned more
about how refugees are benefiting from
the use of smartphones.] •

• Use of "have learned" to signpost that the speech is wrapping up

CONCLUSION

I. We have seen that smartphones are a prized possession for many migrants, how they help emigrants with the logistics of their journey through
Europe, and how they are a valued asset in times of
danger. •

• Efficient summary of main points

II. We'll end with the experience of Mohamed, a
twenty-seven-year-old former deejay, as related
on October 3, 2015, by reporter Mallika Rao in the
World Post. •

A. He was adrift with fifty migrants in the Mediterranean Sea after their overcrowded boat lost
its engine. Mohamed had the foresight to wrap
his iPhone in sheets of plastic, and despite
the waves, he was able to get a signal. He used
Maps.me to track the group's latitude and longitude and texted the coordinates to his cousin
Danya in Hawaii.

• Use of compelling anecdote for clincher

[SHOW A VISUAL AID OF A COORDINATES EXCHANGE VIA TEXT
MESSAGE.]

B. Danya's family was able to contact the coast
guard on the Greek island of Chios. These are
the texts that were sent to Mohamed:

[SHOW A VISUAL AID OF THIS TEXT MESSAGE: "WE ARE ON THE
PHONE WITH THE COAST GUARD. THEY ARE COMING."]

[SHOW A VISUAL AID OF THIS TEXT MESSAGE: "THEY SAID THEY
CAN SEE YOU."]

C.   After the coast guard transported Mohamed and his group to Chinos, he soon found a hairdryer to dry the ports on his phone and sent Danya a Facebook message explaining how they had survived.

• Full citation of all sources used in speech in Works Cited (Check with your instructor about his or her preferred citation format.)

Works Cited •

Brunwasser, M. "A Twenty-first-Century Migrant's Essentials: Food, Shelter, Smartphone." *New York Times*, August 26, 2015, A1.

Dearden, L. "Syrian Refugee Tells How He Survived Boat Sinking in Waters Where Aylan Kurdi Drowned." *The Independent*, September 3, 2015, http://www.independent.co.uk/news/world /europe/syrian-refugee-tells-how-he-survived-boat-sinking-in -waters-where-aylan-kurdi-drowned-10484607.html.

Dewast, L. "Volunteers Bring Wi-Fi to Refugees in Europe on Backpacks." *ABC News*, September 22, 2015, http://abcnews .go.com/International/volunteers-bring-wi-fi-refugees-europe -backpacks/story?id = 33953223.

Ensor, J., and M. Samaan. "The Facebook Group Helping Migrants Reach Europe." *The Telegraph*, September 20, 2015, http://www.telegraph.co.uk/news/worldnews/europe /croatia/11877508/The-Facebook-group-helping-migrants -reach-Europe.html.

Graham, L. "How Smartphones Are Helping Refugees in Europe." *CNBC*, September 11, 2015, http://www.cnbc.com/2015/09/11 /how-smartphones-are-helping-refugees-in-europe.html.

International Committee of the Red Cross. *Trace the Face: People Looking for Missing Migrants in Europe*, August 27, 2015, https://www.icrc.org/en/document/trace-face-people-looking -missing-migrants-europe.

International Rescue Committee. *Refugee Info*, 2015, https:// refugeeinfo.eu/.

Kaufman, G. "Young Refugees Are Using Their Smartphones for Way More Than Snapchatting and Selfies." *MTV News*, October 9, 2015, http://www.mtv.com/news/2285755 /refugees-europe-facebook-smartphones-wifi/.

Kozlowska, H. "The Most Crucial Item That Migrants and Refugees Carry Is a Smartphone." *Quartz*, September 14, 2015, http://qz.com/500062/the-most-crucial-item-that-migrants -and-refugees-carry-is-a-smartphone/.

Price, R. "Google Maps Is Putting Europe's Human-Traffickers Out of Business." *Business Insider*, September 9, 2015, http://www .businessinsider.com/refugee-crisis-how-syrian-migrants-use -smartphones-avoid-traffickers-2015-9?r=UK&IR=T.

Ram, A. "Smartphones Bring Solace and Aid to Desperate Refugees." *Wired*, December 5, 2015, http://www.wired.com/2015/12/smartphone-syrian-refugee-crisis/.

Rao, M. "Lost at Sea and Texting for Help." *TheWorldPost*, October 3, 2015, http://www.huffingtonpost.com/entry/syrian-refugees-technology_560c13e2e4b07681270024d9.

Watson, I., C. Nagel, and Z. Bilginsoy. "'Facebook Refugees Chart Escape from Syria on Cell Phones." *CNN*, September 15, 2015, http://www.cnn.com/2015/09/10/europe/migrant-facebook-refugees/.

Witty, P. "Searching for Signal: The Smartphone Is the Refugee's Best Friend." *Time*, October 19, 2015, 56.

⊚ HOW EMIGRANTS USE SMART-PHONES: FULL-LENGTH SPEECH

Imagine that you are a refugee from a war-torn country, trying to migrate across Europe with what you can carry in your backpack. What would be the most important possession to bring with you? Most of you have one with you right now. And although your water bottle and the California roll you brought for lunch would help, I'm not referring to these necessities. The answer, for many emigrants, is a smartphone.

Mia gains audience attention with a rhetorical question.

Today, we'll take a look at how smartphones are central to the success of emigrants' journeys. Many members of this class have their own stories of how their families came to the United States. And most of you are very familiar with a multitude of apps on your own smartphones. So let's put these two ideas together and see why smartphones are

Mia uses facial expressions to reinforce her point.

so useful for migrants. I have always been interested in my own family's story of emigration through Europe and on to North America and have been fascinated while researching the twenty-first-century version of this narrative. We'll get that narrative going by first taking a look at the widespread use of smartphones by emigrants; next, considering how smartphones are vital to emigrants' journeys; and finally,

Mia's gestures help convey her idea.

seeing how smartphones are especially essential in dangerous situations. So let's begin by observing that smartphones are extensively used during emigration.

Smartphones are one of the most important possessions of many college students, and our class surveys indicated that many of you spend hours each day on yours. Smartphones are even more vital for emigrants. Hannah Kozlowska, staff reporter for *Quartz*, indicated on September 14, 2015, that "more than a billion people around the world rely on smartphones and their ubiquitous messaging and social media apps, but none more so than the hundreds of thousands of people who are fleeing war, hunger, and famine in the Middle East and Africa."

In an October 9, 2015, *MTV News* article, Melita Šunjič, a United Nations Relief and Works Agency senior public information officer, stated that at refugee camps, emigrants not only ask about where to eat and sleep but also "where they can get WiFi" and "is it possible to help them charge their phones."

For example, a music teacher named Osama Aljasem, who migrated from Syria to Belgrade, Serbia, told the *New York Times* on August 25, 2015, that "every time I go to a new country, I buy a SIM card and activate the Internet and download the map to locate myself." Mr. Aljasem acknowledges that "I get stressed out when the battery even starts to get low."

Mia speaks extemporaneously, glancing at her notes occasionally for reference.

The need for Internet access can spur creative solutions. When refugees experienced connectivity problems after crossing the border into Croatia, Louise Dewast, a digital news associate for *ABC News*, described a unique fix on September 22, 2015. Otvorena Mreža (Project Open Network), a tech start-up, sent "volunteers carry[ing] backpacks with mobile Wi-Fi devices," creating human hotspots.

Now that you have seen that many emigrants rely on smartphones, let's take a look at how and why these phones are so helpful.

Imagine that you have just arrived in a country for the first time and you need to cross it on your journey. You don't speak the language, could be all alone, have no local currency, and don't know where you can stay or how to travel safely. What apps on your phones might you use? Don't say "Order a pizza" because the closest Domino's is over one hundred miles away and they won't deliver. And what new apps would you download before you left? Your phone could be your lifeline.

Communicating with family members is one important use of smartphones. In *Time* magazine, October 19, 2015, news photographer Patrick Witty tells the story of Rami Shahhoud, who uses his phone to connect with his wife and family back in Damascus. Rami explains that "if it were five years ago, they'd maybe be thinking what's happening to me and I'd be wondering what's happening to them. . . . But now, thank God for this technology." Emigrants who have become separated from family members can use the Red Cross Web site Trace the Face: People Looking for Missing Migrants in Europe to post their own picture or search for pictures of loved ones that have been posted.

Another helpful app is a foreign currency conversion calculator. Picture yourself newly arrived in Macedonia with $1,000—your life savings. If a trader offers you 30,000 denars for these dollars, the right decision could determine whether you can afford to make it through Macedonia and on to your ultimate destination. That sounds like a lot of denars. Should you make this deal?

Mia maintains eye contact while explaining a presentation aid.

The answer is no!

If you accepted the 30,000 denars for your $1,000, you would get only about half of what your money was worth. No emigrant could finance travel for long at this rate. Fortunately, as Rob Price, a technology reporter, writes in *Business Insider*, September 9, 2015, "foreign currency conversion calculators are [a] popular choice, helping people to avoid getting ripped off as they cross borders and currency areas."

After obtaining the right currency, another question is where to eat and stay. Emigrants share this information with one another online. For instance, on September 15, 2015, *CNN* reported the experience of Kenan al Beni and six friends, who relied on the Facebook pages of other migrants. These pages included advice about which tent to purchase and directions to a reasonably priced Athens hotel. They relied on social media sites for "everything we need," according to Kenan.

Nonprofit organizations' sites also can be accessed. The International Rescue Committee's Web site, Refugee Info, can be accessed to find information about lodging, services, and food in a number of different European cities. In *Wired*, December 5, 2015, Rey Rodrigues, the organization's technology coordinator, states that "We're trying to reach as many people in as many spots as possible, to make sure it's not outdated information. . . . My team then goes in to map those services and validate it across peer groups in each city."

The next morning, it may be time to move on toward the ultimate destination, and again smartphones play a useful role. Investigative journalist Matthew Brunwasser wrote in the *New York Times*, August 25, 2015, that emigrants "share photos and videos of their journeys taken on their smartphones" with Facebook groups such as How to Emigrate to Europe, which has over 39,000 members.

In *The Telegraph*, September 20, 2015, reporters Josie Ensor and Magdy Samaan describe a 120,000-member Facebook group, Karajat Al Mushuntiteen (Travelers Platform) as "an eBay or one-stop shop for migrants" from Africa and the Middle East. On this site, members provide maps with "the best routes and good stopping points on the way." When one route is closed off, this is noted, and new options are suggested.

We have seen how emigrants use smartphones to take care of daily needs. Next, let's look at uses of these phones in riskier situations.

One problem is coping with traffickers. In his *Business Insider* article, Rob Price noted that thanks to apps such as Google Maps, "refugees are able to make their own way like never before, without having to rely on the high prices and often horrendous conditions offered by people-traffickers." In the previously cited *New York Times* article, Mohammed Haj Ali of the Adventist Development and Relief Agency concurs that "the traffickers are losing business because people are going it alone, thanks to Facebook."

Smartphones also provide vital information for emigrants who decide to rely on traffickers for all or part of their journey. Many members of our class have relied on reviews on sites such as Uber and Yelp to make decisions as consumers. And according to social media manager Alessandra Ram in *Wired*, December 5, 2015, social media allows migrants to review trafficking services and to compare prices. Matthew Brunwasser, previously cited, provides an example of one trafficker who offered a half-price discount for young children and received thirty-nine Facebook "likes." In a September 11, 2015, *CNBC* article, Kate Coyer, director of the Civil Society and Technology Project at Central European University, indicates that although online tools may not bring an end to trafficking, they can reduce the "costs and dangers of trafficking."

A second danger is crossing the high seas, often in substandard and overcrowded watercraft. In the *World Post*, October 14, 2015, International Rescue Committee press manager Paul Donohoe reports that "the mobile phone has also become a 'fundamental' tool in surviving the harrowing watercrossing from Turkey to Greece, which has claimed almost 3,000 lives in 2015 alone, according to the U.N. Human Rights Council."

Mia's presentation aid conveys the danger of the situation that she describes.

In *The Independent*, September 3, 2015, reporter Lizzie Dearden related the story of a twenty-year-old emigrant that she calls Firas (Dearden kept the man's real name private). He described the experience of being on a boat that was heading to Greece when the engine died after one half hour at sea:

> Quickly the boat became full of water and started to sink. . . . So I sent a Whatsapp message giving my GPS and asking them [the Greek coast guard] to help us. . . . Me and my three friends from Syria jumped into the sea. We didn't have any life jackets, just two children's rubber rings for the four of us. . . . The water was very cold, and the waves were very strong. . . . But I never lost my faith or my hope. . . . I was picked up by the coast guard after seven hours of swimming. . . . I've managed to call my mother and tell her I made it.

So you can see that a smartphone can literally make the difference between life and death.

Today, I hope you have learned more about how refugees are benefiting from the use of smartphones. We have seen that smartphones are a prized possession for many migrants, how they help emigrants with the logistics of their journey through Europe, and how they are a valued asset in times of danger.

Mia's nonverbal expressions enhance her delivery.

Mia concludes with a compelling narrative.

We'll end with the experience of Mohamed, a twenty-seven-year-old former deejay, as related on October 3, 2015, by reporter Mallika Rao in the *World Post*. He was adrift with fifty migrants in the Mediterranean Sea after their overcrowded boat lost its engine. Mohamed had the foresight to wrap his iPhone in sheets of plastic, and despite the waves, he was able to get a signal. He used Maps.me to track the group's latitude and longitude and texted the coordinates to his cousin Danya in Hawaii. Danya's family was able to contact the coast guard on the Greek island of Chios. They texted Mohamed. After the Greek coast guard transported Mohamed and his group to Chinos, he soon found a hairdryer to dry the ports on his phone and sent Danya a Facebook message explaining how they had survived.

WHY STUDENT ATHLETES SHOULD BE PAID: SPEECH OUTLINE

As you have progressed through the chapters in Speak Up, *you also have followed the story of Jacob and his persuasive speech assignment. Unfortunately, Jacob did not invest as much time as Mia did in preparing his speech, and he did not make as much of an effort as she did to follow the instructor's directions or the advice provided in class and in the textbook. As a result, Jacob did not follow an outline format, which made the structure of his presentation hard to determine. The limited research that he did was not properly cited or quoted in the speech, care was not taken in selecting supporting materials, and his message was not tailored to his audience.*

INTRODUCTION •

My favorite college basketball team is the Kentucky Wildcats, and when they won the national championship game sixty-seven to fifty-nine over Kansas in 2012, their star player Anthony Davis filled up the stats sheet with six points, sixteen rebounds, five assists, six blocked shots, and three steals. Nobody had done that in any college game since Minnesota's Joel Prizybilla in 2000. • The only bad thing about that is that after just one year in college, Anthony Davis left school to turn pro, signing a multimillion-dollar contract with the New Orleans Hornets. If only he could have been paid to continue playing college ball! This shows why we need to pay college athletes in revenue-producing sports—because they are the men who make the big bucks and receive so little in return. •

I am credible on this topic because I know a lot about sports. I played baseball in high school, and I interviewed my roommate, who used to play football for our school. I watched *Last Week with John Oliver* and read a *Forbes* online article by a commentator on sports legal issues and did some more research. • And I know you guys agree with me because look at how many people go to football, basketball, and baseball games at our school. •

[TRANSITION] •

I don't think there is any doubt that players in revenue-producing sports give up a lot to play their sports. According to my research: •

- The typical Division I college football player devotes 43.3 hours per week to his sport—3.3 more hours than the typical American workweek.
- Although the NCAA claims that college athletes are just students, the NCAA's own tournament schedules require college athletes to miss classes

---

Margin notes:

• Specific purpose not included

• No source cited for statistics

• Parts of the introduction should be labeled I, II, III, IV, and V.

• The list of sources is insufficient. Sources must be cited where used in speech.

• No preview of main points

• Transitions should be word-for-word, and main points should be a single sentence.

• Research for these facts is not cited, and quotation marks are not used for directly quoted material.

for nationally televised games that bring in revenue.

- Currently, the NCAA Division I football championship is played on a Monday night. This year, the national football championship game required Florida State football players to miss the first day of spring classes.

• The speech structure should be in alphanumeric format, not bullet points.

- Meanwhile, the annual NCAA men's basketball tournament affects more than six days of classes (truly "Madness" if the players aren't "employees"). •

• No title for this main point, nor is it labeled "II"

[TRANSITION Who gets rich off college sports? Not the guys who make it happen on the field.] •

- The NCAA currently produces nearly $11 billion in annual revenue from college sports—more than the estimated total league revenues of both the National Basketball Association and the National Hockey League.

- This year, the University of Alabama reported $143.3 million in athletic revenues—more than all thirty NHL teams and twenty-five of the thirty NBA teams. •

• Source not cited for these facts and statistics

- The year that Boston College quarterback Doug Flutie won the Heisman Trophy as the nation's outstanding college football player, Boston College's undergraduate admissions increased by twenty-five points, and its average SAT score of admitted freshmen skyrocketed by 110 points.

- Of course, there are many colleges that use their athletes as core marketers of the university. If not for college basketball players, think about how much more money Gonzaga University would need to spend on building name recognition to prospective students not located on the West Coast.

• Interview research should be directly quoted in the outline.

This is my roommate's point, too—the one who played football for our school. (Talk about what my roommate said) •

•The lack of outline format makes it unclear which ideas are main points or subpoints.

Here's another problem: •

- At other schools, college coaches regulate student-athlete speech on Facebook and Twitter—even when their sport is not in session.

This is America, and the last time that I checked, we have freedom of speech. Americans fought and died for freedom of speech. It just isn't right to tell athletes what they can and cannot say on social media. • It is none of the school's business. Nobody tells students on an art scholarship or a band scholarship or a math scholarship what they can and cannot say on Facebook. This is discrimination, and it isn't right.

•The social media point is not subordinate to the thesis.

So the question is, "What are we going to do about it?" I'll tell you what we need to do about it. These guys are being treated unfairly. They sacrifice everything for the game, and they get little to nothing in return. • Revenue-producing sports should not be propping up the rest of the athletic department. The football team averages 29,517 fans, men's basketball gets 11,583, and baseball draws 5,973. How do our untraditional sports draw? Not even half that many. I'm not trying to be rude or offend anyone, but let's face it: not every sport is exciting. Players who are bringing in the fans are the ones who deserve to be paid for their hard work. •

• Frequent references to "guys" and "men" disrespects female athletes and other women in the audience.

My solution. Players in the revenue-producing sports should be paid a salary of $35,310. I got this amount because it is three times the federal poverty level, according to healthcare.gov. • And their tuition should be free. I'm not saying that college players need to be millionaires. I am saying that this would be a reasonable amount of money to live off of while you are in school. And I am saying when you are working a full-time job for your college, you deserve to get paid full-time wages. •

• The speech needs a full transition to the next main point.

• The research source is not fully cited.

So I'll tell you what I am trying to say. Right now, players in revenue-producing sports are making a lot of money for their schools. They are working a full-time job, and their colleges are getting rich off of them. • The conclusion is obvious. Student athletes need to be paid a salary. That's what I have to say. •

• No transition to conclusion

• No clear summary of main points

• The clincher does not provide a memorable end to the speech.

• Reference
format
inconsistent,
no style manual
followed

Bibliography •

Marc Edelman (Jan. 30, 2014). 21 Reasons Why Student Athletes
    are Employees and should be allowed to Unionize, Forbes
    .com
Last Week with John Oliver, 2015
Interview with my roommate Rick

• Citations are
incomplete.

healthcare.gov •
"UK's Anthony Davis Leaves his mark, espn.com
@MarkKobaCNBC, What a College Athlete is Worth on the open
    Market, 12 Apr 2014 •

• This source
was not used in
the speech and
should not be in
the works cited.

▶ STUDENT ATHLETES SHOULD BE PAID: FULL-LENGTH SPEECH

Jacob presents his attention-
getter with enthusiasm.

Jacob's facial expressions
convey his interest in the topic.

My favorite college basketball team is the
Kentucky Wildcats. And when they won
the national championship game with a
score of sixty-seven to fifty-nine over Kansas
in 2012, their star player Anthony Davis
filled up the stats sheet with six points, sixteen rebounds, five assists, six blocked shots,
and three steals. Nobody had done that in
any college game since Minnesota's Joel
Prizybilla in 2000.

The only bad thing about that is that
after just one year in college, Anthony
Davis left school to turn pro, signing a multimillion-dollar contract with the New Orleans Hornets. If only he could have been
paid to continue playing college ball! This
shows why we need to pay college athletes
in revenue-producing sports—because they
are the men who make the big bucks and
receive so little in return.

I am credible on this topic because I know a lot
about sports. I played baseball in high school, and I interviewed my roommate, who used to play football for our
school. I watched *Last Week with John Oliver*, read a *Forbes*
online article by a commentator on sports legal issues, and
did some more research.

And I know you guys agree with me because look at how many people go to football, basketball, and baseball games at our school.

I don't think there is any doubt that players in revenue-producing sports give up a lot to play their sports. According to my research,

- The typical Division I college football player devotes 43.3 hours per week to his sport—3.3 more hours than the typical American work- week.

Jacob checks his note cards to get his statistics right.

- Although the National Collegiate Athletic Association (NCAA) claims that college athletes are just students, the NCAA's own tournament schedules require college athletes to miss classes for nationally televised games that bring in revenue.
- Currently, the NCAA Division I football championship is played on a Monday night. This year, the national football championship game required Florida State football players to miss the first day of spring classes.
- Meanwhile, the annual NCAA men's basketball tournament affects more than six days of classes (truly "Madness" if the players aren't "employees").

Who gets rich off college sports? Not the guys who make it happen on the field.

The NCAA currently produces nearly $11 billion in annual revenue from college sports—more than the estimated total league revenues of both the National Basketball Association (NBA) and the National Hockey League (NHL).

Jacob holds his notes in one hand and gestures with the other.

This year, the University of Alabama reported $143.3 million in athletic revenues—more than all thirty NHL teams and twenty-five of the thirty NBA teams.

The year that Boston College quarterback Doug Flutie won the Heisman Trophy as the nation's outstanding college football player, Boston College's undergraduate admissions increased by twenty points, and its average SAT score of admitted freshmen skyrocketed by 110 points.

Of course, many colleges use their athletes as core marketers of the university. If not for college basketball players, think about how much more money Gonzaga University would need to spend on building name recognition to prospective students not located on the West Coast.

Jacob's eye contact keeps him connected to the audience.

This is my roommates' point too—the one who played football for our school. He says, "Yeah, athletes should be paid. Going to practice and playing games feels like a full-time job. We fill up the stadium, and they make millions of dollars. The scholarships are so low that you always run out of money before the end of the month."

Here's another problem:

At other schools, college coaches regulate student-athlete speech on Facebook and Twitter—even when their sport is not in session.

This is America, and the last time that I checked, we have freedom of speech. Americans fought and died for freedom of speech. It just isn't right to tell athletes what they can and cannot say on social media. It is none of the school's business. Nobody tells students on an art scholarship or a band scholarship or a math scholarship what they can and cannot say on Facebook. This is discrimination, and it isn't right.

So the question is, "What are we going to do about it?" I'll tell you what we need to do about it. These guys are being treated unfairly. They sacrifice everything for the game, and they get little to nothing in return. Revenue-producing sports should not be propping up the rest of the athletic department. The football team averages 29,517 fans, men's basketball gets 11,583, and baseball draws 5,973. How do our untraditional sports draw? Not even half that many. I'm not trying to be rude or offend anyone, but let's face it: not every sport is exciting. Players who are bringing in the fans are the ones who deserve to be paid for their hard work.

Jacob models extemporaneous delivery, looking up from his notes often.

My solution: Players in the revenue-producing sports should be paid a salary of $35,310. I got this amount because it is three times the federal poverty level, according to healthcare.gov. And their tuition should be free. I'm not saying that college players need to be millionaires. I am saying that this would be a reasonable amount of money to live off of while you are in school. And I am saying when you are working a full-time job for your college, you deserve to get paid full-time wages.

So I'll tell you what I am trying to say. Right now, players in revenue-producing sports are making a lot of money for their schools. They are working a full-time job, and their colleges are getting rich off of them. The conclusion is obvious. Student athletes need to be paid a salary. That's what I have to say.

Jacob wraps up his speech with confidence.

APPENDIX B
Additional Sample Speeches

SAMPLE PERSUASIVE SPEECH

Ⓒ CHILD SLAVERY AND THE PRODUCTION OF CHOCOLATE

David Kruckenberg
Santiago Canyon College

Student David Kruckenberg presented this speech in the finals of the Phi Rho Pi National Tournament in 2007. David uses a problem-cause-solution format to address the compelling issue of child labor in the production of chocolate. He uses diverse reasoning strategies and consistently documents his claims with evidence. David's speech is well organized, with a clear preview and transitions between each main point. His audience-centered solution demonstrates how each of us can be personally involved in addressing the problem.

I was forced to stay in a large room with other children from a neighboring plantation. I tried to run away, but I was caught. As punishment they cut my feet; I had to work for weeks while my wounds healed.

• Attention-getter: A shocking first-person quotation plus evidence that the problem is growing

This moving testimony may sound like past history, when slavery was prevalent. But these words are not a reminder of the past. They're found in the April 24, 2006, issue of *Forbes* magazine. These are the words of an enslaved boy working in the cocoa fields of the country of Côte d'Ivoire, also known as the Ivory Coast. And he is not alone. UNICEF reports in February 2006 that child trafficking is on the rise in this African region. •

A-22

It may surprise you to learn that the last chocolate you ate may well have been tainted with child slavery. Despite the promises and agreements made in recent years by chocolate companies, they continue to use child labor in the production of their chocolate. We as consumers must communicate that this is unacceptable. •

To do so, we will first reveal the connection between chocolate and child slavery, second examine why the problem continues, and finally discover just how much power we have in bringing child slavery to an end.

How are chocolate and child slavery connected? •

Cocoa bean production is limited to areas near the equator, such as Central America, Indonesia, and the Ivory Coast. The International Cocoa Initiative Web site, last updated on February 8, 2007, explains that with almost a million acres devoted to growing cocoa, the Ivory Coast accounts for more than 40 percent of world cocoa production. According to a November 10, 2006, report by the *Vancouver Sun*, because growing cocoa is labor-intensive and labor is a significant part of the cost of production, many farmers in the Ivory Coast have turned to using forced child labor to cut costs.

The conditions of these children are beyond comprehension. The International Cocoa Initiative details the hazards they face each day. They must work long hours in the fields in brutal conditions. They clear fields with machetes and apply pesticides without protective gear. After harvesting the cocoa pods, they must split them open with heavy knives. Once the beans are dried and bagged, they must carry these large loads long distances on their young backs.

Even more alarming is just how many children are forced to live this life. The *New York Times* of October 26, 2006, reports that more than 200,000 children in the Ivory Coast are forced to work in the cocoa fields. The *Chicago Tribune* of May 5, 2006, reports that in contrast to the rest of the world, this region of Africa has the highest rate of child laborers of all children five to fourteen years old; more than one in four are forced to work. Earth Save International, last updated February 14, 2007, says that these children are either enticed with promises of good wages and easy work or outright kidnapped. One example is a boy named Molique, who came to the Ivory Coast at the age of fourteen.

• David connects with the audience and presents his thesis.

• Preview statement and transition to first main point

- Combination of examples to build pathos and statistics to document the extent of the problem

- Transition to main point II

- Causal reasoning

- Blood chocolate: A compelling analogy to blood diamonds

Despite the promises, he was never paid. When he asked to be paid, he was beaten. He had to scavenge for food and at night was locked up with the other kids. The *New York Times* of October 29, 2006, says that almost twelve thousand children in the Ivory Coast have been trafficked far from their families' homes and into slavery. •

The growing use of child slavery is reprehensible, but why is it allowed to continue? The answer is our widespread and growing demand for chocolate. •

Unfortunately, child slavery continues because our demand for chocolate continues, enabling the Ivory Coast and the chocolate companies to ignore the problem. Farmers in the Ivory Coast invest in cocoa for its large profits. In order to maximize their gain, they cut costs by using the forced labor of children. These 600,000 farmers then turn to large export companies in the Ivory Coast to buy their cocoa. The *New York Times* of October 26, 2006, reports that these export companies are able to keep the price that they pay for cocoa low because they have so many farmers to choose from. The exporters then sell their cocoa to large chocolate companies, such as Hershey's, Nestle, M&M/Mars, and Cadbury. •

The *Calgary Herald* of November 17, 2006, tells us that in 2001, almost all of the big chocolate companies signed the Harkin-Engel Protocol, agreeing that by 2005 they would certify that their chocolate was not tainted with child slavery; however, this deadline passed two years ago, with the companies making excuses and saying they need more time. But the September 20, 2006, *Seattle Post-Intelligencer* suggests that they're more concerned about the civil war in the Ivory Coast interfering with their supply of cocoa. Clearly, the civil war is also the top priority with the Ivory Coast government. The Associated Press on June 15, 2006, explains that the government doesn't want to interfere with the supply of cocoa because export taxes are its primary source of revenue. The government uses this money to buy military arms and equipment. The Ivory Coast may not have blood diamonds, but the nation certainly possesses blood chocolate. •

Ultimately, the blame rests on us because consumer demand for chocolate keeps the industry insulated from pressure. The World Cocoa Foundation Web site, last updated February 14, 2007, tells us that North America and Europe consume nearly two-thirds of all cocoa products and that demand for confectionary products containing chocolate rises 4 to 5 percent each year. The sad truth is that most consumers are not aware of chocolate's connection to child slavery. Because we continue to buy its chocolate, the industry feels no urgency to change. •

Now that we understand the problem and why it continues, we must ask what we can do, and the answer is simple. We must stop buying slave-produced chocolate.

But don't worry, I'm not suggesting that we stop buying chocolate altogether. There is an alternative, and it's called fair trade chocolate. TransFair USA, a nonprofit organization, is the only independent third-party certifier of fair trade products in the U.S. It allows companies to display the fair trade–certified label on products that meet strict standards. Some of these standards found on the organization's Web site, last updated November 16, 2006, include a prohibition on forced child labor, safe working conditions, living wages, environmentally safe farming methods, a guaranteed minimum price, and direct trade between the farmers and chocolate companies, thus eliminating the manipulative exporters. •

If we as consumers change how we buy chocolate, the industry will have to respond. Currently, companies are trying to distance themselves from the bad press associated with slave labor, and as a result the Ontario *Guelph Mercury*, February 3, 2007, reports that some have begun to buy into the fair trade market. For example, *Business Wire*, October 11, 2006, reports that Ben and Jerry's is expanding its fair trade–certified ice cream flavors. *Forbes* magazine, previously cited, says that fair trade has even made inroads into the Ivory Coast but still accounts for only about 1 percent of cocoa exports. •

Economics teaches us that demand controls supply; they can only sell what we buy. A perfect example of this is the industry's response to the rise in demand for organic food products. The *Boston Herald* on October 16, 2006, reports that organic food sales have risen more than 15 percent in the last two years. According to the September 20, 2006,

• Evidence shows that the speaker and audience members are part of the problem.

• How the audience can be personally involved in the solution

• David explains how one solution can reduce the problem.

Sacramento Bee, with a multibillion-dollar market, big companies like Walmart and Frito-Lay have made organic food mainstream. If we demand more fair trade chocolate, the industry will have to supply it, and when the chocolate companies start buying more slave-free cocoa, farmers in the Ivory Coast will have to abandon slavery to keep their buyers. •

• Analogy to consumer-generated demand for organic products

Today we have exposed the connection between chocolate and child slavery, examined why the problem continues, and finally discovered how we can bring it to an end. The next time you go to buy chocolate, remember the words of a child, quoted in the November 10, 2006, *Toronto Star*: "When the rest of the world eats chocolate, they're eating my flesh." The Ivory Coast may be seven thousand miles away, but we have a responsibility to protect all children. Fair trade chocolate may cost us a little more money, but that's a small price to pay to free thousands of children from slavery. •

• The clincher includes another compelling quotation that connects to the introduction.

SAMPLE PERSUASIVE SPEECH

RECLAIMING PUBLIC SPACES FOR THE EMPOWERMENT OF WOMEN AND GIRLS

Michelle Bachelet

Michelle Bachelet, former executive director of UN Women (2010–2013) and the first female president of Chile, presented this speech during a Side Event for the Commission on the Status of Women, March 7, 2013.

Ladies and gentlemen,

I am pleased to be with you as we gather to talk about a subject critical to the well-being of millions of women and girls around the globe. This subject seems, at first glance, so simple and straightforward that we take it often for granted. It is about the ability of women and girls to be safe in public spaces. • It's about being able to wait for a bus, ride a subway, sell goods in a marketplace, walk to school, be in the school or a store or a voting booth, swim in a pool, visit a

• Here Bachelet gives a precise topic statement.

friend—safely and peacefully. • But so often, women and girls are in fear of public spaces: they get accosted, threatened, harassed, or assaulted.

• This sentence lists the ways that women should be able to occupy a public space. Each example reinforces and explains the main topic statement.

Violence against women and girls takes place every day in public spaces around the globe. Most cases, however, remain hidden—unspoken, unreported, unaddressed. But sometimes . . . sometimes . . . the acts are so horrific that when publicized they draw the outcry, the revulsion, and condemnation of people everywhere, and they rally millions to demand change.

You heard me say it before—this happened last October, when Malala Yousafzai, a fourteen-year-old Pakistani girl, was shot by an assailant who boarded her school bus. It happened in December, when a twenty-three-year-old medical student was robbed, gang-raped, and thrown off a bus in New Delhi. All she wanted to do is get home safely after watching a movie. How many of you here in this room take it for granted to get home safely after an evening out with friends?

And it's not just happening in the evening. It happened last month when Kepari Leniata, a twenty-year-old Papua New Guinea mother, accused of witchcraft, was tortured and burned alive on a public street in broad daylight.

• In this paragraph (and the ones before it), the speaker offers examples of women around the world who paid a price for trying to occupy a public space. These examples qualitatively enrich the significance of her claims.

And it happens everywhere! More than 1 million women are stalked in the United States each year. Women and girls are kidnapped and sold into sexual slavery in Europe. Indigenous women disappear along British Columbia's notorious Route 16, now called "the Highway of Tears." •

Instead of letting ourselves be overwhelmed by the staggering number of these incidents, instead of being paralyzed by the heart-rending stories of each individual victim, instead of being disheartened by what the prevalence of such violence might say about the state of humanity in the twenty-first century . . .

• This comes across as a clear action step. It is direct and memorable.

Let us speak; let us act; let us rise. •

Events like our being together today allow us to share our experiences, our ideas, and our recommendations to aid women and girls, our fellow human beings at risk around the world. • If I have one hope, it is that when you leave this room after our meeting you are determined to take ACTION—to do what you can do to put an end to this.

• Here the use of words like *our* and *us* allow the speaker to suggest common ground with her audience.

We find ourselves at a unique global moment and opportunity. The momentum is there to break through the barriers to ending sexual violence and harassment in public spaces. Research sponsored by the UN Safe Cities Global Initiative, for example, reveals that women and girls identify sexual harassment and fear of violence in public spaces as inhibiting their lives, and they are ready to break their silence about it and collectively move to action. At UN Women, we are committed to working with the members of this panel, the members of this audience, and all people of goodwill to bring experiences, diverse resources, and determination to the table to maximize our impact and serve as a catalyst for change.

UN Women works collaboratively with UN-Habitat, UNICEF, UN Development Programme, and numerous global and local partners—including Huairou Commission, Women in Cities International, Women and HABITAT Network–Latin America, and GROOTS International. We work with many partners in cities across regions to develop innovative strategies to tackle this most important issue. We do this because we know that we have to unite to have greater and faster impact.

New cities are joining in our work all the time—including, most recently, Dublin, Ireland. In fact, our goal was to involve thirty-five cities by 2017, but that goal will be reached this year, in 2013.

And the Safe Cities program is already making a difference. In Quito, Ecuador, for example, women were encouraged to break the silence about their experiences through a public awareness letter-writing campaign. Some ten thousand letters were submitted and resulted in an amended city ordinance recognizing violence against women in public spaces. •

- By including examples of solutions from around the world, the speaker offers a symmetry to her earlier examples of problems from around the world.

In Rio de Janeiro, it's making a difference through the use of mapping technologies to identify safety concerns in ten of the city's high-risk areas.

And it's making a difference in Port Moresby, Papua New Guinea, where women organized a market vendor association, and local government invested in improvements to ensure safety and a cleaner working environment.

I am excited and encouraged every day by the progress I see around me in this area. I know we have a long way to go, but change is happening. I thank you for being here, and I thank you for all you do. I look forward to our conversation today and tomorrow and to our actions for many days to come. Let us work together for freedom and justice for all women and girls.

NOTES

Chapter 1

1. J. Williams, "Malala Yousafzai and the BBC," *BBC News*, October 19, 2012, http://www.bbc.co.uk/blogs/theeditors/2012/10/malala_yousafzai_and_the_bbc.html.

2. "Desmond Tutu Announces Nominees Children's Peace Prize 2011," *Kids Rights*, October 25, 2011, http://www.kidsrights.org/News/tabid/121/articleType/ArticleView/articleId/43/Desmond-Tutu-announces-nominees-Childrens-Peace-Prize-2011.aspx.

3. M. Gibson, "Malala Yousafzai Gives Her First Public Address Just Months after Being Shot in the Head by the Taliban," *Time NewsFeed*, February 4, 2013, http://newsfeed.time.com/2013/02/04/watch-malala-yousafzai-gives-her-first-public-address-just-months-after-being-shot-in-the-head-by-the-taliban.

4. M. Yousafzai, "Nobel Lecture," *Nobelprize.org*, December 10, 2014, http://www.nobelprize.org/nobel_prizes/peace/laureates/2014/yousafzai-lecture_en.html.

5. NACE, "Employers Cite Communication Skills as Key, but Say Many Job Seekers Lack Them," *NACEWeb*, April 26, 2006, http://www.naceweb.org/press/display.Asp?year + &prid + 235.

6. R. H. Whitworth and C. Cochran, "Evaluation of Integrated versus Unitary Treatments for Reducing Public Speaking Anxiety," *Communication Education* 45 (1996): 306.

7. D. J. DeNoon, "Help for Public-Speaking Anxiety," *CBS News Healthwatch*, April 20, 2006, http://www.cbsnews.com/stories/2006/04/20/health/webmd/main1523045.shtml.

8. G. D. Kuh, N. Jankowski, S. O. Ikenberry, and J. Kinzie, *Knowing What Students Know and Can Do: The Current State of Student Learning Outcomes Assessment in U.S. Colleges and Universities* (National Institute for Learning Outcomes Assessment, January 2014), 14.

9. National Association of Colleges and Employers, "The Skills/Qualities Employers Want in New College Graduates," November 18, 2014, https://www.naceweb.org/about-us/press/class-2015-skills-qualities-employers-want.aspx.

10. Heldrich Center for Workforce Development and Center for Survey Research and Analysis, "Making the Grade? What American Workers Think Should Be Done to Improve Education," June 2000, 14.

11. Copley News Service, "Communication Skills Help Win, Keep Health-Care Job," *Fresno Bee*, February 26, 2012, D2.

12. L. Gehrig, "C250 Celebrates Columbians ahead of Their Time," *Columbia 250* (2004), http://c250.columbia.edu/c250_celebrates/remarkable _columbians/lou_gehrig.html.

13. K. Cheney, "Tammy Duckworth Running for Senate," *Politico*, March 30, 2015, http://www.politico.com/story/2015/03/tammy-duckworth-2016 -illinois-senate-bid-116507.html.

14. L. S. O'Leary, "Civic Engagement in College Students: Connections between Involvement and Attitudes," *New Directions for Institutional Research* 162 (2014): 55, 61.

15. M. I. Finley, *Politics in the Ancient World* (New York: Cambridge University Press, 1983), 59, 73.

16. D. Bodde, *China's First Unifier* (Hong Kong: Hong Kong University Press, 1967), 181.

17. A. A. Boahen, "Kingdoms of West Africa," in *From Freedom to Freedom*, ed. M. Bain and E. Lewis (New York: Random House, 1977), 69.

18. G. Welch, "The Authors Who Talked," in Bain and Lewis, *From Freedom to Freedom*, 39.

19. R. T. Oliver, *Culture and Communication: The Problem of Penetrating National and Cultural Boundaries* (Springfield, IL: Charles C. Thomas, 1962), 141.

20. C. Brooks, R. W. B. Lewis, and R. P. Warren, *American Literature: The Makers and the Making*, vol. 1, *Beginnings to 1861* (New York: St. Martin's Press, 1973), 1179.

21. "Lincoln-Douglas Debates of 1858," *Illinois in the Civil War*, 2000, http:// www.illinoiscivilwar.org/debates.html.

22. E. C. DuBois, *The Elizabeth Cady Stanton–Susan B. Anthony Reader* (Boston: Northeastern University Press, 1992), 8.

23. A. Ayres, ed., *The Wisdom of Martin Luther King, Jr.* (New York: Penguin Books, 1993).

24. M. Z. Muhammad, "Students Are the Vanguard of Million Woman March," *Black Collegian* 28 (February 1998): 10; "Million Man March Draws More Than One Million Black Men to Nation's Capital," *Jet*, October 30, 1995, 4.

25. R. M. Berko, A. D. Wolvin, and D. R. Wolvin, *Communicating: A Social and Career Focus*, 3rd ed. (Boston: Houghton Mifflin, 1985), 42.

26. J. Stewart, *Bridges, Not Walls,* 7th ed. (New York: McGraw-Hill, 1999), 16.

27. M. W. Lustig and J. Koester, *Intercultural Competence: Interpersonal Communication across Cultures* (New York: HarperCollins, 1993), 31.

28. "Calvin Coolidge Delivers First Presidential Address on Radio," *New York Times*, December 6, 2011, http://learning.blogs.nytimes .com/2011/12/06/dec-6-1923-calvin-coolidge-delivers-first-presidential -address-on-radio.

29. "First Presidential Speech on TV," http://www.history.com/this-day-in -history/first-presidential-speech-on-tv (accessed May 23, 2012).

30. R. Wolf, "What Will Hillary Clinton's Diplomatic Legacy Be?," *USA Today*, May 18, 2012, 6A.

31. J. H. Bodley, "An Anthropological Perspective," *What Is Culture?*, 1994, http://www.wsu.edu/gened/learn-modules/top_culture/culture-definitions /bodley-text.html.

32. R. Trousen, "13 Percent in U.S. Foreign Born, a Level Last Seen in 1920," *Los Angeles Times*, May 11, 2012.

33. D. Cohn, "Falloff in Births Slows Shift to a Majority-Minority Youth Popula- tion," *Pew Research Center,* June 26, 2014, http://www.pewresearch.org /fact-tank/2014/06/26/falloff-in-births-slows-shift-to-a-majority-minority -youth-population.

34. A. R. Williams, "What's in a Surname?," *National Geographic*, January 19, 2011, http://ngm.nationalgeographic.com/2011/02/geography/usa -surnames-interactive.

35. N. P. Retsinas, "The New Homeowners," *Boston Globe*, July 8, 2007, http:// boston.com/news/globe/editorial_opinion/oped/articles/2007/07/08/the _new_homeowners.

36. Lustig and Koester, *Intercultural Competence*, 11.

37. M. Anderson, "Young Adults More Likely to Say Vaccinating Kids Should Be a Parental Choice," *Pew Research Center,* February 2, 2015, http://www .pewresearch.org/fact-tank/2015/02/02/young-adults-more-likely-to-say -vaccinating-kids-should-be-a-parental-choice.

38. Ibid.; P. J. Smith, S. G. Humiston, E. K. Marcuse, Z. Zhao, C. G. Dorell, C. Howes, and B. Hibbs, "Parental Delay or Refusal of Vaccine Doses, Childhood Vaccination Coverage at Twenty-four Months of Age, and the Health Belief Model," *Public Health Reports* 126 (Suppl. 2) (2011): 135–46.

39. Ibid.

40. J. Bell, *Evaluating Psychological Information: Sharpening Your Critical Thinking Skills,* 2nd ed. (Boston: Allyn and Bacon, 1995), 72, cited in J. Bell, *Critical Thinking as Described by Psychologists,* December 15, 1996, http://academic .pg.cc.md.us/~ wpeirce/MCCCTR/bell1.html (accessed June 12, 2006).

41. C. Morris, *Psychology,* 1993, xv–xvi, cited in Bell, *Critical Thinking as Described by Psychologists.*

42. NCA, "NCA Credo for Ethical Communications," 1999, www.natcom.org /uploadedFiles/About_NCA/Leadership_and_Governance/Public_Policy _Platform/PDF-PolicyPlatform-NCA_Credo_for_Ethical_Communication.pdf.

43. P. Bizzell and B. Herzberg, *The Rhetorical Tradition* (Boston: Bedford/St. Martin's, 1990), 35.

44. Gallup, "Confidence in Institutions," June 5–8, 2014, http://www.gallup .com/poll/1597/confidence-institutions.aspx.

Chapter 2

1. L. G. Davis, *I Have a Dream: The Life and Times of Martin Luther King, Jr.* (Westport, CT: Greenwood Press, 1973).

2. A. Ayres, ed., *The Wisdom of Martin Luther King, Jr.* (New York: Penguin Books, 1993).

3. Davis, *I Have a Dream*, 137.

4. K. D. Miller and E. M. Lewis, "Touchstones, Authorities, and Marian Anderson: The Making of 'I Have a Dream,'" in *The Making of Martin Luther King and the Civil Rights Movement*, ed. B. Ward and T. Badger (New York: New York University Press, 1996), 151.

5. Ayres, *Wisdom of Martin Luther King, Jr.*, 62–63.

6. E. Rothstein, "A Resonance That Shaped a Vision of Freedom," *New York Times*, June 29, 2006, B7.

7. J. F. Wilson and C. C. Arnold, *Public Speaking as a Liberal Art*, 3rd ed. (Boston: Allyn and Bacon, 1974), 337.

8. P. Bizzell and B. Herzberg, *The Rhetorical Tradition* (Boston: Bedford/St. Martin's, 1990), 32, 310.

9. K. K. Dwyer and M. M. Davidson, "Is Public Speaking Really More Feared Than Death?," *Communication Research Reports* 29, no. 2 (2012): 99–107, 106.

10. H. Liao, "Examining the Role of Collaborative Learning in a Public Speaking Course," *College Teaching* 62, no. 2 (2014): 47–54, doi: 10.1080/87567555.2013.855891.

11. Dwyer and Davidson, "Is Public Speaking Really More Feared Than Death?," 100.

12. K. E. Menzel and L. J. Carrell, "The Relationship between Preparation and Performance in Public Speaking," *Communication Education* 43, no. 1 (1994): 17, 24.

13. R. R. Behnke and C. R. Sawyer, "Milestones of Anticipatory Public Speaking Anxiety," *Communication Education* 48, no. 2 (1999): 165, 171.

14. J. C. McCroskey, *An Introduction to Rhetorical Communication* (Englewood Cliffs, NJ: Prentice-Hall, 1986), 31.

15. A. N. Finn, C. R. Sawyer, and P. Schrodt, "Examining the Effect of Exposure Therapy on Public Speaking State Anxiety," *Communication Education* 58, no. 1 (2009): 92–109, 104.

16. C. W. Choi, J. M. Honeycutt, and G. D. Bodie, "Effects of Imagined Interactions and Rehearsal on Speaking Performance," *Communication Education* 64, no. 1 (2015): 25–44, doi: 10.1080/03634523.2014.978795.

17. Ibid., 41.

18. J. Ayres, "Comparing Self-Constructed Visualization Scripts with Guided Visualization," *Communication Reports* 8 (1995): 193–99.

19. C. R. Sawyer and R. R. Behnke, "State Anxiety Patterns for Public Speaking and the Behavior Inhibition System," *Communication Reports* 12 (1999): 34.

20. D. D. Deiters, S. Stevens, C. Hermann, and A. L. Gerlach, "Internal and External Attention in Speech Anxiety," *Journal of Behavior Therapy and Experimental Psychiatry* 44, no. 2 (2013): 143–49, doi: http://dx.doi.org /10.1016/j.jbtep.2012.09.001.

21. C.-F. Hsu, "The Relationships of Trait Anxiety, Audience Nonverbal Feedback, and Attributions to Public Speaking State Anxiety," *Communication Research Reports* 26, no. 3 (2009): 237–46, 244.

Chapter 3

1. See C. G. Christians, "Primordial Issues in Communication Ethics," in *The Handbook of Global Communication and Communication Ethics*, ed. R. S. Fortner (Hoboken, NJ: Blackwell, 2011), 5: "For cultural relativism, morality is a social product. Whatever the majority in a given culture approves is a social good. Since all cultures are presumed to be equal in principle, all value systems are equally valid. Cultural relativity now typically means moral relativism. Contrary to an ethnocentrism of judging other groups against a dominant Western model other cultures are not considered inferior only different."

2. Reuben Navarette, "Donald Trump: A Mexican-American's Take on Businessman's Clownish Presidential Bid," June 24, 2014, http://www.foxnews .com/opinion/2015/06/24/donald-trump-mexican-americans-take.html.

3. Brian Stelter, "Univision Dumps Trump, Cancels Miss USA over His Comments about Mexicans," http://money.cnn.com/2015/06/25/media /univision-donald-trump-mexicans.

4. *Black's Law Dictionary*, 9th ed., s.v. "plagiarism."

5. See N. Granitz and D. Loewy, "Applying Ethical Theories: Interpreting and Responding to Student Plagiarism," *Journal of Business Ethics* 72 (2007): 293: "Through online paper mills (http://www.cheater.com, http://www .schoolsucks.com), Google searches, as well as access to library databases, students literally have a world of information at their fingertips."

6. N. P. Lewis and B. Zhong, "The Personality of Plagiarism," *Journalism and Mass Communication Educator* 66 (December 2011): 327; J. M. Stephens, M. F. Young, and T. Calabrese, "Does Moral Judgment Go Offline When Students Are Online? A Comparative Analysis of Undergraduates' Beliefs and Behaviors Related to Conventional and Digital Cheating," *Ethics and Behavior* 17 (July 2007): 233–54.

7. United States National Park Service, "History Continued," *Statue of Liberty National Monument*, August 14, 2006, http://www.nps.gov/stli/historyculture /history-continued.htm (accessed May 16, 2013).

Chapter 4

1. J. Stewart, *Bridges Not Walls*, 4th ed. (New York: Random House, 1986), 181.

2. G. D. Bodie, D. Worthington, M. Imhof, and L. O. Cooper, "What Would a Unified Field of Listening Look Like? A Proposal Linking Past Perspectives and Future Endeavors," *International Journal of Listening* 22 (2008): 105. For more on this, see also B. R. Burelson, "A Constructivist Approach to Listening," *International Journal of Listening* 25 (2011): 27–41. Burelson describes listening as "a process that involves the interpretation of messages that others have intentionally transmitted in an effort to understand those messages and respond to them appropriately" (27).

3. L. K. Steil, "Listening Training: The Key to Success in Today's Organizations," in *Listening in Everyday Life: A Personal and Professional Approach*, ed. M. Purdy and D. Borisoff (Lanham, MD: University Press of America, 1997), 215.

4. Ibid.

5. O. Hargie, *Skilled Interpersonal Communication: Research, Theory and Practice* (New York: Routledge, 2011), 179–81.

6. Ibid., 180.

7. J. D. Boudreau, E. Cassell, and A. Fuks, "Preparing Medical Students to Become Attentive Listeners," *Medical Teacher* 31 (2009): 22–29.

8. Study by TCC Consulting (San Francisco) undertaken between 1987 and 1997.

9. M. K. Johnston, J. B. Weaver, K. W. Watson, and L. B. Barker, "Listening Styles: Biological or Psychological Differences?," *International Journal of Listening* 14 (2000): 36.

10. E. Langer, "Rethinking the Role of Thought in Human Interaction," in *New Directions in Attribution Research*, vol. 2, ed. H. Hurvey, W. Ickes, and R. Kidd (Hillside, NJ: Erlbaum 1980), 35–38.

11. Johnston et al., "Listening Styles," 37.

12. K. W. Watson and L. L. Barker, *The Listening Style Inventory* (New Orleans: SPECTRA, 1985).

13. K. Watson, L. Barker, and J. Weaver, "The Listening Styles Profile (LPP16): Development and Validation of an Instrument to Assess Four Listening Styles," *International Journal of Listening* 9 (1995): 1–13.

14. Johnston et al., "Listening Styles," 37.

Chapter 5

1. See D. Paul-Pertaub, M. Slater, and C. Barker, "An Experiment on Public Speaking Anxiety in Response to Three Different Types of Virtual

Audience," *Presence* 11, no. 1 (2002): 69: "The smaller the size of the audience, the more the interaction approximates a conversational paradigm."

2. For more on using demographics to craft messages, see D. Therkelsen and C. Fiebach, "Message to Desired Action: A Communication Effectiveness Model," *Journal of Communication Management* 5, no. 4 (2001): 376.

3. Kevin T. Jones, Instructor's Corner #2: "What Presidential Speeches Can Teach Us about Audience Analysis," *Communication Currents* 10, no. 3 (June 2015), http://www.natcom.org/CommCurrentsArticle.aspx?id=6143: "Good audience analysis begins with a clear demographic assessment—age, sex, religion socio-economic status, etc. From this basic assessment, the speaker develops a psychological profile of the audience that identifies beliefs, attitudes and values."

4. Valentina Zarya, "Here's Why Tesla Is Wooing Women—and Will Probably Win Them Over," *Fortune*, September 18, 2015, http://fortune.com/2015/09/18/tesla-model-x-women.

5. The 2015 decision was *Obergefell et al. v. Hodges, Director, Ohio Department of Health* and is available at http://www.supremecourt.gov/opinions/14pdf/14-556_3204.pdf.

6. G. P. Quinn, M. B. Schabath, J. A. Sanchez, S. K. Sutton, and B. L. Green, "The Importance of Disclosure: Lesbian, Gay, Bisexual, Transgender/Transsexual, Queer/Questioning, and Intersex Individuals and the Cancer Continuum," *Cancer* 121, no. 8 (2015): 1160–63, http://onlinelibrary.wiley.com/doi/10.1002/cncr.29203/full4147202169140546.

7. G. Quinn, http://www.jpost.com/Diaspora/Jews-Catholics-celebrate-50th-anniversary-of-Nostra-Aetate-430321.

8. Although Obama and Romney often spoke about middle-class job creation and economic growth, they rarely mentioned the existing poverty rate. See, for example, B. Calvin, "Little Mentioned on Trail, Poverty Widening in US," *Boston Globe*, September 10, 2012, http://www.bostonglobe.com/news/politics/2012/09/09/for-advocates-country-poor-presidential-campaign-gives-little-clarity-addressing-poverty/sZhd9i4Z0gMGahFKxknDXM/story.html.

9. A. Chozick, "Middle Class Is Disappearing, at Least from Vocabulary of 2016 Contenders," *New York Times*, May 11, 2015, http://www.nytimes.com/2015/05/12/us/politics/as-middle-class-fades-so-does-use-of-term-on-campaign-trail.html?_r = 0.

10. Common ground is critical not only because it enhances a speaker's credibility but also because it makes a speech easier to understand. See S. R. Fussell and R. M. Krauss, "Understand Friends and Strangers: The Effects of Audience Design on Message Comprehension," *European Journal of Social Psychology* 19 (1989): 510.

11. For more, see J. S. Tuman, *Communicating Terror: The Rhetorical Dimensions of Terrorism*, 2nd ed. (Thousand Oaks, CA: Sage, 2010), 113:

"Next the creator of the speech may inquire: is there any possibility for common ground between the speaker and the audience?"

12. For more on this speech, go to http://www.americanrhetoric.com /speeches/tedkennedytruth&tolerance.htm.

13. See http://www.religiousherald.org/index.php?option=com_content&task =view&id=3677&Itemid = 53.

Chapter 6

1. S. Liu, "Catching FIRE: Seven Strategies to Ignite Your Team's Creativity," *Quality Progress* 47, no. 5 (2014): 18–24.

2. M. C. Bell, N. Kawadri, P. M. Simone, and M. Wiseheart, "Long-term Memory, Sleep, and the Spacing Effect," *Memory* 22, no. 3 (2014): 276–283, doi: 10.1080/09658211.2013.778294.

3. Illumine Training, "How to Make a Mind Map®," 2015, http://www .mindmapping.co.uk/mind-mapping-information-and-advice/how-to -make-a-mind-map.

4. B. Kirchner, "Mind-Map Your Way to an Idea: Here Is One Approach to Rooting Out Workable Topics That Move You," *Writer* 122, no. 3 (2009): 28–29.

5. J. F. Wilson and C. C. Arnold, *Public Speaking as a Liberal Art*, 3rd ed. (Boston: Allyn and Bacon, 1974), 70–71.

Chapter 7

1. R. D. Rieke and M. O. Sillars, *Argumentation and Critical Decision Making*, 5th ed. (New York: Addison Wesley Longman, 2001), 136.

2. J. C. Reinard, *Foundations of Argument* (Dubuque, IA: Brown, 1991), 113.

3. E. Brynjolfsson, L. M. Hitt, and H. H. Kim, "Strength in Numbers: How Does Data-Driven Decisionmaking Affect Firm Performance?," working paper, April 22, 2011, http://ssrn.com/abstract=1819486.

4. Ibid.

5. J. P. Biddix, J. C. Chung, and H. W. Park. "Convenience or Credibility? A Study of College Student Online Research Behaviors," *Internet and Education* 14 (2011): 176.

6. S. Miller and N. Murillo, "Why Don't Students Ask Librarians for Help? Undergraduate Help-Seeking Behaviors in Three Academic Libraries," in *College Libraries and Student Culture: What We Now Know*, ed. L. Duke and A. Asher (Chicago: American Library Association, 2012), 53.

7. Reinard, *Foundations of Argument*, 115.

8. N. Pastore and M. W. Horowitz, "The Influence of Attributed Motive on the Acceptance of a Statement," *Journal of Abnormal and Social Psychology* 51 (1955): 331–32.

9. "Predictions with a Purpose: Why the Projections of Ebola in West Africa Turned Out Wrong," *The Economist*, February 7, 2015, http://www.economist.com/news/international/21642242-why-projections-ebola-west-africa-turned-out-wrong-predictions-purpose.

10. J. Erickson, "Faulty Modeling Studies Led to Overstated Predictions of Ebola Outbreak," *Michigan News*, March 31, 2015, http://ns.umich.edu/new/releases/22783-faulty-modeling-studies-led-to-overstated-predictions-of-ebola-outbreak.

11. A. J. Head, *Learning the Ropes: How Freshmen Conduct Course Research Once They Enter College*, Project Information Literacy Research Report, December 5, 2013, 10, 13.

12. Pew Internet and American Life Project, *The Internet Goes to College: How Students Are Living in the Future with Today's Technology*, September 15, 2002, http://www.pewinternet.org/PPF/r/71/report_display.asp, 2–3.

13. Primary Research Group, *The Survey of American College Students: Who Goes to the College Library and Why?*, April 2009, http://www.researchandmarkets.com/reportinfo.asp?report_id=888965&t=d&cat_id=.

14. P. Lyman and H. Varian, "How Much Information?," School of Information Management and Systems, University of California at Berkeley, 2003, http://www2.sims.berkeley.edu/research/projects/how-much-info-2003.

15. Netcraft, *January 2015 Web Server Survey*, 2015, http://news.netcraft.com/archives/2015/01/15/january-2015-web-server-survey.html.

16. M. J. Metzger, A. J. Flanagin, and L. Zwarun, "College Student Web Use, Perceptions of Information Credibility, and Verification Behavior," *Computers and Education* 41, no. 3 (November 2003): 271–90.

17. D. Westerman, P. R. Spence, and B. Van Der Heide, "A Social Network as Information: The Effect of System Generated Reports of Connectedness on Credibility on Twitter," *Computers in Human Behavior* 28, no. 1 (2012): 199–206.

18. W. L. Lym, "Tempting Students with Scholarly Research: Breaking the Fast-Food Research Diet," *College Teaching* 57 (Fall 2009): 237.

19. C. Chen et al., "An Assessment of the Completeness of Scholarly Information on the Internet," *College and Research Libraries* 70 (July 2009): 237.

20. E. Fahy et al., "Quality of Patient Health Information on the Internet: Reviewing a Complex and Evolving Landscape," *Australasian Medical Journal* 7, no. 1 (2014): 24–28, doi: 10.4066/amj.2014.1900; R. Hirasawa et al., "Quality and Accuracy of Internet Information Concerning a Healthy Diet," *International Journal of Food Sciences and Nutrition* 64, no. 8 (2013): 1007–13, doi: 10.3109/09637486.2013.812620; B. Reichow, A. Shefcyk, and M. B. Bruder, "Quality Comparison of Websites Related to Developmental Disabilities," *Research in Developmental Disabilities* 34, no. 10 (2013): 3077–83, doi: 10.1016/j.ridd.2013.06.013.

21. ICANN, "Glossary," 2013, www.icann.org/en/about/learning/glossary.

22. J. Newman, "Top-Level Domain Name Grab: ICANN Reveals Results," *PC World*, June 13, 2012, http://www.pcworld.com/article/257549/toplevel _domain_name_grab_icann_reveals_ results.html.

23. C. Barth, "Amazon Just Spent Millions Applying for Domain Names. Why?," *Forbes*, June 13, 2012, http://www.forbes.com/sites/chrisbarth/2012/06/13 /amazon-just-spent-millions-applying-for-domain-names-why.

24. R. Berkman, "Internet Searching Is Not Always What It Seems," *Chronicle of Higher Education* 46 (July 28, 2000): B9.

25. The Virtual Chase, "How to Evaluate Information—Checklist," March 6, 2006, http://virtualchase.justia.com/how-evaluate-information-checklist.

26. H. Francke and O. Sundin, "Negotiating the Role of Sources: Educators' Conceptions of Credibility in Participatory Media," *Library and Information Science Research* 34, no. 3 (2012): 169–75.

27. A. R. Brown, "Wikipedia as a Data Source for Political Scientists: Accuracy and Completeness of Coverage," *PS: Political Science and Politics* 44, no. 2 (2011): 339.

28. Ibid., 340.

29. C. Royal and D. Kapila, "What's on Wikipedia, and What's Not . . . ?," *Social Science Computer Review* 27, no. 1 (2009): 146.

30. "Wikipedia: Academic Use," *Wikipedia*, en.wikipedia.org/wiki/Wikipedia: Academic_use (page last modified May 15, 2013).

31. D. Sullivan, "How Search Engines Work," *Search Engine Watch*, October 14, 2002, http://searchenginewatch.com/webmasters/article.php/2168031.

32. D. Sullivan, "How Search Engines Rank Web Pages," *Search Engine Watch*, July 31, 2003, http://searchenginewatch.com/webmasters/article .php/2167961.

33. comScore, "comScore Releases March 2015 U.S. Desktop Search Engine Rankings," April 15, 2015, http://www.comscore.com/esl/Insights/Market -Rankings/comScore-Releases-March-2015-US-Desktop-Search-Engine -Rankings.

Chapter 8

1. K. E. Rowan, "A New Pedagogy for Explanatory Public Speaking: Why Arrangement Should Not Substitute for Invention," *Communication Education* 44, no. 3 (1995): 236, 241.

2. C. Heath and D. Heath, *Made to Stick: Why Some Ideas Survive and Others Die* (New York: Random House, 2007), 110–11.

3. Ibid., 111.

4. C. C. Mann, *1491: New Revelations of the Americas before Columbus* (New York: Knopf, 2005), 345–49.

5. J. A. Herrick, *Understanding and Shaping Arguments* (State College, PA: Strata Press, 2011), 44.

6. N. Singer, "They Loved Your G.P.A. Then They Saw Your Tweets," *New York Times*, November 9, 2013, 3.

7. C. Choi, "Five Best Practices for Lawfully Monitoring Your Employees' Social Media Activities," *Philadelphia Business Journal*, October 27, 2014, http://www.bizjournals.com/philadelphia/blog/guest-comment/2014/10/5-best-practices-for-lawfully-monitoring-your.html.

8. R. Gallagher, "U.S. Cities Embrace Software to Automatically Detect 'Suspicious' Behavior," *Slate*, June 11, 2012, http://www.slate.com/blogs/future_tense/2012/06/11/aisight_from_brs_labs_ and_other_technologies_to_detect_suspicious_behavior_.html.

9. A. Hicks, "Public Fears Invasion of Privacy by Smart TVs," *Peninsula Press*, February 13, 2015, http://peninsulapress.com/2015/02/13/smart-tvs-privacy.

10. *Cambridge Dictionaries Online*, s.v. "Zoroastrianism," accessed January 31, 2007, http://dictionary.cambridge.org.

11. M. Boyce, *Zoroastrians: Their Religious Beliefs and Practices* (London: Routledge, 1979), 2.

12. Ibid., 2.

13. Ontario Consultants on Religious Tolerance, "Zoroastrianism," Religious-Tolerance.org, March 24, 2005, http://www.religioustolerance.org/zoroastr.htm.

14. College Board, "Average Estimated Undergraduate Budgets, 2014–15," *Trends in Higher Education*, 2015, http://trends.collegeboard.org/college-pricing/figures-tables/average-estimated-undergraduate-budgets-2014-15.

15. J. Reinard, *Foundations of Argument* (Dubuque, IA: Brown, 1991), 111.

16. W. R. Fisher, *Human Communication as Narration: Toward a Philosophy of Reason, Value, and Action* (Columbia: University of South Carolina Press, 1987).

17. S. Buhr, "So I Flew in an 'Uber for Tiny Planes,'" *TechCrunch*, June 20, 2014, http://techcrunch.com/2014/06/20/uber-for-x-in-a-tiny-plane.

18. Cornelia Dean, "In Road-Building, Black Soldiers Defied Prejudice," *New York Times*, July 24, 2012, D4.

19. Rowan, "New Pedagogy," 245.

20. "Science Café: What Is the Higgs Boson?," North Carolina Museum of Natural Sciences, July 13, 2012, http://naturalsciences.org/about-us/news/science-cafe-what-higgs-boson.

21. "New Data from VTTI Provides Insight into Cell Phone Use and Driving Distraction," Virginia Tech Transportation Institute, July 27, 2009, http://www.vtti/vt.edu/PDF/2-22-09-VTTI-Press_Release_Cell_phones_and_Driver_Distraction.pdf.

22. R. M. Felder and B. A. Soloman, "Learning Styles and Strategies," North Carolina State University, http://www.ncsu.edu/felder-public/ILSdir/styles.htm (accessed April 17, 2006).

23. Ibid.

24. R. M. Felder and L. K. Silverman, "Learning and Teaching Styles in Engineering Education," *Engineering Education* 78, no. 7 (1988): 677.

25. S. Gillette, "The Effects of Seductive Details in an Inflatable Planetarium," *Planetarian* 43, no. 4 (December 2014): 26–30.

Chapter 9

1. J. C. McCroskey, *An Introduction to Rhetorical Communication*, 5th ed. (Englewood Cliffs, NJ: Prentice Hall, 1986), 185.

2. J. C. McCroskey, "The Effects of Disorganization and Nonfluency on Attitude Change and Source Credibility," *Speech Monographs* 36 (March 1969): 13–21; and H. Sharp Jr. and T. McClung, "Effect of Organization on the Speaker's Ethos," *Speech Monographs* 33 (June 1966): 182–83.

3. L. M. Simons, "Inside Bollywood," *Smithsonian* 31 (January 2001): 50.

4. C.S.N.H. Murthy, O. B. Meitei, and A. Barua, "Breaking Western Filmmaking Models: An Unexplored Indian Frame of Film Communication—Evidence from Telugu Cinemas," *Journal of Communication Inquiry* 39, no. 1 (January 2015): 38–62.

5. Simons, "Inside Bollywood," 49.

6. T. Ganti, "No Longer a Frivolous Singing and Dancing Nation of Movie-Makers: The Hindi Film Industry and Its Quest for Global Distinction," *Visual Anthropology* 25, no. 4 (July 2012): 340–65.

7. C. S. Hemphill and J. Suk, "The Law, Culture, and Economics of Fashion," *Stanford Law Review* 61 (March 2009): 1147–99, 1158, 1168.

8. T. Ferris, "Planet Fever," *Smithsonian* 43, no. 5 (2012): 32–36.

9. A. Linn, "How to Manage, or Better Yet Avoid, Student Loan Debt," NBCNEWS.com, August 3, 2012, http://lifeinc.today.msnbc.msn.com/_news/2012/03/28/10890912-how-to-manage-or-better-yet-avoid-student-loan-debt?lite.

Chapter 10

1. P. Bizzell and B. Herzberg, *The Rhetorical Tradition* (New York: St. Martin's Press, 1990), 429.

2. K. K. Campbell, *The Rhetorical Act*, 2nd ed. (Belmont, CA: Wadsworth, 1996), 264–65.

3. V. Havel, "Playwright-Dissident Vaclav Havel Assumes the Presidency of Czechoslovakia," in *Lend Me Your Ears: Great Speeches in History*, ed. W. Safire (New York: Norton, 1992), 629–34.

4. United States Department of Agriculture, "ChooseMyPlate." http://www.choosemyplate.gov (accessed July 20, 2015).

5. The Ethicist, "May I Post a Photo of a Bad Driver on Social Media?," *New York Times Magazine*, July 19, 2015, 15.

4. W. Neuman, "Nutrition Plate Unveiled, Replacing Food Pyramid," *New York Times*, June 3, 2011, B3.

5. C. Harada, "A Novel Idea for Cleaning Up Oil Spills," July 2012, http://ted.com/talks/cesar_harada_a_novel_idea_for_cleaning_up_oil_spills.html.

6. C. D'Aniello, "The Wikipedia, Possibilities and Opportunities," January 20, 2012, http://libweb.lib.buffalo.edu/blog/history-us/?p = 1264.

7. L. M. Forquer et al., "Sleep Patterns of College Students at Public University," *Journal of American College Health* 56 (March–April 2008): 563.

8. M. al-Sharif, "The Drive for Freedom," Speech, Oslo Freedom Forum, May 8, 2012, http://www.oslofreedomforum.com/speakers/manal-al-sharif.html.

9. S. Ride, "Shoot for the Stars," May 25, 2012, http://eloquentwoman.blogspot.com/2012/05/famous-speech-friday-sally-rides-shoot.html.

10. R. Clark, *Einstein: The Life and Times* (London: Hodder and Stoughton, 1973), 26.

Chapter 12

1. See also A. A. Braga, D. M. Hureau, and A. V. Papachristos, "Deterring Gang-Related Gun Violence: Measuring the Impact of Boston's Operation Ceasefire on Street Gang Behavior," *Journal of Quantitative Criminology* 30, no. 1 (March 2013): 113–39.

2. One influential industry publication says that the cloud is a "communications network. The word 'cloud' often refers to the Internet, and more precisely to some datacenter full of servers that is connected to the Internet. However, the term 'cloud computing' refers to the software and services that have enabled the Internet cloud to become so prominent. . . . A cloud can be a wide area network (WAN) like the public Internet or a private, national or global network. The term can also refer to a local area network (LAN) within an organization." See Encyclopedia, *PC Magazine* (2015), http://www.pcmag.com/encyclopedia/term/39847/cloud.

3. See "Text of Mayor de Blasio's State of the City Address," *New York Times*, February 3, 2015, http://www.nytimes.com/2015/02/04/nyregion/new-york-mayor-bill-de-blasios-state-of-the-city-address.html?_r=0.

4. See, for example, K. Murdock, "Recovering the Classical in the Common: Figures of Speech in 'A Scandal in Bohemia,'" *Minnesota English Journal* 47 (2012): 85–89. See also http://www.changingminds.org/techniques/language/figures_speech/figures_speech.htm.

5. To see an illustration of antithesis, consider how politicians use it in their speeches. See, e.g., Q. Zhou and B. Kazemian, "A Rhetorical Identification Analysis of English Political Public Speaking: John F. Kennedy's Inaugural

Address," *International Journal of Language and Linguistics. Special Issue: Critical Discourse Analysis, Rhetoric, and Grammatical Metaphor in Political and Advertisement Discourses* 4, no. 1 (2015): 10–16, doi: 10.11648 /j.ijll.s.2016040101.12.

6. For more on metaphors, see B. Forgács et al., "Metaphors Are Physical and Abstract: ERPs to Metaphorically Modified Nouns Resemble ERPs to Abstract Language," *Frontiers in Human Neuroscience* 9 (2015): 28, http://doi.org/10.3389/fnhum.2015.00028.

7. C. R. Jorgensen-Earp and A. Q. Staton, "Student Metaphors for the College Freshman Experience," *Communication Education* 42 (1993): 125.

8. J. L. Stringer and R. Hopper, "Generic *He* in Conversation?," *Quarterly Journal of Speech* 84, no. 2 (1998): 209–21.

9. D. Cameron, *Feminism and Linguistic Theory* (New York: St. Martin's Press, 1985), 68.

Chapter 13

1. Research has shown that along with desensitization (relaxation, deep breathing, visualization), cognitive restructuring (identifying what causes your anxiety and developing coping strategies), *learning, knowing, and practicing* your speech are the best ways to reduce speech anxiety. For more, see T. Docan-Morgan and T. Schmidt, "Reducing Public Speaking Anxiety for Native and Non-Native Speakers: The Value of Systematic Desensitization, Cognitive Restructuring, and Skills Training," *Cross Cultural Communication* 8, no. 5 (2012): 16–19. For more on speech preparation, see H. Liao, "Examining the Role of Collaborative Learning in a Public Speaking Course," *College Teaching* 62, no. 2 (2014): 47–54.

2. See, for example, http://www.merriam-webster.com/dictionary/nuclear. See also M. Reed and J. Lewis, *The Handbook of English Pronunciation* (Malden, MA: Wiley-Blackwell, 2015).

3. J. S. Tuman and Reverend Paul Levine, personal communication, 1976.

4. D. Matsumoto and H. S. Hwang, "Body and Gestures," in *Nonverbal Communication: Science and Applications*, ed. D. Matsumoto, M. Frank, and H. S. Hwang, 75–96 (Thousand Oaks, CA: Sage, 2013), 75.

5. V. Manusov, "Perceiving Nonverbal Messages: Effects of Immediacy and Encoded Intent on Receiver Judgments," *Western Journal of Speech Communication* 55, no. 3 (1991): 236.

6. For more on gestures, see A. Hostetter, "When Do Gestures Communicate? A Meta-analysis," *Psychological Bulletin* 137 (2011): 297–315.

7. For more on co-speech gestures, see L. Marstaller and H. Burianova, "The Multisensory Perception of Co-Speech Gestures: A Review and Meta Analysis of Neuroimaging Studies," *Journal of Neurolinguistics* 30 (2014): 69–77.

8. J. K. Burgoon and B. A. LePoire, "Nonverbal Cues and Interpersonal Judgments: Participant and Observer Perceptions of Intimacy, Dominance, Composure, and Formality," *Communication Monographs* 66 (1999): 107.

9. Much of the original research on proxemics was pioneered by anthropologist Edward T. Hall: E. T. Hall, *The Hidden Dimension* (New York: Doubleday, 1966). See also M. L. Patterson, "Spatial Factors in Social Interactions," *Human Relations* 21 (1968): 351–61.

10. Patterson, "Spatial Factors," 351–61.

11. J. K. Burgoon et al.,"Relational Messages Associated with Nonverbal Behaviors," *Human Communication Research* 10 (1984): 351–78.

12. E. T. Hall, *Hidden Differences: Doing Business with the Japanese* (New York: Doubleday, 1987).

13. Communication scholars note that other elements of physical appearance—such as physiognomy, hair color, and height—also can affect how audiences respond to speakers. For more, see J. K. Burgoon, L. K. Guerrero, and V. Manusov, "Nonverbal Signals," in *The Sage Handbook of Interpersonal Communication*, 4th ed., ed. M. L. Knapp and J. A. Daly, 239–80 (Thousand Oaks, CA: Sage, 2011), 241.

14. L. J. Smith and L. A. Malandro, "Personal Appearance Factors Which Influence Perceptions of Credibility and Approachability of Men and Women," in *The Nonverbal Communication Reader*, ed. J. A. DeVito and M. L. Hecht (Prospect Heights, IL: Waveland Press, 1990), 163.

Chapter 14

1. E. Bohn and D. Jabusch, "The Effect of Four Methods of Instruction on the Use of Visual Aids in Speeches," *Western Journal of Communication* 46 (1982): 253–65.

2. H. E. Nelson and A. W. Vandermeer, "The Relative Effectiveness of Several Different Sound Tracks Used on an Animated Film on Elementary Meteorology," *Speech Monographs* 20, no. 4 (1953): 261–67.

3. See, e.g., S. E. Secur, M. Sahin, and B. Alci, "Investigating the Effect of Audio Visual Materials as Warm Up Activity in Aviation English Courses on Students' Motivation and Participation at High School Level," *Procedia: Social and Behavioral Sciences* 199 (2015): 120–38, http://ac.els-cdn.com/S1877042815044985/1-s2.0-S1877042815044985-main.pdf?_tid=b0548796-9083-11e5-8509-00000aacb35d&acdnat=1448133277_549c28b365b09162066c3c8d3f3dafd2.

4. See, e.g., A. Kumar et al., "Students' Views on Audio Visual Aids Used during Didactic Lectures in a Medical College," *Asian Journal of Medical Science* 4, no. 2 (2013): 36–40.

5. In a study examining student learning and retention of information, it was determined that audience memory retention was greatest for information

extracted from visual materials. See P. Baggett and A. Ehrenfeucht, "Encoding and Retaining Information in the Visuals and Verbals of an Educational Movie," Technical Report No. 108-ONR, Institute of Cognitive Science, University of Colorado, 1981, 1. See also M. A. Defeyter, R. Russo, and P. L. McPartlin, "The Picture Superiority Effect in Recognition Memory: A Developmental Study Using the Response Signal Procedure," *Cognitive Development* 24, no. 3 (2009): 265–73.

6. To watch a video presentation of Herr's TED talk on bionic limbs, go to http://www.ted.com/talks/hugh_herr_the_new_bionics_that_let_us_run _climb_and_dance#t-425338.

7. PowerPoint is used for millions of presentations globally every day, and its software is found on hundreds of millions of computers. For more, see S. M. Kosslyn et al., "PowerPoint® Presentation Flaws and Failures: A Psychological Analysis," *Frontiers in Psychology* 3 (2012): 230.

8. Although this kind of presentation software has become very popular, it also has its critics. Supporters claim that it improves learning, creates greater audience interest, and helps explain complex subjects. Critics argue that it can inhibit audience/speaker interactions, limit the number of details that are presented, and even limit the analytical details that might be required in a technical presentation. For more, see A. Savoy, R. W. Proctor, and G. Salvendy, "Information Retention from PowerPoint™ and Traditional Lectures," *Computers and Education* 52 (2009): 858–67.

Chapter 15

1. K. Parker, A. Lenhart, and K. Moore, *The Digital Revolution and Higher Education: College Presidents, Public Differ on Value of Online Learning* (Washington, DC: Pew Research Center, August 28, 2011), 1.

2. For more on massive open online courses, see H. McCleod, "Emerging Patterns in MOOCs: Learners, Course Designs and Directions," *TechTrends* 59, no. 1 (January–February 2015): 56–62.

3. P. Moore, "Productivity by Camera," *NZ Business*, July 2011, 43.

4. For more, see "Video Conferencing Market: Global Opportunity, Trends, Forecast 2015–2019, *Technavio Report*, http://www.technavio.com/report /video-conferencing-market-global-opportunity-trends-forecast-2015-2019.

5. For more see K. Finnell, "UC Briefs: Video Conferencing Services Grow Worldwide," *TechTarget* (July 2015), http://searchunifiedcommunications. techtarget.com/news/4500249537/UC-briefs-Video-conferencing-services -grow-worldwide.

6. J. Eberbach, "Detroit City Council to Skype Public Meetings," *21c3* (blog), Michigan Municipal League, March 10, 2011, http://www.mml.org /resources/21c3/post/2011/03/10/Detroit-City-Council-to-Skype-Public -Meetings.aspx.

7. For more, see G. H. Olivera and E. W. Welch, "Social Media Use in Local Government: Linkage of Technology, Task, and Organizational Context," *Government Information Quarterly* 30, no. 4 (2013): 397–406.

8. J. M. Denstadli, T. E. Julsrud, and R. J. Hjorthol, "Videoconferencing as a Mode of Communication: A Comparative Study of the Use of Videoconferencing and Face-to-Face Meetings," *Journal of Business and Technical Communication* 26, no. 1 (2012): 71.

9. Ibid., 84–85.

10. R. van der Kleij, R. M. Paashuis, and J. M. Schraagen, "On the Passage of Time: Temporal Differences in Video-Mediated and Face-to-Face Interaction," *International Journal of Human-Computer Studies* 62, no. 4 (2005): 528.

11. Ibid., 539.

12. N. Kock, "Information Systems Theorizing Based on Evolutionary Psychology: An Interdisciplinary Review and Theory Integration Framework," *MIS Quarterly* 33, no. 2 (2009): 406–7.

13. N. Kock, "Media Richness or Media Naturalness? The Evolution of Our Biological Communication Apparatus and Its Influence on Our Behavior toward E-Communication Tools," *IEEE Transactions on Professional Communication* 48, no. 2 (2005): 121.

14. Kock, "Information Systems," 407.

15. See T. M. Wells and A. R. Dennis, "To Email or Not to Email: The Impact of Media on Psychophysiological Responses and Emotional Content in Utilitarian and Romantic Communication," *Computers in Human Behavior* 54 (2016): 1–9.

16. J. K. Burgoon et al., "Testing the Interactivity Principle: Effects of Mediation, Propinquity, and Verbal and Nonverbal Modalities in Interpersonal Interaction," *Journal of Communication* 52, no. 3 (2002): 662.

17. A. Lyons, S. Reysen, and L. Pierce, "Video Lecture Format, Student Technological Efficacy, and Social Presence in Online Courses," *Computers in Human Behavior* 28, no. 1 (2012): 182.

18. Burgoon et al., "Testing the Interactivity Principle," 662.

19. W. Turmel, *Ten Steps to Successful Virtual Presentations* (Alexandria, VA: ASTD Press, 2011), 8.

20. Z. Guo et al., "Improving the Effectiveness of Virtual Teams: A Comparison of Video-Conferencing and Face-to-Face Communication in China," *IEEE Transactions on Professional Communication* 52, no. 1 (2009): 1–16.

21. Kock, "Media Richness," 121.

22. Denstadli, Julsrud, and Hjorthol, "Videoconferencing as a Mode," 66.

23. Van der Kleij, Paashuis, and Schraagen, "On the Passage of Time," 523.

24. J. Gendelman, *Virtual Presentations That Work* (New York: McGraw-Hill, 2010), 35–36.

25. R. F. Adler and R. Benbunan-Fich, "Juggling on a High Wire: Multitasking Effects on Performance," *International Journal of Human-Computer Studies* 70, no. 2 (2012): 156.

26. Turmel, *Ten Steps*, 8.

27. Ibid., 125–26.

28. R. McCammon, "Is There Proper Etiquette for Videoconferencing?," *Entrepreneur*, November 2011, 22.

29. T. J. Koegel, *The Exceptional Presenter Goes Virtual* (Austin: Greenleaf Book Group Press, 2010), 98.

30. Guo et al., "Improving the Effectiveness," 3.

31. C. A. Noble, "From China's Great Wall to Hollywood's Great Spy: The Story of Military Smokes and Obscurants," in *Aerosol Science and Technology: History and Reviews*, ed. D. S. Ensor, 377–88 (Research Triangle Park, NC: RTI International, 2011), 377.

32. Turmel, *Ten Steps*, 8.

33. S. Stockman, *How to Shoot Video That Doesn't Suck* (New York: Workman, 2011), 92.

34. Turmel, *Ten Steps*, 93.

35. Stockman, *How to Shoot Video*, 12–13, 120.

36. Gendelman, *Virtual Presentations That Work*, 66.

37. McCammon, "Is There Proper Etiquette for Videoconferencing?" 20.

38. Turmel, *Ten Steps*, 93.

39. Koegel, *Exceptional Presenter*, 114.

40. Stockman, *How to Shoot Video*, 41.

41. Ibid., 150.

Chapter 16

1. See A. Myles, "Get a Flu Shot before It Is Too Late," *Auburn Plainsman* (student newspaper), October 27, 2015, http://www.theplainsman.com /article/2015 /10/get-a-flu-shot-before-it-is-too-late.

2. Flag-folding etiquette is detailed by the American Legion at http://www .legion.org/flag/folding (accessed March 23, 2010).

3. U.S. Code, title 4, chapter 1, sections 3, 8(d), via Cornell University Law School, http://www.law.cornell.edu/uscode/html/uscode04/usc _sup_01_4_10_1.html (accessed March 23, 2010).

4. D. Russakoff, "Building a Career Path Where There Was Just a Dead End," *Washington Post*, February 26, 2007, A1. In 2013, Per Scholas was recognized for inclusion in the S&I (Social Impact) 100 List, recognizing nonprofits that provide high-impact solutions to America's problems. For more, see http://www.socialimpactexchange.org/exchange/si-100.

5. For more, see Editorial Board, "A Football Player's Safe Exit," *New York Times*, March 21, 2015, http://www.nytimes.com/2015/03/22/opinion /sunday/a-football-players-safe-exit.html?_r=0.

6. D. M. Fraleigh and J. S. Tuman, *Freedom of Speech in the Marketplace of Ideas* (New York: St. Martin's Press, 1997).

7. J. S. Tuman, *Communicating Terror: The Rhetorical Dimensions of Terrorism* (Los Angeles: Sage, 2004).

8. K. E. Rowan, "A New Pedagogy for Explanatory Public Speaking: Why Arrangement Should Not Substitute for Invention," *Communication Education* 44 (July 1995): 236–50.

Chapter 17

1. R. E. Petty and J. T. Cacioppo, *Communication and Persuasion: Central and Peripheral Routes to Attitude Change* (New York: Springer-Verlag, 1986).

2. J. K. Clark, A. T. Evans, and D. T. Wegener, "Perceptions of Source Efficacy and Persuasion: Multiple Mechanisms for Source Effects on Attitudes," *European Journal of Social Psychology* 41, no. 5 (2011): 596–607; R. L. Holbert, R. K. Garrett, and L. S. Gleason, "A New Era of Minimal Effects? A Response to Bennett and Iyengar," *Journal of Communication* 60, no. 1 (2010): 25.

3. Petty and Cacioppo, *Communication and Persuasion*, 7.

4. I. M. Handley and B. M. Runnion, "Evidence That Unconscious Thinking Influences Persuasion Based on Argument Quality," *Social Cognition* 29, no. 6 (2011): 677.

5. Ibid., 669.

6. Holbert, Garrett, and Gleason, "A New Era of Minimal Effects?," 25.

7. M. B. Wanzer, A. B. Frymier, and J. Irwin, "An Explanation of the Relationship between Instructor Humor and Student Learning: Instructional Humor Processing Theory," *Communication Education* 59, no. 1 (2010): 5.

8. M. A. Yeh and R. D. Jewell, "The Myth/Fact Message Frame and Persuasion in Advertising: Enhancing Attitudes toward the Mentally Ill," *Journal of Advertising* 44, no. 2 (2015): 161–72.

9. M. Sherif and C. I. Hovland, *Social Judgment, Assimilation, and Contrast Effects in Communication and Attitude Change* (New Haven: Yale University Press, 1961), 195–96.

10. Ibid.

11. D. K. O'Keefe, *Persuasion: Theory and Research* (Newbury Park, CA: Sage, 1990), 36–37.

12. Petty and Cacioppo, *Communication and Persuasion*, 81.

13. A. H. Maslow, "A Theory of Human Motivation," *Psychological Review* 50 (1943): 370–96.

14. V. Packard, *The Hidden Persuaders* (New York: Pocket Books, 1964).

15. M. Rokeach, *Understanding Human Values* (New York: Free Press, 1979), 2.

16. J. S. Tuman, "Getting to First Base: Prima Facie Arguments for Propositions of Value," *Journal of the American Forensic Association* 24 (Fall 1987): 86.

17. M. Rokeach, *Beliefs, Attitudes, and Values: A Theory of Organization and Change* (San Francisco: Jossey-Bass, 1968).

18. J. Hornikx and D. J. O'Keefe, "Adapting Consumer Advertising Appeals to Cultural Values," *Communication Yearbook* 33 (2009): 38–71.

19. For an analysis of how this argument and other strategies may influence a change in audience values, see N. Rescher, "The Study of Value Change," *Journal of Value Inquiry* 1 (1967): 12–23.

20. D. Hample and J. M. Hample, "Persuasion about Health Risks: Evidence, Credibility, Scientific Flourishes, and Risk Perceptions," *Argumentation and Advocacy* 51 (Summer 2014): 17–29; A. Svokos, "College Students Don't Get Flu Shots and That's a Real Problem," *Huffington Post College*, October 31, 2014, http://www.huffingtonpost.com/2014/10/30/college-flu -shots_n_6054946.html.

21. Rokeach, *Beliefs, Attitudes, and Values*, 3.

22. M. Fishbein and I. Ajzen, *Belief, Attitude, Intention, and Behavior: An Intro- duction to Theory and Research* (Reading, MA: Addison-Wesley, 1975).

23. K. Horneffer-Ginter, "Stages of Change and Possible Selves: Two Tools for Promoting College Health," *Journal of American College Health* 56, no. 4 (2008): 351–58.

24. M. Allen, "Comparing the Persuasive Effectiveness: One- and Two-Sided Message," in *Persuasion: Advances through Meta-Analysis*, ed. M. Allen and R. W. Preiss (Cresskill, NJ: Hampton Press, 1998), 96.

25. R. Hamill, T. Wilson, and R. Nesbit, "Insensitivity to Sample Bias: General- izing from Atypical Cases," *Journal of Personality and Social Psychology* 39 (1980): 578–89.

26. C. Hoyt, "The Sources' Stake in the News," *New York Times*, January 17, 2010, WK8.

27. L. Grossman, "A Star Is Born," *Time*, November 2, 2015, 30–39.

28. A. Monroe, *Principles and Types of Speech* (New York: Scott, Foresman, 1935).

29. R. E. McKerrow et al., *Principles and Types of Public Speaking*, 16th ed. (Boston: Pearson Education, 2007), 168.

Chapter 18

1. J. C. Reinard, *Foundations of Argument* (Dubuque, IA: William C. Brown, 1991), 353–54.

2. Aristotle, *On Rhetoric*, trans. G. A. Kennedy (New York: Oxford University Press, 1991), 1378a.

3. J. C. McCroskey and J. J. Teven, "Goodwill: A Reexamination of the Construct and Its Measurement," *Communication Monographs* 66, no. 1 (1999): 92.

4. S. Wheaton, "Missouree? Missouruh? To Be Politic, Say Both," *New York Times*, October 13, 2012, A1.

5. H. Flesher, J. Ilardo, and J. Demoretcky, "The Influence of Field Dependence, Speaker Credibility Set, and Message Documentation on Evaluations of Speaker and Message Credibility," *Southern Communication Speech Journal* 34 (Summer 1974): 400.

6. J. C. McCroskey, "A Summary of Experimental Research on the Effects of Evidence in Persuasive Communication," *Quarterly Journal of Speech* 55 (April 1969): 172.

7. Ibid., 175.

8. D. J. DeNoon, "Drink More Diet Soda, Gain More Weight?," June 13, 2005, http://www.webmd.com/content/article/107/108476.htm#.

9. R. E. Nisbett and L. Ross, *Human Interference: Strategies and Shortcomings of Social Judgment* (Englewood Cliffs, NJ: Prentice Hall, 1980).

10. D. Hample and J. M. Hample, "Persuasion about Health Risks: Evidence, Credibility, Scientific Flourishes, and Risk Perceptions," *Argumentation and Advocacy* 51 (Summer 2014): 17–29.

11. Tr'ondëk Hwëch'in Heritage Sites, "Fortymile Caribou Herd," 2012, http://trondekheritage.com/our-places/forty-mile/what-makes-forty-mile-special/fortymile-caribou-herd.

12. National Park Service (Yosemite), "Special Status Bird Species," January 6, 2016, http://www.nps.gov/yose/learn/nature/ss-bird-species.htm.

13. U.S. Fish and Wildlife Service, "Chart and Table of Bald Eagle Breeding Pairs in Lower Forty-eight States," April 20, 2015, http://www.fws.gov/Midwest/eagle/population/chtofprs.html.

14. M. DeLisi et al., "Violent Video Games, Delinquency, and Youth Violence: New Evidence," *Youth Violence and Juvenile Justice* 11, no. 2 (2013): 138.

15. B. Kiviat, "How to Create a Job," *Time*, March 29, 2010, 18.

16. S. Callahan, "The Role of Emotion in Ethical Decision Making," *Hastings Center Report* 18, no. 3 (1988): 9.

17. G. Anders, *Health against Wealth: HMOs and the Breakdown of Medical Trust* (Boston: Houghton Mifflin, 1996), 108–9.

18. K. Witte and K. Morrison, "Examining the Influence of Trait Anxiety/Repression-Sensitization on Individuals' Reactions to Fear Appeals," *Western Journal of Communication* 64 (Winter 2000): 1.

19. P. A. Mongeau, "Another Look at Fear-Arousing Persuasive Appeals," in *Persuasion: Advances through Meta-Analysis*, ed. M. Allen and R. W. Preiss (Cresskill, NJ: Hampton Press, 1998), 66.

20. Ibid.

21. D. Westen, "Health Care Reform: It's How You Say It," *StarTribune*, July 1, 2009, http://www.startribune.com/opinion/49631647.html.

22. D. Westen, *The Political Brain: The Role of Emotion in Deciding the Fate of the Nation* (New York: Public Affairs, 2007).

23. Chris Moody, "How Republicans Are Being Taught to Talk about Occupy Wall Street," *Yahoo! News*, December 1, 2011, http://news.yahoo.com /blogs/ticket/republicans-being-taught-talk-occupy-wall-street-133707949. html.

24. J. G. Hodge Jr. and D. Campos-Outcalt, "Legally Limiting Lies about Vaccines," *Jurist*, November 17, 2015, http://jurist.org/forum/2015/11/hodge -campos-vaccines-speech.php.

25. "Off-Base Camp: A Mistaken Claim about Glaciers Raises Questions about the UN's Climate Panel," *Economist* 394 (January 23, 2010): 76–77.

26. W. DeJong and L. Wallack, "A Critical Perspective of the Drug Czar's Antidrug Media Campaign," *Journal of Health Communication* 4 (1999): 155–60; D. R. Buchanan and L. Wallack, "This Is the Partnership for a Drug-Free America: Any Questions?," *Journal of Drug Issues* 28, no. 2 (1998): 329–56.

27. A. Lang and N. S. Yegiyan, "Understanding the Interactive Effects of Emotional Appeal and Claim Strength in Health Messages," *Journal of Broadcasting and Electronic Media* 52, no. 3 (2008): 432–47.

28. U.S. Department of Agriculture, "What Foods Are in the Fruit Group?," http://www.choosemyplate.gov/food-groups/fruits.html (accessed September 25, 2013).

29. K. D. Brownell et al., "The Public Health and Economic Benefits of Taxing Sugar-Sweetened Beverages," *New England Journal of Medicine* 361 (October 15, 2009): 1599–605.

Chapter 19

1. Aristotle, *On Rhetoric*, trans. G. A. Kennedy (New York: Oxford University Press, 1991), 1358a–b.

2. Ibid., 7, 47.

3. See D. J. Ochs, *Consolatory Rhetoric: Grief, Symbol, and Ritual in the Greco-Roman Era* (Columbia: University of South Carolina Press, 1993).

4. W. D. Hansen and G. N. Dionisopoulos, "Eulogy Rhetoric as a Political Coping Mechanism: The Aftermath of Proposition 8," *Western Journal of Communication* 76, no. 1 (2012): 26.

5. To review some of Twain's famous after-dinner speeches, see B. Blaisdell, ed., *Great Speeches by Mark Twain* (Mineola, NY: Dover Publications, 2013).

Chapter 20

1. B. R. Patton and K. Giffen, *Decision-Making Group Interaction*, 2nd ed. (New York: Harper & Row, 1978), 2.

2. I. Janis, *Victims of Groupthink* (Boston: Houghton Mifflin, 1972).

3. See B. Kennedy, "The Hijacking of Foreign Policy Decision Making: Groupthink and Presidential Power in the Post 9/11 World," *Southern California Interdisciplinary Law Journal* 21 (2012): 637.

4. W. E. Watson, K. Kumar, and L. K. Michaelson, "Cultural Diversity's Impact on Interaction Processes and Performance: Comparing Homogeneous and Diverse Task Groups," *Academy of Management Journal* 36 (1993): 590–602.

5. K. D. Benne and P. Sheats, "Functional Roles of Group Members," *Journal of Social Issues* 1, no. 4 (1948): 41, 49. For a modern look at types of roles for group members, consider A. N. Novak, C. M. Mascaro, and S. P. Goggins, "Virtual Play and Communities: The Evolution of Group Roles in Electronic Trace Data," in *Proceedings of the 2012 iConference on Culture, Design and Society* (New York: ACM, 2012), 490–91, http://dl.acm.org /citation.cfm?id = 2132260.

6. L. Hambley, T. O'Neil, and T. Kline, "Virtual Team Leadership: Perspectives from the Field," *International Journal of e-Collaboration* 3 (2007): 40–64.

7. J. H. Waldeck, P. Kearney, and T. G. Plax, *Business and Professional Communication in a Digital Age* (Boston: Cengage Learning, 2013).

8. The reflective-thinking process was developed from the ideas of John Dewey, an American philosopher who was interested in problem solving.

GLOSSARY

abstract A summary of an article's contents, often included in library indexes.

abstract word A term that refers to intangible things, like feelings, ideals, concepts, and qualities. An abstract word can be too general or confusing for an audience. To say "I have a pet" is less informative than saying "I have a gray tabby cat."

academic research The study of a topic by experts who have education and experience in the topic area with a goal of undercovering facts or principles. An expert's academic research generally is reviewed by other authorities in the field.

action-oriented listening A style of listening in which the listener focuses on immediately getting to the meaning of a message and determining what response is required.

***ad hominem* (personal attack) fallacy** An error in reasoning in which the speaker tries to persuade an audience to dislike someone by targeting his or her character rather than the relevant issues.

***ad populum* (bandwagon) fallacy** An error in reasoning in which the speaker tries to persuade an audience to accept an argument by claiming that a fact is true because many or most people believe that it is true. Another form of this logical fallacy (often used in advertising and marketing) is to imply that because many people are engaging in an activity, everyone should engage in the activity. Bandwagoning is unethical if speakers fail to provide support for their claims.

advanced search A feature that is provided by many search engines and that allows users to narrow or broaden their Web searches.

age A demographic consideration that affects an audience's response to and understanding of a speaker's message. For example, avoiding popular culture references that are too old or too young for an audience is a good way to take age into consideration.

agenda-driven listening Focusing only on delivery of one's speech instead of also acknowledging the audience's questions and comments.

analogy A comparison of two things—one that is familiar to an audience and one that is less familiar—that is based on their similarities and that helps listeners use their existing knowledge to absorb new information.

anaphora   A repetition of a word or phrase at the beginning of successive phrases, clauses, or sentences. It is used to emphasize, clarify, and deliver a rhetorical sense of style.

antithesis   The opposition of one clause to another, usually to distinguish between choices, concepts, and ideas.

appeal to tradition fallacy   An error in reasoning in which the speaker tries to persuade an audience to believe that a practice or policy is good by claiming that people have followed it for a long time.

argumentative listening   Focusing on a message only long enough to get material to feed one's own argument.

arrangement   The effective organization of ideas to present them to an audience. It is one of the five classical canons of rhetoric.

articulation   Speaking that is crisp and clear so that listeners can distinguish separate words, syllables, and vowel or consonant sounds within words.

atlas   A reference work that collects maps, charts, and tables that relate to different geographic regions.

attention-getter   The material at the start of a speech that is intended to capture an audience's interest. The speaker can get an audience's attention by telling a story or an anecdote, offering a striking or provocative statement, building suspense, letting listeners know he or she is one of them, using humor, asking a rhetorical question, or providing a quotation.

attitude   The audience's favorable or unfavorable feelings toward your thesis.

audience analysis   The process of learning about an audience's interests and backgrounds in order to create or adapt a speech to their wants and needs.

audience size   The number of people who will be present for a speech.

audience surveillance   The speaker's analysis of an audience's nonverbal and verbal responses while listening to a speech.

bandwagon fallacy   See *ad populum* (bandwagon) fallacy.

bar graph   A graph that compares several pieces of information by showing parallel bars of varying height or length.

belief   An audience's acceptance of something as existing or as true.

biased language   Words, phrases, and expressions that suggest prejudice against or preconceptions about other people, usually referring to race, ethnicity, gender, sexuality, religion, or mental or physical ability.

bibliographic information   The important facts about a researched source, including author, title, publication date, and page numbers or URL.

body   The main part of a speech. The body falls after the introduction and before the conclusion and includes all the main points and the material that supports them.

body clock (chronemics)   The time of day or day of the week when an audience is listening to a presentation. An audience is more prone to distraction at certain times of the day, such as lunchtime, and certain days of the week, such as Friday.

boomerang effect   An audience's return to its previously held beliefs when a speaker chooses a position that falls on the extreme end of the audience's latitude of rejection. See also **latitude of rejection**.

brainstorming   A strategy for generating topic ideas by listing every idea that comes to mind—without evaluating its merits—in order to develop a long list of ideas quickly.

brief example   A short instance that supports or illustrates a more general claim.

categorical (topical) pattern   A model for speech organization in which each main point emphasizes one of the most important aspects of the speaker's topic. This pattern often is used when a speaker's topic does not easily conform to the other speech organization patterns— spatial, temporal, causal, comparison, problem-cause-solution, criteria-application, or narrative.

causal pattern   A model for speech organization that explains cause-and-effect relationships in which each main point is either an event that leads to a situation or a link in a chain of events between a catalyst and a final outcome.

causal reasoning   Arguing that one event has caused another.

central route   According to the elaboration likelihood model, one of two ways that audience members may evaluate a speaker's message. This route denotes a high level of elaboration—a mental process that involves actively processing a speaker's arguments. See also **peripheral route**.

channel   The medium through which a source delivers a message, such as voice, microphone, radio, television, or Internet.

chronological (temporal) pattern   A model for speech organization in which the speaker presents information in the order that events occurred, with each main point addressing a particular time within the chronology.

circle graph See **pie chart (circle graph)**.

citation The important facts about a researched source, including author, title, publication date, and page numbers or URL.

civic engagement Active public participation in political affairs and social and community organizations.

classical canon of rhetoric According to Cicero, one of the five concepts that effective speakers must attend to while preparing a speech. These concepts are invention, arrangement, style, memory, and delivery.

clincher A closing comment in a speech that leaves a lasting impression in listeners' minds. This comment or call to action should be as compelling as the speech's attention-getter and usually appears as the second element in a speech conclusion. To leave the audience thinking, a speaker can extend a story that was used at the start of the speech, relay a new story or anecdote, end with a striking phrase or sentence, or conclude with an emotional message.

common ground The collection of beliefs, values, and experiences that a speaker shares with an audience. A speaker seeks to establish common ground with an audience, whether verbally or nonverbally, so that listeners will be more receptive to his or her message.

common knowledge Widely known information that can be found in many sources and that does not require citation.

comparison pattern A model for speech organization that discusses the similarities and differences between two events, objects, or situations. This pattern is especially useful when comparing a new subject to one that is known to the audience.

comparison reasoning Arguing that two instances are similar enough that what is true for one is likely to be true for the other. If a speaker argues that U.S. residents will eventually accept mandatory health insurance because they accepted mandatory car insurance, the speaker is using comparison reasoning.

competence Knowledge and experience in a subject.

conclusion The final part of a speech, in which the speaker summarizes the main points and leaves the audience with a clincher, such as a striking sentence or phrase, an anecdote, or an emotional message.

concrete word A word or phrase that describes what can be experienced by one or more of the senses. For example, to say a man was wearing a "dark blue suit" (which mentions a color) is more concrete than saying he was wearing "clothes."

connotative meaning An association that comes to mind when a person hears a word. For example, saying "He tackled the project" brings to mind football and is a more vivid way to convey enthusiasm than saying "He was excited to start the project and tried to do a good job."

constructive criticism Thoughtful and tactful suggestions for improvement that take into account what a speaker is trying to accomplish. Speakers can use these kinds of suggestions to make improvements for future presentations.

content-oriented listening Focusing on the depth and complexity of information and messages.

context The occasion, surrounding environment, and situation in which a speaker gives a presentation.

coordination The connection of two or more ideas of equal weight and importance. In a well-organized speech, all points at the same level share the same significance. Each main point is coordinate with other main points, each subpoint with other subpoints, and each sub-subpoint with other sub-subpoints.

core belief A deeply held viewpoint about the self and the world that is particularly immune to persuasion.

credibility The perception of an audience that a speaker is prepared and qualified to speak on his or her topic. Trustworthiness, dynamism, and goodwill are also elements of a speaker's credibility. See also ethos (credibility).

credible source An author or organization that can be reasonably trusted to be accurate and objective in presenting information.

criteria-application pattern A model for speech organization that proposes standards for a value judgment that a speaker is making and then applies those standards to a related topic. For example, a speaker who argues that a city should budget money to restore a crumbling historic neighborhood would first define the criteria for a "historic neighborhood" and then discuss how the city's neighborhood is historic and therefore worth restoring.

critical thinking The analysis and evaluation of one's own ideas and others' ideas, based on reliability, truth, and accuracy.

culturally relative Varying according to the norms of individual societies.

culture The values, traditions, and rules for living that are passed from generation to generation. Culture is learned, not innate, and influences all aspects of a person's life.

decode To interpret a message by making sense of a source's verbal and nonverbal symbols. Decoding is performed by a receiver.

defeated listening Pretending to understand a message while actually being overwhelmed by or uninterested in the subject matter.

definition A statement that explains the essence, meaning, purpose, or identity of something.

delivery A speaker's varied and appropriate use of vocal and nonverbal elements, such as voice, hand gestures, eye contact, and movement. It is one of the five classical canons of rhetoric.

delivery reminder A bracketed instruction in a speaking outline that reminds the speaker about body language, pauses, special emphasis, and presentation aids.

demographics The characteristics of audience members, including age, gender, sexual orientation, race, ethnicity, religious orientation, socio-economic background, and political affiliation.

demonstration A technique used in informative speeches that involves both physical modeling and verbal elements and that teaches an audience how a process or set of guidelines works.

denotative meaning The literal dictionary definition of a word.

description The use of words to paint a mental picture for audience members so that they can close their eyes and imagine what a speaker is saying.

designated leader A person who is chosen by an authority figure to help a group move quickly forward with its mission.

diagram A drawing that details an object or action and shows arrangements and relations among its parts.

diction See **word choice (diction)**.

dictionary A reference work that offers definitions, pronunciation guides, and sometimes etymologies of words.

dictionary definition The meaning of a term as it appears in a general or specialized dictionary.

direct quotation An author's exact words. Quotation marks must be put around quotations to avoid plagiarism.

disposition An audience's likely attitude toward a message. In most cases, an audience can be divided into three groups—sympathetic, hostile, and neutral.

divergent thinking Employed in the brainstorming process of a speech, a path of thinking that generates diverse and creative ideas.

elaboration likelihood model A dual-process theory that shows that audience members may evaluate a persuasive speaker's message according to two routes—the central and peripheral routes. See also **central route** and **peripheral route**.

emergent leader   A person who comes to be recognized as a leader by a group's members over time.

encode   To choose verbal or nonverbal symbols to organize and deliver one's message.

encyclopedia   A reference work that offers relatively brief entries that provide background information on a wide range of alphabetized topics.

epideictic   Praising or blaming.

ethical absolutism   A code of behavior that a person adheres to in all circumstances. See also **situational ethics**.

ethical audience   An audience that exhibits courtesy, open-mindedness, and a willingness to hold the speaker accountable for his or her statements.

ethical speech   Language that incorporates ethical decision making, follows guidelines to tell the truth, and avoids misleading the audience.

ethics   A set of rules and values that are shared by members of a group and that help them guide conduct and distinguish between right and wrong.

ethnicity   The part of a person's cultural background that usually is associated with shared religion, national origin, and language.

ethos (credibility)   An appeal to ethics; the quality of being worthy of trust. A credible speaker inspires audience members to believe his or her claims by conveying a sense of the speaker's knowledge, honesty, trustworthiness, experience, authority, or wisdom.

etymological definition   An explanation of the linguistic origin of a term. It is useful when the term's origin is interesting or will help the audience understand the word.

eulogy   A speech that comments on the death of an individual, celebrates his or her life, and often shares personal reflections and stories about the deceased.

evidence   Information gathered from credible sources that helps a speaker support his or her claims.

example   A sample or an instance that supports or illustrates a general claim.

example reasoning   Presenting specific instances to support a general claim and to convince listeners that the claim is reasonable or true.

expert definition   A statement that provides the meaning of a term as presented by a person who is a credible source of information on a particular topic.

expertise   The knowledge necessary to offer reliable facts or opinions about a topic.

expert testimony   Statements made by credible sources who have in-depth knowledge of a topic.

explanation   An analysis of something that traces a line of reasoning or a series of causal connections between events.

export (citations)   To move source citations from a computer-based library index to a digital file.

extemporaneous delivery   The presentation of a speech smoothly and confidently from a speaking outline without reading from it.

extended example   A detailed narrative that serves as a sample or an instance to support or illustrate a general claim.

external noise   A distraction in the external speech environment that disrupts communication between source and receiver. For example, a speech might be drowned out by a fleet of jets roaring overhead. Also known as an *external distraction*.

eye contact   The act of looking directly into each other's eyes. This occurs between a speaker and an audience as they are speaking or listening.

fact claim   A statement that asserts that something is true or false. For example, "Animal experimentation is necessary for human survival."

fallacious (faulty) reasoning   Presenting a weak link between a claim and its supporting material.

false dilemma fallacy   An error in reasoning in which the speaker incorrectly claims that there are only two possible choices to solve a problem, that one of them is wrong, and that the audience therefore should support the speaker's solution. This fallacy usually can be detected when listeners know there are more than two choices.

false inference   Presenting information that leads an audience to an incorrect conclusion.

fear appeal   An argument that arouses fear in the minds of audience members. It is a form of pathos.

feedback   An audience's verbal and nonverbal responses to a source's message.

figurative analogy   An analogy in which the two entities being compared are not in the same category.

figurative language   Words and phrases that employ certain techniques to describe claims or ideas in order to make them more clear, memorable, or rhetorically stylistic. Examples include **anaphora**, **antithesis**, **metaphor**, and **simile**.

fixed-response question A survey question that provides a set of specific answers for the respondent to choose from. Examples include true/false, multiple-choice, and select-all-that-apply questions.

flowchart A diagram with text labels that demonstrates the direction of information or ideas or illustrates the steps in a process.

forum (location) The setting where a speaker delivers a speech and an audience listens to it.

freedom of expression The right to share one's ideas and opinions free from censorship.

full disclosure The acknowledgment of any potential conflicts of interest in a topic before a speaker presents his or her arguments.

full-text source The complete text of a published article that is mentioned in a speech. It often is located by a link in a library's online periodical index.

functional definition An explanation of how something is used or what it does.

gender composition A demographic characteristic that considers how many men and women will be in an audience.

gender-neutral term A word that does not suggest male or female.

gender stereotype An oversimplified, often distorted view of what it means to be male or female.

gesture A hand, head, or face movement that emphasizes, pantomimes, demonstrates, or calls attention to something.

goodwill Friendly or helpful feelings toward another person. Good speakers want what is best for their audience rather than what would most benefit themselves.

graph A visual representation of the relationship between different numbers, measurements, or quantities. See also **bar graph**, **line graph**, and **pie chart (circle graph)**.

group dynamics The ways in which the members of a group relate to one another and view their functions.

groupthink The tendency of group members to accept some ideas and information uncritically because they have strong feelings of loyalty or single-mindedness.

half-truth A statement that deceives an audience by stating part of the truth but mixing it with a lie.

hasty generalization   An error in reasoning that asserts that a piece of evidence that applies to one case applies to all cases.

hearing   Passively receiving messages without trying to interpret or understand them.

heterogeneity   Diversity among members of a group.

hierarchy of needs   A theory that people's most basic needs must be met before they can focus on less essential ones. Psychologist Abraham Maslow's hierarchy of needs begins with physiological needs and is followed by safety, love/belonging, self-esteem, and self-actualization needs.

homogeneity   Similarity among members of a group.

hostile audience   A group of listeners who oppose a speaker or a speaker's message and resist listening to the speech.

hypothetical example   An imagined example or scenario that a speaker presents to help an audience follow a complicated point.

imagery   Mental pictures or impressions painted with vivid language.

imagined interaction   The mental delivery of a speech to an audience. The speaker practices delivering a speech silently and pictures a positive interaction with the audience (such as applause).

implied leader   A person who has preexisting authority or skills that make him or her likely to be recognized as a leader by a group, even if leadership has not been formally assigned.

impromptu delivery   Generating the content for a speech in the moment, without advance preparation.

inductive reasoning   Generalizing from facts, instances, or examples and then making a claim based on that generalization. If people have two bad experiences in a row at the same restaurant, they might conclude that they always will have a bad experience at that restaurant.

informative purpose   The intent to educate and increase an audience's understanding and awareness of a topic. It is one of three possible rhetorical purposes.

interactive listening   The process of a receiver filtering out distractions, focusing on what others have said, and communicating that he or she has paid attention.

internal noise   A thought that distracts a sender or receiver from processing and retaining a message. Also known as *internal distraction*.

internal preview   A short list of ideas that summarizes the points that will follow. Using an internal preview in a speech gives the audience an advance warning of what is to come.

internal summary   A quick review of what has just been said in a speech's main point or subpoint. It is used to help an audience remember a particularly detailed point.

interruptive listening   Interjecting questions or comments before a sender is finished speaking. Both audience members and speakers can be guilty of interruptive listening.

interview   A meeting of people face-to-face to gather information for research or audience analysis. A speaker speaks with experts or select members of a future audience and records their responses. The interview can be conducted in person, by e-mail, or by instant message.

introduction   The beginning of a speech. It gains the audience's attention, presents the thesis statement, builds common ground with the audience, establishes speaker credibility, and previews the speech's main points.

invention   The use of a variety of techniques and sources to gather and choose ideas for a speech. It is one of the five classical canons of rhetoric.

jargon   Specialized or technical words or phrases that are familiar only to people who work in a specific field or belong to a specific group.

key word   An important word or term that relates to a topic, including a synonym of the word. *Keywords* are often used in online or database searches.

latitude of acceptance   The range of positions on a given issue that are acceptable to an audience.

latitude of rejection   The range of positions on a given issue that are unacceptable to an audience.

lay testimony   Statements about a topic that are made by persons with no special expertise in the subject they are discussing.

legally protected speech   The expression of any opinion in public without censorship by the government. When speakers use legal protection as a guiding principle for a speech—telling or withholding information based on whether the law allows it—they can technically stay within the bounds of what is lawful but still speak unethically.

line graph   A graph that compares the relationships between two elements by plotting data points on a vertical axis and a horizontal axis and connecting the points with a line.

listening   Actively receiving and processing messages to understand their meaning and remember their content.

list of works cited   An alphabetized list of the sources that a speaker cites in his or her speech. It usually is formatted according to a particular style of documentation, such as the American Psychological Association (APA) style or the Modern Language Association (MLA) style.

literal analogy   A comparison based on similarities between two entities in the same category.

loaded language   Emotionally charged words that convey meanings that cannot be supported by facts.

loaded language fallacy   An error in reasoning in which the speaker tries to persuade an audience by using emotionally charged words to convey a meaning that is not supported by factual evidence.

location   See **forum (location)**.

logos   An appeal to logic; the sound reasoning that supports a speaker's claims and makes an argument more persuasive to an audience.

main point   A key idea that supports a thesis and helps an audience understand and remember what is most important about a speaker's topic. Main points are supported by subpoints. See also **subpoints**.

marking a special occasion   Honoring a person or an event by entertaining, inspiring, or emotionally moving an audience. It is one of three possible rhetorical purposes.

mediated communication   The transmission of a message through either a mechanical or an electronic medium.

mediated presentation   A speech that is transmitted through either a mechanical or an electronic medium.

memory   The process of preparing and practicing a speech to ensure confident and effective delivery. It is one of the five classical canons of rhetoric. Although this canon originally referred to learning a speech by heart, today using notes and other memory aids is usually preferred.

message   The verbal or nonverbal ideas that a source conveys to an audience through the communication process.

metaphor   A comparison of unlike objects that identifies one object with another. For example: "Her adviser was a *fount of knowledge*."

mind mapping   Generating topic ideas by writing down an initial word or phrase and then surrounding it with additional words, pictures, and symbols to create an interconnected map of ideas.

mobile audience   Listeners who do not have to sit or stand during a speech. Mobile audiences might be found at an exhibitor's booth, on a town common, or on a city sidewalk.

moderator The person who introduces the participants in a panel discussion and facilitates the discussion.

monotone Unchanging in pitch or tone.

motivated sequence A model for persuasive speech organization that inspires people to take action. This popular organizational pattern was developed by Alan Monroe and has five main points—attention, need, satisfaction, visualization, and action.

multimedia presentation A presentation that employs various forms of supporting materials, such as video clips, PowerPoint slides, and illustrations.

multitasking Engaging in several different activities at once, often including the use of technological devices. This speech distraction is more likely to occur during a presentation in which the speaker is in a remote location than when he or she is in the same physical space with the audience.

narrative A story that a speaker tells to share information and capture an audience's attention. In informative speeches, the story can be a personal remembrance, a humorous anecdote, or a serious account of an event that happened in someone else's life.

naturalness The extent to which a communication medium matches the features of face-to-face interaction.

need An object that an audience desires or a feeling that must be satisfied.

nervous listening Talking through silences in conversation.

neutral audience A type of audience that has neither negative nor positive opinions about a speaker or message.

noise (interference) External or internal phenomena that disrupt communication between a source and a receiver. External sources include nearby loud noises, and internal sources include the wandering thoughts of the source or receiver.

nonlistening Failing to pay attention to what one is hearing and thus failing to process, understand, and retain the message.

nonverbal delivery skill The use of eye contact, gestures, or other techniques—such as physical movement, proxemics, and personal appearance—to deliver a speech.

nonverbal symbol A means of communicating without using words. Examples include hand gestures, eye contact, and facial expressions.

objectivity   A quality of being impartial. In research, credible sources show objectivity when they avoid bias—that is, prejudice or partisanship.

observational capacity   The ability to witness a situation for oneself, thus increasing reliability.

omission   A form of false inference that deceives an audience by withholding important information.

open-ended question   A survey question that invites respondents to give answers of their own choosing, rather than offering them a limited set of responses.

outline   A written means of organizing a speech by using sentences, phrases, or key words. An outline includes the main ideas of a speech's introduction, body, and conclusion.

outlining   Organizing the points of a speech into a structured form that lays out the sequence and hierarchy of a speaker's ideas.

panel discussion   A form of group presentation in which group members engage in discourse with one another while they are observed by an audience.

panelist   A participant in a panel discussion.

panning   A form of nonverbal delivery in which a speaker looks at and surveys all audience members. As the speaker looks back and forth across the audience, he or she pauses and makes extended eye contact with an individual listener for a few moments before moving on to do the same with another listener.

paraphrase   To put someone else's ideas into one's own words and give appropriate credit to the original source.

participatory (or social) media   Online communication methods that allow users to create and share material or participate in social networking. Information that is posted on social media is not reviewed by editors or other readers, so speakers should proceed with caution before using it in a speech.

pathos   An appeal to emotion; an attempt to persuade an audience by creating an emotional response.

pausing   Leaving strategic gaps of silence between the words and sentences of one's speech.

peer review   The evaluation of an author's professional work by other experts in a particular field.

people-oriented listening   Investing time and attention in communication because of an interest in supporting one's friends and strengthening relationships.

periodical   A weekly, monthly, quarterly, or annual publication, including scholarly journals and news and topical-interest magazines.

peripheral belief   A viewpoint that is not held as closely or as long as a core belief and that may be open to persuasion. See also **core belief**.

peripheral route   According to the elaboration likelihood model, one of two ways that audience members may evaluate a speaker's message. This route uses tangential cues (low elaboration), such as attractiveness of the speaker, flashy presentation aids, or certain aspects of the speaker's delivery. See also **central route**.

personal appearance   The impression that speakers make on an audience through their clothing, jewelry, hairstyle, and grooming.

persuasive purpose   The intent to strengthen listeners' commitment, weaken listeners' commitment, or promote a particular action. It is one of three possible rhetorical purposes.

persuasive speech   Language that aims to influence audience members' beliefs, attitudes, or actions by employing strategic discourse and calling for the audience to accept fact, value, and policy claims.

physical movement   The bodily activity that a speaker engages in while giving a presentation.

pie chart (circle graph)   A graph that arranges information to resemble a sliced pie to clarify how proportions and percentages relate to one another and add up to a whole.

plagiarism   The presentation of another person's words or ideas as one's own.

policy claim   A statement that advocates that organizations, institutions, or members of the audience should take action. For example: "Anyone opposed to animal experimentation should join an activist organization, such as the Humane Society, to help put a stop to this cruel and unnecessary practice."

political affiliation   A person's political beliefs and positions.

post hoc **fallacy**   An error in reasoning that incorrectly states that a second event is caused by the event that immediately preceded it.

power wording   The paraphrasing of evidence in a way that supports one's own claim but misrepresents a source's point of view. It is considered unethical.

precise evidence   Specific dates, places, numbers, and other facts that are presented as supporting materials.

prerecorded (asynchronous) presentation   A speech that is recorded by the speaker for later viewing by one or more audiences.

presentation aid Anything beyond spoken words that a speaker uses to help the audience understand and remember his or her message. Presentation aids include materials that can be seen, heard, or touched.

presentation software A computer program that enables users to create, edit, and present information, usually in a slide-show format.

presentation time The length of time that a speaker has to deliver his or her speech.

preview A brief statement of the main points that a speaker will present in his or her speech. The preview tells audience members what to expect and helps them visualize the structure of a speech. It sometimes is referred to as a *road map* for the speech.

prior exposure The extent to which an audience has already heard a speaker's message, which affects the audience's interest or belief in what the speaker is saying.

problem-cause-solution pattern A model for speech organization that identifies a problem, explains the problem's causes, and proposes one or more solutions, which often include asking an audience to support a policy or take a specific action.

processing Thinking about the meaning of the verbal and nonverbal components of a message that one is receiving. Processing is the first step in effective listening.

projection The act of "booming" one's voice across a speaking forum to reach all audience members.

pronunciation The way that a person says words.

proxemics The use of space and distance between a speaker and an audience.

quotation book A reference work that includes famous or notable quotations on a variety of subjects.

race A common heritage based on the genetically shared physical characteristics of people in a group.

rate of delivery The speed at which a person speaks while giving a presentation.

real-time (synchronous) presentation A speech that is delivered directly to the audience as the speaker presents the message from a remote location.

receiver The person who processes a message to perceive its meaning.

recency   The state of having just happened. Because of society's many and rapid changes, newer evidence is generally considered more reliable and credible than older evidence.

reference work   A compilation of background information on major topic areas that is useful for doing introductory research or discovering a specific fact.

reflective-thinking process   A five-step strategy for group decision making that includes defining the problem, analyzing the problem, establishing criteria for solving the problem, generating possible solutions, and selecting the best solution.

relaxation strategy   A technique that can be performed before giving a speech to help relieve muscle tension and banish negative thoughts. Relaxation strategies include deep breathing and tensing and releasing one's muscles.

religious orientation   A person's set of religious beliefs, which can shape his or her responses to a speech.

representative example   An instance that is typical of the class it represents. For example, a speaker who is arguing that Americans are getting tired of corrupt politicians might cite instances of like-minded Americans from several regions rather than from only one or two states.

research   The process of gathering information from libraries, the Internet, and interviews to increase a speaker's credibility and understanding of a topic.

research librarian   A career professional who is hired to assist students and teachers with their research.

research objective   A goal that someone wants to accomplish with research.

research plan   A strategy for finding and keeping track of the information (in books, periodicals, Web sites, and other sources) that a speaker might use to prepare a presentation.

retention   The ability to remember what one has heard. It is the second step in effective listening and is directly related to how much attention someone pays during an event. The more attentive that a listener is, the more he or she will remember.

reversed causality   A situation where what appears to be an effect of an event is actually the cause of the event.

rhetorical purpose   The speaker's intended effect on the audience. There are three possible rhetorical purposes for a presentation—to inform, to persuade, or to mark a special occasion.

rhetorical question A question that a speaker expects listeners to answer in their heads. It is used to capture an audience's attention and lead them to think about a speaker's topic.

scaled question A survey question that measures the intensity of a respondent's feelings on an issue by offering a range of fixed responses. These can take the form of a numerical scale (for example, the numbers one to ten) or a list of options ("strongly agree," "agree," "neutral," "disagree," or "strongly disagree").

script A typed or handwritten document that contains the entire text of a speech.

search engine An online program that allows users to conduct keyword searches and access links to relevant Web pages. Examples include Google (www.google.com), Yahoo! (www.yahoo.com), Bing (www.bing.com), and Ask (www.ask.com). It also is referred to as a *spider* or *crawler*.

sexist language Words that reveal a bias for or against one gender.

sexual orientation A demographic characteristic that considers whether audience members may be straight, gay, lesbian, bisexual, transgendered, or questioning.

shared meaning A common understanding that decreases confusion and misinterpretations among speakers and listeners. Achieving shared meaning is a priority of the transactional model of communication.

signpost A word or phrase within a sentence that informs the audience about the direction and organization of a speech.

sign reasoning Arguing that a fact is true because indirect indicators are consistent with that fact. For example, a speaker might argue that the United States is in a recession, supporting that claim with evidence that people are taking out more payday loans.

simile A comparison of objects that uses the word *like* or *as*. For example: "My grandmother's lap was *as soft as a pillow*."

situational audience analysis The process of learning about an audience's interests and backgrounds just before or during a speech. It usually is conducted when speakers discover that the makeup of an audience is different from what they expected or when the audience appears to be confused, lost, or hostile.

situational characteristic A factor in a specific speech setting that a speaker can observe or discover before giving the speech. Examples include audience size, time, location (forum), and audience mobility.

situational ethics The belief that ethical behavior can be informed by a person's circumstances, especially when those circumstances are extreme or unusual. See also **ethical absolutism**.

slippery slope fallacy   An error in reasoning in which the speaker argues against a policy because he or she assumes (without proof) that the first policy will lead to a second, undesirable outcome. For example, "If we legalize marijuana, that will be the first step toward legalization of all drugs, which would create a public health catastrophe."

small group   A limited number of people (three or more) who have gathered for a specific purpose.

social judgment theory   A theory stating that receivers decide to accept or reject a persuasive thesis by comparing it to their own position on the issue.

socioeconomic status   A measure of the financial resources, education, and occupation of people compared to other individuals.

source   In models of communication, a person who creates and sends a message to receivers.

spatial pattern   A model for speech organization in which the main points represent important aspects of a topic and are thought of as adjacent to one another in location or geography. A speaker who is discussing historical sites in a state's three largest cities might use a spatial pattern of organization.

speaking outline   A type of outline that contains words or short phrases that represent the speaker's key ideas and give reminders of delivery guidelines.

specific purpose   A concise phrase that states the rhetorical purpose and objective of a speech. For example, the specific purpose of a speech about traveling in the Yucatan Peninsula might be: "To inform my audience about the educational and recreational opportunities as well as the health and safety hazards of traveling in the Yucatan Peninsula."

speech anxiety (stage fright)   The nervousness that a person experiences before giving a speech. It can result in a variety of symptoms, such as sweaty palms, dry mouth, nausea, hyperventilation, and panic.

speech critique   The written or oral feedback following a presentation that identifies the presentation's main points and objectives, discusses strengths and weaknesses, and offers suggestions for improvement.

stationary audience   Listeners who are relatively motionless during a speech. Classrooms, lecture halls, and conference rooms generally house stationary audiences.

statistic   A piece of numerical data that helps a speaker quantify points and helps an audience understand how often a given situation occurs.

stereotype   A generalization based on the false assumption that the characteristics displayed by some members of a group are shared by all members of that group.

strategic discourse The process of selecting arguments that will best achieve a speaker's rhetorical purpose in an ethical manner.

straw person fallacy An error in reasoning in which the speaker makes a weak claim that he or she can easily refute, rather than making a strong claim that he or she cannot easily refute. For example, if a mayor proposes adding bike lanes to a city's main streets but the city council argues that it would be too expensive to add bike lanes to every street in the city, the city council is committing this fallacy (the mayor proposed adding bike lanes only to main streets, not to every street).

style A speaker's choice of language that best expresses his or her ideas to the audience. It is one of the five classical canons of rhetoric.

subordination The act of making one thing secondary to another thing. This principle of outlining dictates the hierarchy in the relationship of main points and supporting materials. Each subpoint must support its corresponding main point, and each sub-subpoint must support its corresponding subpoint. In an outline, supporting points are written below and to the right of the point they support. See also **subpoints** and **sub-subpoints**.

subpoint An idea that is gathered from brainstorming and research and that explains, proves, and expands on a speech's main points.

sub-subpoint An idea that is gathered from brainstorming or research that explains, proves, and expands on a speech's subpoints.

summary A brief review of a speech's main points. It is used in the conclusion of a speech to help audience members remember what they have heard.

superficial listening Pretending to pay attention while actually succumbing to internal or external noise, such as wandering thoughts, cell phones, or conversation.

supporting materials (supporting points) The examples, definitions, testimony, statistics, narratives, and analogies that support or illustrate a speaker's main points.

survey A series of written questions that a speaker asks audience members to answer in advance of the presentation.

sympathetic audience An audience that already agrees with a speaker's message or holds the speaker in high esteem and will respond favorably to the speech.

symposium A method of group presentation in which group members take responsibility for delivering different parts of the presentation.

takeaway   A memorable phrase or sentence that captures the essence of a speech and can be repeated at key points in the speech.

taking evidence out of context   Selectively choosing from a source's data or statements and presenting the information in a manner that is inconsistent with the source's beliefs or conclusions.

testimony   Statements that are provided by other people and that often are researched in a library, found online, or recorded in an interview.

thesis statement   A single sentence that conveys the topic and purpose of a speech. All the different parts of a speech, such as the main points and subpoints, should tie into the thesis statement. It sometimes also is referred to as the *central idea* or *topic statement*.

time-oriented listening   A style of listening in which listeners are concerned with managing, conserving, and protecting their time.

tone   The high and low qualities of a person's speaking voice. Moderate tonal variety is preferable to using a single tone—known as **monotone**—which is usually either low and mumbling or high-pitched and annoying.

topic   The subject of a speech. Speakers should choose a topic that is based on their own and their audience's interests and knowledge level, as well as their ability to cover the topic during the allotted time frame.

top-level domain   The designation at the end of a Web address that indicates the site sponsor's affiliation. Some common domains are commercial (.com), nonprofit (.org), educational (.edu), government (.gov, .uk), and other organization (.net). The top-level domain alone cannot be used to determine whether an online source is credible. The credibility of the person or organization that created the site must be assessed.

transaction   A communicative exchange in which all participants continuously send and receive messages.

transition   A sentence that smoothly connects one idea or part of a speech to another.

trustworthiness   The characteristic of exhibiting honesty and fairness. Often seen as one component of a speaker's ethos.

two-sided argument   An argument in which the speaker acknowledges an argument against his or her thesis and then uses evidence and reasoning to refute that argument.

unprocessed note taking   Writing down a speech word-for-word without thinking about what is being said. Unprocessed note taking hampers retention.

value One of a person's "core conceptions" about what is desirable for his or her own life and for society. Values guide people's judgments and actions.

value claim A statement that attaches a judgment—such as deeming something good, bad, moral, or immoral—to a subject. For example: "Animal experimentation is inhumane."

verbal chart Words arranged in a certain format, such as a bulleted list or columns, to explain ideas, concepts, or general information.

verbal clutter Extraneous words that make a presentation hard to follow. To say *"In spite of the fact that* you disagree with me" is more verbally cluttered than *"Although* you disagree with me."

verbal delivery skill The use of one's voice to deliver a speech effectively. A speaker should consider volume, tone, rate of delivery, projection, articulation, pronunciation, and pausing.

verbal filler A word or phrase such as *you know* or *like* that a speaker uses to fill uncomfortable silences.

verbal symbol A spoken, written, or recorded word that a source uses to convey a message.

verbal tic A sound such as *um* or *ah* that speakers use when searching for a correct word or when they have lost their train of thought.

visualization A method of easing speech anxiety in which the speaker imagines him- or herself giving a relaxed, well-received speech from start to finish.

vivid language Attention-grabbing and descriptive words and phrases that appeal to the senses.

volume The loudness or softness of a speaker's voice when delivering a speech.

word association A method for generating topic ideas in which one idea leads to another, then another, and so on, until the speaker generates an appropriate topic.

word choice (diction) The selection of language for a speech that considers the audience, occasion, and nature of one's message.

working outline An outline that contains full sentences or detailed phrases of all the main points, subpoints, and sub-subpoints in a speech. It also is referred to as a *detailed outline* or *preparation outline*.

worldview The "lens" through which a person sees and interprets reality. Listeners' worldviews will affect how they respond to a source's message.

yearbook A reference work that is updated annually and contains statistics and other facts about social, political, and economic topics.

INDEX